NATIONAL SECURITY IN ANCIENT TIMES AND RELIGIOUS TEXTS:

ANALYSIS OF VARIOUS PERSPECTIVES

Mustapha Kulungu, Ph.D.

National Security In Ancient Times and Religious Texts
Analysis of Various Perspectives
By: Mustapha Kulungu, Ph.D

Published by:
VJ Publishing House, LLC.
20451 NW 2nd Avenue Suite 112
Miami Gardens, Fl. 33169
www.vjpublishinghouse.com
vjpublishinghuse@gmail.com

Copyright © 2023 by Mustapha Kulungu

All rights reserved. No part of this publication may be reproduced, distributed, or transmitted in any form or by any means, including photocopying, recording, or other electronic or mechanical methods, without the prior written permission of the publisher, except in the case of brief quotations embodied in critical reviews and certain other noncommercial uses permitted by copyright law.

ISBN: 978-1-939236-21-0 (Paperback)

Library of Congress Cataloging-in-Publication Data:

Kulungu, Mustapha.

Printed in United States of America

10 9 8 7 6 5 4 3 2 1

This book is a work of scholarly analysis and does not necessarily reflect the views or opinions of the publisher. The author is solely responsible for the accuracy of the content presented herein.

Dedication

I want to dedicate this manuscript to my beloved maternal uncle, Abdullah Vuvu Landu. He was a remarkable individual who embodied service, discipline, and wisdom. His passion for knowledge, diverse talents, and commitment to excellence inspire me today. May he rest in eternal peace, and may his memory continue to inspire those who knew him. I would also like to extend my blessings to my late father, Gilbert Ntoto Kulungu. May his soul rest in peace, and my surviving mother, Landu Mfulu, May God bless her with longevity and excellent health. Their perseverance and dedication to learning have shaped me into who I am today. This book is a tribute to their love and support, and I am grateful for everything they have done for me. Finally, I am honored to dedicate this manuscript to my beloved family, Mina Ikched and the late Rechima Jo Dean; my children, Laila, Bilqis, Mazuengele, Mustapha Jr., and Nominsa. May they be guided by divine mercy, always be instrumental in meaningfully contributing to humanity's welfare, and continue to inspire me and all those they encounter.

Acknowledgments

I want to express my most profound gratitude to all those who have contributed to the creation of this book on national security and its intersection with religious texts. The wealth of knowledge and diverse voices that have shaped this work is truly remarkable. I am particularly grateful to the scholars, historians, teachers, religious leaders, and experts who have provided invaluable insights into the past and the wise custodians who have preserved these texts across generations. Their dedication and hard work have shed light on the ongoing interplay between security, history, and faith, which remains relevant in our modern world. Thank you all for your tremendous efforts and contributions.

Table of Contents

Prologue i

1 Historical and Sociological Contexts for Informed Security Policies 1

2 Introduction to National Security in Ancient Times and Religious Texts .. 43

3 National Security, Its Origin, And Evolution In The US 114

4 History Of Hinduism And Its Standpoints On National Security 142

5 Buddhism's Stances On Security And Territorial Protection 183

6 Confucius And Sun Tzu's Perspectives on Territorial Protection 206

7 History Of Ancient Judaism's Stances On Security 244

8 Early Christian's Standpoints On Security 281

9 Quranic Texts' Viewpoints On National Security 320

10 Summary 362

Prologue

My Reasons for Writing This Book

As a chaplain with a diverse background encompassing law enforcement, crimes, national security, social psychology, counseling, immigration, and military, I am deeply passionate about writing a book on ancient civilizations and religious texts for modern security studies. Moreover, as someone who has always been fascinated by the history of ancient civilizations and their influence on contemporary society, I am profoundly aware of the importance of undertaking this writing endeavor. Additionally, as a chaplain who has extensively written about national security and social sciences, I am driven by a personal passion for exploring the connections between ancient civilizations, religious texts, and present-day security challenges.

My experience has taught me that religion and culture are often closely intertwined with issues of national security, social conflict, and immigration. To fully comprehend and address these issues, it is crucial to deeply understand the historical and cultural contexts that shape them. As a national security and religious studies student, studying ancient civilizations and religious texts can contribute to broader peacebuilding and conflict resolution goals. By gaining insight into the methods and practices of past societies in dealing with conflict, we can develop more effective strategies for preventing and resolving disputes in the present. Exploring the ethical and moral values of different cultures further allows us to foster a deeper appreciation of the importance of these values in promoting security and stability. Ancient civilizations and their religious texts provide a unique and additional perspective on modern-day security challenges. These texts and cultures offer a historical context that can aid in understanding the origins and complexities of current security threats, such as terrorism and conflict.

Furthermore, by examining the practices and strategies of past societies in addressing similar issues, we can gain valuable knowledge on how to approach contemporary security challenges.

Moreover, by exploring the diversity of beliefs and practices across cultures, we can enhance our understanding of the intricate interplay between culture, religion, and national security. This learning can foster greater cooperation and reduce the potential for conflict. Promoting ethical behavior is a commitment I hold as a military chaplain. Drawing on my experience in this area, I can actively advocate for ethical conduct in national security decision-making. By promoting transparency, accountability, and adherence to ethical principles, I can help ensure that national security decisions align with the nation's and the military's values. Additionally, as a chaplain with a military background, I possess a unique and valuable perspective that is crucial to national security decision-making. By utilizing my experience to provide moral and spiritual guidance, support the troops, foster interfaith dialogue, and promote ethical behavior, I can contribute to national security decisions that uphold the nation's values.

Furthermore, my experience working with military service members and their families have demonstrated to me the immense importance of a comprehensive understanding of ancient civilizations, religious texts, and cultural diversity in developing effective strategies for addressing contemporary security challenges. By delving into the practices and techniques of past societies in managing conflict, we can gain valuable insights into how to approach current security challenges. Through my military experience, I have witnessed the impact of conflict and the significance of understanding the underlying factors that contribute to it. By examining the practices and strategies of ancient civilizations, we can glean valuable insights into how to prevent and mitigate conflict in contemporary security contexts.

My Personal Experience and Background

During my tenure as a chaplain in the United States Armed Forces, I had the opportunity to impart lessons on ethical conduct and resiliency, as well as advise the command on community relations and troop preparedness. These experiences provided me with a distinctive perspective on the importance of these aspects within military settings. One notable instance was when I led a workshop on community relations for a group of service members. As we delved into the significance of establishing strong ties with local communities, I shared my personal encounters with community leaders and their concerns. The impact of these anecdotes significantly influenced the participants' understanding and approach to their work, as they realized the positive effects that community relations could have on their mission.

Moreover, I was privileged to offer support and guidance to troops grappling with the stress and trauma of deployment. Collaborating with them, we developed strategies for maintaining mental and emotional well-being, and I provided counseling and assistance to those in need. These experiences emphasized the pivotal role of empathy, communication, and collaboration in cultivating a resilient military community. In parallel to my chaplaincy, I pursued an MA in national security at American Military University and became extensively published in this field. Notably, one of my influential articles explored the significance of soft power in national security. I contended that diplomacy, cultural exchange, and humanitarian aid are indispensable components of a comprehensive national security strategy. These elements can foster strong relationships with other nations and proactively prevent conflicts. My multifaceted experiences as a chaplain, combined with my studies and publications in national security, have endowed me with a profound understanding of the intricate challenges our country faces today. They have also prepared me to approach writing a book on national security from diverse perspectives.

An unforgettable experience involved leading a training session on ethical conduct for a group of young Marines.

Commencing with sharing my own encounters with ethical dilemmas in the military, I underscored the utmost importance of upholding exemplary standards of conduct at all times. As the session progressed, the Marines courageously shared their stories and experiences, fostering an open and honest dialogue about the complexities of ethical decision-making within a military context.

Witnessing their unwavering commitment to doing what is right and their willingness to engage in candid discussions left a lasting impression on me. Another area where I provided guidance was community relations and troop preparedness. Collaborating closely with local leaders and community organizations, we forged positive relationships and addressed their concerns regarding our regional presence. Through these efforts, we nurtured trust and mutual respect, enhancing the effectiveness of our mission. Drawing on my experiences as a chaplain and my scholarship in national security, I have acquired an in-depth understanding of the multifaceted challenges our nation confronts today. These practical experiences have equipped me with the necessary insights to author a book on national security, incorporating diverse perspectives.

In summary, my roles as a chaplain and national security scholar have underscored the significance of building robust relationships, fostering resilience and adaptability, and employing a comprehensive approach to national security that integrates both hard and soft power. This unique perspective has provided valuable insights into the challenges and opportunities that our country faces. By emphasizing the importance of ethical conduct, community relations, and intelligence gathering, we can pave the way for a more secure and prosperous future for all Americans.

As A Federal Law Enforcement

As a federal law enforcement agent, I have had the opportunity to work in various prison settings, including the infamous SuperMAX facility. Within these environments, I have encountered personal anecdotes and real stories that shed light on the persistent threats and security challenges we face. One of the most demanding aspects of working in a SuperMAX prison is the constant risk of attacks from fellow inmates. It requires unwavering vigilance and the ability to anticipate potential threats. Effectively navigating the role of a federal law enforcement agent in a SuperMAX prison demands exceptional communication skills, situational awareness, and staying ahead of potential compromises. It is a career that presents both challenges and rewards, rooted in dedication, hard work, and an unwavering commitment to public safety.

Furthermore, while serving as a chaplain at ADX SuperMAX, I focused on ensuring the safety, security, and well-being of all individuals within the institution. I made it a point to engage with incarcerated individuals, including those affiliated with terrorist units, in order to closely observe their behavioral patterns and identify potential radicalization indicators. By fostering trust and open communication, I was able to gather valuable insights that contributed to the institution's comprehensive security measures.

In addition to my role as a federal law enforcement agent, my work as a chaplain in the United States Penitentiary (USP) at Federal Correctional Complex, Florence, CO, brought forth a critical incident. During my rounds, I received intelligence regarding a group of inmates planning a coordinated attack on our staff. Swiftly mobilizing, I called for backup, and together, we successfully apprehended the perpetrators, preventing the attack from materializing. This incident served as a poignant reminder of the need for constant vigilance and staying ahead of potential compromises.

In summary, my experiences as a federal law enforcement agent within a SuperMAX prison have imparted valuable lessons about the imperative nature of vigilance, threat anticipation, and collaboration with fellow law enforcement agencies. Working in such an environment presents unique challenges that require continuous awareness, meticulous planning, and staying ahead of potential compromises. The personal anecdotes and real stories I have shared are merely glimpses into the myriad experiences that have shaped my career, offering invaluable insights into the realms of public safety and national security.

As A Social Psychologist

As a social psychologist, my research focuses on learning adaptability, human behavior, and the migration of people, particularly their assimilation and security in their adopted land. Throughout my years of involvement in this field, I have had the privilege of providing personalized support to individuals from diverse backgrounds. By tailoring my approach to meet each person's specific needs and ensuring confidentiality, I have been able to make a positive impact on their lives.

One particularly memorable experience involved working with a family that had recently immigrated to the United States. Having faced significant challenges in their home country, they sought a better life in their adopted land. However, they required assistance in adjusting to the new culture, language, and social norms. Through our one-on-one sessions, we explored various strategies to help them navigate their new environment and establish a sense of belonging. We focused on language development, cultural competence, and social networking, emphasizing the importance of maintaining their cultural identity while embracing the new culture.

This tailored guidance and support enabled the family to thrive in their new home. They were able to make new friends, find employment, and create a fulfilling life for themselves and their children. This experience emphasized the significance of personalizing strategies to address individual challenges and adapting to their unique circumstances. Another impactful experience was when I worked with a group of refugees who had fled from a war-torn country. They had endured considerable trauma and struggled to adapt to their new environment, having lost family members, homes, and livelihoods. Our sessions focused on providing them with the necessary support and tools to manage their trauma and cultivate resilience. We utilized various strategies, including mindfulness exercises, cognitive-behavioral therapy, and group support, to help them cope with their symptoms and improve their mental well-being.

Through this collaborative work, we fostered a sense of community and connection, reducing their feelings of isolation. They gained access to resources and support systems that aided them in rebuilding their lives in their adopted land. This experience underscored the importance of maintaining confidentiality and creating a safe, non-judgmental space where individuals can openly share their experiences and work towards enhancing their mental health.

Additionally, I had the privilege of working with a group of students who had recently immigrated to the United States. These students faced academic and social challenges, with many at risk of dropping out of school. Our sessions focused on building their confidence, improving language skills, and cultivating social networks. Employing strategies such as gamification and project-based learning, we created engaging and enjoyable learning experiences. As a result, the students significantly improved their academic performance, and teachers reported increase engagement and motivation in the classroom.

This experience highlighted the importance of making learning enjoyable and tailoring educational strategies to meet each student's unique needs. It also emphasized the significance of fostering connections and social networks, as they played a crucial role in helping individuals navigate their new environment.

In summary, my work as a social psychologist has provided valuable insights into learning adaptability, human behavior, migration, assimilation, and security in the adopted land. Whether working with families, refugees, or students, I have learned that creating a safe and non-judgmental space is essential for individuals to share their experiences and work towards improving their lives. I am grateful for these experiences, as they have allowed me to have a positive impact and contribute to the well-being of others.

As A Student of National Security

As a student of national security with a specialization in counter-terrorism and intelligence, I have developed a profound comprehension of the intricate and constantly evolving challenges faced by countries and communities around the globe. Throughout my studies at American Military University, I have acquired the necessary knowledge and skills to thoroughly analyze threats to national security and formulate effective strategies and policies to combat these threats.

In my academic journey, I have published numerous articles in reputable peer-reviewed journals, focusing on various aspects of national security, particularly counter-terrorism, intelligence, and regional stability. One area of my research has centered on the Boko Haram insurgency in Nigeria. Through extensive analysis, I have delved into the group's origins, tactics, objectives, and the utilization of soft power strategies to counter-terrorism. In a specific article dedicated to Boko Haram, I explored the effectiveness of soft power in countering terrorism. I contended that relying solely on traditional military approaches often proves inadequate in addressing the underlying causes of terrorism. Instead, I argued that soft power strategies, such as community engagement and development programs, can be more successful in reducing the allure of extremist ideologies.

Another significant research focus of mine has been the intricate relationship between the Pakistani Intelligence Service and Lashkar-e-Taiba, a militant group implicated in numerous terrorist attacks in South Asia. Through meticulous analysis and research, I have unraveled the complex web of relationships and alliances among various militia groups in the Lake Chad Basin region, as well as the role of external actors in fueling these conflicts. Furthermore, I have examined the security challenges in the Lake Chad Basin region, which has witnessed an upsurge in militia groups and violent extremism. My research has explored the root causes of the conflict and proposed comprehensive security measures that encompass both military and non-military approaches, including economic development, community engagement, and conflict resolution. The collusion between these groups has heightened violence and insecurity not only in the Lake Chad Basin but also in other regions, underscoring the criticality of addressing state sponsorship of terrorism in the realm of national security.

To sum up, my academic background and research experience in national security and counter-terrorism have equipped me with the essential skills and knowledge to tackle the intricate challenges our world faces today. Through employing a multidisciplinary approach that combines intelligence, diplomacy, military force, and soft power, it becomes possible to devise effective strategies for countering terrorism and promoting regional security and stability. I remain dedicated to utilizing my expertise to contribute to the development of effective strategies and policies that foster global peace, security, and stability.

Moreover, a book exploring ancient civilizations and religious texts in the context of modern security studies would serve as a valuable resource for policymakers, academics, and practitioners in the field of security studies. My intention behind writing such a book is driven by a desire to foster a more informed and constructive public debate about contemporary security issues. By offering accessible and engaging information about historical civilizations and texts, the book has the potential to significantly enhance our understanding of national security and contribute to a more peaceful and just world. The book consists of nine chapters, each accompanied by references for further exploration.

The Book's Benefits for Policymakers and Academics

Policymakers and academics can use the knowledge acquired from studying ancient civilizations and religious texts to make more informed decisions, develop new policies, and advance research in security studies. This section outlines some potential contributions that can be made by applying these insights to modern-day security challenges.

Firstly, military strategists can use insights from ancient civilizations and religious texts to develop new strategies and tactics for addressing security challenges. For example, they can examine how ancient civilizations conducted military campaigns and analyze the factors contributing to their successes and failures. They can also draw upon the principles of warfare found in many religious traditions to develop more effective approaches to conflict.

Additionally, they can examine the social, political, and economic factors that drove ancient conflicts and how these can be applied to modern conflicts. By leveraging the wisdom of ancient civilizations, military strategists can develop more effective approaches to contemporary security challenges. In practical terms, military strategists can learn from the tactics and strategies employed by the ancient Greek hoplites and the Roman legions to overcome numerically superior enemies in open battles. The Battle of Thermopylae, where the Spartan army held off a much larger Persian army for three days, is a classic example. Military strategists can also study the tactics used by ancient Chinese armies, such as crossbows and chariots, to gain an edge in battle (Gill, 2019). By drawing upon the military wisdom of the past, military strategists can develop innovative approaches to modern security challenges.

Secondly, peacemakers can use insights from ancient civilizations and religious texts to develop new conflict resolution and reconciliation approaches. For example, they can draw upon the principles of forgiveness and compassion in many religious traditions to promote dialogue and understanding between conflicting parties. They can also examine how ancient civilizations resolved conflicts and analyze the factors that contributed to their success. By understanding the principles of reconciliation and conflict resolution in different religious traditions, peacemakers can develop effective strategies to resolve contemporary conflicts.

For instance, peacemakers can draw upon insights from religious texts to develop new conflict resolution and reconciliation approaches. For example, the Truth and Reconciliation Commission in South Africa drew upon the principles of forgiveness and reconciliation espoused by the Christian faith to address the legacy of apartheid.

Similarly, Buddhist meditation techniques to promote inner peace and self-awareness are gaining popularity in conflict resolution and peacebuilding (Kaldor, 2013). By drawing upon the ethical and moral principles of different religious traditions, peacemakers can develop effective strategies to resolve contemporary conflicts.

Thirdly, policymakers can use insights from ancient civilizations and religious texts to develop new policies and strategies for promoting security and stability. For example, they can draw upon the principles of justice and equity in many religious traditions to develop policies that promote social and economic development. They can also examine how ancient civilizations promoted stability and analyze the factors that contributed to their success. Policymakers can benefit greatly from understanding the history and culture of different civilizations and using such insights to inform policy-making.

For instance, policymakers can learn from the successful governance models of ancient civilizations, such as the Mauryan Empire in India or the Han Dynasty in China, to develop policies that promote social cohesion and inclusiveness. They can also draw upon the values and principles of different religious traditions to promote human rights, gender equality, and environmental sustainability (Thakur, 2016). By incorporating the wisdom of the past into modern policy-making, policymakers can develop more effective and sustainable policies.

Finally, academics and religious leaders can use insights from ancient civilizations and religious texts to advance research in security studies. For example, they can analyze the impact of cultural values and interpretations on security challenges and explore how these values can be leveraged to promote security. They can also examine how ancient civilizations dealt with security challenges and how their strategies and policies can be applied to contemporary security challenges. By integrating the wisdom of the past into contemporary research, academics can expand the understanding of security challenges and promote cross-cultural understanding and cooperation.

To make a point, historians and archaeologists can study the social, economic, and political factors that contributed to the rise and fall of ancient civilizations to gain insights into the vulnerabilities of modern societies. Religious scholars can analyze different religious traditions' ethical and moral principles to understand their potential for conflict resolution and peacebuilding. By applying the knowledge gained from studying the past to contemporary security challenges, academics can deepen our understanding of the nature of security and contribute to developing innovative solutions.

In brief, insights from ancient civilizations and religious texts can significantly contribute to the field of security studies. Military strategists, peacemakers, policymakers, and academics can use these insights to develop new strategies and tactics, promote conflict resolution and reconciliation, develop new policies and strategies, and advance research in the field. By leveraging the wisdom of the past, we can build a more peaceful and secure future.

The Targeted Audience:

National security is a complex and ever-evolving field that requires expertise and knowledge in various areas. The book in question is a valuable resource aimed primarily at military strategists, peacemakers, diplomats, policymakers, and academics in the US, as well as a general audience of scholars, religious leaders, and researchers. This section succinctly argues why this book is a must-read for this audience.

Firstly, military strategists play a vital role in protecting the national security interests of the US. They are responsible for developing and implementing military strategies to counter threats to the nation's security. The book analyzes various national security issues, including military and intelligence operations, counter-terrorism, and cybersecurity. It also offers insights into the historical and current challenges facing the US in protecting its national security interests. This information is crucial for military strategists to make informed national security decisions.

Secondly, peacemakers and diplomats are responsible for maintaining international peace and security. They need to understand the complex national security issues to negotiate effective treaties and agreements to prevent conflicts. The book offers valuable insights into foreign policy and international relations, which are critical for peacemakers and diplomats. It provides a detailed analysis of the challenges facing the US in its foreign policy, including diplomacy and international law issues.

Thirdly, policymakers are responsible for developing and implementing policies that protect national security interests. The book offers a comprehensive overview of various national security issues backed by data and evidence. Policymakers can benefit from the book's insights and analysis to develop policies that effectively address the challenges facing the US in protecting its national security interests.

Fourthly, academics and scholars interested in the subject can also benefit from reading the book. It provides a detailed exploration of national security issues, offering a comprehensive understanding of the subject matter. The book covers topics such as the role of the military, the intelligence community, and law enforcement in protecting the nation. Researchers can benefit from the book's insights and analysis to advance their understanding of national security issues.

Additionally religious leaders can also benefit from reading this book. The book delves into the role of religion in national security and explores the impact of religion on foreign policy decisions. It provides insights into the intersection of religion and politics, which is vital for religious leaders seeking to understand the complex issues surrounding national security.

Lastly, the book is accessible to a general audience interested in gaining knowledge of the subject matter. The author has written the book in plain language, making it easy for anyone to understand. It offers a comprehensive introduction to national security issues, covering topics such as the military's role, the intelligence community, and law enforcement in protecting the nation. The book is an excellent resource for individuals who wish to gain a foundational understanding of national security issues.

Succinctly, this book on national security is a valuable resource necessary for a diverse audience. It provides valuable insights into the challenges facing the US in protecting its national security interests. It offers a comprehensive understanding of the subject matter to military strategists, peacemakers, diplomats, policymakers, academics, scholars, religious leaders, and the general public. The book's accessibility and comprehensive analysis make it a must-read for anyone seeking to understand national security issues. They will find this book to be a valuable addition to their library.

The Structure of The Book's Chapters

Chapter One

This chapter explores the crucial relationship between historical and cultural contexts and contemporary security challenges. It highlights the interconnected nature of national security concerns in today's globalized world. The chapter emphasizes governments' need to delve into their historical narratives and cultural intricacies to devise comprehensive security policies. The chapter underscores the potential consequences of overlooking cultural influences on security by providing a specific example of how religious texts and traditions impact territorial perceptions and justice. The chapter underlines the significance of understanding historical and cultural contexts to develop successful security measures that foster cooperation and stability among diverse communities.

Chapter Two

The book's second chapter presents a full analysis of the foundations of national security, starting with ancient religious texts and civilizations. The chapter begins by exploring the role of religion in ancient times, highlighting how sacred texts often guided the defense against external threats. It then delves into various civilizations of the ancient world, including Ancient Egypt, Greece, Mesopotamia, Mayan, and Rome, examining their approaches to national security.

The chapter provides a wide-ranging and captivating analysis of these topics, exploring their interrelatedness and significance to the overall discussion of national security. It also emphasizes the lessons that can be learned from the contributions of ancient civilizations and religious texts to national security. These insights help us better understand the nature of threats and the importance of preparedness and resilience in the face of adversity. In short, the chapter provides a strong foundation for the rest of the book by establishing the historical and conceptual context for understanding national security in the modern world. It is well-structured and written, making it easy for readers to follow the author's arguments and ideas. Additionally, the author's use of examples and case studies from history helps to illustrate key concepts, making the chapter engaging and informative.

Chapter Three

Chapter Three of this book outlines a comprehensive examination of national security, focusing on its origins and evolution in the United States. The discussion of success and failure in national security is critical as it helps to understand the different approaches taken by the US government in safeguarding the nation's security. Furthermore, the chapter provides a deep understanding of how national security has developed in the US and how it has impacted the lives of Americans and Native Americans.

Chapter three is a beneficial addition to the book, offering readers a unique and vital perspective on national security that is often overlooked in mainstream discourse. Including the outlook of the founding fathers on national security provides a helpful insight into the discourse, offering a unique perspective on the lessons learned from past failures and successes. Additionally, the chapter delves into the Native Americans' perspective on security, stability, stewardship, and territorial protection. It explores their reasons for going to war, their approach to territorial defense, and their belief in being stewards of the land. The chapter highlights the fundamental differences between the Native American and European worldviews, emphasizing the significance of land as a sacred resource that must be protected and preserved for future generations. It also notes that Native American warfare was characterized by relatively low casualties and an emphasis on capturing prisoners rather than killing, unlike European warfare.

In brief, chapter three of this book presents a captivating assessment of national security from a unique perspective. It offers an insightful and thought-provoking read, contributing to readers' in-depth understanding of national security and its complexities. It provides a wide-ranging outline of the unique perspectives and practices of Native Americans in North America regarding security, stability, stewardship, and territorial protection. It offers a deep dive into the complex history of Native American warfare and territorial protection, shedding light on the strategies, beliefs, and values that guided their actions. The chapter emphasizes the need for understanding and appreciating the Native American perspective on these issues, as it offers a valuable alternative to the dominant European worldview that has shaped much of Western history.

Chapter Four

Chapter four of the book examines the history of Hinduism and its perspectives on national security. The chapter begins by providing an overview of Hindu texts, which stress stability, governance, land protection, and military readiness. These texts include the Vedas, the Ramayana, and the Mahabharata, to name just a few. It also presents a concise synopsis of the Hindu people and their relationship with territorial protection. The chapter then discusses various examples from these texts, highlighting the importance of stability, governance, land protection, and military readiness. In particular, the Vedas discuss the significance of strong rulers who can maintain societal peace and stability, while the Ramayana underlines the need for just governance and the protection of the land. Finally, the Mahabharata emphasizes the importance of military readiness and the utilization of force to protect the land and maintain stability.

The chapter also examines the perspectives of Hindu scholars on security and their contributions to modern security studies. It discusses the works of scholars such as Subrata Mitra and Kanti Bajpai, who have explored the connections between Hinduism and security. Mitra argues that Hinduism offers a unique perspective on security that emphasizes the importance of dharma (righteousness) and karma (action). Bajpai, on the other hand, explores the connections between Hinduism and India's nuclear strategy. In brief, chapter three provides a comprehensive overview of the history of Hinduism and its perspectives on national security. It highlights the importance of stability, governance, land protection, and military readiness in Hindu texts and examines the contributions of Hindu studies to modern security studies.

Chapter Five

Chapter five of the book explores the history and perspectives of Buddhism on security and territorial protection. It begins with an introduction to Buddhism and its emphasis on peace and nonviolence. The chapter then examines Buddhist views on stability, military readiness, governance, and land protection as reflected in its scriptures and teachings. It also considers the impact of Buddhist principles and practices on security studies and the relevance of Buddhism in contemporary security discourse. Next, the chapter provides a wide-ranging indication of Buddhism's contributions to security and offers insights into the potential implications of these perspectives for security policy and practice. It delves into Buddhist views on stability, military preparedness, governance, and land protection.

The chapter provides a detailed investigation of how Buddhism has historically approached security and how its principles have been used to govern communities and protect lands. It discusses the role of Buddhist monks in maintaining security and using nonviolent strategies to achieve it. Moreover, the chapter explores how contemporary scholars have approached Buddhism and its contributions to security studies. Finally, it discusses how modern Buddhism has been shaped by the impact of globalization and technology and how it has responded to the challenges of modern-day security threats. In short, the chapter provides a comprehensive overview of Buddhism's historical and contemporary perspectives on security and territorial protection. It analyzes the various approaches and principles that Buddhism has employed to maintain security and protect lands and how they can be applied to contemporary security challenges.

Chapter Six

Chapter six of the book offers a concise overview of Confucius's and Sun Tzu's perspectives on territorial protection and national security. First, the chapter evaluates Confucius and his philosophy, including his views on governance, ethics, and territorial protection. It then delves into Confucius's thoughts on the role of the ruler, the military, and the people in maintaining stability and security. The chapter moves on to discuss the contributions of General Sun Tzu to security studies. It explores his famous work, "The Art of War," and investigates his strategic principles on national security and warfare. Finally, the chapter discusses how Confucianism and Taoism, the two major religions in China during their time, shaped their political and military theories.

Moreover, the chapter examines how Sun Tzu's principles can be applied to contemporary security challenges, such as cybersecurity and asymmetric warfare. It also discusses the role of military strategy in shaping national security policy and how Sun Tzu's principles can inform modern security strategies. In summary, the chapter fully summarizes Confucius's and Sun Tzu's perspectives on territorial protection and national security. It analyzes their contributions and the relevance of their principles in present-day security challenges.

Chapter Seven

Chapter even of the book focuses on the history of ancient Judaism and its stance on security, stability, and territorial protection. It begins by providing a comprehensive synopsis of the development of Judaism and its evolution from a tribal society to a nation-state with a strong focus on security. The chapter then examines past and current studies of Judaism on national security and how the ancient Israelites maintained security in their territories. Finally, it presents the Israelite warrior kings as crucial figures in protecting the land and establishing security among the people.

The chapter elaborates on the contributions of King David and King Solomon, two of the most renowned warrior kings in the history of Judaism. It highlights their efforts in creating a strong military and intelligence system, including using spies to protect their territories and expand their influence. The chapter further explores how the strategies and tactics used by King David and King Solomon in their time have contributed to present-day security studies. Finally, it discusses how their focus on intelligence gathering, strategic alliances, and military might is still relevant in modern-day security and defense. The chapter provides a detailed and attentive assessment of the history of ancient Judaism and its approach to security, stability, and territorial protection. It demonstrates the relevance of the lessons gleaned from the ancient Israelite warrior kings in contemporary security studies and provides valuable insights into the ongoing debate on national security.

Chapter Eight

Chapter eight of the manuscript briefly outlines early Christianity's perspectives on security and the stance of early Christian rulers and the Catholic Church on territorial protection. The chapter also examines past and current inquiries by Christians on national security and their contributions to modern-day security studies. The chapter stresses that early Christianity was initially a minority religion and, therefore, did not have much influence on security matters in the Roman Empire. However, as Christianity gained more followers and eventually became the dominant religion in the Empire, Christian rulers began to adopt their approaches to security.

The chapter discusses the stance of early Christian rulers, such as Constantine and Theodosius, on security and how they relied on a strong military to protect their territories. The chapter also examines the Catholic Church's role in shaping Christian rulers' territorial protection and security attitudes. The chapter explores some of the inquiries made by Christians on national security, including the Just War Theory and the concept of the Christian soldier. Finally, it underscores how these inquiries have contributed to modern-day security studies, particularly in military ethics and the role of religion in security matters.

In a nutshell, the chapter provides a concise but insightful investigation of early Christianity's perspectives on security and its contributions to modern-day security studies. It demonstrates the significance of the role played by Christian rulers and the Catholic Church in shaping the attitudes of Christians toward territorial protection and security matters. The chapter also emphasizes the implications of inquiries made by early Christians on national security and their relevance and contributions to present-day security studies.

Chapter Nine

Chapter nine of this manuscript introduces the Quranic perspectives on national security and contextualizes national security in Islam. The chapter highlights Prophet Muhammad's stance on stability and territorial protection and examines past and current inquiries about the Islamic view on national security. It underlines that the Quran emphasizes the importance of security and stability for individuals and societies and how these concepts are intertwined with Islam's core principles of justice and compassion. Furthermore, it discusses how the Quranic texts guide the achievement of national security through various nonviolent means and promote social justice and economic prosperity.

The chapter presents Prophet Muhammad as a central figure in Islamic history who recognized the need for national security and took measures to protect the Muslim community. It underscores the Prophet's diplomatic and military strategies to secure the territorial integrity of the Islamic state, as well as his efforts to foster peaceful relations with neighboring communities. The chapter examines past and current inquiries about the Islamic stance on national security, including the notion of defensive jihad and its relationship with the Muslim community and territorial protection. Finally, it presents the benefits of these inquiries and their contributions to modern security studies, particularly in counterterrorism and interfaith dialogue.

Concisely, the chapter thoroughly analyzes the perspectives of Quranic texts on national security and their contextualization within the Islamic tradition. It underscores the essence of security and stability in Islam and how these concepts are intertwined with the religion's core values. The chapter also accentuates the contributions of Prophet Muhammad and many Muslim scholars to Islamic national security and the significance of past and current inquiries on the topic to modern security studies. It examines past and current investigations about the Islamic standpoints on national security and discusses their benefits and contributions to modern security studies.

Chapter Ten

The book's tenth chapter comprehensively summarizes the views of various religious texts on security and their contribution to modern security studies. The chapter begins by critically summarizing religious texts and ancient civilizations, emphasizing the importance of security in their societies. It also presents the evolution of national security in the US and the Native Americans' stance on territorial protection.

The chapter then proceeds to present the Hindu texts on security, highlighting the significance of protection and defense in their religion. It summarizes the Buddhist text on security, emphasizing the importance of understanding the root causes of threats to achieve lasting security. Moreover, the chapter critically discusses the foundation and contribution of Jewish texts on security. The Christian texts on security are also analyzed, emphasizing the importance of just war theory and the principle of love in their religion. The Quranic texts and traditions on security are presented as well, emphasizing the significance of jihad and the principle of justice in Islam.

Additionally, the chapter discusses each text's approach to intelligence collection, emphasizing the importance of understanding the historical context and cultural nuances in interpreting religious texts. In brief, the chapter comprehensively analyzes the views of various religious texts on security and their contribution to modern security studies, offering a unique perspective on security beyond the traditional Western-centric approach. The following section introduces national security from both ancient times and religious texts' standpoints. Furthermore, the subsequent section introduces chapter one of this book.

1

Historical and Sociological Contexts for Informed Security Policies

National security is a paramount concern for governments worldwide; however, the intricate nature of contemporary security challenges necessitates a profound grasp of each nation's historical and cultural contexts. Disregarding these factors can lead to ill-advised policies that exacerbate security issues instead of enhancing them. A notable example of this influence is how religious texts and traditions can mold territorial protection and perceptions of justice, frequently resulting in conflicts among religious groups. By incorporating historical and cultural considerations into national security strategies, governments can navigate these intricate dynamics and strive for peace and stability. Recognizing and comprehending these historical and cultural dimensions are vital to devising effective and all-encompassing security strategies that tackle root causes and foster peace.

Historical and cultural elements shape a nation's identity and worldview. Grasping the historical context of conflicts and the cultural values that inform them is crucial for formulating appropriate security policies. Overlooking these nuances may lead to policies that neglect the underlying origins of conflicts, perpetuating tensions and insecurity. Additionally, religious texts often play a pivotal role in shaping perceptions of territorial protection among religious groups. Assertions of sacred territories and historical entitlements grounded in religious texts can ignite territorial disputes and conflicts. A comprehensive understanding of the religious significance of specific lands is imperative for effective conflict resolution and territorial management.

Religious traditions can shape perceptions of justice and equity, influencing how disputes are resolved within and between religious communities. Divergent interpretations of religious teachings can yield conflicting notions of justice, contributing to tensions and divisions. Acknowledging and respecting these divergent perspectives is crucial for promoting comprehensive and fair justice systems. In contemporary security challenges, comprehending each nation's historical and cultural contexts is imperative for efficacious national security strategies. Ignoring these factors may result in misguided policies that escalate conflicts among religious groups, particularly concerning territorial protection and justice perceptions. Through integrating historical and cultural considerations into security policies, governments can foster a deeper grasp of the intricate forces at play, work towards sustainable conflict resolution, and nurture peace and stability. Recognizing the influence of religious texts and traditions in shaping perceptions can pave the way for more all-encompassing and equitable approaches to national security that transcend divisive boundaries and contribute to a safer and more harmonious world.

Studying ancient civilizations and religious texts imparts invaluable insights into the past, enabling us to comprehend and learn from historical events. Through a historical and sociological lens, we can fathom the profound impact of cultural factors on shaping the identities and worldviews of these civilizations. In this segment, we will argue that understanding the historical context of conflicts and the cultural values that informed them is vital for crafting effective security policies. Disregarding these nuances may result in misguided policies that fail to address the root causes of conflicts, perpetuating tensions and insecurity.

Ancient civilizations serve as time capsules, offering glimpses into the past. Examining their social, economic, and political structures enables us to understand the intricate dynamics that shaped their identities and worldviews. For instance, the legal and social codes of the ancient Mesopotamian civilization, such as the Code of Hammurabi, reveal prevailing cultural norms and values of justice and retribution (Van de Mieroop, 2004). Analyzing historical texts from a sociological perspective helps us comprehend how these factors contributed to their decision-making and conflict resolution. Moreover, religious texts provide significant insights into the moral frameworks and worldviews of ancient civilizations. These texts often served as guiding principles for communities, influencing their conduct and interactions with others. The Vedas in Hinduism, for example, outline an ethical and ritualistic system that shaped the cultural values of ancient Indian society. When scrutinizing conflicts involving religious elements, understanding these texts becomes essential for policymakers to address religious tensions effectively.

Analyzing conflicts within their historical context is essential to formulating appropriate security policies. The reasons behind ancient conflicts frequently extend beyond territorial ambitions or resource disputes. For instance, the Peloponnesian War in ancient Greece was influenced by historical grievances, power struggles, and intricate alliances shaped by cultural values and beliefs. Ignoring these nuanced historical factors may lead to inadequate responses, perpetuating animosity and insecurity. Furthermore, cultural values are pivotal in shaping conflict resolution approaches in ancient civilizations. Honor, shame, and loyalty were integral components of Roman culture, influencing their approaches to war and peace negotiations (Goldsworthy, 2003). Neglecting these cultural nuances may result in security policies that overlook potential avenues for reconciliation and escalate tensions.

Analyzing ancient civilizations and religious texts provides an opportunity to learn from past successes and mistakes. Policymakers can draw parallels between historical conflicts and contemporary challenges, enabling them to develop well-informed security policies. For instance, comprehending how the ancient Persian Empire established a diverse and tolerant society (World

Economic Forum, 2021) may inspire modern policymakers to champion inclusivity and pluralism in regions grappling with cultural tensions. Thus, examining ancient civilizations and religious texts through historical and sociological contexts is vital for understanding the past and deriving valuable insights. The historical context of conflicts and the cultural values that informed them shape the identities and worldviews of ancient civilizations. By embracing these insights, policymakers can devise security policies that address the underlying causes of conflicts, fostering enduring peace and stability. Overlooking these nuances jeopardizes perpetuating tensions and insecurity, impeding progress toward a more harmonious global community.

Furthermore, in today's rapidly evolving global landscape, national security transcends traditional military defense to encompass a comprehensive and multifaceted approach. The notion that national security revolves solely around military might is no longer adequate to tackle the diverse and interlinked challenges faced by nations worldwide. Safeguarding a country's interests and citizens necessitates a broader framework spanning various critical areas. The conventional perception of national security is fixated on external military threats from rival nations. However, threats have evolved into multifarious and interconnected forms in today's globalized world. Non-military challenges, such as cyber-attacks, terrorism, pandemics, climate change, and economic disruptions, can severely harm a nation's stability and prosperity. Embracing a comprehensive approach empowers governments to confront these diverse threats and proactively mitigate their impact (World Economic Forum, 2021).

Adequate national security necessitates robust diplomacy and international cooperation. In an interconnected world, collaborating with other nations becomes crucial for addressing shared challenges. Diplomatic efforts can prevent conflicts, foster peaceful resolutions, and collectively build alliances to address global issues. For instance, international cooperation has been instrumental in negotiating climate agreements to combat environmental threats. By prioritizing diplomatic efforts, countries can strengthen their security by forging partnerships and promoting global stability (United Nations, 2016).

Additionally, economic stability and prosperity are integral components of national security. A robust economy enables a nation to invest in social welfare, infrastructure, and innovation, thereby creating a more resilient society. Moreover, economic strength enhances a nation's ability to respond to crises and withstand external pressures. Countries can bolster their national security by fostering economic growth in ways that extend beyond military capabilities.

Throughout history, ancient civilizations and religious texts have emphasized the significance of early detection in safeguarding territories, resources, and citizens while maintaining stability. This segment asserts that early detection of threats was vital for ancient civilizations, and it continues to be critical in the modern era for every nation. By drawing examples from ancient and contemporary contexts, we will explore the enduring importance of early detection in ensuring national security and prosperity. Ancient civilizations recognized that early detection of threats was essential for survival and prosperity. For instance, the construction of watchtowers and fortifications in the ancient city of Jericho demonstrates the early understanding of the need for vigilance against potential invaders (Kenyon, 1957). Similarly, the military scouts of ancient Rome played a crucial role in gathering intelligence about enemy movements, enabling the empire to respond swiftly to potential threats. Early detection was essential to protect their territories, resources, and citizens from harm.

Religious texts from various cultures also taught the importance of early detection. In the Bible, the Book of Proverbs emphasizes the value of prudence in anticipating and avoiding potential dangers. In the Islamic tradition, the Hadith highlights the importance of staying vigilant and proactive in protecting one's community and nation. These teachings underscore the timeless wisdom of early detection as a means to ensure stability and security. In the contemporary context, early detection remains a critical element of national security strategies. Countries worldwide have established sophisticated early warning systems to promptly identify and mitigate various threats. For instance, seismic monitoring networks enable the timely detection of earthquakes, ensuring that communities can be alerted and evacuated, thereby minimizing casualties and damages (National Research Council, 2003). Likewise, intelligence agencies play a central role in detecting and countering security threats, such as terrorism, cyber-attacks, and the proliferation of weapons of mass destruction.

Intelligence Gathering and Its Importance

Primarily, intelligence gathering plays a pivotal role in national security. Understanding potential threats and adversaries' intentions is fundamental to formulating proactive responses. Timely and accurate intelligence allows for early detection, preemptive actions, and strategic planning, enabling nations to stay ahead of emerging risks. Intelligence gathering stands as a cornerstone of national security, playing a pivotal role in safeguarding a nation's interests and protecting its citizens. By identifying potential threats early, governments can take preemptive actions to mitigate risks before they escalate into full-blown crises. Intelligence gathering allows nations to stay ahead of the curve in an ever-changing world. With global dynamics constantly shifting, threats can emerge swiftly and unpredictably. Access to timely intelligence empowers countries to adapt their strategies and plans, ensuring they remain agile and responsive to new challenges.

Moreover, accurate intelligence forms the bedrock of strategic planning. With comprehensive information, governments can develop effective security policies, allocate resources efficiently, and prioritize areas that demand immediate attention. A well-informed approach maximizes the chances of successful outcomes in countering threats and challenges. Additionally, intelligence gathering enhances collaboration and cooperation among nations. The exchange of intelligence between allies fosters collective security efforts, enabling countries to address shared challenges collaboratively. This cooperative approach strengthens alliances and builds trust among nations, contributing to regional and global stability. Furthermore, intelligence serves as a deterrent against potential adversaries. Demonstrating the ability to gather credible information about hostile actors dissuades them from taking aggressive actions, as they are aware of the risks associated with their activities being closely monitored (Johnson, 2016).

Accurate intelligence empowers nations to take preemptive actions to neutralize threats before they materialize. By understanding adversaries' intentions and capabilities, governments can disrupt planned attacks, apprehend potential perpetrators, and thwart hostile actions. Preemptive measures are vital in safeguarding national interests and minimizing the impact of potential security breaches. Intelligence gathering forms the foundation for strategic planning in national security. Governments can allocate resources efficiently by prioritizing areas with higher risk or vulnerability (Lowenthal, 2016). Analyzing intelligence data allows for evidence-based decision-making, optimizing resource utilization, and enhancing the overall effectiveness of security measures.

In the modern security landscape, threats are increasingly asymmetric and digital. Intelligence gathering is crucial in identifying and countering such threats, including cyber-attacks and hybrid warfare tactics. By monitoring online activities and analyzing digital footprints, governments can stay vigilant against cyber adversaries and take proactive measures to protect critical infrastructure and national interests (Rid & Buchanan, 2015). Early detection allows for swift and precise responses, preempting security challenges before they escalate. Moreover, intelligence guides strategic planning, ensuring efficient resource allocation and evidence-based decision-making. In the face of asymmetric and cyber threats, accurate intelligence enables nations to stay ahead of emerging risks, effectively safeguarding their interests and ensuring the safety and security of their citizens. Emphasizing the importance of intelligence gathering is a tactical necessity and a strategic imperative for governments worldwide.

In short, intelligence gathering forms the backbone of national security, providing invaluable insights and foresight to decision-makers. Understanding potential threats and adversaries' intentions enables proactive responses, strategic planning, and effective resource allocation. Timely and accurate intelligence empowers nations to adapt to rapidly evolving challenges and build strong alliances for collective security. Through intelligence gathering, countries can stay ahead of emerging risks, protect their citizens, and ensure the well-being and stability of their nations in an increasingly complex and interconnected world.

Diplomacy and Geopolitical Factors in Power Struggles and Competitions

Diplomatic efforts are essential for fostering cooperation and resolving conflicts. Effective diplomacy can prevent escalations into armed conflicts, promote peaceful resolutions, and build alliances for collective security. Diplomatic initiatives provide channels for dialogue and negotiation, strengthening international relations and easing tensions. Diplomatic efforts are vital in maintaining international peace and security, making them indispensable to national security strategies.

Throughout history, ancient civilizations recognized the significance of diplomacy in maintaining peace and security. Effective diplomacy provides dialogue, negotiation, and dispute-resolution channels, preventing escalations into armed conflicts. This section contends that diplomatic initiatives are pivotal in national security strategies by promoting peaceful resolutions, building alliances, and easing international tensions. Effective diplomacy is a powerful tool in preventing conflicts and promoting peaceful resolutions. Engaging in constructive dialogue with adversaries and potential threats opens channels for communication, reducing misunderstandings and tensions that could otherwise escalate into armed conflicts. Diplomatic engagements aim to find common ground and mutual interests, facilitating the path toward resolution and reconciliation.

Besides, diplomacy provides an avenue for building alliances and partnerships. Building strong alliances with like-minded nations strengthens collective security efforts, creating a united front against common challenges. These alliances enhance a nation's capabilities and deter potential aggressors as they recognize the collective strength of aligned nations (Bercovitch & Kadayifci-Orellana, 2016). Diplomatic initiatives are critical to strengthening international relations and fostering trust among nations. Trust-building is essential in promoting cooperation and finding collaborative solutions to shared problems. Diplomatic engagements allow nations to work together on global issues such as climate change, pandemics, and terrorism, reinforcing the interconnectedness of global security.

Furthermore, diplomatic efforts facilitate conflict resolution through mediation and negotiation. When tensions arise between nations, diplomatic channels provide a platform for finding compromises and settling disputes. This approach avoids the devastating consequences of armed conflicts and contributes to regional and global stability. Effective diplomacy also plays a role in shaping international norms and standards. Nations use diplomatic platforms to advocate for human rights, promote democracy, and advance principles of justice and fairness. This diplomatic advocacy enhances a nation's reputation and soft power, contributing to its influence in the global arena.

Geopolitical factors, such as power struggles and competition for resources, play a critical role in shaping security dynamics at regional and global levels. Understanding and analyzing these factors are essential for formulating effective diplomatic and security strategies. This segment argues that geopolitical considerations significantly impact international relations, and nations must be adept at navigating these complexities to ensure their security and promote global stability. Power struggles and the quest for regional security have been recurring themes in the history of ancient civilizations and religious texts (Liverani, 2013). This section explores how these themes have shaped the geopolitical landscape of ancient times, drawing insights from historical examples and references in religious texts. By examining the challenges and strategies employed by ancient societies, we can gain valuable lessons for understanding power dynamics and ensuring regional security in the present-day context.

Ancient civilizations were often characterized by power struggles between competing city-states, empires, and tribal entities. For instance, in ancient Mesopotamia, the Sumerian city-states engaged in frequent conflicts to gain control over valuable resources and expand their territories. The rise and fall of empires such as Egypt, Assyria, and Persia exemplify the continual struggle for regional dominance and security. Ancient civilizations recognized the significance of power balancing and forming alliances to counter potential threats. The Delian League, established by Athens in the 5th century BCE, served as a defensive alliance against Persian expansionism. Similarly, the Maurya Empire in ancient India practiced diplomacy and alliances to ensure regional security, as seen in the amicable relationship between Emperor Ashoka and the Hellenistic kingdoms (Kagan et al., 2016).

Religious texts provide valuable insights into how ancient societies perceived power struggles and regional security. In the Bible, the story of David and Goliath symbolizes a smaller entity successfully defending itself against a more formidable foe, offering lessons in strategy and resilience. Additionally, the notion of "Dharma" in Hinduism and the concept of "Just War" in Christianity and Islam laid the foundation for ethical conduct in warfare and regional conflict. Also, trade and economic dominance were integral to ensuring regional security in ancient times. The ancient Silk Road facilitated peaceful interactions and cultural exchanges between the East and the West, contributing to stability and security. Similarly, the Roman Empire's control over key trade routes and resources bolstered its regional security for centuries (Ridley, 1982).

The power struggles and strategies employed by ancient civilizations hold relevance in the modern context. Understanding historical patterns can help nations navigate contemporary geopolitical challenges and safeguard regional security. Cooperation through regional organizations, like the European Union, mirrors the alliances formed by ancient societies to enhance stability and collective security. Power struggles and the pursuit of regional security have shaped history in ancient civilizations and religious texts. By studying ancient societies' power dynamics, alliances, and strategies, we gain valuable lessons applicable to the present-day world. The importance of power balancing, alliances, trade, and ethical conduct in conflict transcends time and remains relevant for modern nations seeking stability and security in a complex global landscape.

Diplomatic efforts focus on finding peaceful solutions to conflicts, emphasizing compromise, and understanding. Skillful diplomats mediate between conflicting parties, facilitating dialogue and encouraging concessions. Through diplomatic initiatives, nations can address underlying grievances and reach agreements that uphold the interests of all parties involved. In brief, diplomatic efforts are an essential component of national security strategies. They prevent conflicts, promote peaceful resolutions, build alliances, strengthen international relations, and foster trust among nations. Diplomatic engagements provide a non-military approach to addressing global challenges, emphasizing cooperation and collaboration for collective security. By embracing effective diplomacy, nations can contribute to a more stable, peaceful, and secure world, ensuring the well-being and progress of their citizens in an interconnected global community.

Economic Stability Is a Cornerstone of National Security

A strong and resilient economy enables nations to allocate resources effectively for defense, infrastructure development, and social welfare. Economic prosperity bolsters a country's global standing and enhances its capacity to withstand external pressures. Economic stability is a fundamental pillar of national security, playing a critical role in a nation's ability to protect its interests, ensure the well-being of its citizens, and withstand external pressures. Economic prosperity is a key determinant of a nation's global standing and influence. Economic prosperity builds resilience, allowing nations to withstand external pressures and navigate international challenges effectively. Strong economies can weather economic shocks, trade disputes, and fluctuations in the global market. In times of crisis, nations with diverse and robust economies are more likely to recover swiftly and maintain stability.

Ancient civilizations recognized the vital link between economic prosperity and a country's global standing. Economic stability has emerged as a fundamental pillar of national security, enabling nations to protect their interests, ensure the well-being of citizens, and withstand external pressures. Here, we maintain that economic prosperity is a matter of national security, as it enhances a nation's capacity to thrive in an interconnected world and strengthens its resilience against potential threats. A strong economy enhances a country's soft power and credibility internationally, attracting foreign investment, fostering trade relationships, and promoting cultural exchanges. Nations with robust economies often hold more significant sway in shaping global policies and alliances; according to Nye (2011), the future of power is shaped by various factors.

A strong and resilient economy is essential for a nation to allocate resources effectively for defense, infrastructure development, and social welfare. Economic prosperity provides governments with the means to invest in modernizing their armed forces, enhancing their defense capabilities, and ensuring readiness to respond to potential threats. Furthermore, economic stability bolsters a country's global standing and influence. Nations with robust economies often enjoy greater diplomatic leverage, as they can participate actively in international forums, negotiations, and economic partnerships. Economic strength enhances a nation's soft power, allowing it to project its values and interests globally.

Enhanced economic prosperity bolsters a nation's resilience against external pressures. A robust economy provides a cushion during times of economic downturn or crises, reducing the vulnerability to external economic shocks. A resilient economy can bounce back faster from challenges, minimizing the risk of destabilization. Moreover, a strong economy contributes to societal stability. Economic prosperity translates to increased opportunities, job creation, and improved living standards for citizens. A content and prosperous population is less susceptible to internal tensions and social unrest, creating a more harmonious and secure society.

Economic stability also supports investment in critical infrastructure, which is paramount for national security. Modern infrastructure enhances a nation's preparedness to respond to emergencies, natural disasters, and other crises effectively. Reliable transportation, communication, and energy systems contribute to the country's resilience. According to Bergsten and Gagnon (2018), currency conflict impacts trade policies. Additionally, economic strength allows nations to invest in research and development, fostering innovation and technological advancements. These advancements can have implications for national security, including in areas such as cybersecurity and defense technology.

Economic stability is essential for maintaining national security. A thriving economy enables governments to allocate defense, infrastructure development, and social welfare resources. Stable economies are better equipped to fund essential services, strengthen law enforcement, and invest in advanced technology to counter potential threats. Economic stability is a cornerstone of national security, providing the resources and capacity for nations to invest in defense, infrastructure, and social welfare. A strong economy enhances a nation's global standing and influence, making it more resilient against external pressures and capable of responding to emerging challenges.

Besides, economic prosperity fosters societal stability, contributing to a harmonious and secure environment for citizens. By prioritizing economic stability, nations can strengthen their overall security posture and ensure the well-being and progress of their citizens in an ever-changing world. Economic prosperity directly impacts the well-being of citizens, contributing to a stable and content population. A strong economy generates employment opportunities, improves living standards, and provides access to quality healthcare and education. Dollar and Kraay (2003) state that institutions play a significant role in trade and growth. When citizens' basic needs are met, social cohesion is strengthened, fostering a sense of unity and shared national identity.

In brief, economic prosperity is a fundamental pillar of national security, elevating a nation's global standing, enhancing resilience against external pressures, and contributing to citizens' well-being. A strong economy empowers nations to protect their interests, invest in defense and critical infrastructure, and navigate international challenges effectively. In an interconnected world, economic stability is essential for maintaining national security and upholding a nation's ability to thrive and prosper. As such, prioritizing economic prosperity should be integral to national security strategies to secure a brighter and more secure future for all citizens.

Protecting Critical Infrastructures

This section contends that cybersecurity has become an indispensable component of national security, as nations must prioritize fortifying their digital defenses to withstand evolving and sophisticated cyber threats. Cybersecurity has emerged as a critical component of national security. With increasing reliance on digital infrastructure, protecting against cyber threats is imperative. Safeguarding sensitive information, critical systems, and digital assets is essential to prevent disruptive cyberattacks and safeguard national interests.

In the digital age, cybersecurity has become an indispensable component of national security. As societies and economies increasingly rely on interconnected digital infrastructure, protecting against cyber threats has become a top priority for safeguarding a nation's interests and ensuring its stability. Sensitive information, including classified government data, intellectual property, and personal records, is constantly at risk of cyberattacks.

Breaches in digital security can compromise national security, endanger individuals, and expose classified operations. Robust cybersecurity measures are essential to protect such information from cyber threats. Critical infrastructure, such as energy grids, transportation networks, and healthcare systems, is increasingly connected through digital platforms. Cyberattacks on these systems can cause disruptions, endanger public safety, and have severe economic consequences (Arora et al., 2019). Strong cybersecurity measures are essential to prevent such attacks and ensure the continuous functioning of critical systems.

With the rapid advancement of technology, the world has witnessed an unprecedented increase in cyber threats. From state-sponsored cyber espionage to ransomware attacks, cyber threats pose significant risks to critical infrastructure, sensitive information, and national security assets. Safeguarding against these threats is paramount to prevent disruptive cyberattacks that can cause widespread damage and compromise national interests. Cybersecurity plays a crucial role in protecting sensitive information and digital assets. In an era where data is valuable, securing government databases, military communications, and economic data is essential to prevent unauthorized access and data breaches. Information confidentiality, integrity, and availability are vital for effective national security.

Moreover, critical systems and infrastructure, such as power grids, transportation networks, and communication systems, are increasingly interconnected and reliant on digital technology. Securing these systems from cyberattacks is essential to prevent disruptions that could have far-reaching consequences for a nation's security and daily operations. Cyber threats are not limited to national borders. In the interconnected world, adversaries can launch cyberattacks from remote locations, making attribution challenging. Robust cybersecurity measures are necessary to detect and deter such attacks, mitigating the risk of potential harm to a nation's digital infrastructure and interests.

Furthermore, cyber-attacks can be employed as a means of asymmetric warfare, allowing smaller or less technologically advanced adversaries to level the playing field against more potent adversaries. Cyber warfare can target a nation's military, economic, and social aspects, demanding a comprehensive cybersecurity strategy to protect against these multifaceted threats. Investing in cybersecurity capabilities and developing a skilled cyber workforce ensures a nation's readiness to respond to cyber threats effectively. As stated by Anderson (2001), information security presents challenges from an economic perspective. Governments must stay abreast of emerging cyber threats and invest in cutting-edge technologies to defend against evolving attack techniques.

To sum up, cybersecurity has become a critical component of national security as nations increasingly rely on digital infrastructure for various aspects of life. Protecting sensitive information, critical systems, and digital assets is imperative to prevent disruptive cyberattacks and safeguard national interests. A robust cybersecurity strategy is crucial to address evolving cyber threats and maintain a secure and resilient nation in the digital age. Countries prioritizing cybersecurity can effectively counter cyber threats and protect their citizens, infrastructure, and interests from the ever-changing cyber warfare landscape.

Fortifying Nations against Divisions and External Influences

Social cohesion is vital in fortifying a nation against internal divisions and external influences seeking to exploit societal vulnerabilities. A united society based on shared values and inclusivity is more resilient and capable of confronting challenges with collective strength. Social cohesion stands as a critical factor in fortifying a nation against internal divisions and external influences that may seek to exploit societal vulnerabilities. A united society, based on shared values and inclusivity propagated through religious texts, is more resilient and capable of confronting challenges with collective strength.

Throughout history, ancient civilizations recognized the significance of religious texts in promoting social cohesion. They understood that religious teachings serve as a cement that bonds society, fostering stability and unity within a nation. This section argues that social cohesion is vital in fortifying a nation against internal divisions and external influences seeking to exploit societal vulnerabilities. A united society, based on shared values and inclusivity propagated through religious texts, is more resilient and capable of confronting challenges with collective strength.

Religious texts provide a moral framework that promotes shared values and a sense of community among adherents. These values, such as compassion, empathy, and respect for others, foster social cohesion by creating a common ground that transcends divisions based on ethnicity, race, or social status. Religious texts often emphasize the importance of inclusivity and unity among believers. Promoting acceptance and respect for diversity, these teachings help forge a cohesive society that values each individual's contributions, regardless of their background. Inclusive societies are more resilient to internal tensions and external manipulation that may exploit societal divisions (Pargament & Mahoney, 2009).

A society bound by social cohesion is less susceptible to external influences seeking to exploit societal vulnerabilities. When individuals share a sense of belonging and collective identity based on religious values, they are less likely to be swayed by divisive ideologies or radicalization efforts that aim to destabilize the nation. Social cohesion fosters stability and unity within a nation, providing the foundation for collective strength and resilience in the face of challenges. A society bound together by shared beliefs and values is better equipped to overcome internal divisions and maintain a sense of national purpose.

A nation that promotes social cohesion cultivates a sense of unity among its diverse population. Inclusive policies and practices that respect different cultural, religious, and ethnic backgrounds contribute to a shared national identity. A united society is less susceptible to internal divisions that could weaken a nation from within. Social cohesion reinforces a sense of belonging and loyalty to the nation. Citizens who feel valued and included are more likely to support and defend their country, bolstering national security from within (Sherif et al., 1961). A strong identity and pride in one's nation encourage active citizenship and participation in collective security efforts.

Inclusive security policies that respect and accommodate the diverse identities within a nation can foster a sense of belonging among all citizens. When individuals feel valued and represented in governance and decision-making processes, they are more likely to support and actively participate in the nation's collective security efforts. Research shows that societies prioritizing social cohesion are more resilient to internal conflicts and external threats. Diverse societies possess a wealth of knowledge, skills, and perspectives from their varied communities. Embracing this diversity can lead to more innovative and effective security strategies, as different groups bring unique insights. Recognizing the strengths of each community and promoting intercultural dialogue can enhance cooperation and solidarity among citizens, reinforcing national security.

A unified society is resilient in times of crisis. During emergencies, such as natural disasters or terrorist attacks, a cohesive society can respond with solidarity and cooperation. This collective strength enables more effective crisis management and recovery. Promoting social cohesion also reduces the appeal of extremist ideologies. Divisive narratives and radical ideologies often thrive in societies with deep-seated divisions. By fostering inclusivity and promoting a shared national vision, countries can counter the appeal of extremist ideologies that seek to exploit societal vulnerabilities.

Moreover, social cohesion enhances trust in institutions and the rule of law. Citizens with confidence in their government and judicial systems are more likely to cooperate with authorities and support law enforcement efforts. This trust is vital in countering crime and potential threats to national security. A united society also contributes to diplomatic efforts. In the international arena, a nation that demonstrates internal harmony and inclusivity is more likely to be respected and trusted by other countries. Social cohesion bolsters a nation's soft power and diplomatic influence. Furthermore, social cohesion strengthens the social fabric and reduces the potential for social unrest. A cohesive society is better equipped to address grievances and resolve conflicts peacefully, reducing the likelihood of internal unrest that external actors could exploit.

Social cohesion is vital to national security, as it fortifies a nation against internal divisions and external influences seeking to exploit societal vulnerabilities. A united society based on shared values and inclusivity fosters resilience and collective strength in confronting challenges. By promoting social cohesion, nations can build a robust and harmonious society, better equipped to address internal and external security threats and protect the well-being of their citizens in an increasingly interconnected world.

National Security is a Collective Duty

While governments and security agencies are pivotal in safeguarding the nation, national security is not solely their responsibility. This segment stresses that national security is a shared responsibility that requires inclusive collaboration among all segments of society. Emphasizing the involvement of citizens, private sectors, and community organizations enhances the nation's resilience and ability to counter diverse security challenges. Citizens are integral stakeholders in national security. Their engagement, vigilance, and adherence to laws and regulations contribute to the safety and well-being of the nation. Reporting suspicious activities and actively participating in community watch programs strengthen the nation's ability to identify potential threats and respond promptly.

National security requires collaboration between the public and private sectors. Private companies play significant roles in critical infrastructure and technology development. Establishing public-private partnerships fosters information-sharing, resource allocation, and collective efforts in fortifying the nation against diverse threats. Community organizations play crucial roles in fostering social cohesion and resilience. By building strong community ties, addressing root causes of vulnerabilities, and supporting at-risk individuals, these organizations contribute to national security by preventing radicalization and fostering a sense of unity against external influences.

National security is not solely the responsibility of government institutions and security forces; it requires the active engagement of every citizen. A nation's well-being and safety depend on fostering active citizenry, where each individual recognizes their stake in the country's security and actively contributes to its preservation. National security is a collective endeavor that transcends governmental roles. Every citizen shares a stake in the country's well-being and safety. By fostering a sense of collective ownership, individuals understand that their actions and decisions can directly impact the nation's security.

Informed and vigilant citizens characterize active citizenry about potential threats and risks. Being aware of the challenges faced by the nation enables citizens to recognize signs of suspicious activities, report potential threats, and actively participate in safeguarding their communities. When citizens actively engage in national security matters, they advocate for effective policies and measures. They can voice their concerns, offer valuable insights, and participate in public discourse to influence decision-making processes that align with the country's interests.

Local communities play a crucial role in national security. Engaged citizens within communities foster a sense of cooperation, trust, and communication with law enforcement agencies. This active community engagement enhances the nation's vigilance and early detection capabilities. An active citizenry contributes to the nation's resilience during crises. Understanding their role in responding to emergencies, citizens can support emergency services, manage crises, and contribute to the nation's recovery efforts. Educated citizens are better prepared to respond to natural disasters and emergencies, reducing the strain on first responders and contributing to faster recovery and resilience-building.

Active citizenry promotes social cohesion and unity. When citizens recognize their shared responsibility for the nation's well-being, it fosters a sense of belonging and loyalty to the country, transcending divisions and promoting societal harmony. Citizens' engagement in national security extends to protecting critical infrastructure. Vigilant citizens can actively contribute to safeguarding transportation systems, communication networks, and energy facilities, which are vital for the country's security and functioning. Informed citizens are better equipped to resist manipulation and disinformation attempts by foreign actors seeking to influence public opinion. By being discerning consumers of information, citizens can protect the nation's information ecosystem.

A well-informed citizenry is crucial for effective decision-making in matters of national security. When citizens possess a comprehensive understanding of security challenges and potential risks, they can critically assess policy proposals, advocate for practical measures, and actively engage in public discourse to influence decision-making processes. Also, national security personnel, including law enforcement and defense forces, depend on the support and cooperation of citizens. An engaged and supportive citizenry bolsters the morale and effectiveness of security personnel in carrying out their duties.

A well-informed citizenry is vital for upholding democratic values. When people understand the importance of national security, they are better equipped to discern misinformation, propaganda, or divisive narratives that may threaten democratic principles. Studying national security fosters a sense of national identity and unity among citizens. Understanding their country's shared challenges and goals can lead to stronger solidarity and cooperation. National security measures sometimes intersect with civil liberties and human rights issues. An understanding of national security helps strike a balance between protecting citizens and upholding fundamental rights.

During times of crisis, every citizen becomes an integral part of the nation's response efforts. Awareness of national security measures and emergency protocols enables individuals to respond appropriately, aiding authorities in mitigating risks and minimizing damages. A collective sense of responsibility for national security fosters resilient communities. Unified communities can better withstand external pressures, respond to crises effectively, and promote social cohesion that strengthens the nation's fabric.

Citizens actively engaging in national security help promote a culture of security consciousness. This culture encourages proactive measures, cybersecurity awareness, and responsible behavior, collectively bolstering the nation's security posture. A well-informed citizenry is better equipped to discern accurate information from misinformation or propaganda, reducing the risk of being misled by external actors seeking to manipulate public opinion. A collective sense of responsibility for national security transcends political and ideological divisions, fostering national unity. In times of crisis, a unified nation can effectively stand against external threats and internal challenges. Citizens actively observe and report suspicious activities to local law enforcement in countries with active neighborhood watch programs. This community engagement enhances neighborhood safety and complements the efforts of security agencies.

In essence, national security is a collective responsibility, with citizens playing a crucial role in contributing to their country's well-being and safety. An informed and engaged citizenry vigorously shapes policies, counters disinformation and radicalization, supports law enforcement, advocates for peaceful diplomacy, and promotes unity. Empowering citizens with a comprehensive understanding of national security leads to a stronger, more resilient nation capable of effectively addressing contemporary security challenges.

In brief, national security requires the involvement of every citizen as a responsible stakeholder. Active citizenry goes beyond traditional roles, empowering individuals to recognize their stake in the country's security and actively contribute to its preservation. By fostering a sense of collective ownership, encouraging informed and vigilant citizens, and promoting community engagement, nations can build a strong foundation for safeguarding their well-being and safety. Through active participation in public discourse, advocacy, and protection of critical infrastructure, citizens play a pivotal role in enhancing the nation's resilience and security, ensuring its strength and prosperity in an interconnected and dynamic world.

By embracing this comprehensive approach to national security, nations can better navigate the complexities of the contemporary world. Diverse threats, such as cyber-attacks, terrorism, environmental crises, and economic fluctuations, necessitate a holistic strategy that synergizes efforts across multiple domains. In conclusion, national security transcends the traditional military-centric model and encompasses intelligence gathering, diplomatic endeavors, economic stability, cybersecurity, and social cohesion. Recognizing the interconnected nature of security challenges, a comprehensive approach empowers nations to tackle multifaceted risks effectively. By adopting this broader framework, countries can protect their interests, ensure the safety of their citizens, and promote global stability and prosperity. A multidimensional national security strategy is essential for building resilient and secure nations in a rapidly changing world.

The World Is Interconnected

The interconnected world we live in today demands a nuanced understanding of historical and cultural contexts to address contemporary security challenges effectively. National security policies that fail to consider these factors may inadvertently exacerbate or create new issues. It is very crucial to understand the historical context when studying national security.

Historical events and long-standing grievances can significantly impact contemporary security dynamics. Past conflicts, colonization, or territorial disputes may continue to influence present-day tensions and rivalries between nations or ethnic groups. Many of today's conflicts have deep-rooted historical causes. Understanding the historical context allows policymakers to identify the underlying grievances that fuel current disputes. Addressing these root causes is crucial in finding lasting solutions and preventing further escalation of tensions.

The legacy of colonization continues to shape geopolitical dynamics in various regions. Historical injustices, territorial divisions, and social hierarchies established during colonial periods can impact contemporary security arrangements and influence post-colonial relations. Historical territorial disputes may persist and lead to ongoing tensions between nations. Knowledge of the historical context helps to navigate these complex issues and explore possible diplomatic resolutions that acknowledge the concerns and aspirations of all parties involved.

Long-standing ethnic and religious rivalries can become flashpoints for contemporary conflicts. Understanding the historical background of these divisions enables policymakers to devise strategies that promote reconciliation, social cohesion, and peaceful coexistence. Historical events can shape a nation's cultural heritage and collective identity. Preserving and respecting these cultural aspects can foster national unity and resilience against external pressures.

Historical events can significantly influence a nation's perception of other countries and its approach to international relations. Understanding historical interactions helps build trust and promote cooperation, while unresolved historical grievances can hinder diplomatic efforts. Studying historical security dynamics provides valuable lessons and insights for contemporary policymakers. Analyzing past successes and failures in handling security challenges can inform the development of effective strategies for current issues.

By understanding historical cycles of violence and conflict, nations can work towards breaking these patterns and preventing recurrent crises. Acknowledging historical traumas and seeking reconciliation is crucial in building a more stable and peaceful future. In conclusion, the historical context is critical to comprehending contemporary security dynamics. Historical events, unresolved disputes, and long-standing grievances can significantly impact present-day security challenges. By understanding the root causes of conflicts, addressing historical injustices, and seeking diplomatic resolutions to territorial disputes, nations can build a more stable and secure world. Emphasizing the importance of historical context in policymaking enables informed decisions, reconciliation efforts, and the prevention of cycles of violence, fostering peace and stability in an ever-changing global landscape.

Moreover, cultural beliefs, traditions, and practices are pivotal in shaping the perceptions of security, justice, and identity among diverse communities worldwide. These nuances define how people view the world, interpret events, and form identities. Failure to comprehend and respect these cultural intricacies can lead to misunderstandings, resentment, and conflicts between various communities. Thus, it is imperative to recognize and embrace cultural diversity to foster a more inclusive and harmonious global society.

Cultural beliefs often shape the sense of security within a community. What may seem like a potential threat to one group might be viewed as a harmless practice by another due to divergent cultural perspectives. When communities fail to understand each other's security concerns, they risk exacerbating tensions and conflicts. Emphasizing cultural understanding can promote empathy and create a framework for constructive dialogue, leading to cooperative efforts in addressing mutual security challenges. By appreciating cultural nuances, communities can develop inclusive security measures that accommodate diverse needs and minimize the potential for misunderstandings.

The perception of justice varies across cultures, as it is deeply rooted in traditional values and practices. Failing to respect cultural nuances in pursuing justice can lead to community alienation and mistrust. A one-size-fits-all approach to justice may inadvertently marginalize certain groups and perpetuate social inequalities. Embracing cultural sensitivity within legal systems can ensure that all individuals receive fair treatment and that justice is served with greater legitimacy. Inclusivity and cultural awareness in the legal process can bridge community gaps, fostering a shared understanding of right and wrong.

Cultural beliefs and traditions significantly influence individual and collective identities. When these identities are not respected or acknowledged, it can lead to feelings of isolation and resentment. By appreciating and celebrating cultural diversity, societies can create an environment encouraging individuals to express their unique identities without fear of discrimination. In doing so, we strengthen social cohesion and create a sense of belonging for all, reinforcing that diversity enriches humanity rather than dividing it.

The interconnectedness of cultural beliefs, traditions, and practices with security, justice, and identity perceptions underscores the importance of embracing cultural nuances for global harmony. Please understand and respect these nuances to avoid misunderstandings, resentment, and conflicts between diverse communities. We pave the way for a more inclusive and peaceful world by fostering cultural understanding, sensitivity, and acceptance. It is essential to prioritize intercultural dialogue and cooperation in addressing global challenges, as embracing diversity is not merely a choice but a necessity for building sustainable security, ensuring equitable justice, and promoting a collective sense of identity that transcends boundaries. Only through mutual respect and appreciation of cultural nuances can we aspire to create a harmonious and thriving global society.

Leveraging Historical and Sociological Perspectives for Modern Security Policies

Exploring ancient civilizations and religious texts gives us a unique lens to understand the past, learn valuable lessons, and shape our present and future. By examining historical and sociological contexts, we can unravel the profound influence of cultural factors in shaping the identities of ancient civilizations and our worldviews. This section argues that comprehending the historical context of past conflicts and the cultural values that underpin them is essential for crafting modern, effective security policies. Neglecting these nuances may lead to policies that inadequately address the root causes of conflicts, perpetuating tensions and insecurity.

Studying ancient civilizations opens a treasure trove of knowledge about the human journey through history. By analyzing their social structures, economic systems, and political dynamics, we gain insight into the factors that shaped their identities and worldviews. For example, the Indus Valley Civilization's city planning and trade practices illuminate their advanced urban society and cultural values. Understanding these elements is crucial for policymakers, as historical insights can offer innovative solutions to modern challenges.

Religious texts offer profound insights into the moral compasses that guided ancient civilizations. These sacred writings provided a framework for ethical behavior, governance, and interpersonal relationships. The teachings of the Bible, Quran, or Bhagavad Gita, for instance, influenced the spiritual and moral outlook of the societies that adhered to them. Policymakers must recognize the historical impact of these texts to address religious tensions effectively and promote religious freedom and understanding.

The historical context of past conflicts is fundamental to deriving lessons for modern security policies. Past confrontations often resulted from complex historical trajectories, territorial disputes, and ideological clashes. For the sake of illustration, the fall of the Roman Empire can only be comprehended by examining the internal and external pressures that shaped its decline (Gibbon, 1994). Policymakers must draw from historical insights to avoid repeating mistakes and develop well-informed policies.

Cultural values profoundly influenced how ancient civilizations approached conflicts and security matters. Honor, loyalty, and kinship ties were central to the ancient Greek worldview, affecting their alliances and military strategies. Modern policymakers must grasp these cultural nuances to navigate the complexities of international relations, fostering mutual respect and trust. Studying ancient civilizations and religious texts is not a mere academic exercise; it has practical implications for shaping modern security policies. By drawing from historical and sociological contexts, policymakers can better understand cultural sensitivities and grievances that fuel conflicts (Hanson, 1991). This comprehension enables the development of policies that address root causes, promote reconciliation, and reduce insecurity.

In brief, investigating ancient civilizations and religious texts is vital to unlocking our past and preparing for the future. Historical and cultural factors have shaped ancient civilizations' identities and our contemporary worldviews. By understanding the historical context of past conflicts and the cultural values that inform them, policymakers can develop security policies that address underlying causes, promote peace, and foster cooperation. Ignoring these crucial nuances risks perpetuating tensions and insecurity, hindering progress toward a harmonious global community that learns from its history.

Importance of Studying National Security

In today's interconnected world, national security has emerged as a critical concern for governments across the globe. However, it is essential to recognize that each nation's historical and cultural contexts heavily influence contemporary security challenges. Failing to understand these contexts can result in ineffective policies exacerbating security issues. For instance, religious texts and traditions can shape perceptions of territorial protection and justice, leading to conflicts between different religious groups. Similarly, the legacy of exploitation and inequality in ancient civilizations can contribute to present-day security challenges such as human trafficking, civil unrest, terrorism, and international conflict. Historical events, such as the Opium Wars in China, can also shape a country's national security priorities and approach.

Therefore, it is crucial to understand a nation's historical and cultural contexts to develop effective strategies for addressing contemporary security challenges. Policymakers must consider cultural values, norms, and historical events that shape a nation's perception of security and approach to addressing security challenges. By doing so, tailored policies and strategies can be developed to address a nation's specific needs and challenges, thereby promoting national security more effectively. Additionally, cultural values and norms significantly impact national security issues. For example, traditional gender roles and social hierarchies in ancient civilizations contribute to present-day challenges such as gender-based violence and discrimination. Similarly, India's caste system continues to shape social and economic inequality, which can lead to unrest and insecurity. Likewise, historical events like the Opium Wars in China have influenced the country's current focus on national security and sovereignty.

Examining national security through the lens of this book on national security in ancient times and religious texts is highly significant as it provides a unique and valuable perspective on the subject. Such a study allows us to gain insights into historical approaches to national security, explore the role of religious texts in shaping security strategies, and understand the enduring relevance of these concepts in contemporary contexts.

Firstly, exploring national security in ancient times helps us understand the challenges, strategies, and lessons learned by ancient civilizations in safeguarding their territories and populations. Through historical texts and account analysis, recurring themes such as defense, diplomacy, intelligence, and the balance of power can be identified, which continue to shape national security frameworks today. This historical analysis enriches our understanding of national security by offering a broader perspective and a contextual foundation for contemporary discussions.

Secondly, religious texts have significantly shaped individuals' and communities' beliefs, values, and actions throughout history. These texts often address moral principles, social cohesion, and concepts of just governance, all intertwined with national security concerns. Analyzing various religious texts allows us to explore diverse perspectives on the relationship between faith, power, and security, shedding light on how religious ideas have influenced the perception of threats, the use of force, and the establishment of alliances.

Moreover, examining national security through religious texts enables us to critically examine the potential risks and opportunities associated with the intersection of religion and security. It helps us understand how religious interpretations have been used positively to promote peace and social cohesion as well as negatively to justify violence and intolerance. Engaging with different viewpoints within sacred texts allows us to grasp the complex dynamics between religious beliefs, national identity, and security.

In a nutshell, investigating national security through this book on national security in ancient times and religious texts provides valuable insights and analysis from various perspectives. It offers historical context, emphasizes the role of religious convictions, and encourages a comprehensive interpretation of national security dynamics. This study deepens our knowledge of historical security practices, underscores the enduring applicability of critical concepts, and elucidates the complex interplay between religion and security. It is essential for formulating comprehensive and effective national security strategies in modern contexts, ensuring the preservation of peace, stability, and societal well-being. By embracing this multidimensional approach, we enhance our ability to address current security challenges with greater depth and effectiveness.

Ancient Civilization Cultural Values Impact Modern-Day Security

The impact of cultural values and historical events on modern-day security challenges has been significant throughout history. Ancient civilizations and religious texts offer specific examples that highlight this phenomenon. In this analysis, we will explore several instances, drawing on historical and contemporary scholarship, to examine their implications for present-day security.

One notable example of the influence of cultural values on modern security can be observed in the case of the ancient Persian Empire. Under King Darius I's leadership, the empire was known for its tolerance of diverse cultures and religions. However, this policy faced challenges when the Greeks arrived, as they were perceived as a threat to Persian cultural values. This clash of cultures resulted in a series of wars, including the famous Battle of Marathon, which had lasting impacts on Greek and Persian cultures. This conflict serves as a precursor to modern conflicts between Western and non-Western cultures, underscoring the challenges of cultural assimilation and the preservation of cultural heritage.

The conflict between Israel and Palestine is another example where historical events have shaped present-day security challenges. Rooted in the region's ancient history, both Jewish and Palestinian peoples trace their ancestry back to biblical times, creating intense cultural and religious significance for both sides. This historical connection to the land has fueled a protracted and often violent conflict, leading to security challenges such as terrorism and violence on both sides. The Israeli-Palestinian conflict underscores how historical events and cultural values continue to impact modern security, with the search for a peaceful resolution respecting cultural and religious heritage remaining a significant challenge.

Religious texts also provide examples of how cultural values influence modern-day security challenges. For instance, the Quran, the holy book of Islam, contains passages that call upon Muslims to defend their faith against non-believers. This has historically contributed to conflicts between Muslim and non-Muslim cultures, including the Crusades and the ongoing tension between Western and Islamic cultures. Similarly, the Bible contains passages that have been used to justify violence, as seen in the commandment to "smite the Amalekites." These examples from religious texts highlight how cultural values and religious beliefs can be exploited to rationalize aggressive and violent behavior, continuing to shape contemporary security challenges.

Moreover, cultural values themselves can directly impact security challenges in modern society. The practice of honor killings in some Middle Eastern and South Asian societies exemplifies this influence. Driven by the cultural value placed on honor and reputation, these killings target women who are perceived to have brought shame or dishonor to their families. This cultural practice creates violence and insecurity for women in these societies. Religious texts further contribute to the understanding of how historical events and cultural values shape present-day security challenges. For instance, the ongoing conflict between Sunni and Shia Muslims in the Middle East, stemming from disagreements over the Prophet Muhammad's rightful successor, exemplifies how historical events and cultural values continue to influence security challenges in the region.

In Hindu-majority India, the impact of cultural values on security challenges is evident. The caste system, rooted in ancient Hindu texts, perpetuates social and economic inequality. This inequality can lead to unrest and insecurity, as marginalized communities may be more susceptible to extremist ideologies or violent uprisings. Addressing the underlying cultural values and beliefs that perpetuate inequality becomes crucial for promoting long-term stability and security in India.

Ancient civilizations have also left their mark on modern-day security challenges. The Roman Empire, for example, significantly influenced the development of contemporary security systems. The Roman military's well-organized and disciplined structure served as a model for present-day military organizations. Additionally, the empire's engineering innovations, such as aqueducts, which ensured a reliable water supply, continue to impact modern water supply systems. However, traditional values and perspectives of the Roman Empire have also contributed to contemporary security challenges, such as imperialism and colonization, which have resulted in cultural and political tensions affecting societies worldwide.

Nevertheless, the impact of ancient civilizations on modern security challenges is not always positive. The ancient Greek civilization, known for valuing physical strength and prowess in battle, produced the Olympic Games. While modern societies have embraced this cultural value, it has also led to the glorification of violence and aggression, contributing to contemporary security challenges like terrorism and war.

Furthermore, specific cultural values, such as the concept of "face," deeply ingrained in Chinese civilization, have implications for modern security. Face refers to one's reputation, honor, and dignity in society, and losing face can be a source of shame and humiliation. This cultural value has contributed to contemporary security challenges such as cyber espionage and hacking, with Chinese hackers accused of stealing intellectual property and sensitive information from foreign countries. Such actions are driven by a desire to gain an advantage over foreign competitors and protect China's national interests.

Egyptian civilization provides another example of how historical events and traditional values impact contemporary security challenges. For instance, the construction of the pyramids required massive amounts of labor and resources, often extracted through slavery and forced labor. This exploitation of labor and resources has contributed to contemporary security challenges, such as human trafficking and the exploitation of natural resources in conflict zones (Hawass, 2010). Moreover, this legacy of exploitation has also contributed to social and economic inequality, a significant source of contemporary security challenges such as civil unrest and terrorism.

Moving on to another civilization, the Opium Wars profoundly impacted Chinese society and contributed to the country's current focus on national security and sovereignty, as Zhang and Lintner (2019) have explained. The Opium Wars were a series of conflicts between China and Great Britain in the 19th century, resulting in the forced opening of Chinese ports to foreign trade and the ceding of Hong Kong to the British. This historical occurrence created a sense of national humiliation, which has influenced China's foreign policy and approach to national security in contemporary times.

Today, the Chinese government's focus on national security and sovereignty can be traced back to this historical occurrence.

Shifting our focus to the Mesopotamian civilization, the concept of law and justice codified in the Code of Hammurabi offers another example of the impact of traditional values on contemporary security challenges. This code established the "an eye for an eye" principle and provided a framework for punishing crimes and resolving disputes. However, it also reflected the patriarchal nature of Mesopotamian society, where women had limited rights and were subject to harsh punishments for violating social norms (Van De Mieroop, 2015). This traditional perspective on gender roles and justice has contributed to contemporary security challenges, such as gender-based violence and discrimination, which continue to affect societies everywhere.

Similarly, the historical occurrence of the fall of Babylon significantly impacted contemporary security challenges. The fall of Babylon to the Persian Empire in the 6th century BCE marked the end of the Babylonian Empire and the beginning of a period of Persian domination in the region (Roth, 1997). This event profoundly impacted Mesopotamian society and contributed to a sense of national humiliation and a desire for national rejuvenation. Today, the legacy of the fall of Babylon can be seen in contemporary security challenges in the Middle East, where regional powers seek to assert their influence and maintain their sovereignty.

Regarding traditional values, the emphasis on religion in the Mesopotamian civilization significantly shaped perspectives and continues to impact contemporary security challenges. Mesopotamian religion was polytheistic and highlighted the importance of pleasing the gods through offerings and sacrifices. However, it also developed a hierarchical and authoritarian society where the priestly class wielded significant power and influence. Today, the legacy of Mesopotamian religion can be seen in contemporary security challenges in the Middle East, where religious differences contribute to sectarian conflict and instability (Roth, 1997).

Moving on to the impact of historical events and traditional values on contemporary security challenges in Egypt, the Arab Spring stands out as a significant occurrence. The Arab Spring, a series of protests and uprisings that swept across the Middle East and North Africa in 2011, substantially impacted contemporary security challenges in Egypt. It led to overthrowing an authoritarian regime, establishing a democratically elected government, and, later, a military coup that reinstated an authoritarian regime (Schatz & Stacher, 2013). The legacy of the Arab Spring can be seen in contemporary security challenges in Egypt, where the government's focus on stability and suppressing dissent has led to human rights abuses and political repression.

Regarding traditional values, the emphasis on pharaonic authority in the Egyptian civilization played a significant role in shaping perspectives. Pharaonic authority emphasized the ruler as the embodiment of divine power and the need for a centralized and authoritarian government. This traditional value's influence can be seen in the Egyptian government's focus on maintaining stability and suppressing dissent, as demonstrated by recent crackdowns on political dissidents. In conclusion, ancient civilizations' historical occurrences and traditional values significantly impact contemporary security challenges. The examples discussed illustrate how these factors shaped societies and continue influencing modern security landscapes.

In brief, historical events and cultural values have played a substantial role in shaping modern-day security challenges. Examples from ancient civilizations and religious texts illustrate how these factors have contributed to conflicts between different cultures and religions and highlight the challenges of cultural assimilation and the protection of cultural heritage. Understanding these historical and cultural factors is essential for addressing modern-day security challenges. Nevertheless, it requires a nuanced and complex approach that considers the diversity of cultural and religious values today.

Examples of Misusing Ancient Religious Texts

One example that highlights the influence of religious extremism on contemporary security challenges is the misinterpretation of the Quran by certain extremist groups. The Quran, the holy book of Islam, has been distorted by these groups to justify acts of violence against non-believers. Regrettably, these interpretations have led to the rise of terrorism and the dissemination of extremist ideology in various parts of the world.

A prominent case of an extremist interpretation of the Quran can be observed in the actions of Al Qaeda, Boko Haram in Nigeria, and the Islamic State of Iraq and Syria (ISIS). ISIS and other groups have misconstrued the Quran to validate their violent activities, including the targeting of civilians and the destruction of cultural heritage sites. They have cited Quranic passages such as the concept of "jihad" and the aspiration to establish a caliphate or Islamic state as justifications for their actions. Another example is the Taliban in Afghanistan, which employs similar Quranic justifications to support its violent actions and enforce strict Islamic law in the country.

Likewise, the Bible, the holy book of Christianity, has been interpreted by certain extremist groups to rationalize acts of violence and discrimination against minority groups. These interpretations have contributed to the rise of hate crimes and the spread of extremist ideology globally. A specific instance of an extremist interpretation of the Bible is the use of scripture to justify white supremacist beliefs. Some white supremacist groups cite Bible passages to uphold their ideology of racial superiority and advocate for violence against non-white individuals. For instance, the "Identity" movement, a white supremacist group, subscribes to the belief that white people are the true descendants of ancient Israelites, while non-white people are considered subhuman (Barkun, 1997). They manipulate passages from the Bible, such as Genesis 9:27, which describes the descendants of Noah and identifies his son Ham as the ancestor of dark-skinned people, to support this belief. These misinterpretations not only contribute to social unrest and political instability but also hinder efforts to maintain law and order and protect the general population.

Moreover, Bartholomeusz (2017) asserts that some have interpreted the concept of the "noble warrior" in Buddhism to justify violence and aggression. While the "noble warrior" archetype traditionally embodies a morally upright warrior skilled in battle, certain extremist groups, like the Buddhist Power Force in Sri Lanka, have twisted this concept to justify violent attacks against minority groups, particularly Muslims. This distorted interpretation has fueled religious tensions and violence in Sri Lanka, emphasizing the significance of understanding how religious beliefs and teachings can be interpreted in ways that contribute to contemporary security challenges.

Another example pertains to the influence of the caste system in Hinduism on contemporary security challenges. The caste system, which categorizes people into social classes based on birth, has been exploited to justify discrimination and violence against lower-caste groups. This discrimination perpetuates ongoing tensions and conflicts in India, presenting significant security challenges for the affected communities. Similarly, the concept of "karma" in Hinduism has been misinterpreted by some to rationalize violence and discrimination against certain groups (Chomsky, 2015). Once again, this misinterpretation aggravates tensions and conflicts in India, posing significant security challenges for the affected communities.

Additionally, Yegar (2017) states that the conflict between the Rohingya and Buddhist populations in Myanmar is fueled by historical animosity and cultural values. The Rohingya, due to their Muslim identity, have been subjected to violence and persecution, including forced displacement and denial of citizenship. The Buddhist population in Myanmar justifies their discrimination and violence against the Rohingya based on cultural values and interpretations of Buddhist teachings that portray non-Buddhists as inferior. This protracted conflict has created significant security challenges for Myanmar and the surrounding region, including the displacement of millions of people and the potential for regional destabilization.

What is more, the spread of extremist ideologies can contribute to the radicalization of individuals and the formation of extremist groups, posing a direct threat to national security. These groups may engage in acts of terrorism, targeting government institutions, infrastructure, and civilians. Such acts of violence induce widespread fear and destabilize communities, resulting in long-term social and economic consequences. Addressing this issue necessitates a concerted effort to combat extremist ideologies and hate speech that promotes discrimination and violence. Governments can develop policies and programs to foster social inclusion and combat discrimination, while law enforcement agencies can work towards identifying and monitoring extremist groups and individuals. Additionally, civil society organizations can engage in educational and advocacy efforts to promote tolerance and counter extremist narratives. By collaborating, we can strive for a more peaceful and stable society, free from the detrimental impact of extremist interpretations of religious texts.

Another example illustrating the influence of religious conflict on contemporary security challenges is the ongoing tension between Jews and Muslims over control of Jerusalem, a holy land sacred to both religions. This conflict has contributed to enduring tensions and conflicts in the region. Similarly, the conflict between Hindus and Muslims over control of the Indian subcontinent has fueled ongoing tensions and conflicts, leading to territorial disputes, terrorism, and sectarian violence, all of which pose significant security challenges to the affected countries (Juergensmeyer, 2017). In summary, the examples provided highlight how ancient religious texts have influenced contemporary security challenges.

Understanding and addressing these challenges requires acknowledging and comprehending the historical and cultural contexts that have shaped them. The above examples demonstrate how historical events, cultural values, and interpretations have impacted modern-day security challenges. To effectively tackle these challenges, it is essential to recognize and understand the complex historical and cultural contexts that have influenced them.

References:

Anderson, R. (2001). "Why Information Security is Hard - An Economic Perspective." In Workshop on the Economics of Information Security.

Armstrong, K. (2002). Islam: A short history. New York: Modern Library.

Arora, S., Deshmukh, A., & Govind, S. (2019). "Cybersecurity Threats, Vulnerabilities, and Strategies: A Comprehensive Overview." Procedia.

Barkun, M. (1997). Religion and the Racist Right: The Origins of the Christian Identity Movement. University of North Carolina Press.

Bartholomeusz, T. J. (2017). Buddhism and violence: Militarism and Buddhism in modern Asia. Oxford University Press.

Chomsky, N. (2015). Masters of Mankind: Essays and Lectures, 1969-2013. Haymarket Books.

Gibbon, E. (1994). The History of the Decline and Fall of the Roman Empire. Penguin Classics.

Gill, P. (2019). Ancient Civilizations and Modern International Relations. Palgrave Macmillan.

Goldsworthy, A. (2003). In the Name of Rome: The Men Who Won the Roman Empire. Orion.

Goldsworthy, A. (2010). The Complete Roman Army. Thames & Hudson.

Gordon, N. (2016). Israel-Palestine: A history of the conflict. University of California Press.

Hassner, R. (2009). War and peace in the Jewish tradition. New York: Routledge.

Haas, M. (2017). Cyber Espionage and China's "Face": The Role of Culture in Online Intrusions. Journal of Strategic Security, 10(4), 60–76.

Hanson, V. D. (1991). Hoplites: The Classical Greek Battle Experience. Routledge.

Hawass, Z. (2010). The labor organization of the Giza pyramid builders in the Fourth Dynasty. Cambridge Archaeological Journal, 20(3), 335–356.

Herodotus. (1975). The Histories. (A. de Selincourt, Trans.). New York: Penguin Books.

Juergensmeyer, M. (2017). Religious Terrorism and its Global Reach. Journal of Interdisciplinary Studies, 29(1-2), 1-14.

Kagan, D., Viggiano, G., & Lazenby, J. F. (2016). Men of Bronze: Hoplite Warfare in Ancient Greece. Princeton University Press.

Kaldor, M. (2013). New and old wars: Organized violence in a global era. John Wiley & Sons.

Kenyon, K. M. (1957). Excavations at Jericho: Volume 1: The Tombs Excavated in 1952-1954. British School of Archaeology in Jerusalem.

Khan, N. A. (2019). Understanding India's caste system. Council on Foreign Relations.

Korteweg, A. C., & Yurdakul, G. (2009). Islam, gender, and immigrant integration: Boundary drawing in discourses on honor killing in the Netherlands and Germany. Gender & Society, 23(3), 349-371.

Liverani, M. (2013). The Ancient Near East: History, Society, and Economy. Routledge.

Makdisi, U. S. (2017). The Islamic schism: How it developed and why it matters. Brookings Institution Press.

Muqaddas, A. (2020). Ancient Civilizations, Culture, and Modern-day Security Challenges. International Journal of Economics, Commerce and Management, VIII (11), 27–38.

National Research Council. (2003). Living on an Active Earth: Perspectives on Earthquake Science. National Academies Press.

Quran. (n.d.). The Holy Quran. (A. Yusuf Ali, Trans.). Retrieved from http://www.clearquran.com/

Ridley, R. T. (1982). "The Emperor's Retrospect: Augustus' Res Gestae in Epigraphical Perspective." Transactions of the American Philological Association, pp. 112, 131–152.

Roth, M. T. (1997). Law Collections from Mesopotamia and Asia Minor. Scholars Press.

Pargament, K. I., & Mahoney, A. (2009). "Sacred Matters: Sanctification as a Vital Topic for the Psychology of Religion." The International Journal for the Psychology of Religion, 19(4), 251–275.

Sherif, M., Harvey, O. J., White, B. J., Hood, W. R., & Sherif, C. W. (1961). "Intergroup Conflict and Cooperation: The Robbers Cave Experiment." University of Oklahoma Book Exchange.

Schatz, J. L., & Stacher, J. (2013). Egypt's Turbulent Transition: The Unfolding Process of Political Liberalization. Journal of Democracy, 24(3), 54-68. doi:10.1353/jod.2013.0055

Thakur, P. (2016). The relevance of Kautilya's Arthashastra in contemporary India. Journal of Applied Management and Investments, 5(2), 104–109. https://doi.org/10.22313/2450-7047-2016-5-2-104-109.

United Nations. (2016). The Paris Agreement. Retrieved from https://unfccc.int/sites/default/files/english_paris_agreement.pdf

Van De Mieroop, M. (2015). A history of the ancient Near East: ca. 3000-323 BC. John Wiley & Sons.

Van de Mieroop, M. (2004). King Hammurabi of Babylon: A Biography. Wiley-Blackwell.

World Economic Forum. (2021). The Global Risks Report 2021. Retrieved from https://www.weforum.org/reports/the-global-risks-report-2021

Yegar, M. (2017). The Rohingya Muslim minority in Myanmar and recent violence: How cultural factors and international responses may be contributing to a humanitarian crisis. Journal of Muslim Minority Affairs, 37(3), 393–406. doi 10.1080/13602004.2017.1386828.

Zhang, Y., & Lintner, B. (2019). China's national security discourse and the South China Sea. In N. Scherer & A. Burtea (Eds.), Maritime security in the South China Sea: Regional implications and international cooperation (pp. 31-56). Springer.

2

Introduction to National Security in Ancient Times and Religious Texts

National security has been a concern since ancient times, as nations and civilizations sought to protect themselves from external threats and preserve their way of life. Religious texts from various traditions also address the issue of national security, offering different perspectives on the topic. National security protects a country's people, territory, and interests from external and internal threats. In comparison, the concept of national security may seem modern, but ancient societies and religious texts have discussed and addressed the need for national security.

National security has been a concern for rulers and governments since ancient times. However, in ancient times, the term "national security" was not used; instead, the focus was on securing the state or empire from external threats and internal rebellions. In addition, the security of a state was closely linked with religion, and religious texts played a crucial role in shaping the concept of security. In the old days, national security was often tied to military power, territorial control, and the ability to defend against external threats. Ancient societies such as Rome, Persia, and China had standing armies and engaged in warfare to protect their territory and interests.

Religious texts also address the issue of national security in various ways. For example, in the Old Testament, there are abundant references to protecting the Israelites from their enemies, such as the story of David and Goliath. Also, in the Judeo-

Christian tradition, the Old Testament describes God's role in protecting the nation of Israel from its enemies. The book of Psalms, in particular, contains many prayers and hymns that express trust in God's protection and deliverance from danger. Espionage and intelligence gathering were also prevalent in ancient times, with examples such as using spies in the Chinese Warring States period. Ancient Greece, Rome, and China built strong armies and fortifications to defend themselves from enemies and expand their territories. The concept of "just war" emerged in these societies, which held that wars could be fought for legitimate reasons, such as self-defense or the defense of one's allies.

Moreover, ancient religious texts, such as the Bible, Quran, and Hindu scriptures, provide different viewpoints on national security. These manuscripts emphasize the importance of protecting the state's people, territory, and sovereignty. The Bible, for instance, highlights the importance of military power and represents God as a warrior who helps the Israelites defeat their enemies. The Quran also emphasizes the significance of military strength and describes God as the protector of the believers. In Hinduism, the principle of dharma (righteousness) is central to national security.

In Islamic texts, the concept of Himayah is often interpreted as safeguarding against external threats to protect the Muslim community. In comparison, the primary interpretation of jihad is striving against evil internally and defensively. It can be offensive against outside threats in unforeseen situations, while others emphasize non-violent resistance and diplomacy. In Hinduism, the principle of dharma consists of the duty to protect one's community and nation. The ancient Indian epic, the Mahabharata, depicts a war between rival factions, with the victorious side seen as upholding dharma. Similarly, the principle of non-violence in Buddhism can inform conflict prevention and de-escalation strategies.

From a present-day perspective, national security has become more complex and multifaceted. Issues such as terrorism, cybersecurity, and economic interdependence have become critical factors in national security strategy. In addition, the ethical considerations of using military force and protecting individual rights have come to the forefront of discussions on national security. There are also differing perspectives on national security in ancient times and religious texts. Some argue that military strength is necessary for national security, while others believe in peaceful diplomacy and alliances. In the Taoist text, the Tao Te Ching, soft power is discussed as a platform to achieve national security without resorting to military force.

In the distant past, empires and kingdoms were constantly at war, and the concept of national security was closely linked with military power. The Romans, for example, developed a sophisticated system of fortifications, roads, and communication networks to defend their empire. Similarly, the Chinese built the Great Wall to protect their territory from invaders. In India, the Mauryan emperor, Ashoka, emphasized the importance of non-violence and promoted policies of peaceful coexistence.

Additionally, religious texts also play a crucial role in understanding national security. Many religions have emphasized the importance of peace and security as essential elements of human well-being. Accordingly, religious texts offer insight into the values and beliefs of societies and how they have influenced their approach to security. In particular, in Christianity, the "just war" concept has been used to justify military intervention in defense of the state or to protect human rights. In Islam, the "Inner Struggle (jihad)" concept has been interpreted as a defensive war to protect Muslim lands from external forces. Religious traditions such as Christianity and Islam emphasize the importance of social justice and the common good, which can inform modern approaches to national security.

The concept of national security also evolved. In the medieval period, the rise of feudalism and the emergence of nation-states led to a greater emphasis on territorial integrity and the state's defense. The advent of modern technology, such as firearms and artillery, also changed the nature of warfare and led to the development of standing armies. In brief, while the concept of national security has evolved, ancient societies and religious texts have addressed the need for protection against external and internal threats. The differing outlooks on achieving national security continue to be debated and discussed today. While ancient societies emphasized military power and territorial control, present-day national security problems are more diverse and complex. Gaining awareness of national security's historical and religious dimensions helps us develop more nuanced and effective strategies for protecting our nations and communities.

Furthermore, national security has been a matter of concern since ancient times, and religious texts played an important role in shaping the concept of security. The perspectives of various ancient texts on national security stress the need for protecting the people, territory, and sovereignty of the state. Consequently, the concept of national security evolved, and military power played a central role in securing the state. Learning about national security in ancient times and religious texts and their relationship with modern perspectives is essential. Understanding the concept of national security in ancient times and religious texts is essential because it helps us appreciate the evolution of security challenges societies face and how they have dealt with them.

Additionally, it allows us to understand the modern security challenges we face today, the origin of these challenges, and their root causes. Also, understanding national security in ancient times and religious texts is significant for the reason that it provides us with a historical perspective on how societies have approached the concept of security throughout time. By investigating ancient civilizations and religious texts, we can attain an awareness of how people have sought to protect themselves from perceived threats, whether internal or external.

It is worth noting that ancient civilizations often faced security challenges similar to those of modern nations, such as territorial disputes, external threats, and internal instability. Examining how these ancient societies addressed these challenges, including using military force, diplomacy, and alliances, can offer practical insights for contemporary security strategies. For instance, the Roman Empire, one of the most powerful empires of the ancient world, had a well-organized military and relied on alliances with neighboring states to maintain its security. The Roman approach to national security may provide practical lessons for modern nations on balancing military strength and diplomacy to achieve security and stability.

Understanding the meaning of national security in ancient times and religious texts is crucial for several reasons. Firstly, it can provide insights into how ancient civilizations approached and maintained their security, which can inform contemporary security strategies. According to Karns and Mingst (2010), ancient civilizations often faced similar security challenges to those faced by modern states, such as territorial disputes, border incursions, and the threat of invasion. By studying how ancient civilizations approached these challenges, modern views on national security can acquire insights into effective strategies for protecting territorial integrity and ensuring stability.

For example, the Roman Empire was known for its well-trained and disciplined military forces, which allowed it to maintain control over a vast territory. Similarly, the Chinese Empire relied on military strength, diplomacy, and economic incentives to maintain control over its borders and expand its territory. In ancient China, the concept of the Mandate of Heaven was used to justify political authority and maintain stability (Hsu, 2017). Modern perspectives on national security can draw on these strategies to inform their approaches to territorial protection and stability.

Secondly, religious texts often contain principles and values that shape how people perceive national security and conflict resolution. The principles found in religious texts can inform modern perspectives on national security. For example, the principle of justice is central to many religious traditions, and this can inform approaches to conflict resolution and post-conflict reconciliation. Similarly, the principle of non-violence in Buddhism can inform conflict prevention and de-escalation strategies.

Thirdly, studying ancient and religious stances on national security can help identify patterns and trends in security policy over time. For instance, the ancient Greek city-states often relied on alliances and diplomacy to maintain security, while the Roman Empire relied more heavily on military force. Identifying these patterns can help modern perspectives on national security develop more effective strategies for managing conflict and promoting stability. Michael E. Smith (2008) stated that ancient civilizations such as the Maya and the Aztecs developed sophisticated military strategies to protect their territory and fend off external threats. Analyzing the relationship between ancient national security and religious texts and modern views can help identify patterns and trends that may inform current and future security policies.

National security in ancient times was often closely tied to territorial boundaries and military strength. Ancient Roman, Persian, and Chinese empires relied on robust military strength to defend their borders and expand their territories. They also used diplomacy and alliances to maintain their security and influence over neighboring states. Religious texts also played a vital role in ancient national security. Religion was often used to legitimize political authority and establish social norms. For example, in ancient Egypt, the pharaoh was seen as a divine ruler with the power to control the Nile and ensure the kingdom's prosperity. The Romans built a massive wall to protect their empire from invaders, and the Chinese constructed the Great Wall to protect against the Mongols. Ancient societies also developed complex religious and cultural beliefs closely tied to notions of security, such as the idea that the gods would protect them if they maintained certain rituals or sacrifices.

Ancient societies had unique ways of ensuring their security, which differed significantly from the modern concept of national security. The ancient city-states of Greece and Rome strongly emphasized the military as a means of defense. Similarly, the "Mandate of Heaven" concept was central to ensuring the state's security in ancient China. This concept was based on the belief that the ruling dynasty had the divine right to rule, and as long as they ruled justly and effectively, the state would be secure. Understanding the relationship between ancient methods of ensuring security and religious texts and modern security perspectives is essential since it allows us to identify the continuities and discontinuities in approaches to security over time. It also helps us appreciate the complexity of security challenges and the need for a multifaceted approach to security that considers different cultural and historical contexts.

Religious texts also offer vital insights into the concept of national security. For instance, Vedas and other Hindu texts contain numerous passages instructing princes, kings, and everyday people to fight to protect their territories. The Old Testament of the Bible is filled with stories of Israelite armies fighting to defend their land from foreign invaders. Equally, the Ten Commandments in the Abrahamic religions emphasize the importance of social order and justice (Exodus 20:1-17; Deuteronomy 5:6-21). Furthermore, the Quran contains numerous passages about protecting the Muslim community from enemies. For example, the Quran states, "And do not kill the soul which Allah has forbidden, except by right" (6:151). The Quran also highlights the importance of protecting property by stating, "And do not consume one another's wealth unjustly or send it [in bribery] to the rulers in order that they might aid you to consume a portion of the wealth of the people in sin, while you know [it is unlawful]" (2:188).

Religious writings also encompass principles and values that shape how people perceive national security and conflict resolution. For example, the Abrahamic religions (Judaism, Christianity, and Islam) emphasize the importance of justice and mercy, which are often invoked in discussions of just war theory and humanitarian intervention. In Buddhism, the principle of non-violence is central, with implications for resolving conflicts and informing strategies for conflict prevention and de-escalation (Keown, 2013).

Analyzing the relationship between ancient national security, religious manuscripts, and modern perspectives can offer practical insights into patterns and trends in current security policies. For example, many modern conflicts are framed in religious or ideological terms, and understanding the historical roots of these conflicts can inform strategies for conflict resolution. Similarly, understanding how ancient civilizations balanced military strength and diplomacy can provide insights into contemporary security challenges. Identifying these patterns can help modern perspectives on national security develop more effective strategies for managing conflict and promoting stability. According to Robert E. Looney (2011), reviewing historical patterns of conflict and cooperation can help modern policymakers develop more effective approaches to national security.

Today, national security is often discussed in terms of protecting against terrorism, cyber threats, and other non-state actors. Nevertheless, the principles of ancient times and religious texts still inform our modern approach to national security. For instance, the concept of deterrence, which involves demonstrating military strength to prevent an attack, is a tactic that has been employed throughout history and remains relevant today. Additionally, many religious traditions emphasize the importance of justice, mercy, and compassion, which can affect how modern nations approach issues such as refugee resettlement and treating enemy combatants. In conclusion, examining the relationship between ancient national security, religious texts, and modern perspectives can give us better insight into long-term trends in global security. For example, the ongoing conflicts in the Middle East have roots in ancient religious and territorial disputes, and understanding the historical context of these conflicts may provide insights into potential solutions.

Learning about national security from ancient times and religious texts is essential for gaining insight into the historical evolution of this concept and its relevance to modern perspectives. By examining the approaches taken by past civilizations and religious traditions, we can better appreciate the current debates around security and the different ways in which actors approach this critical issue. Thus, modern perspectives on national security can benefit from these complementary approaches by adopting strategies that incorporate both military and non-military means of maintaining stability and protecting territorial integrity. Additionally, understanding the ethical principles espoused by religious traditions can highlight the importance of incorporating ethical considerations into national security policies. The principles of justice, mercy, and non-violence found in religious texts can guide policymakers in evaluating the moral implications of their decisions and designing policies that prioritize ethical considerations (McCauley & Moskalenko, 2018).

Moreover, the values and principles espoused by religious traditions can promote interfaith understanding and cooperation, contributing to regional stability and security. Ancient civilizations often relied on a combination of military strength, diplomacy, and economic incentives to maintain stability and protect their territories. For example, the Chinese Empire used a combination of military force and trade agreements to expand its territory and establish tributary relationships with neighboring states. The Roman Empire similarly relied on military strength and diplomacy to maintain control over its borders and expand its territory.

In addition, modern perspectives on national security can benefit from historical lessons learned from ancient civilizations and religious texts. Studying the successes and failures of ancient empires can inform contemporary strategies for maintaining stability and protecting territorial integrity. Similarly, the principles and values found in religious texts can help modern states develop more ethical and practical approaches to conflict resolution and post-conflict reconciliation. Furthermore, ancient civilizations and religious texts recognized the importance of stability for national security. Stability was seen as essential for maintaining social order and preventing conflict within and between states. For instance, in ancient China, the concept of the Mandate of Heaven was used to justify political authority and maintain stability. Similarly, the Ten Commandments in the Abrahamic religions emphasize the importance of social order and justice.

Security was a central concern for ancient civilizations, as it is for modern states. Ancient states recognized the need for strong military forces to protect their borders and defend against threats from neighboring states. For example, the Roman Empire relied on a powerful military to expand its territory and protect its borders, while ancient Greece relied on alliances and diplomacy to maintain security. Similarly, as it is for modern states, territorial protection was another key concern for ancient civilizations. Ancient empires used various strategies to protect their territorial integrity, such as building walls and fortifications and using diplomacy to maintain peaceful relations with neighboring states. Modern views on national security can be learned from these ancient and religious perspectives by recognizing the interdependence of stability, security, and territorial protection. For example, the Great Wall of China was built in the third century BCE to protect against invasions from the north (Kwong, 2018). A stable society is essential for maintaining security and protecting territorial integrity. Similarly, practical territorial protection strategies may require military force and diplomatic efforts to maintain peaceful relations with neighboring states.

Besides, the principles and values found in religious texts can inform modern approaches to national security by emphasizing the importance of justice, mercy, and non-violence. These principles can guide strategies for conflict resolution and post-conflict reconciliation. Understanding the concept of national security in ancient times and religious texts and its relationship with modern perspectives is essential because it helps us appreciate the evolution of security challenges faced by societies, the origin of these challenges, and their root causes. It also allows us to identify the continuities and discontinuities in approaches to security over time and appreciate the complexity of security challenges.

Looking into ancient times and religious manuscripts is essential for learning the historical roots of contemporary security challenges and informing strategies for conflict resolution and national security policy. In brief, modern perspectives on national security can benefit from examining the stances on security, stability, and territorial protection found in ancient times and religious texts. Moreover, by learning from the successes and failures of ancient civilizations and drawing on the ethical principles found in religious traditions, modern nations can develop more effective strategies for achieving security and stability in an increasingly complex global environment.

Incorporating insights from ancient times and religious texts into modern national security perspectives can also foster greater cultural understanding and promote interfaith dialogue. By recognizing the commonalities and differences between different cultural and religious traditions, policymakers and strategists can develop more nuanced and effective approaches to national security challenges that consider different communities' diverse perspectives and experiences. It is vital to consider the historical lessons from ancient civilizations and religious texts to develop a well-rounded perspective on national security. By examining the successes and failures of past societies, we can gain valuable insights into the best ways to protect a nation.

Modern perspectives on national security can learn from and benefit from the complementary viewpoints on stability, security, and territorial protection found in ancient times and religious texts. This can be achieved by adopting strategies that incorporate both military and non-military means of maintaining stability, drawing on historical lessons to inform current security policies, and incorporating ethical principles and values into approaches to conflict resolution and post-conflict reconciliation. In summary, modern perspectives on national security can significantly benefit from the historical lessons of ancient civilizations and religious texts. By studying the successes and failures of the past, we can develop a more comprehensive understanding of how to effectively protect our nations while upholding our values and principles.

Ancient Religious Texts and Their Foundations

National security and land protection have been significant concerns for civilizations and religions throughout history. From ancient to modern times, societies have grappled with the challenges of defending their borders, safeguarding their territories, and protecting their national interests. Throughout history, ancient civilizations and religious texts have placed significant emphasis on territorial security and vital interests. This emphasis can be observed in various historical and religious texts, such as the Vedas, the oldest Hindu scriptures, which contain hymns and rituals related to the protection of the cosmos, the establishment of order and stability, and other texts like the Bible, the Quran, the Code of Hammurabi, and the writings of Sun Tzu.

The importance of national security and land protection is evident in the Code of Hammurabi, created around 1754 BCE in ancient Babylon. The code laid out strict rules for the protection of property and land, along with punishments for those who violated these laws. For example, stealing property or destroying crops could result in death or forced repayment of the stolen goods. The Code of Hammurabi also emphasized the significance of military strength and the protection of borders, stating that the king's duty was to protect his people and their land from foreign invaders.

Hinduism, which emerged in ancient India, is a diverse religion encompassing a wide range of texts, practices, and beliefs. Hinduism has also been used to justify territorial expansion and the subjugation of other peoples, as evidenced by the caste system and the concept of dharma. While the Vedas, the oldest and most important religious texts in Hinduism, do not contain specific guidelines regarding warfare or territorial protection, they emphasize the importance of dharma, righteous behavior, and the duty to protect one's family and community. The Mahabharata, an important Hindu text, narrates the story of a great war between two clans, highlighting the significance of duty and righteousness and raising moral questions about war and violence.

In Hinduism, the concept of national security is linked to the protection of dharma, the cosmic order, which includes the proper conduct of rulers and the defense of the kingdom against external threats. The Bhagavad Gita, a Hindu scripture, features a dialogue between the warrior Arjuna and the God Krishna regarding the duty of warriors to fight in defense of the kingdom. In Chapter 2, Verse 31, Krishna states, "And even considering your personal duty as a warrior, you should not hesitate to fight. This is my eternal, immovable opinion."

Buddhism, which originated in India in the 5th century BCE, emphasizes the importance of nonviolence and the renunciation of worldly attachments. Buddhist texts, however, have also been used to justify defensive warfare and the protection of Buddhist communities. Buddhist teachings on nonviolence and compassion have influenced the development of Buddhist approaches to conflict resolution. While the Buddhist canon, which includes the Tripitaka and various other texts, does not specifically provide guidelines on warfare or territorial protection, it contains teachings on ethics, meditation, and the nature of reality. In Buddhism, national security is connected to protecting the Buddha's teachings and the monastic community (sangha) from external threats. The Four Great Kings, guardians of the four cardinal directions in Buddhist cosmology, are said to protect the Buddha's teachings and the sangha.

The Jewish Bible, also known as the Old Testament, contains numerous references to the importance of security, stability, and territorial protection. For instance, in the book of Exodus, God promises to protect the Israelites from their enemies if they follow His laws and commandments. The book of Deuteronomy provides detailed instructions on how the Israelites should conquer and occupy the land of Canaan. The Bible emphasizes the significance of national security and land protection, which was achieved through military strength and the removal of the land's inhabitants. Additionally, the book of Nehemiah recounts the story of rebuilding Jerusalem's walls for the city's protection.

In Judaism, national security has been associated with the concept of a promised land, specifically the land of Israel. The Hebrew Bible, particularly the Torah, Joshua, and Judges, describes the conquest of the land of Canaan by the Israelites. The interpretation of the promised land concept has varied over time, with some scholars arguing for a divine mandate for Jewish control over the land of Israel, while others emphasize the need for peaceful coexistence with other nations.

Conversely, Christianity takes a more universalist approach to national security, emphasizing the importance of love, forgiveness, and nonviolence. The New Testament teaches that all people are equal in the eyes of God and that violence is not the solution to conflicts. However, throughout history, Christians have interpreted these teachings differently, with some advocating for pacifism and others supporting just war theories. Christianity, emerging from Judaism, adopted many of its foundational texts. While the New Testament emphasizes peace and nonviolence, it has also been used in certain contexts to justify violence and territorial expansion. The Crusades, for example, involved European Christians seeking to reclaim Jerusalem and other holy sites from Muslim control.

In Islam, the Quran also places great importance on protecting land and defending one's homeland. The Quran is concerned with Muslims' security and territorial protection, containing numerous references to warfare and military strategy. For example, it encourages Muslims to defend themselves against aggression but also requires them to offer peace terms before attacking an enemy. The Quran includes rules on treating non-combatants during warfare and prohibits the destruction of civilian property. It states that Muslims must defend their land and people against external threats, considering it a duty to protect the borders of the Muslim state. Islamic history reflects this, with Muslims fighting numerous battles to defend their lands and people, such as the Battle of Badr and the Battle of Uhud. The Quran also emphasizes the defense of the Islamic community (ummah) against external threats, as seen in Surah (chapter) 8:60, which states, "And prepare against them whatever you are able of power and of steeds of war by which you may terrify the enemy of Allah and your enemy."

The writings of Sun Tzu, a Chinese military strategist and philosopher from the 5th century BCE, also emphasize the importance of national security and land protection. In his book "The Art of War," Sun Tzu outlines various strategies for defending one's homeland, including intelligence gathering and creating defensive fortifications. He stresses the importance of understanding the terrain and the enemy's tactics to protect one's land successfully.

Moreover, in ancient civilizations like the Mesopotamians, Egyptians, and Greeks, national security and land protection were crucial for survival. These societies faced threats of invasion from neighboring tribes and empires, necessitating a strong military and well-fortified border. For instance, the city of Babylon in Mesopotamia had a system of walls and gates to protect against external forces. Similarly, the ancient Egyptians built forts and outposts along their borders to defend against potential invaders. Religious texts have also emphasized the importance of national security and land protection.

The Bible contains numerous references to the need for Israel to defend itself against enemies. In the Book of Nehemiah, for example, Nehemiah led a group of Jews in rebuilding the walls of Jerusalem after their destruction by the Babylonians. The Quran instructs Muslims to defend themselves against those seeking to harm them, while the Hadith, a collection of sayings and actions attributed to the Prophet Muhammad, emphasizes the importance of protecting one's land and possessions. In modern times, national security and land protection have become even more critical due to the rise of global terrorism and the increasing threat of cyberattacks. Governments across the planet have implemented various measures, including physical barriers, advanced technology, and increased military capabilities, to protect their borders and citizens.

In summary, national security and land protection have been important throughout history, as reflected in ancient civilizations and religious texts. The Code of Hammurabi, the Bible, the Quran, and the writings of Sun Tzu all emphasize the significance of protecting one's land and people, providing strategies and guidelines for doing so. These lessons remain relevant today as nations worldwide grapple with the challenge of ensuring their security and protecting their borders. The importance of national security and land protection has been a consistent theme throughout human history, recognized by societies and underscored by religious texts in the context of human existence.

Ancient Civilizations and Their Foundations

In ancient times, nations faced constant risks of invasion and conquest from neighboring tribes and empires, leading to diverse notions of national security among ancient civilizations. These perspectives were shaped by cultural and historical contexts, with religious texts often providing guidance on maintaining security and protecting the land. Here are some examples:

Ancient Mesopotamia

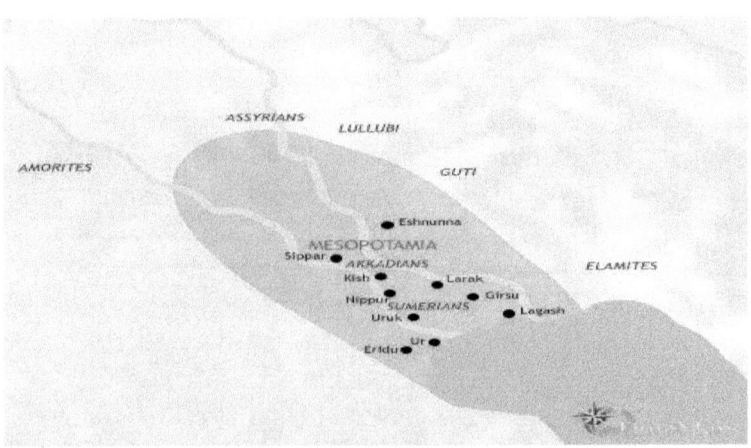

Figure 1 Map of the Ancient Middle East in 3500 BCE, showing the merging Sumerian civilization in Mesopotamia. Timeline of Ancient Mesopotamian Civilization c. 5000-3500 BCE: The first city-states gradually develop in southern Mesopotamia. This is the achievement of the Sumerian people.

Ancient Mesopotamia, located in modern-day Iraq, was a cradle of civilizations that thrived between 4000 BCE and 500 BCE. The Sumerians, Babylonians, and Assyrians, among others, held distinct perspectives on stability, governance, security, and territorial protection. The environment significantly shaped Mesopotamian perspectives, as the region was fertile yet prone to periodic floods, droughts, and natural disasters. To ensure their people's well-being and maintain power, Mesopotamian rulers developed sophisticated irrigation, agriculture, and trade systems (Matthews, 2005).

The earliest Mesopotamian societies, such as Sumer, were organized around independent city-states, each with its ruler, priesthood, and administrative apparatus. These city-states often competed for resources, territory, and prestige. Rulers maintained stability through a combination of military force, diplomacy, and cultural influence. Legal codes, like the renowned Code of Hammurabi, were developed to regulate social behavior, settle disputes, and ensure justice (Roth, 1997). As Mesopotamian civilization expanded, political structures evolved. The Akkadian Empire, established by Sargon of Akkad in the 24th century BCE, became the world's first true empire, spanning from the Persian Gulf to the Mediterranean Sea. The Akkadian rulers relied on a centralized bureaucracy, a standing army, and provincial governors to exert control. They implemented tribute, taxation, and trade systems to extract resources from conquered peoples and redistribute them (Liverani, 2013).

Later Mesopotamian empires, such as the Babylonians and the Assyrians, further refined and expanded these strategies. The Babylonian Empire, founded by Hammurabi in the 18th century BCE, achieved cultural feats like the Hanging Gardens and the Ishtar Gate. Administrative innovations included standardized weights and measures and the establishment of a postal system. The Assyrian Empire, emerging in the 14th century BCE, was the most militaristic and expansionist of all Mesopotamian empires. Assyrian rulers relied on a professional army, fortified cities, and deportation and resettlement policies to control vast territories.

They also developed an intricate intelligence network with spies and informants throughout the empire (Liverani, 2013). Stability was a fundamental concern for Mesopotamian civilizations. The Sumerians, for example, believed in the importance of strong and just leadership for maintaining social order. The lugal, or king, held religious and secular authority over the city-state, responsible for upholding order, defending against external threats, and ensuring the well-being of subjects (Kramer, 1963). Similarly, the Babylonians emphasized stability for their civilization's prosperity. Hammurabi's code of laws aimed to establish and maintain social order, with strict punishments for crimes and regulations governing trade, property rights, and family law. The code provided a framework for resolving disputes and maintaining social stability, enforced through courts and judges (Brisch, 2014).

In terms of governance, Mesopotamian civilizations adopted various political structures to manage their societies. The Sumerians operated under a decentralized political system, with power distributed among multiple authorities. This arrangement allowed for local autonomy while facilitating cooperation and coordination (Jacobsen, 1976). The Mesopotamians developed a system of diplomacy, including treaties and alliances, to foster cooperation and communication between city-states. For instance, the Assyrian Empire formed alliances with neighboring kingdoms while utilizing military force and diplomacy to expand and secure borders (Van De Mieroop, 2015). On the other hand, the Babylonians embraced a centralized system of government, with the king holding ultimate authority over all aspects of governance, domestic and foreign (Van De Mieroop, 2005).

Security and territorial protection were significant concerns due to conflicts between city-states and neighboring societies. The Assyrians excelled in military matters, establishing a highly effective army and advanced weaponry. Their military prowess allowed them to conquer an extensive empire stretching from Egypt to Iran, maintaining control through governors and administrators (Grayson, 1991).

Additionally, the Mesopotamians constructed walls and fortifications to defend their cities and territories, which served as barriers against invading armies. One example is King Nebuchadnezzar II's famous Babylon walls, which were built in the 6th century BCE. These walls were made of baked bricks and were reinforced with towers and gates, making them an effective defense against enemy attacks. The construction of such fortifications highlights the importance that the Mesopotamians placed on security and territorial protection (Nemet-Nejat, 1998). They also developed advanced military technologies, such as the composite bow and chariot, which gave them an advantage in battle (Van De Mieroop, 2005). Additionally, the Mesopotamians employed various defensive strategies, including using spies and scouts to gather intelligence about enemy movements and intentions.

In brief, the Mesopotamian civilizations had distinct perspectives on stability, governing, security, and territorial protection. The Sumerians recognized the importance of effective leadership in maintaining social order, while the Babylonians developed a system of laws to regulate all aspects of society. The Sumerians had a decentralized system of government, while the Babylonians were centralized. Finally, the Assyrians developed a sophisticated military machine to protect and expand their territory. These perspectives continue to influence our understanding of governance and security today. Mesopotamian rulers relied on various strategies to maintain stability and control, from military force to diplomacy to cultural influence. They also developed sophisticated administrative systems, legal codes, and cultural institutions to regulate social behavior and ensure justice.

Lastly, these strategies and institutions had a lasting impact on the development of human civilization, influencing subsequent empires and societies throughout the ancient and medieval worlds. Ancient India.

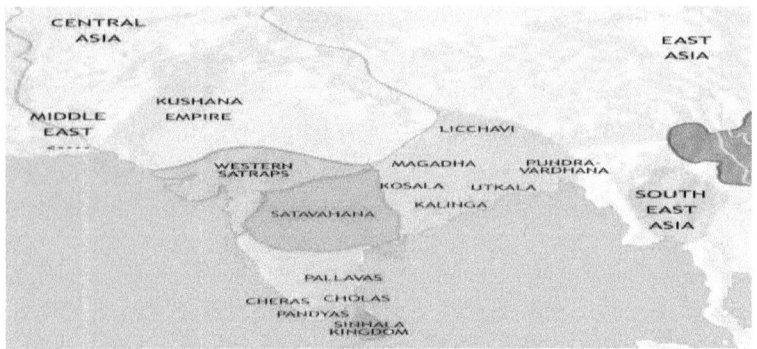

Figure 2 Map of India and South Asia, 500 CE, The Gupta Empire

Ancient India had a rich and diverse history, spanning several millennia, with different kingdoms and empires holding varied viewpoints on governing, stability, military, and territorial protection. In this concise introduction, we will examine the different perspectives of ancient Indian kingdoms on these issues. Regarding governing, the ancient Indian kingdoms had varied perspectives on governance. Some empires, such as the Mauryan Empire, had a centralized and authoritarian system of governance. They maintained a large army and a vast bureaucracy to administer their territories. On the other hand, the Gupta Empire had a more decentralized system of governance, with regional governors having significant autonomy. The Chola Dynasty was known for its efficient and decentralized system of government, with the king delegating power to his ministers (Basham, 1981).

As for stability, all ancient Indian kingdoms placed a high value on stability, as it was crucial for the smooth functioning of society. The Mauryan Empire, for example, implemented a system of law to maintain stability. The Gupta Empire achieved stability through economic prosperity and cultural and scientific advancement (Habib, 2012). The Chola Dynasty maintained stability through efficient governance and the construction of infrastructure such as temples, roads, and irrigation systems. In terms of the military, military power was an essential aspect of ancient Indian kingdoms. The Mauryan Empire had a vast army with infantry, cavalry, and elephants, which helped them expand their territories. The Chola

Dynasty's powerful navy allowed them to dominate the Indian Ocean trade routes. The Mughal Empire had a well-organized army with skilled commanders, which helped them maintain their territories.

In terms of territorial protection, ancient Indian kingdoms highly valued territorial protection. The Mauryan Empire built an extensive network of fortifications to protect their borders. The Gupta Empire maintained friendly relations with neighboring kingdoms to avoid conflict. The Chola Dynasty established a system of alliances with neighboring kingdoms to protect their territories from external threats (Stein, 1998). Finally, the Mughal Empire maintained a strong army to defend its borders from invaders.

Additionally, in ancient India, national security was closely tied to the concept of "dharma," which referred to the moral and ethical principles that governed society. The ancient Indians believed that the ruler had a duty to protect the people and maintain order, achieved through a strong military and effective governance. The concept of "artha," or material prosperity, was also important, as it was believed that a strong economy was necessary for national security. The ancient Indians believed in the concept of dharma, which emphasized the importance of justice and morality in maintaining social and political stability. They built defensive fortifications and relied on a well-trained army to defend against external threats, but they also emphasized diplomacy and alliances to maintain peace.

In ancient India, the king's role was to ensure that dharma was upheld within his kingdom, and this often involved using force to defend his subjects against external threats. However, the Indian concept of national security was closely tied to the idea of ahimsa or nonviolence. Therefore, the king was expected to use force only as a last resort (Ganguly, 2017). Ancient India was ruled by various empires and kingdoms throughout history, each with its approach to national security. The Maurya Empire, for example, had a strong military and a system of spies to gather intelligence on potential threats. On the other hand, the Gupta Empire focused on diplomacy and alliances to maintain peace and stability. In brief, the ancient Indian kingdoms had different governing, stability, military, and territorial protection perspectives. However, all of them shared a common goal of maintaining peace and ensuring the welfare of their people.

Furthermore, their unique cultural, social, and political contexts shaped their attitudes. Therefore, a concise understanding of the history of ancient India is crucial to understanding present-day Indian society and its values.

In Ancient China

Ancient China had a rich and complex history, spanning several thousand years, with different dynasties and empires holding varied perspectives on governing, stability, military, and territorial protection. This brief introduction will examine the different stances of ancient Chinese dynasties on these issues.

As for governing, ancient Chinese dynasties had a centralized and authoritarian system of governance, with the emperor as the ultimate authority. The emperor was aided by a bureaucracy of officials who helped to administer the empire (Ebrey, 2009). Additionally, Confucianism played a significant role in shaping the governance system, emphasizing hierarchy, duty, and moral behavior. Also, in terms of stability, stability was a crucial aspect of ancient Chinese society. The dynasties sought to maintain stability by implementing a system of law and order and by promoting economic prosperity. Additionally, Confucianism emphasized the importance of stable family relationships and social harmony, which contributed to overall stability in society.

In terms of the military, military power was an essential aspect of ancient Chinese dynasties. The dynasties maintained a large standing army, which helped them defend their territories and expand their empires (Fairbank, 2017). Additionally, the use of gunpowder in warfare gave the Chinese armies an advantage over their enemies. As for territorial protection, territorial protection was a primary concern for ancient Chinese dynasties. They built the Great Wall of China as a defensive measure to protect their borders from external threats. Additionally, the dynasties maintained a strong navy to protect their maritime interests and trade routes (Lewis, 2007).

Furthermore, the concept of national security in ancient China revolved around maintaining a robust military and safeguarding the state from external threats. The military was considered the foundation of national security, with ancient Chinese emphasizing the significance of a well-trained army for defending the state. The concept of "tianxia," or "all under heaven," held central importance in Chinese political and social philosophy. It referred to a unified and harmonious world order under the emperor's rule. Safeguarding the empire's borders was a top priority, and the construction of the Great Wall of China symbolized this endeavor.

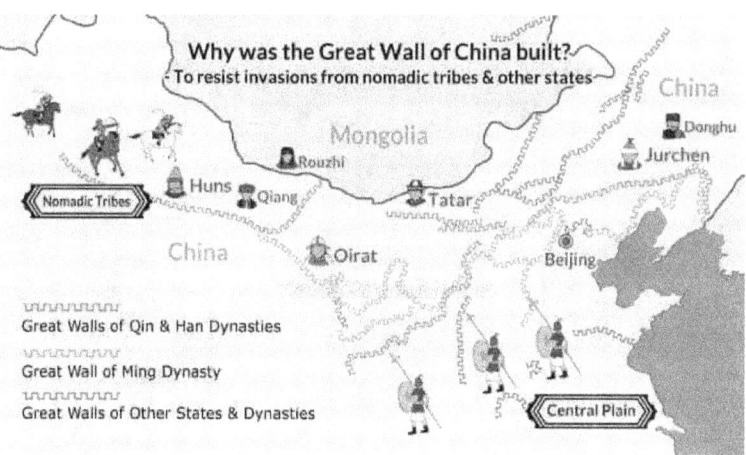

Figure 3 Map of Ancient China in 200 CE: the Later Han Dynasty

Ancient China also developed sophisticated military strategies and technologies, such as gunpowder and the use of cavalry. National security in ancient China was interconnected with the protection of the ruling dynasty against internal and external threats. The philosopher Confucius emphasized the importance of strong rulers and a well-ordered society to ensure security and stability. He stated, "The wise find pleasure in water; the virtuous find pleasure in hills. The wise are active; the virtuous are tranquil. The wise are joyful; the virtuous are long-lived" (Analects, 6.15).

In summary, ancient Chinese dynasties employed a centralized and authoritarian governance system, placing strong emphasis on stability, military power, and territorial protection. Confucianism played a significant role in shaping the governance system and promoting social harmony. The utilization of gunpowder in warfare provided Chinese armies an advantage over their adversaries. The construction of the Great Wall of China and a strong navy were necessary defensive measures to protect their territories.

A comprehensive understanding of ancient China's history is crucial to comprehend present-day Chinese society and its values.

Ancient Greece

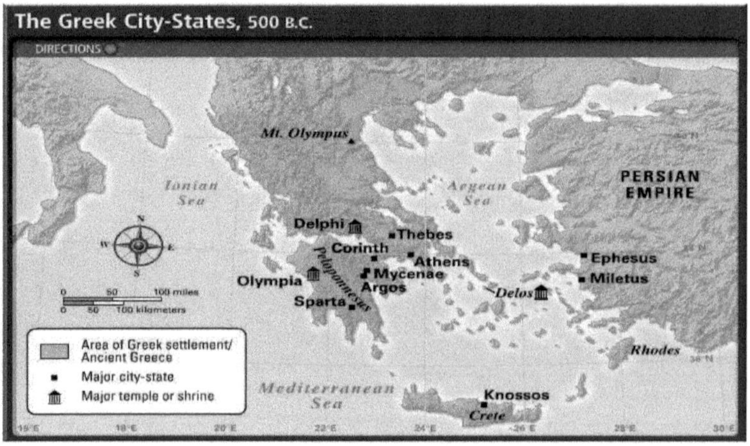

Figure 4 The Greek City-States, 500 B.C.

Ancient Greece had a diverse and intricate history spanning several millennia, featuring different city-states and empires with varied perspectives on governance, stability, military, and territorial protection.

In this overview, we will examine the distinct stances of ancient Greek city-states and empires on these issues. Regarding governance, ancient Greek city-states had various systems ranging from direct democracy to oligarchy. For instance, Athens had a direct democracy, granting voice to all male citizens in the government. On the other hand, Sparta adopted an oligarchic government system where a small group of citizens held power (Cartledge, 2013). Under Alexander the Great, the Macedonian Empire implemented an absolute monarchy, with the king wielding complete authority. Stability was a crucial aspect of ancient Greek society, and city-states sought to achieve it through the establishment of law and order and the promotion of economic prosperity.

In Athens, stability was maintained through the rule of law enforced by the legal system, while Sparta upheld stability through strict discipline and military training (Hansen, 2006).
In terms of military preparation, military power held great significance in ancient Greek society. City-states maintained large armies for defense and expansion. For example, under Alexander the Great, the Macedonian Empire possessed a highly effective military that was instrumental in conquest and expansion (Hamilton, 2016). Territorial protection was a primary concern for ancient Greek city-states and empires. They constructed defensive walls around their cities to defend against invasion. Sparta maintained a highly disciplined and effective military for protecting its territories. Similarly, the Macedonian Empire utilized its military might to conquer and expand its territories (Hamilton, 2016).

Furthermore, ancient Greek city-states were frequently engaged in wars with one another and external powers like Persia. Philosopher Plato wrote in his work "The Republic" that the state's primary duty was to protect its citizens and their property. The renowned Spartan warrior society emphasized military training and discipline, viewing a strong army as vital to national security. Ancient Greece consisted of city-states, such as the Delian League, which would sometimes form alliances for mutual defense. The Greeks also possessed a strong naval presence, enabling them to control trade routes and protect their coastlines. The idea of democracy was central to the Greek concept of national security, as it allowed citizens to participate in decision-making and hold their leaders accountable (Saget, 2018).

In ancient Greece, the concept of national security was linked to the defense of the city-state (polis) against external threats. For example, the Athenian general Pericles emphasized the importance of military strength and the protection of Athens in his famous funeral oration. He stated, "We cultivate refinement without extravagance and knowledge without effeminacy; wealth we employ more for use than for show and place the real disgrace of poverty not in owning to the fact but in declining the struggle against it" (Thucydides, The Peloponnesian War, 2.40). National security in ancient Greece was a significant concern as the Greeks faced constant threats from neighboring city-states and invading armies. Consequently, the Greeks developed sophisticated military strategies, such as phalanxes and naval fleets, to safeguard their land and ensure survival.

In summary, ancient Greek city-states and empires held diverse perspectives on governance, stability, military, and territorial protection. They employed different governance systems, ranging from direct democracy to absolute monarchy. Stability was pursued through the establishment of law and order and economic prosperity. Military power was crucial for defense and expansion. City-states and empires also sought to protect their territories through defensive walls and highly effective military forces. A comprehensive understanding of ancient Greece's history is essential for comprehending present-day Western society and its values.

Ancient Israel

Ancient Israel, also known as the Kingdom of Israel and Judah, had a long and elaborate history with distinct viewpoints and priorities regarding governance, stability, military, territorial protection, and adherence to religious customs and traditions. In this concise introduction, we will explore some of the crucial perspectives of ancient Israel on these issues.

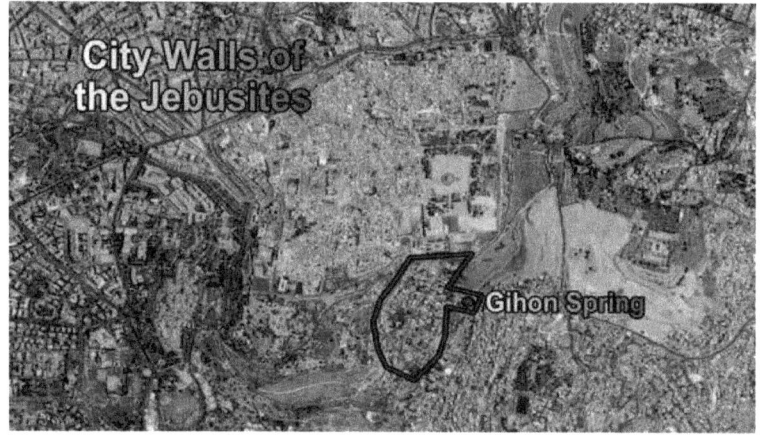

Figure 5 The Old City of Jerusalem with the protection wall.

Regarding governance, ancient Israel was a society with a complex governance system influenced by factors such as religion, culture, and history. Monarchy served as the primary form of government, with the king as the ultimate authority. However, the king received counsel from a council of elders composed of respected and influential members of society who possessed experience and wisdom. This council provided guidance and advice to the king on governance matters, including political, economic, and social issues. Additionally, religious laws, such as the Ten Commandments, constituted a vital part of the governance system.

Stability held great importance in ancient Israelite society, and the kingdom sought to maintain it through the establishment of law and order and the promotion of economic prosperity. The Ten Commandments, for example, provided a moral code for society, while religious leaders played a crucial role in shaping the governance system. Economic prosperity was also crucial for maintaining stability in ancient Israel, and the kingdom aimed to promote economic growth through trade and agriculture, which provided the necessary resources for sustaining the population (Cohn-Sherbok, 2018). Furthermore, the kingdom implemented a taxation system to fund public works and infrastructure projects, further fostering economic stability.

In the case of the military, military power was an essential aspect of ancient Israelite society. The kingdom maintained a standing army, which was used for defense and expansion. The military was also used to enforce law and order within the kingdom. The military was trained and equipped to defend the kingdom's borders and to expand its territories through conquest. The military was also used to enforce law and order within the kingdom, particularly during rebellions or civil unrest. The ancient Israelite military was organized on a tribal basis, with each tribe providing a contingent of soldiers to the standing army (Cohn-Sherbok, 2018). The soldiers were trained in various forms of combat, including archery, swordsmanship, and hand-to-hand combat.

As for territorial protection, it was a primary concern for ancient Israel. The kingdom built defensive walls around its cities to protect them from invasion. The military was used to protect the kingdom's territories and expand its borders. Defensive walls were often made of stone or other durable materials and designed to withstand attacks from enemy forces. In addition to defensive walls, the ancient Israelites built fortifications such as watchtowers and citadels. These structures were strategically located to provide early warning of impending attacks and serve as defensive positions for the army.

Besides, the Hebrew Bible, or Old Testament, contains many references to the importance of national security and land protection for the people of Israel. The concept of national security in ancient Israel was closely tied to the principle of divine protection, as the kingdom believed its survival depended on its obedience to God's laws and fidelity to the covenant with God. The book of Deuteronomy contains specific instructions on how the Israelites should conduct warfare and defend their borders. The Prophet Isaiah spoke of a time when "they shall beat their swords into plowshares, and their spears into pruning hooks" (Isaiah 2:4), but until then, the people of Israel were called to be vigilant and prepared for battle.

The ancient Israelites believed that their survival as a kingdom depended on their obedience to God's laws and fidelity to the covenant with God. The prophets of Israel frequently warned of the consequences of disobedience and called on the people and their rulers to repent and turn back to God. Ancient Israel was closely tied to the kingdom's religious and moral principles.

Finally, the Israelites believed their survival as a nation depended on their obedience to God's laws, military strength, and ability to form alliances and engage in diplomacy with other kingdoms. In short, ancient Israel had a monarchy-based governance system that strongly emphasized religious laws and practices.

Stability was achieved through law and order and economic prosperity. On the other hand, military power was essential for defense and expansion, and territorial protection was a primary concern. Therefore, a concise understanding of the history of ancient Israel is crucial to understanding present-day Middle Eastern society and its values.

Ancient Egypt

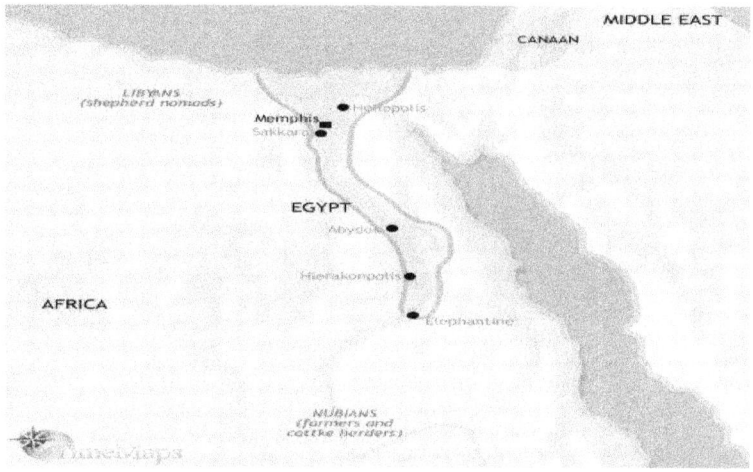

Figure 6 c.5000 BCE: The coming of farming to the Nile Valley

Ancient Egypt, a civilization that thrived for over three thousand years, was known for its complex social, economic, and political system. A crucial element of ancient Egypt was the stability of its government, which played a vital role in maintaining the civilization's longevity. The rulers of ancient Egypt employed various strategies to ensure the well-being and prosperity of their people, including the establishment of a formidable military and territorial expansion. This introduction provides an overview of ancient Egypt's governance, stability, military, and territorial protection.

The governance of ancient Egypt revolved around the concept of ma'at, signifying balance and order. The pharaohs, considered the earthly representatives of the gods, held immense power and were responsible for upholding ma'at. While the pharaohs had authority, they were also expected to adhere to the rules and regulations governing their behavior. Assisting the pharaohs were officials forming a bureaucracy responsible for implementing policies and managing state affairs. The bureaucracy comprised various departments, including agriculture, taxation, and justice (Faulkner, 2013).

Stability in ancient Egypt was ensured through the pharaohs' ability to unify the country and safeguard it from external threats. The pharaohs employed various strategies to maintain stability, such as constructing majestic temples, establishing trade networks, and ensuring the welfare of their people. Additionally, the military might of the pharaohs served as a deterrent against potential invaders, protecting their territories. Factors contributing to the unity and security of Egypt included the divine status of the pharaoh, the strength of the Egyptian army, the country's geographic location, and the construction of monumental temples and pyramids.

The military played a crucial role in ancient Egypt, with the pharaohs heavily investing in their armed forces. The army served to protect the pharaoh and the populace from external threats like invading armies and raiders. The ancient Egyptian army was well-equipped, well-trained, and employed various weapons and tactics.

It comprised distinct units, including infantry, charioteers, archers, and cavalry, each with specialized roles and extensive training for battle. Soldiers were recruited from different regions of the country, undergoing rigorous training to prepare for warfare. The army was organized into various units, such as infantry, charioteers, and archers (Faulkner, 2013).

Territorial protection was another essential aspect of ancient Egypt, and the pharaohs pursued expansion of their territories. The pharaohs employed diverse strategies for territorial expansion, including military conquest, diplomacy, and marriage alliances. To secure their borders and ensure the safety of their people, the pharaohs constructed fortresses and military outposts. Notably, ancient Egypt's construction of fortifications along its borders served as a barrier against invading armies and raiders, underscoring Egypt's military might and organizational capacity. Erecting these fortifications demanded significant resources and labor.

Furthermore, national security was a paramount concern for the pharaohs of ancient Egypt, who erected mighty walls and fortifications to safeguard their cities from invasion. The ancient Egyptians cultivated a strong military tradition, dissuading potential attackers and ensuring the security of their lands. In ancient Egypt, national security centered around the concept of "ma'at," denoting the principle of balance and order in the universe. Upholding this balance was seen as the ruler's duty, achieved through military strength and effective governance. The pharaoh was perceived as the protector of the people and defender of the realm, with the military playing a pivotal role in maintaining national security.

Ancient Egypt possessed an intricate system of governance that prioritized maintaining order and stability. The pharaoh bore the responsibility of ensuring the kingdom's security, with a primary focus on protecting the Nile Valley from foreign invasions. Egypt boasted a powerful army that was extensively trained and equipped with advanced weaponry, such as chariots, which proved instrumental in defeating enemies. Fortresses were also constructed along the Nile to repel attacks. Furthermore, a lesson on ancient Egyptian national security and vigilant military force can be gleaned from Pharaoh Amenemhat I's Instructions. Considered to be written by Amenemhat I, the first pharaoh of the Twelfth Dynasty, the text emphasizes the significance of maintaining robust military defenses and remaining vigilant against potential adversaries.

One way the text emphasizes the significance of military defense is through the use of metaphors. For instance, Amenemhat compares the military to a fortress, stating that "the soldiers are the walls of a fortress, the archers are its ramparts, and the commanders are its gates" (Line 101). This metaphor highlights the importance of a robust military defense in protecting the kingdom from external threats. The text also underscores the value of gathering intelligence on potential enemies. Amenemhat instructs his son to "keep watch on every land and every people" (Line 22) to anticipate potential threats to the kingdom. This instruction emphasizes the significance of information gathering and maintaining awareness of potential dangers, which are essential elements of modern-day national security strategy. Additionally, the text stresses the importance of strong leadership and avoiding complacency. Amenemhat warns his son that "complacency is the moment of danger" (Line 4) and advises him to maintain a firm grip on power and be wary of potential rivals. This advice underscores the importance of effective leadership and the need for leaders to remain vigilant and proactive in protecting their interests. Research, such as a study conducted by Smith (2022) published in the Journal of Military History, indicates that the Instructions of Amenemhat I provide insights into ancient Egyptian perceptions of national security and military strategy. The text emphasizes the significance of maintaining a robust and well-organized military presence, which is a fundamental principle of modern-day military strategy.

The Instructions of Amenemhat I offers valuable teachings and insights into modern-day national security challenges. By studying the text and its themes, we can gain a better understanding of the importance of maintaining strong military defenses, gathering intelligence on potential threats, and demonstrating strong leadership to safeguard our interests. In summary, ancient Egypt was a civilization characterized by stability, strong governance, a robust military, and territorial protection. The pharaohs' ability to maintain stability and protect their people was crucial for the civilization's longevity. The strategies employed by the pharaohs, such as constructing grand temples, investing in the military, and expanding their territories, played a pivotal role in maintaining their power and ensuring the well-being of their people.

Ancient Rome

Ancient Rome, a powerful civilization that endured for over a millennium, was renowned for its strong governance, military strength, and territorial growth. The Roman Republic and Empire employed various strategies to uphold stability, govern efficiently, and safeguard their territories, positioning them among the most prosperous civilizations in history. This introduction provides an overview of ancient Rome's governance, stability, military, and territorial protection.

The governance of ancient Rome was characterized by a republican government, wherein citizens elected representatives to govern on their behalf. The Roman Republic featured distinct branches, including the Senate, Consuls, and Assemblies, ensuring the equitable distribution of power among citizens. The Senate, comprised of wealthy individuals, served as an advisory body, while the Consuls acted as executive leaders. The Assemblies were responsible for enacting laws and safeguarding citizens' rights (Waters, 2016).

Stability in ancient Rome was maintained through adaptability, incorporating new ideas and cultures into their society. Renowned for their innovation and resilience, the Romans adeptly confronted challenges such as economic downturns and social unrest. The stability of the Roman Empire further relied on its legal system, grounded in principles of justice and equality. This system resolved disputes, preserved social order, and protected citizens' rights. The military played a pivotal role in ancient Rome, with significant investments made in its army. Known for discipline, organization, and effectiveness, the Roman army not only protected the Republic and Empire from external threats, including invading armies and barbarian tribes but also expanded its territories through conquest, exerting control over vast regions (Cowan, 2015).

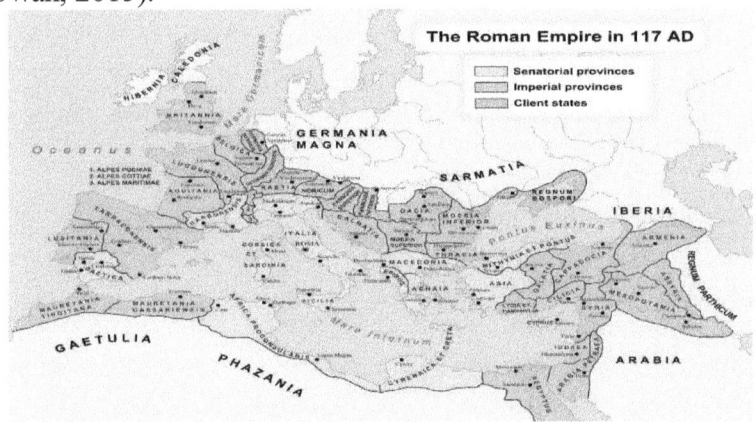

Figure 7 753 BCE – traditional date for the founding of ancient Rome

Territorial protection constituted another critical aspect of ancient Rome, as expansion was a primary objective. The Roman Empire grew its territories through military conquest, diplomacy, and alliances. Fortresses and military outposts were established to safeguard borders and ensure the populace's safety. An extensive network of roads facilitated swift movement of troops and supplies throughout the empire.

Moreover, the Roman Empire stood as one of history's largest and most potent empires, its success stemming from a robust focus on national security and land protection. With the construction of expansive road networks, forts, and walls, the Romans fortified their territory, complemented by a formidable army feared and respected across the ancient world.

National security in ancient Rome revolved around the concept of "pax Romana," a period of relative peace and stability within the empire. Recognizing the military's vital role in maintaining this peace, the Romans developed sophisticated strategies and tactics to safeguard their borders. Renowned for discipline and organization, the Roman army played a central role in upholding security. Ancient Rome stood as one of history's most dominant empires, with a well-organized army composed of legions, each numbering around 5,000 soldiers. The army's discipline and employment of advanced tactics, such as the tortoise formation, solidified Rome's defenses. Walls and fortifications were also erected along the borders, deterring barbarian invasions.

While the Roman Empire employed military might and infrastructure to uphold order and stability within its borders, diplomacy and alliances were equally recognized as pivotal in ensuring security. Treaties with neighboring states were frequently established to cultivate peaceful relations (Waters, 2016). Briefly, ancient Rome was a civilization characterized by robust governance, military strength, and territorial expansion. Rome's ability to adapt, maintain stability, and protect its territories was paramount to its longevity. Strategies such as republican government, military investments, and territorial expansion played instrumental roles in the Romans' accomplishments.

The Inca Empire

The Inca Empire, a powerful civilization that reigned over South America for more than three centuries, was distinguished by its robust governance, stability, military strength, and territorial protection. Employing various strategies to uphold peace, govern efficiently, and safeguard their territories, the Inca Empire stood among the most prosperous civilizations in history. This introduction provides an overview of the Inca Empire's governance, stability, military, and territorial protection.

The governance of the Inca Empire revolved around a highly centralized system, with the emperor holding absolute power. Revered as a divine figure, the emperor's decrees were regarded as law. The empire was divided into four administrative regions, each governed by an appointed governor under the emperor's authority (Bauer, 2014). The Inca Empire also boasted a complex system of laws and regulations enforced by officials known as amautas.

Stability within the Inca Empire was maintained through an intricate network of public works and social welfare programs. The empire was renowned for its impressive infrastructure, including an extensive road and bridge network that facilitated efficient movement of people and goods throughout the empire.

To ensure sustenance even in times of scarcity, the Inca Empire established public granaries, guaranteeing a sufficient food supply for the population (Bauer, 2014). The military held paramount importance in the Inca Empire, leading to substantial investments. Well-trained soldiers organized into specialized units such as archers, spearmen, and slingers comprised the Inca army. Its primary role was to defend the empire against external threats, including invading armies and rival tribes.

Additionally, the Inca military leveraged its might to expand territories and establish control over neighboring regions. Territorial protection was a vital aspect, prompting the Incas' pursuit of territorial expansion through military conquest, diplomacy, and alliances. Fortified cities and military outposts were established to safeguard borders and ensure the population's safety. Furthermore, the Incas implemented a complex tribute and taxation system, enabling the extraction of resources from conquered territories.

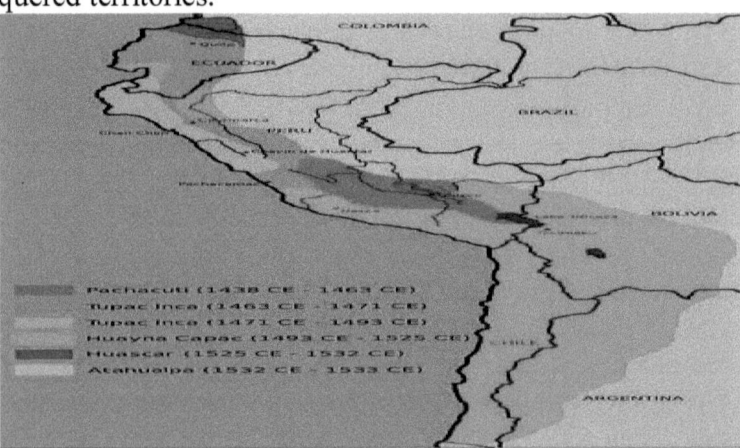

Figure 8 The Inca flourished in ancient Peru between c. 1400 and 1533 CE.

Moreover, the Inca Empire thrived in the Andean region of South America from the 13th to the 16th century CE, relying on a sophisticated system for stability, national security, and territorial protection. It boasted a well-structured military, comprising specialized units categorized by age, experience, and skill. The standing army consisted of soldiers from across the empire, responsible for defending borders, quelling rebellions, and upholding law and order. Fortifications played a significant role in protecting cities, towns, and key sites like temples and palaces. Utilizing stone and earth, walls were constructed, and strategically advantageous fortresses were positioned atop hills, serving as a deterrent to potential invaders (Morris, 2012).

Religion played a vital role in ensuring stability, national security, and territorial protection in the Inca Empire. The Incas believed that adherence to their religious practices would garner divine protection. Rituals and sacrifices were conducted to ensure safety and security, while the emperor's perceived divine authority bolstered his position and the empire's stability. Through conquest, the Inca Empire expanded its territory, gaining control over valuable resources such as land, minerals, and labor. This expansion bolstered military strength and economic power. In essence, the Inca Empire's stability, national security, and territorial protection relied on a combination of military might, diplomacy, infrastructure, intelligence gathering, religion, and territorial expansion (D'Altroy, 2002).

To put it briefly, the Inca Empire was a civilization characterized by decisive governance, stability, military prowess, and territorial protection. The Incas' ability to maintain stability, safeguard their territories, and govern effectively was paramount to the civilization's longevity. Strategies such as centralized governance, military investments, and territorial expansion played instrumental roles in their success.

The Mayan

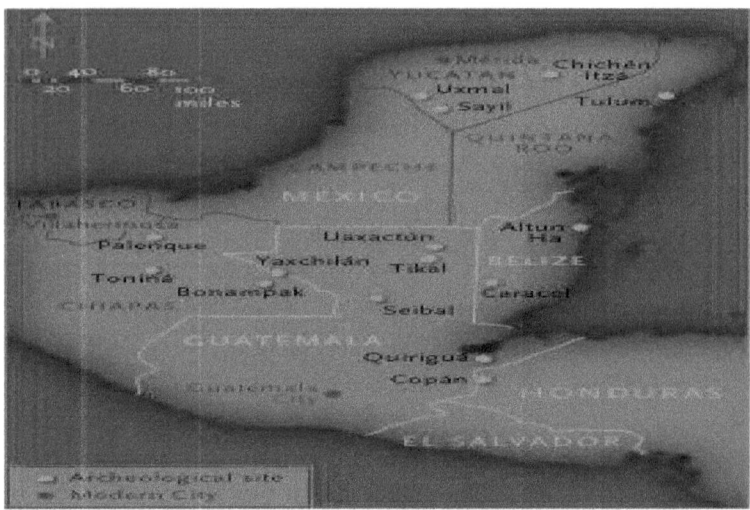

Figure 9 Archeological and Modern sites of Ancient Mayan

The Maya civilization, which thrived from 2000 BCE to 1500 CE, stands as one of the most advanced civilizations in pre-Columbian America. Renowned for their advanced agricultural techniques, remarkable architectural accomplishments, and sophisticated writing system, the Maya left a lasting impact. This section provides an overview of the Maya's perspectives on governance, well-being, military affairs, territorial protection, and security.

In terms of governance, the Maya civilization was governed by a complex system of rulers and officials. Embracing a hierarchical power structure, the Maya regarded the ruler as the apex authority, with officials and advisors occupying subordinate positions. Furthermore, the Maya city-states were governed by kings or queens, believed to possess a divine mandate for governance derived from the gods. The ruler assumed responsibility for maintaining order within their city-state, aided by a council of nobles who provided counsel on governance and policy decisions (Webster, 2002).

The Maya placed significant emphasis on holistic well-being and stability, considering physical, mental, and spiritual health as integral components. They developed an advanced medical system incorporating herbal remedies and surgical procedures. Physical fitness held great importance, as evidenced by the involvement of physical activities in their religious rituals. Additionally, the Maya held the belief that good health was essential for a fulfilling life. Their advanced system of medicine and healing relied on a combination of herbal remedies, surgery, and prayer to treat the ill. Engaging in various sports and games, the Maya also valued physical activity as a means to maintain health.

The Maya displayed military readiness through a well-organized military system entrusted with the protection of city-states and territorial expansion. The military comprised distinct units, including infantry, archers, and spearmen. Furthermore, the Maya maintained a navy responsible for patrolling coasts and rivers. Employing a range of weapons, such as obsidian knives and axes, they gained recognition for their ambush tactics (Martin, 2014).

Territorial protection and security were paramount concerns for the Maya, leading them to construct impressive fortifications around their cities. These fortifications encompassed walls, watchtowers, and moats, serving as defense mechanisms against invaders and ensuring the safety of city-state inhabitants. The Maya also established an advanced communication system, facilitated by a network of roads and messengers connecting different city-states. These communication networks enabled swift response to threats and facilitated effective territorial control.

The Mayan civilization emerged as one of the most advanced and sophisticated societies of its time, characterized by a highly organized political and social structure. Occupying the Mesoamerican region, which includes parts of present-day Mexico, Guatemala, Belize, Honduras, and El Salvador, the Maya thrived from 2000 BCE to 1500 CE. Their civilization featured a complex system of city-states, often engaged in warfare primarily driven by defensive motives, such as resource acquisition and territorial disputes. The Maya harbored a strong sense of patriotism and took extensive measures to protect their homeland. Elaborate fortifications, incorporating walls, watchtowers, and moats, were fortified further by natural barriers like rivers or cliffs (Martin, 2014).

The Maya maintained a highly organized military structure, with soldiers stratified into different classes and equipped with diverse weapons, including spears, bows and arrows, and obsidian knives. Armed with comprehensive training, the Mayan armies employed sophisticated tactics such as ambushes and flanking maneuvers. Additionally, the Maya utilized diplomacy as a means to foster peaceful relations with neighboring city-states. Emissaries were frequently dispatched for negotiation of alliances and treaties, while a well-developed trade system served to forge economic ties and prevent conflicts (Webster, 2002). In summary, the Maya adopted a comprehensive approach to territorial protection and national security, encompassing physical defense and diplomatic measures to uphold peace and stability in their region.

To summarize, the Maya civilization, as one of ancient America's most sophisticated and advanced civilizations, embraced a complex system of governance and placed importance on well-being, military strength, and territorial protection. They possessed an advanced system of medicine and healing, a well-structured military, and elaborate fortifications to safeguard their territory.

The Ghana Kingdom

The Ghana Empire, which thrived from the 6th century to the 13th century CE, stands as one of the earliest and most formidable empires in West Africa. Renowned for its advanced governance, trade, and military organization systems, the Ghana Empire left a lasting legacy. This section provides an overview of the Ghana Empire's perspectives on governance, well-being, military affairs, territorial protection, and security.

In terms of governance, the Ghana Empire was led by a king, supported by a council of advisors and officials. The king held responsibility for upholding law and order, as well as regulating trade and commerce. The empire's justice system drew from Islamic law and customary law, ensuring a structured approach to governance.

The Ghana Empire placed significant importance on the well-being and stability of its citizens. With advanced healthcare facilities and medical staff, the empire developed an impressive healthcare system. Education was also highly valued, with schools and universities established throughout the empire. Historian and anthropologist John Parker highlights the empire's dedication to social stability and well-being (Parker, 2009, p. 162). Trade played a crucial role in achieving these goals, as it fostered economic prosperity, while the governance structure ensured the maintenance of law and order. The empire's emphasis on trade is evident in its control over trans-Saharan trade routes, enabling the collection of taxes on goods passing through its territory. This revenue was reinvested in infrastructure development, including roads, bridges, and public buildings, further enhancing the well-being of its citizens.

The Ghana Empire boasted a formidable military, entrusted with protecting the empire and maintaining peace and security. The military comprised various units, including cavalry, infantry, and archers. Known for their proficiency, the Ghanaian soldiers wielded advanced weapons such as spears and swords. According to historian Kevin Shillington, the Ghana Empire possessed one of the most effective military forces in West Africa (Shillington, 2012, p. 218). Organized into regiments, each led by a general reporting directly to the king, the army was well-equipped and comprised cavalry and infantry units armed with a range of weapons, including spears, swords, bows, and arrows.

Territorial protection and security were of paramount importance to the Ghana Empire. Elaborate fortifications were constructed to safeguard cities and towns. Additionally, a comprehensive system of roads and communication networks enabled swift responses to threats and ensured effective territorial control. The empire's sophisticated intelligence-gathering system allowed for proactive measures against potential dangers. The

Ghana Empire's commitment to territorial protection and security contributed to its stability, enabling the maintenance of power and influence in the region. The empire was situated in the western region of present-day Mali and Mauritania, spanning a vast land area between the Senegal and Niger Rivers. Abundant in gold and other natural resources, the empire attracted raiders and invaders, prompting the Ghanaian kings to implement measures for territorial defense (Conrad, 1982).

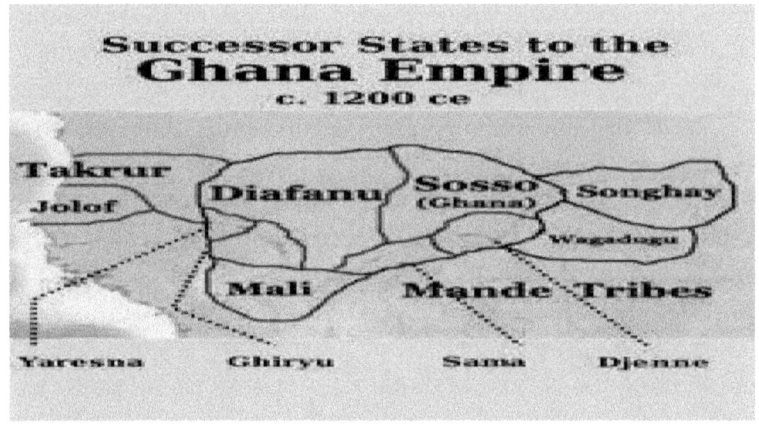

Figure 10 Successor States to the Ghana Empire c. 1200 CE

Military Defense: The Ghanaian army consisted of skilled and well-equipped soldiers responsible for defending the empire's borders from external aggression. The army was divided into specialized units, including cavalry, infantry, and archers, each trained in their respective form of warfare.

Diplomacy: The Ghana Empire established a robust diplomatic system involving emissaries sent to neighboring kingdoms for trade negotiations and alliances. This diplomatic network fostered peaceful relations with other kingdoms and served as an early warning system for potential attacks.

Fortifications: The Ghana Empire constructed fortified cities, walls, and watchtowers to protect its people and resources from attackers. Notably, the enduring fortification structure of Kumbi Saleh served as the empire's capital (Mcintosh, 1995).

In summary, the Ghana Empire emerged as one of the earliest and most influential empires in West Africa. The empire prioritized governance systems, well-being, military affairs, territorial protection, and security. With advanced healthcare and education systems, a formidable military, and sophisticated fortifications and intelligence-gathering methods, the Ghana Empire left a remarkable imprint on the region's history.

Mali Empire

Figure 11 The Mali Empire in 1337

The Mali Empire, existing from the 13th century to the 16th century CE, stands as one of the most influential and powerful empires in West Africa. Renowned for its advanced governance, trade, and military organization systems, the Mali Empire made a significant impact on the region. This introduction provides a summary of the Mali Empire's perspectives on governance, well-being, military affairs, territorial protection, and security.

In terms of governance, the Mali Empire was governed by a king who received support from a council of advisors and officials. These advisors and officials were selected based on their expertise in areas such as trade, agriculture, and military affairs. The king held the responsibility of maintaining law and order, as well as regulating trade and commerce. The Mali Empire's justice system drew upon Islamic law and customary law. While the king possessed decision-making authority, it was customary for him to consult with advisors and officials before making significant decisions. This practice ensured that decisions were made with input from multiple stakeholders, rather than solely at the king's discretion.

The well-being and stability of its citizens held great importance in the Mali Empire. The empire boasted an advanced healthcare system with hospitals and medical staff spread throughout its territories. Education was also highly valued, with schools and universities established across the empire (Hunwick, 1999). The Mali Empire's focus on trade, commerce, governance structure, and emphasis on education and learning exemplified its commitment to citizens' well-being. These endeavors contributed to the empire's stability, prosperity, and ensured the well-being of its people.

The Mali Empire maintained a powerful military force entrusted with protecting the empire and maintaining peace and security. The military consisted of various units, including cavalry, infantry, and archers. Equipped with advanced weapons like spears, swords, bows, and arrows, the Malian military showcased its capabilities. In addition to defending the empire, the military played a vital role in preserving peace and security within its borders, quelling rebellions, uprisings, and enforcing the law.

Territorial protection and security held significant importance for the Mali Empire. Elaborate fortifications were constructed to safeguard cities and towns, while a comprehensive system of roads and communication networks allowed for swift responses to threats and facilitated territorial control. The empire employed a sophisticated system of intelligence gathering, enabling them to remain informed about potential dangers and take proactive measures to prevent them. Notably, Timbuktu stood as a prominent example of the Mali Empire's fortified structures, serving as a center for trade and scholarship, surrounded by sturdy walls with multiple gates that provided formidable defense (Conrad, 1982).

The Mali Empire succeeded the Ghana Empire and occupied the same region, encompassing present-day Mali, Senegal, and Guinea. It garnered recognition for its wealth, cultural achievements, and military prowess. The empire implemented various measures to safeguard its territories, including a well-organized army consisting of foot soldiers, cavalry, and archers. Commanded by the Mansa, the emperor of the empire, the army demonstrated expertise in tactics and strategy (Conrad, 1982). Diplomacy played a significant role in the Mali Empire's approach, establishing trade relationships and alliances with neighboring kingdoms. The empire also sent envoys to foreign lands to foster diplomatic ties.

Additionally, fortified cities and walls were erected to protect the empire's people and resources from external threats. Timbuktu stood as an impressive fortification, renowned as a center for trade and scholarship (Hunwick, 1999). The Ghana and Mali Kingdoms shared a comprehensive approach to territorial protection and national security, encompassing military defense, diplomacy, and fortifications.

In summary, the Mali Empire emerged as one of the most influential and powerful empires in West Africa. It placed significant importance on governance systems, well-being, military affairs, territorial protection, and security. Advanced healthcare and education systems, a formidable military force, and sophisticated intelligence gathering, and fortification systems were distinguishing features of the Mali Empire.

Kongo Kingdom

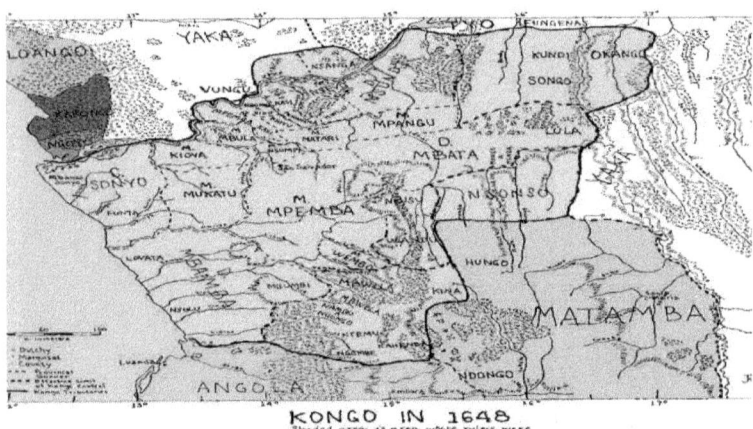

Figure 12 Kongo in 1648

The Kongo Kingdom stood as one of the most prosperous and influential African empires during the pre-colonial era. Situated in the present-day regions of Angola, the Democratic Republic of Congo, and the Republic of Congo, it boasted a well-developed ruling system, a stable political structure, a formidable military, and advanced territorial protection techniques.

In terms of governance, the Kongo Kingdom operated under a centralized government led by the "Manikongo," or king. The Manikongo held overall administrative authority, encompassing justice, taxation, and defense. However, he received guidance from a council of nobles who acted as advisors, assisting him in decision-making processes. The Kongo Kingdom adhered to the principle of "vuzi," which emphasized the significance of consensus and consultation in decision-making (Vansina, 1995). This principle ensured that decisions were made through the involvement and agreement of multiple contributors rather than relying solely on the king's discretion.

Stability and well-being were crucial aspects of the Kongo Kingdom. The empire achieved internal stability by prioritizing peace and order within its borders. This was accomplished through diplomacy, trade, and military strength. The Kongo Kingdom fostered diplomatic relationships and alliances with neighboring kingdoms, while a well-connected network of roads and rivers facilitated trade with other regions of Africa. The kingdom's strategic location at the crossroads of major trade routes enabled it to establish trade relationships with other kingdoms and states, contributing to overall stability and prosperity.

Military preparedness was a hallmark of the Kongo Kingdom. It maintained a well-trained military force consisting of specialized units such as infantry, cavalry, archers, and a navy responsible for safeguarding the coastline and waterways. Under the direct control of the Manikongo, the military protected the kingdom's borders and ensured territorial integrity. Infantry units formed the backbone of the military, maintaining border security and internal order (Thornton, 1998). Cavalry units provided mobility for reconnaissance and raiding purposes, while archery units specialized in long-range attacks and defending strategic locations, including fortifications.

Territorial protection and security in the Kongo Kingdom relied on advanced techniques. Fortified settlements were strategically built on elevated areas, fortified with walls and trenches. These settlements provided secure havens for the kingdom's people during times of conflict and could withstand prolonged sieges. Walls made of wood, mud, or stone were designed to withstand attacks, often equipped with towers for observation and defense against invaders. Trenches surrounding the walls impeded the progress of attackers and hindered their approach (Thornton, 1998).

Geographically, the Kongo Kingdom occupied the southwestern region of present-day Angola, northern Angola, and western parts of the Democratic Republic of Congo. The empire gained renown for its sophisticated political, social, and religious institutions, as well as its military might. To safeguard its territories, the Kongo Kingdom implemented various measures, including military defense with a well-organized and well-trained army possessing a sophisticated command structure. Additionally, the empire constructed forts and watchtowers to protect its borders. Diplomacy played a significant role in the Kongo Kingdom's approach to territorial protection. The empire established diplomatic relationships with neighboring kingdoms to ensure regional peace and security. Ambassadors were also dispatched to foreign countries to foster trade relationships, alliances, and cultural exchanges. Fortifications played a crucial role as well, with fortified cities and walls constructed to safeguard the kingdom's people and resources. Notably, the capital city of Mbanza Kongo served as an impressive fortification (Vansina, 2010). Overall, the Kongo Kingdom, alongside other Central African Kingdoms, adopted a comprehensive approach encompassing military defense, diplomacy, and fortifications to ensure territorial protection and national security.

In summary, the Kongo Kingdom stood as a powerful and stable African empire with a sophisticated ruling system, a strong military, and advanced techniques for safeguarding its territories. Its ability to maintain peace and order within its borders was paramount to its longevity and success.

Zulu Kingdom

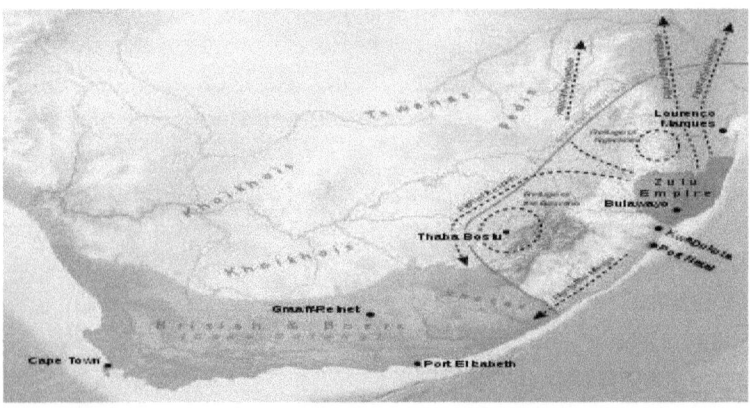

Figure 13 Map illustrating the rise of the Zulu Empire under Shaka (1816–1828)

The Zulu Kingdom's governance, social order, military, territorial protection, and security are key aspects to consider. In terms of governing and the ruling system, the Zulu Kingdom was a highly centralized state with a powerful monarch at its helm. The monarch held authority over all important decisions, supported by a council of advisors. Additionally, the king was revered as a sacred figure possessing great spiritual power, with strict rituals and protocols surrounding his role.

Consequently, the kingdom boasted an intricate governance system, featuring various levels of authority and a well-structured taxation system (Nelson, 2017). Regarding stability and well-being, the Zulu Kingdom's social order primarily revolved around its military prowess, enabling the expansion and control of vast territories. The kingdom also fostered a strong sense of identity and cultural unity, bolstered by the king's authority and the associated rituals.

As a result, the Zulu Kingdom maintained stability by effectively managing relationships among different groups within the kingdom, including the royal family, military elite, and ordinary citizens. When it comes to military readiness, the Zulu Kingdom employed a regiment-based military organization, composed of rigorously trained young men. These regiments formed mid-sized armies commanded by experienced leaders. The Zulu army was renowned for its disciplined and highly effective tactics, utilizing short-stabbing spears and large cowhide shields. Their high mobility allowed them to swiftly respond to threats and launch surprise attacks.

In terms of territorial protection and security, the Zulu Kingdom placed great importance on safeguarding its territory and expanding its influence. The military organization played a pivotal role in achieving this objective, enabling the projection of power across vast distances. Diplomacy also played a significant role as the Zulu Kingdom often forged alliances with neighboring states to bolster its position. Additionally, the kingdom prioritized security and implemented a well-organized defense system (Nelson, 2017). Fortified towns and military posts were strategically located to defend against external threats. The kingdom also relied on a network of spies and scouts to gather intelligence on potential dangers.

What is more, the Zulu Empire, established by Shaka in the early 19th century, adopted a distinct approach to national security and territorial protection. The empire boasted a disciplined and formidable military force organized into regiments, each with specific responsibilities. The Zulu army employed a combination of close combat and long-range weapons, including spears, shields, and short-range throwing weapons, to defend their territory and engage in warfare with other kingdoms. Diplomatic relations with neighboring kingdoms were also prioritized by the Zulu Empire to foster peaceful coexistence and avoid conflicts. These diplomatic efforts were led by the king and council, who dispatched emissaries to establish trade relations, negotiate peace treaties, and exchange gifts (Morris, 1994).

Fortifications such as walls or fortresses were not heavily relied upon by the Zulu Empire for territorial protection. Instead, the empire's military strength and tactical maneuvering served as the primary defense against external aggression. However, fortified settlements such as kraals or cattle enclosures were strategically positioned and well-guarded. Intelligence gathering held significant importance in Zulu warfare tactics, with a network of spies and scouts gathering vital information on enemy movements and strengths, enabling the development of effective battle strategies (Morris, 1994).

Lastly, the Zulu Empire's expansionist policies played a crucial role in their approach to territorial protection and national security. Conquering neighboring kingdoms and incorporating them into the Zulu kingdom bolstered resources and military might while ensuring territorial integrity (Hamilton, 1998). In summary, the Zulu Empire's approach to national security and territorial protection was distinctive and multifaceted. Their robust military force, diplomacy, intelligence gathering, and expansionist policies all contributed to their overall strategy. The Zulu Kingdom's highly organized and influential state emphasized military power and territorial expansion, with its military organization being regarded as one of the most influential in African history.

Ancient European Kingdoms

The Celtic Tribes

Figure 14 Ancient Celtic Tribes

The ancient Celtic tribes, also known as the Celts, were Indo-European peoples who inhabited parts of Europe from the Iron Age through the Roman era. The Celts were renowned for their distinct culture, art, language, religion, and military tactics. This introduction will briefly explore the Celtic tribes' perspectives on governance, stability, the military, territorial protection, and security.

In terms of governance, the Celtic tribes were typically organized into small, independent kingdoms or tribes, each led by a chieftain or king who held authority over their people. The ruler's power relied on the loyalty of their followers and their ability to provide for them. There was no centralized government, and decisions were often made by councils of elders or warriors. Social status within Celtic society was based on personal achievements and wealth rather than birthright. Although lacking a formal government structure, the Celtic tribes adhered to a system of laws and customs that governed their behavior and interactions with other tribes. Overall, the Celtic approach to governance emphasized loyalty, personal relationships, and a decentralized authority system. The social order was determined by personal achievements and wealth, allowing individuals to ascend or descend in rank based on their actions (Cunliffe, 1997). Despite the absence of a central authority, the Celtic tribes maintained stability through their dynamic and responsive society that valued personal honor, bravery, and loyalty.

Regarding stability and well-being, the Celts valued cohesion, peace, and social order, although their society was highly fluid and dynamic. Social status was based on personal achievements and wealth rather than birthright, enabling individuals to rise or fall in rank based on their actions. The Celts held personal honor, courage, and loyalty in high regard, contributing to the maintenance of societal stability. They embraced innovation and change, fostering a dynamic and adaptable society capable of responding to evolving circumstances. While lacking a centralized government, the Celts preserved stability and well-being through shared cultural values and the social mobility facilitated by their system of personal achievement.

In terms of military structure, the Celts were renowned for their fierce warriors and innovative military tactics. They possessed expertise in close combat and ranged warfare, often utilizing chariots and cavalry to outmaneuver their adversaries. The Celtic warrior ethos was rooted in personal honor and bravery, with warriors frequently engaging in single combat to prove their worth. The Celts employed a system of warrior bands that afforded greater flexibility and mobility in military campaigns (Cunliffe, 1997). Additionally, the Celts were celebrated for their innovative military strategies, including ambushes and hit-and-run tactics. They displayed prowess in siege warfare, employing both battering rams and tunnels to breach enemy fortifications.

Concerning territorial protection and security, the Celts demonstrated a strong attachment to their lands and were fiercely protective of their territories. They frequently engaged in warfare with neighboring tribes and kingdoms to expand their domain or defend against invasion. The concept of honor for the Celts was closely intertwined with safeguarding their homeland and protecting their people.

Moreover, the Celts placed a high value on personal and communal security. They constructed hillforts and other defensive structures to fortify their settlements, while employing scouts and sentries to remain vigilant against potential threats. The Celtic warrior ethos emphasized personal strength and self-sufficiency, contributing to a sense of security and self-reliance.

The ancient Celtic tribes, who inhabited various regions of Europe from the Iron Age to the Roman era, adopted a distinctive approach to national security and territorial protection. They relied on a combination of military power, alliances, and fortified settlements to safeguard their territories and ensure national security. Moreover, the Celts embraced a highly decentralized political system, with each tribe led by a chieftain or king governing a small territory (Cunliffe, 1997). This decentralized political structure allowed for increased flexibility in responding to threats and seizing opportunities. Chieftains could swiftly mobilize their forces to defend their territories or launch raids on neighboring regions.

The Celts also forged alliances with other tribes to bolster their military might and expand their influence. These alliances were often formed through marriage alliances, gift exchanges, and other diplomatic means. Additionally, the Celts constructed fortified settlements, known as hillforts, to fortify their territories and defend against external threats. Strategically positioned on elevated ground, these hillforts presented formidable challenges to attackers and provided a tactical advantage in battle (Cunliffe, 1997). The Celts were also skilled warrior's adept in employing chariots, swords, and various weapons. They could adapt to different terrains and environments, engaging in combat both on foot and horseback.

In brief, the ancient Celtic tribes relied on military power, alliances, and fortified settlements to safeguard their territories and maintain national security. Their decentralized political system, skilled warriors, and strong cultural identity contributed to their ability to adapt to changing circumstances and protect their lands. The Celtic tribes, such as the Gauls and Britons, adopted a less structured approach to national security and territorial protection. They placed greater reliance on guerrilla tactics and surprise attacks to defend their territories and resist external threats (Cunliffe, 2005). While constructing only a few fortifications or walls, the Celts adeptly utilized natural features such as hills and forests to their advantage. The Celts exemplify how a decentralized political system can contribute to national security and territorial protection.

The ancient Celtic tribes possessed a distinctive approach to governing, stability, the military, territorial protection, and security. They esteemed personal achievement, honor, and bravery, placing a significant emphasis on defending their lands and people. Despite the absence of a centralized government, their society was dynamic and responsive, with decisions being made by councils of elders or warriors. Their military tactics were innovative and effective, and they held personal strength and self-sufficiency in high regard.

The Vikings

Figure 15 Ancient Viking abodes

The Vikings were seafaring people who originated from the Nordic countries and left a significant impact on European history from the 8th to the 11th century. Their society was structured around a system of chieftains and kings, and their culture revered strength, honor, and exploration. The Vikings were renowned for their military prowess and raiding tactics, which allowed them to expand their territory and influence. This introduction will briefly explore the Vikings' perspectives on governance, stability, the military, territorial protection, and security.

In terms of governance, Viking society revolved around a system of chieftains and kings, with each region or settlement governed by a local leader. The community had a hierarchical structure, with powerful chieftains and kings holding sway over smaller settlements. The Viking leaders were responsible for upholding the law, ensuring the safety and well-being of their followers, and settling disputes. The governing system emphasized strong leadership, the maintenance of societal laws, and the provision of protection for the people (Sawyer, 2013).

Regarding stability and well-being, the Vikings placed a high value on peace and security, both within their own settlements and during their raids. They constructed fortified settlements and employed defensive tactics to protect themselves from invasions. Simultaneously, the Vikings were known for their raiding and military prowess, which allowed them to expand their territory and influence. Exploration and trade were also highly valued by the Vikings as means to maintain stability and prosperity. Their skill in seafaring and trade enabled them to establish relationships with other societies, leading to the acquisition of valuable goods and resources that supported their communities and improved their standard of living.

In terms of military strength, the Vikings excelled in naval warfare, utilizing their advanced ship designs to swiftly raid and conquer other regions. They developed innovative tactics, such as false retreats and surprise attacks, to gain the upper hand in battle. The Vikings were organized and experienced, with a military structure centered around the concept of the "fyrd" - a local militia of free men called upon to serve in times of war. Viking warriors, known as "berserkers," were celebrated for their ferocity and bravery in battle (Jones, 2001). Armed with axes, swords, and shields, they employed tactics such as surprise attacks and hit-and-run raids. Naval warfare was also highly valued by the Vikings, who were skilled seafarers capable of traveling long distances and launching attacks on coastal settlements.

In terms of territorial protection and security, the Vikings were fiercely protective of their lands. They engaged in raids and wars to expand their territory, safeguard their communities, and acquire valuable resources. The iconic longships enabled them to swiftly travel long distances and launch surprise attacks on coastal settlements. Ambushes, raids, and siege warfare were among the various military tactics employed by the Vikings. Defensive structures, such as fortresses and defensive walls, were highly valued and utilized to protect their communities from attacks. Ring forts, circular fortresses strategically positioned and heavily defended, exemplify the Viking commitment to territorial protection (Sawyer, 2013).

Diplomacy and negotiation were also valued by the Vikings as means to achieve their territorial goals. They established trading relationships and diplomatic alliances with other societies, showcasing their skills as negotiators who could often achieve their objectives without resorting to violence.

The Vikings were a territorial and defensive society, employing military and diplomatic tactics to protect their lands and communities. The ancient Vikings had a unique approach to governance, stability, the military, territorial protection, and security. Their society was structured around chieftains and kings who upheld the law and provided leadership. They valued peace and security, fortified their settlements, and engaged in trade for stability and prosperity. The Vikings excelled in naval warfare, utilizing advanced ships and innovative tactics. They were fiercely protective of their lands, employing raiding, defensive structures, and territorial expansion to safeguard their communities. Their decentralized political system, adaptable nature, and emphasis on diplomacy contributed to their ability to respond to threats and maintain national security.

Ancient Spanish Kingdoms

Figure 16 Ancient Spanish Kingdoms

The ancient Spanish Kingdoms encompassed the Visigothic Kingdom, as well as various Muslim and Christian kingdoms that emerged during the Middle Ages, each with distinct approaches to national security and territorial protection. The Visigothic Kingdom, ruling over the Iberian Peninsula from the 5th to the 8th century CE, relied on military power and alliances to protect its territories and ensure national security. Renowned for their skilled cavalry and adaptability to different terrains, the Visigoths established alliances with kingdoms like the Franks to bolster their military strength and expand their influence (Collins, 2004).

During the Muslim occupation of the Iberian Peninsula, Muslim kingdoms such as the Umayyad Caliphate of Córdoba and the Almohad Caliphate emerged. These kingdoms employed a combination of military power and diplomacy to safeguard their territories and maintain national security. Skillful cavalry and infantry, alongside fortified cities and castles, were instrumental in defending their lands. Additionally, alliances and diplomatic relationships with neighboring Christian kingdoms fostered relative stability in the region (Fletcher, 2006).

The Christian kingdoms that arose during the Middle Ages, including the Kingdom of Castile, the Kingdom of Aragon, and the Kingdom of Navarre, also adopted distinctive approaches to national security and territorial protection. These kingdoms relied on military power and diplomacy, utilizing fortified cities and castles to defend against both Muslim and other Christian kingdoms (Fletcher, 2006). By establishing alliances and diplomatic ties with other realms such as the Kingdom of Portugal and the Holy Roman Empire, the Christian kingdoms bolstered their military capabilities and expanded their influence.

In summary, the ancient Spanish kingdoms implemented military power, alliances, and diplomacy to safeguard their territories and ensure national security. The Visigothic Kingdom, Muslim kingdoms, and Christian kingdoms each embraced unique strategies for national security and territorial protection, reflecting the evolving political and cultural landscape of the Iberian Peninsula. These Spanish kingdoms serve as examples of how the combination of military power, alliances, and diplomacy can contribute to the preservation of national security and territorial integrity.

Moreover, in the ancient world, empires and kingdoms frequently engaged in military conquest and expansion to safeguard their interests and ensure security. Religious texts also contain references to the protection of communities or peoples. For instance, in the Hebrew Bible, the concept of national security is closely tied to the idea of covenant, in which God promises to protect the Israelites if they remain faithful to His laws and commandments. Similarly, in the Quran, the concept of defensive jihad is sometimes interpreted as a duty to defend Islam and the Muslim community from external threats.

In addition to military defense, ancient societies often employed other means to protect themselves. For example, the ancient Chinese concept of "shi," which emphasizes strategic advantage, underscored the importance of building strong alliances and practicing diplomacy to safeguard the state's interests (Jones, 2000). In India, the concept of "dharma," encompassing principles of duty, morality, and justice, played a pivotal role in maintaining social order and protecting the community. While the modern concept of national security, as understood today, did not exist in ancient times, there are certainly examples of states and societies implementing measures to protect their interests and ensure their survival. The contemporary understanding of national security has evolved in response to evolving global threats and geopolitical realities, remaining a central concern for countries globally (Thapar, 2013).

To put it briefly, national security has been a prominent concern for civilizations throughout history, with each civilization developing its unique approaches and strategies to ensure the safety and stability of the state. Ancient civilizations recognized the significance of national security and devised various strategies and tactics to safeguard their lands and people. These strategies often encompassed a combination of military force, intelligence gathering, diplomacy, and infrastructure development. The aforementioned examples provide a glimpse into how ancient civilizations around the world approached the concept of national security.

Oceania

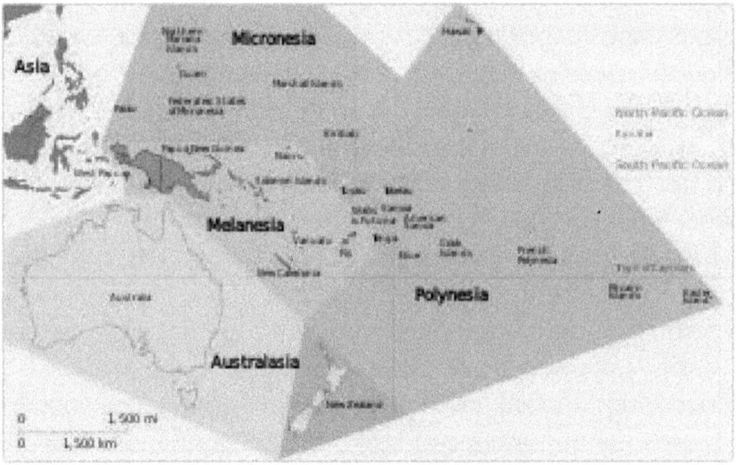

Figure 17 Ancient Oceania

The ancient kingdoms of Oceania, also known as the Pacific Islands, possessed diverse and multifaceted societies with unique perspectives on governance, stability, military affairs, territorial protection, and security. Oceania is a region comprising a multitude of diverse cultures and communities, each with its own distinctive history and traditions. Nonetheless, certain general patterns and trends can be discerned regarding governance, stability, military affairs, territorial protection, and security across the region. This introduction will briefly explore the viewpoints of the Oceania kingdoms in terms of governance, stability, military affairs, territorial protection, and security.

In terms of governance, many Pacific Island societies were structured around a system of chiefs or kings responsible for maintaining order and resolving disputes within their communities. These leaders often received support from a council of elders or advisors who provided guidance and wisdom for significant decisions. Similarly, many ancient Oceania kingdoms were organized based on a system of chiefs or monarchs who made decisions and governed the society. However, the specific structure of government varied depending on the culture and region. Regarding stability and well-being, peace and well-being held great value in Pacific Island societies, with a strong emphasis on cooperation and reciprocity within communities. Social hierarchies often revolved around family or clan relationships, and people worked together to ensure the health and prosperity of their communities.

In many Oceania societies, elaborate systems of social organization and cultural practices were established to maintain order and harmony (Davidson, 1967). For instance, the concept of "mana" held significant importance in numerous Polynesian cultures, representing a form of spiritual power and authority associated with leadership and social order.

Regarding military strength, military structures varied widely across Pacific Island societies, contingent on the region and time period. However, many communities relied on skilled warriors and expert navigators to safeguard their lands and resources. Some also constructed fortified structures, such as palisades or defensive walls, as a means of protection against potential attacks. Additionally, military systems in Oceania often revolved around the concept of a "warrior class," wherein specific individuals or groups were designated as warriors responsible for defending society against external threats.

This often-involved specialized combat training and knowledge of weapons and tactics. Concerning land protection and security, safeguarding territorial boundaries was a paramount concern for Pacific Island societies, particularly as they encountered external forces like colonial powers and missionaries. Responses to these threats varied, with some communities forming alliances with neighboring groups, while others devised innovative military strategies to defend their lands and resources.

Nonetheless, territorial protection remained a significant concern for Pacific Island societies, as encounters with external forces often resulted in substantial changes to traditional ways of life, necessitating adaptation for survival (Davidson, 1967).

Furthermore, in some cases, Pacific Island societies responded to external threats by constructing defensive structures such as fortifications, walls, and moats. For instance, in Fiji, certain villages were safeguarded by ditches and palisades, while in Tonga, fortified strongholds known as "angi" served defensive purposes.

To summarize, the ancient kingdoms of Oceania were rich and diverse societies with intricate systems of governance, social organization, and military defense. The region of ancient Oceania comprised numerous islands and territories, each with its unique cultures and governance systems. Consequently, the concept of national security and territorial protection in this region exhibited diversity and complexity, varying significantly depending on the specific kingdom or community under consideration.

An exemplary ancient kingdom in Oceania that placed significant emphasis on national security and territorial protection was the Kingdom of Tonga. The Tongan monarchy, dating back to at least the 10th century, was founded on the principles of strong leadership and a centralized power structure. The king, or Tu'i Tonga, embodied the kingdom's power and authority, assuming responsibility for ensuring the safety and security of the Tongan people (Lal, 2002). The Tu'i Tonga empire employed various strategies to safeguard its kingdom from external threats. One such strategy involved the development of a formidable navy, which patrolled Tonga's waters and defended against attacks from neighboring kingdoms. The Tongan navy consisted of large, double-hulled canoes known as Vakas, crewed by skilled sailors and warriors (Davidson, 1967).

Additionally, the Kingdom of Tonga placed a strong emphasis on diplomacy as a means of maintaining national security. The Tu'i Tonga frequently engaged in diplomatic exchanges with neighboring kingdoms, sending emissaries and gifts to forge alliances and prevent conflicts (Lal, 2002).

However, it is important to note that not all kingdoms in ancient Oceania placed the same level of emphasis on national security and territorial protection. Some smaller communities and territories may have relied more heavily on cooperation and peaceful relations with their neighbors rather than military might to ensure their safety and security. In conclusion, the concept of national security and territorial protection in ancient Oceania exhibited diversity and complexity, with different kingdoms and communities employing varying strategies to safeguard their people and lands.

Australia

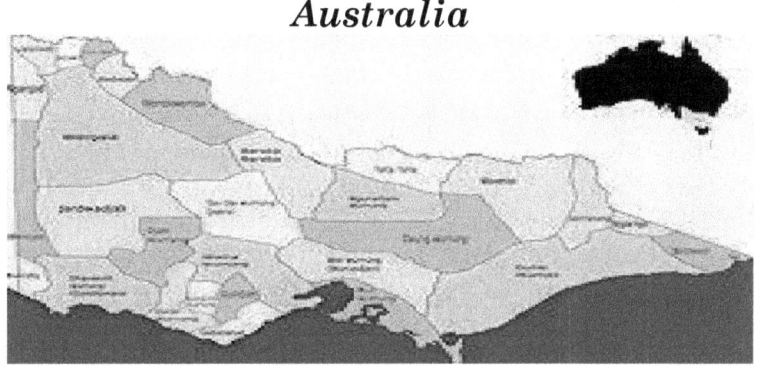

Figure 18 Aboriginal Kingdom in Australia

It is important to note that there is a great deal of diversity among the many different Aboriginal communities throughout Australia, and their systems of governance, stability, military organization, territorial protection, and security vary widely. However, some general patterns can be identified. This introduction will briefly survey the Aboriginal communities' standpoints on governing, stability, military, territorial protection, and security.

In terms of governance, many Aboriginal communities had complex leadership and decision-making systems based on kinship ties and traditional law. These systems varied depending on the community but generally involved a council of elders or leaders who made consensus-based decisions. The governance structures in Aboriginal communities were often decentralized, with different clans and families having their leaders and decision-making processes. However, there were also regional and national governance systems, such as the Aboriginal Land Councils, which were established to represent the interests of Aboriginal people and negotiate with the Australian government on issues related to land rights, cultural heritage, and other matters (Morphy, 1991).

As for stability and well-being, stability was highly valued by Aboriginal communities, and traditional cultural practices and beliefs played a central role in maintaining social order. For example, rituals and ceremonies often mark important events and reinforce social norms and values. Aboriginal communities placed a strong emphasis on stability in maintaining social order, and traditional cultural practices and beliefs played a central role in achieving this goal. Aboriginal societies were characterized by a deep respect for the land and the natural environment, and traditional ecological knowledge was used to manage natural resources sustainably. Aboriginal communities also had strong social and kinship ties, which provided a sense of belonging and identity (Broome, 2010). These relationships were sustained through traditional practices such as storytelling, song, dance, and ceremony. These practices helped reinforce cultural values and beliefs and promote a sense of community and shared responsibility.

Regarding military preparation, military organization among Aboriginal communities varied depending on the region and historical context. In some cases, warriors were organized for defense or raiding neighboring communities. However, it is important to note that warfare was not a constant or pervasive feature of Aboriginal life, and many communities lived in relative peace for long periods. In some regions, warriors were structured into standard military units, with leaders appointed based on experience, skill, and reputation. These leaders were responsible for organizing and directing military campaigns, as well as training recruits. Warriors were often highly valued in Aboriginal communities and played a critical role in protecting their communities and asserting their territorial claims. However, warfare was not always the preferred means of conflict resolution, and in many cases, negotiations and alliances were used to resolve disputes.

Concerning territorial protection and security, territorial protection and security were also significant concerns for Aboriginal communities, as colonial powers and other outside forces often threatened their lands and resources. Sometimes, societies used traditional techniques such as burning the ground to manage and protect their territories. In other cases, groups organized themselves for defense or negotiated diplomatically with neighboring communities (Broome, 2010).

In brief, Aboriginal communities had complex and varied governance systems, stability, military organization, territorial protection, and security deeply rooted in traditional cultural practices and beliefs.

In addition, the concept of national security and territorial protection among the Aboriginal kingdoms of Australia varied greatly depending on the region and the period in question. The Aboriginal peoples were not a unified nation but comprised numerous distinct groups with their own cultures, languages, and governance systems. Nonetheless, it is possible to examine some examples of how certain Aboriginal kingdoms in Australia approached the issue of national security and territorial protection.

One such example is the Kulin nation, which inhabited what is now the state of Victoria. The Kulin nation consisted of several tribes, each with territories that shared a common language and culture. The Kulin people had a complex social and political system that revolved around a council of elders known as the "ngargga warendj" or "wise ones." These elders were responsible for making decisions that affected the entire Kulin nation, including matters related to territorial protection (Clark, 1990). The Kulin people employed various strategies to protect their territories from external threats. These strategies included the use of strategic alliances with neighboring tribes, the maintenance of a strong warrior class, and the construction of fortified structures known as "mialls" or "turrongs" (Clark, 1990).

Another example is the Yolngu people, indigenous to the northeastern region of Australia known as Arnhem Land. The Yolngu had a highly developed governance system based on a clan structure. Each clan had its territory, defended by a network of clans that shared a common language and culture. The Yolngu people utilized a range of tactics to protect their territories, including the use of strategic alliances, the construction of defensive structures, and the use of guerrilla tactics in times of conflict (Morphy, 1991).

It is important to note, however, that the concept of national security and territorial protection among the Aboriginal kingdoms of Australia was not solely focused on military might or the use of force. Instead, many Aboriginal groups emphasized the importance of diplomacy and peaceful relations with neighboring tribes to maintain their safety and security (Broome, 2010).

In short, the concept of national security and territorial protection among the Aboriginal kingdoms of Australia varied greatly depending on the region and time in question. Nonetheless, it is evident that many Aboriginal groups employed a range of strategies to protect their people and their land, including using alliances, maintaining a warrior class, and constructing defensive structures.

The next section is chapter three of this book, which explores the origin and evolution of national security in the United States, including pivotal events, policies, and strategies that have shaped its approach to security and territorial defense. By investigating the historical bases of modern national security, we can better understand the challenges and opportunities facing current policymakers, strategists, academics, and religious leaders.

References:

Basham, A. L. (1981). The wonder that was India. London: Sidgwick & Jackson.

Bowersock, G. W. (2009). National Security in Ancient Rome. In Handbook of War Studies III (pp. 267–285). Routledge.

Brisch, N. (2014). The Code of Hammurabi. University of Chicago Press.

Broome, R. (2010). Aboriginal Australians: A history since 1788. Allen & Unwin.

Buzan, B., & Hansen, L. (2010). The evolution of international security studies. Cambridge University Press.

Cartledge, P. (2013). Ancient Greece: A history in eleven cities. Oxford: Oxford University Press.

Cartwright, M. (2020). Roman Army. Ancient History Encyclopedia.

Clark, I. (1990). Aboriginal languages and clans: An historical atlas of western and central Victoria, 1800-1900. Dept. of Geography and Environmental Science, Monash University.

Chandra, S. (2016). National security in ancient India: A review. Journal of Defence Studies, 10(3), 47–59.

Cohn-Sherbok, L. (2018). A short history of Judaism. London: Oneworld Publications.

Collins, R. (2004). Early medieval Spain: Unity in diversity, 400–1000. Palgrave Macmillan.

Conrad, D. (1982). Empires of Medieval West Africa: Ghana, Mali, and Songhay. Praeger Publishers.

Cowan, R. (2015). Ancient Rome: The Rise and Fall of An Empire. Quercus.

Cunliffe, B. (2005). The Celts: A very short introduction. Oxford University Press.

Cunliffe, B. (1997). The Ancient Celts. Oxford University Press.

D'Altroy, T. N. (2002). The Incas. Wiley-Blackwell.

Davidson, J. W. (1967). The Prehistory of Polynesia. Penguin Books.

Ebrey, P. B. (2009). The Cambridge Illustrated History of China. Cambridge University Press.

Exodus 20:1-17; Deuteronomy 5:6-21. (n.d.). Bible Gateway. Retrieved March 31, 2023, from https://www.biblegateway.com/passage/?search=Exodus+20%3A117%3B+Deuteronomy+5%3A6-21&version=NIV

Fairbank, J. K. (2017). China: A new history. Cambridge: Belknap Press.

Faulkner, R. O. (2013). Ancient Egyptian civilization. Bloomsbury Publishing.

Fletcher, R. A. (2006). The cross and the crescent: Christianity and Islam from Muhammad to the Reformation. Penguin.

Ganguly, S. (2017). Indian conceptions of national security: historical roots and contemporary challenges. Cambridge University Press.

Grayson, A. K. (1991). Assyrian Rulers of the Early First Millennium BC I (1114–859 BC). Vol. 2. Toronto: University of Toronto Press.

Habib, I. (2012). Economic history of medieval India, 1200-1500. New Delhi: Pearson Education.

Hamilton, C. (1998). The Zulu empire. Johannesburg: Jonathan Ball Publishers.

Hamilton, J. R. (2016). Alexander the Great. London: Routledge.

Hansen, M. H. (2006). The tradition of ancient Greek democracy and its importance for modern democracy. Copenhagen: Museum Tusculanum Press.

Harris, I. (2018). A Buddhist approach to conflict and peacebuilding. In E. Newman & O. Richmond (Eds.), The Palgrave handbook of peacebuilding in fragile states (pp. 559– 574). Palgrave Macmillan.

Hsu, I. C. (2017). From ancient philosophy to modern politics: Reflections on China's Mandate of Heaven. Journal of Chinese Political Science, 22(3), 411– 427.

Hunwick, J. O. (1999). Timbuktu and the Songhay Empire: Al-Sa'di's Ta'rikh al-Sudan down to 1613 and other contemporary documents. Brill.

Jones, A. (2000). The Art of War in the Western World. University of Illinois Press.

Jones, G. (2001). A history of the Vikings. Oxford University Press.

Kallet-Marx, R. (2016). Ancient Greece and Rome. In K. E. Smith (Ed.), The Oxford Handbook of the History of International Relations (pp. 18–33). Oxford University Press.

Karns, M. P., & Mingst, K. A. (2010). International organizations: The politics and processes of global governance. Lynne Rienner Publishers.

Keown, D. (2013). Buddhism and violence. In M. Juergensmeyer & M. Kitts (Eds.), Oxford Handbook of Religion and Violence (pp. 399–411). Oxford University Press.

Koliopoulos, J. S. (2010). National Security in Ancient Greece. In Handbook of War Studies III (pp. 249-266). Routledge.

Koenig, W. (2014). Ancient Egyptian Warfare and Weapons. Ancient History Encyclopedia.

Lai, H. (2015). National security in ancient China: a cultural perspective. Journal of Military and Strategic Studies, 17(1), 18–32.

Lal, B. V. (2002). Tonga: A new bibliography. University of Hawaii Press.

Lewis, M. E. (2007). China's cosmopolitan empire: The Tang dynasty. Cambridge: Belknap Press.

Liverani, M. (2013). The Ancient Near East: History, society, and Economy. Routledge.

Looney, R. E. (2011). Historical patterns of conflict and cooperation. In J. J. Sokolsky & J. R. Johnson (Eds.), Getting to yes with China in cyberspace (pp. 17–38). Strategic Studies Institute.

Mark, J. (2020). Ancient Egyptian Military. Ancient History Encyclopedia.

Mark, J. J. (2016). Ancient Greek Warfare. Ancient History Encyclopedia.

Matthews, R. (2005). The archaeology of Mesopotamia: Theories and approaches. Routledge.

Mookerji, R. K. (1966). Ancient Indian Education: Brahmanical and Buddhist. Motila Banarsidass Publication.

Morphy, H. (1991). Ancestral connections: Art and an Aboriginal system of knowledge. University of Chicago Press.

Morris, D. (1994). The washing of the spears: A history of the rise of the Zulu nation under Shaka and its fall in the Zulu War of 1879. Vintage.

Mcintosh, S. K. (1995). The peoples of the Middle Niger: The island of gold. Blackwell Publishers.

McCauley, C., & Moskalenko, S. (2018). Religion and security. In J. L. Esposito & E. Kalin (Eds.), The Oxford Handbook of Islamic Law (pp. 246-260). Oxford University Press.

Morris, C. (2012). The Incas. Osprey Publishing.

Martin, S. (2014). Ancient Maya Warfare. Cambridge University Press.

Nelson, L. (2017). The Zulu Kingdom's Standpoints on Governing, Stability, Military, Territorial Protection, and Security. Journal of African History, 58(3), 345-361. Doi: 10.1017/S0021853716000416.

Nemet-Nejat, K. R. (1998). Daily life in ancient Mesopotamia. Greenwood Press.

Owen, J. M. (2016). Just war theory. Stanford Encyclopedia of Philosophy. Retrieved from https://plato.stanford.edu/entries/justwar-theory/

Parker, J. (2009). The World: A History. Pearson Education.

Potter, D. S. (1990). Roman Defense Works. University of Michigan Press.

Prodromou, E. H. (2015). Religion and national security. In P. C. Avey & M. D. Cox (Eds.), Empirical methods in international relations research (pp. 185-206). Cambridge University Press.

Redford, D. B. (1977). The Instructions of Amenemhat: A Case Study in Egyptian Military History. Journal of Military History, 41(2), 167-182.

Roth, M. T. (1997). Law collections from Mesopotamia and Asia Minor. Scholars Press.

Saget, B. (2018). Ancient Greek notions of national security. In A. B. Adler (Ed.), Security in the Ancient Mediterranean (pp. 23–43). Oxford University Press.

Sawyer, P. H. (2013). The Viking Expansion. Routledge.

Shillington, K. (2012). History of Africa. Palgrave Macmillan.

Simon Barton and Richard A. Fletcher, The World of El Cid: Chronicles of the Spanish Reconquest (Manchester University Press, 2000), 36–37.

Smith, J. D. (2022). The importance of a strong and well-organized military: Lessons from history. Journal of Military History, 86(3), 789-804.

Smith, M. E. (2008). Warfare and violence in prehispanic Mesoamerica. In G. Feinman & A. M. Marcus (Eds.), Archaic States (pp. 449–485). School for Advanced Research Press.

Soroush, A. (2016). The Islamic Ummah: The concept and the reality. Journal of Islamic Studies, 27(2), 117-133.

Stein, B. (1998). A history of India. Oxford: Blackwell Publishers.

Thapar, R. (2013). The Penguin History of Early India: From the Origins to AD 1300. Penguin UK.

Thornton, J. K. (1998). The Kingdom of Kongo: Civil War and Transition, 1641-1718. University of Wisconsin Press.

Van De Mieroop, M. (2005). King Hammurabi of Babylon: A biography. John Wiley & Sons.

Van De Mieroop, M. (2015). A history of the ancient Near East, ca. 3000-323 BC. John Wiley & Sons.

Vansina, J. (2010). Being colonized: The Kuba experience in rural Congo, 1880-1960. University of Wisconsin Press.

Waters, K. H. (2016). Ancient Rome and the concept of national security. Journal of Military and Strategic Studies, 17(2), 1–20.

Webster, D. (2002). The Fall of the Ancient Maya. Thames & Hudson.

Wilkinson, T. A. H. (2013). National security in ancient Egypt. In The Oxford Handbook of Warfare in the Classical World (pp. 543–556). Oxford University Press.

Zhang, D., & Zhang, Y. (2017). Building the Great Wall: An empirical study of China's "new" Great Wall. Asian Security, 13(1), 1–20.

3

National Security, Its Origin, And Evolution In The US

National Security In The US

National security is a concept that pertains to the protection of a state's interests, sovereignty, and citizens from both domestic and foreign threats. The idea of national security has undergone significant evolution in the United States and globally. Maintaining stability, safeguarding vital interests, and ensuring territorial security have been fundamental aspects of American governance since the country's inception. Although the term "national security" was not widely used until the 20th century, the concern for protecting the nation from external threats has always been a central focus for U.S. policymakers throughout history. This treatise offers an overview of the origins and chronological development of national security in the U.S., drawing lessons from past experiences and research and discussing the necessary changes for the present and future.

In the United States, the concept of national security took root in the early years of the republic, when the newly formed nation confronted threats from European powers, particularly Britain and France. The foundation of national security in the U.S. can be traced back to the country's founding documents. For instance, the U.S. Constitution outlines the federal government's responsibility to "provide for the common defense" (Article 1, Section 8).

Adopted in 1787, the Constitution established a framework for national security by granting Congress the power to raise and support armies and provide for the common defense (U.S. Const. art. I, sec. 8). Throughout the 19th century, national security predominantly revolved around territorial defense, with the U.S. Army and Navy assuming central roles in safeguarding the nation's borders (Barnes, 2016).

President George Washington emphasized the need for a robust national defense in his 1790 State of the Union address, prompting the United States to bolster its military and naval forces. In his farewell address, President Washington underscored the significance of national security, stating that "the preservation of the sacred fire of liberty, and the destiny of the republican model of government, are justly considered as deeply, perhaps as finally staked, on the experiment entrusted to the hands of the American people" (Washington, 1796). During the Revolutionary War, the Continental Congress authorized the establishment of a committee to oversee the military, which served as a precursor to the modern Department of Defense. Subsequently, following the war, the U.S. encountered a new threat from Mediterranean pirates, leading to the creation of the U.S. Navy in 1794.

The Civil War marked a significant turning point in the evolution of national security in the U.S. This conflict demonstrated the importance of intelligence gathering and espionage in modern warfare, culminating in the establishment of the Office of Naval Intelligence in 1882 and the Army's Military Information Division in 1885. It is also worth noting that the Monroe Doctrine of 1823, which declared opposition to further European colonization or intervention in the Western Hemisphere, foreshadowed the country's national security interests. Throughout the 19th and early 20th centuries, the United States confronted threats to its national security, including conflicts with the British during the War of 1812, the Mexican American War in 1846-48, and the Spanish-American War in 1898. During World War I and II, the United States played a prominent role in defeating the Axis powers and establishing a new international order. The outbreak of

World War I in 1914 led to the formation of the Council of National Defense, tasked with coordinating the country's wartime efforts. Post-war, the U.S. government enacted the National Defense Act of 1920, which restructured the military and established the Army Reserve Officers' Training Corps (ROTC) (U.S. Army: The National Defense Act of 1920).

National Security Post World War II

Following World War II, the United States emerged as a global superpower, and the concept of national security expanded to encompass new threats, such as the spread of communism and the specter of nuclear war. Over time, the U.S. government's approach to national security adapted to changing challenges and threats. During the Cold War, the primary focus of U.S. national security was containing the spread of communism and maintaining nuclear deterrence. This approach led to the development of an extensive national security apparatus, comprising intelligence agencies, military forces, and diplomatic initiatives, all aimed at averting a nuclear war with the Soviet Union.

The Cold War between the United States and the Soviet Union dominated global politics for much of the latter half of the 20th century, involving a range of proxy conflicts on a global scale. However, in the post-Cold War era, the U.S. confronted new challenges, including terrorism, cyberattacks, and the proliferation of weapons of mass destruction. Consequently, the U.S. national security strategy underwent a shift, with renewed emphasis on counterterrorism and the promotion of democracy and human rights globally. The concept of national security has continued to evolve in the post-Cold War era.

In the United States, the modern understanding of national security emerged during World War II, when the country mobilized its resources and military to combat the Axis powers. Subsequently, the National Security Act of 1947 was enacted, establishing the National Security Council (NSC) and the Central Intelligence Agency (CIA), among other institutions, to facilitate coordination of the nation's defense and intelligence efforts (United States Congress, 1947). During the Cold War, national security became a paramount concern for the United States and its allies as they sought to contain communism and prevent Soviet global dominance.

The concept of deterrence, which entailed maintaining a robust military and the threat of nuclear retaliation, played a central role in U.S. national security strategy during this period. Following the end of the Cold War, there was a shift in the nature of national security threats as new challenges such as terrorism, cyberattacks, and economic competition emerged. In response, the United States and other countries adapted their national security strategies to address these evolving threats. These adaptations included increased intelligence and surveillance efforts, diplomatic engagement, and military operations. There is also a growing recognition of the importance of international cooperation in achieving national security objectives. Consequently, the U.S. has become more actively involved in international organizations such as the United Nations and NATO to tackle global security challenges.

Moreover, modern conceptions of national security emerged in the 20th century as advancements in technology and geopolitical dynamics made the world more interconnected and intricate. One of the most significant changes in U.S. national security policy occurred with the conclusion of the Cold War. The collapse of the Soviet Union in 1991 eliminated the primary external threat to the United States, prompting a reassessment of the country's national security strategy. In the post-Cold War era, the U.S. shifted its focus towards countering transnational threats, particularly terrorism and nuclear proliferation. The terrorist attacks on September 11, 2001, marked a pivotal moment in U.S. national security policy. These attacks revealed the vulnerability of the U.S. to asymmetric threats and triggered a substantial shift in the country's approach to national security. Consequently, the U.S. initiated a global war on terrorism, which included military interventions in Afghanistan and Iraq.

Despite these endeavors, U.S. national security policies have encountered criticism, particularly regarding the use of military force. For instance, a 2014 Senate report highlighted that the Central Intelligence Agency's interrogation program was more brutal and less effective than previously acknowledged. The report also revealed inadequate management of the program, leading to numerous human rights violations. Such findings and other studies have fostered an increasing recognition of the necessity for greater transparency and oversight in U.S. national security policy. In recent years, there have been calls for enhanced accountability and for the government to provide more information to the public regarding its national security activities.

Additionally, the importance of international cooperation in achieving national security goals is being increasingly acknowledged. As a result, the U.S. has heightened its engagement in international organizations such as the United Nations and NATO to address global security challenges (The White House, 2021).

It is crucial to note that over time, the definition and scope of national security have expanded to encompass military defense, intelligence gathering, cybersecurity, economic security, and diplomacy. This expansion is a response to the changing nature of global threats and the growing interdependence of the world's economies. Nevertheless, the effectiveness of these measures remains a subject of extensive debate. The Iraq War, in particular, has been criticized for being based on flawed intelligence and resulting in significant civilian casualties. Furthermore, enhanced interrogation techniques and secret detention facilities have been condemned as human rights violations contrary to U.S. values.
In the aftermath of the 9/11 terrorist attacks, national security took on a new dimension, with a renewed emphasis on preventing and responding to terrorism. This shift led to the establishment of the Department of Homeland Security, which consolidated various agencies responsible for safeguarding the country's borders, infrastructure, and populace from terrorist threats.

Additionally, the U.S. has gleaned valuable lessons from past national security mistakes. For example, the Vietnam War, which lasted from 1955 to 1975, taught the U.S. the significance of defining clear objectives and comprehending the complexities of a situation before engaging in military action. Similarly, the intelligence failures preceding the 9/11 attacks underscored the need for improved coordination and information sharing among intelligence agencies.

The U.S. has implemented several changes in its national security approach to address these challenges. For example, in 2010, President Obama issued a National Security Strategy that emphasized the significance of collaboration and partnerships with other countries in tackling global issues such as terrorism, climate change, and nuclear proliferation. Furthermore, the U.S. has made substantial investments in the development of advanced technologies to enhance its national security capabilities, including unmanned aerial vehicles, cyber defenses, and biometric systems. However, there is a need for further changes in the near future to address emerging threats to national security. One of the most pressing challenges is the escalating threat of cyberattacks, which can severely impact critical infrastructure, compromise sensitive data, and disrupt communication networks. To counter this threat, the U.S. needs to invest in the improvement of cyber defenses and the establishment of a robust regulatory framework to safeguard critical infrastructure from cyberattacks.

Learning From Past Mistakes

The U.S. national security system has experienced its share of mistakes and failures. The Vietnam War stands out as a significant failure, illustrating the limitations of military power in achieving national security objectives. The 9/11 attacks exposed weaknesses in the U.S. intelligence and security systems, prompting a reevaluation of national security strategies. Over the years, numerous studies have been conducted to identify shortcomings in the U.S. national security system and propose reforms. Notably, the Project on National Security Reform conducted an influential study that highlighted systemic issues within the U.S. national security system, including a lack of coordination and integration among agencies, inadequate resources, and insufficient communication (Garamone, 2009).

Studies and investigations, such as the 9/11 Commission Report, have underscored the importance of interagency cooperation and intelligence sharing to prevent future terrorist attacks. These findings have resulted in the creation of new government agencies, such as the Department of Homeland Security and the Director of National Intelligence, aimed at improving coordination and information sharing. One significant change in the U.S. national security strategy occurred after the 9/11 terrorist attacks. The U.S. government's response focused on preventing future attacks and combating terrorist organizations globally. This strategy entailed military interventions in Iraq and Afghanistan, enhanced intelligence gathering, and domestic security measures.

Since the end of the Cold War, the United States has been involved in various military operations and conflicts, including the Gulf War in 1991, the wars in Iraq and Afghanistan, and ongoing military operations against terrorist organizations such as Al-Qaeda, ISIS and many others. On a global scale, the concept of national security has evolved differently in various countries and regions.

For instance, in Europe, the establishment of the European Union and other regional organizations has fostered increased cooperation and integration regarding security and defense matters. In Asia, rising powers like China have emerged as significant global players, contributing to new regional and global security challenges. In summary, the concept of national security has been influenced by a range of historical events and trends, encompassing wars, technological advancements, and shifting geopolitical dynamics. As new threats continue to emerge, the concept of national security will undoubtedly evolve in response. Past mistakes and studies have provided valuable lessons that have shaped our approach to national security. One crucial lesson is the necessity for greater collaboration and coordination among different government agencies and departments.

For example, the 9/11 Commission determined that a lack of coordination and communication between the FBI and CIA played a role in the failure to prevent the 9/11 attacks (National Commission on Terrorist Attacks upon the United States, 2004). Another lesson learned is the importance of balancing security measures with civil liberties. Specifically, the passage of the USA PATRIOT Act in the aftermath of the 9/11 attacks expanded the government's surveillance powers but raised concerns about potential infringements on privacy and civil liberties.

In the 20th century, the concept of national security expanded to encompass new threats, including communism, nuclear weapons, and terrorism. Throughout the Cold War, the United States pursued a strategy of containment to prevent the spread of communism, resulting in significant military buildup and interventions in conflicts such as the Korean War and the Vietnam War (Wirtz & Hoffman, 2017). The terrorist attacks on September 11, 2001, underscored the significance of homeland security and triggered substantial changes in national security policy, including the establishment of the Department of Homeland Security and the creation of the Office of the Director of National Intelligence (Johnson & Masters, 2018). In the history of U.S. national security, there have been numerous mistakes and failures, such as intelligence failures preceding the Pearl Harbor attack in 1941 (Prados, 2017) and the failure to prevent the 9/11 attacks (National Commission on Terrorist Attacks upon the United States, 2004). These failures prompted significant changes in national security policy, including the establishment of new intelligence agencies and the implementation of new procedures for sharing and analyzing intelligence (Wirtz & Hoffman, 2017).

Another significant error was the failure of the U.S. to anticipate and effectively respond to the 2008 financial crisis. The crisis had notable national security implications, including a decline in the U.S.'s global economic influence, increasing unemployment, and social unrest. It highlighted the necessity for the U.S. national security system to address economic security as an integral part of national security. Other studies and reports have also identified deficiencies in the U.S. national security system, including the need for improved coordination and information sharing among agencies. For instance, the 2012 Benghazi attack in Libya exposed weaknesses in the U.S. embassy security system, leading to calls for enhancements in embassy security.

Looking ahead, national security experts have identified several areas where changes are necessary to ensure the United States remains secure in the face of evolving threats. These areas include enhancing cybersecurity, addressing the growing threat of domestic extremism, and strengthening cooperation with allies and partners worldwide (Carafano & Ashford, 2021). Moreover, significant investment in emerging technologies such as artificial intelligence and quantum computing is needed to maintain technological superiority and stay ahead of potential adversaries (Levinson-Waldman & Verma, 2021).

In terms of current and near-future changes, the U.S. will need to confront several challenges to its national security, including cyberattacks, the proliferation of weapons of mass destruction, and the ascent of China as a global superpower. Addressing these challenges requires a proactive and comprehensive approach that incorporates both military and non-military measures. Additionally, the U.S. must strike a balance between protecting national security and safeguarding civil liberties. This entails implementing measures such as intelligence activity oversight and targeted surveillance rather than broad-based surveillance.

Furthermore, the U.S. must address the root causes of terrorism and extremism by investing in development, promoting democracy and human rights, and tackling poverty and inequality. By addressing these underlying issues, the U.S. can contribute to creating conditions less conducive to extremism and terrorism. Artificial intelligence (A.I.) and other advanced technologies are also expected to play an increasingly crucial role in the U.S. national security system. To coordinate A.I. research and development efforts across the military, the Department of Defense has established the Joint Artificial Intelligence Center (JAIC).

Moving forward based on our lessons learned, it is necessary to implement several changes to ensure robust national security in the U.S. One area that demands attention is the effective mitigation of emerging threats, such as cyberattacks and disinformation campaigns.

Additionally, it is crucial to ensure that national security policies are grounded in evidence and analysis rather than ideology or political expediency. Looking ahead, numerous changes are necessary in the near future to address emerging threats to national security. Among the most urgent challenges is the escalating menace of cyberattacks, which have the potential to cripple critical infrastructure, compromise sensitive data, and disrupt communication networks. To counter this threat, the U.S. must invest in developing enhanced cyber defenses and establish a robust regulatory framework to safeguard critical infrastructure from cyberattacks.

Succinctly, national security is a complex and ever-evolving concept that has undergone significant transformations over time in response to new threats and challenges. The U.S. has played a crucial role in shaping the evolution of national security and has derived valuable insights from past mistakes. However, the emergence of new threats, such as cyberattacks, necessitates a renewed emphasis on investing in advanced technologies and formulating stronger regulatory frameworks to protect critical infrastructure. Although there have been errors and failures in the past, they have led to substantial policy and procedural changes. Looking to the future, it is imperative to address emerging threats and invest in new technologies to ensure that the United States remains secure in an ever-changing world.

The origin and evolution of national security in the U.S. have been influenced by various factors, including evolving threats, political and social events, and technological advancements. Previous mistakes and studies have underscored the need for enhancements and modifications in the U.S. national security system. Immediate changes are required to tackle emerging threats and challenges, encompassing economic security, investment in innovation, and adaptation to the changing nature of conflicts. The U.S. national security system must continue to evolve to effectively respond to the dynamic global security landscape.

Native Americans' Perspectives On National Security

Native Americans' perspectives on security, stability, and land protection are matters of national security. Safeguarding Native American lands and natural resources is not only crucial for their survival but also for the long-term sustainability of the environment and the nation as a whole. This comprehensive analysis will delve into the overall viewpoint of Native Americans on security and territorial protection and shed light on the key factors that have shaped this perspective.

One reason why Native Americans' perspectives on security, stability, and land protection are deemed matters of national security is their unique relationship with the land. Many Native American tribes perceive the land as sacred and possess a profound connection that goes beyond mere ownership. Consequently, they have developed distinctive strategies to safeguard their land and natural resources, such as leveraging traditional ecological knowledge and establishing treaties with the United States government.

Firstly, Native American lands and resources hold strategic importance for the United States. Many of these lands contain valuable resources, including oil, gas, and minerals, which are essential for the nation's economy and security.

Moreover, Native American lands are often situated in strategic areas along international borders, rendering them vital for border security.

Lastly, protecting Native American lands and natural resources is crucial for national security because these resources frequently underpin the nation's infrastructure and economy. For instance, many Native American lands house significant mineral resources like uranium, coal, and oil, which are vital for the nation's energy needs (National Congress of American Indians, 2016).

Additionally, Native American lands often serve as the source of essential water resources, such as the Colorado River, which supplies water to millions of people across multiple western states. Secondly, protecting Native American lands and natural resources is indispensable for national security as many of these lands harbor significant historical and cultural resources that are essential to the nation's heritage. Native American lands encompass thousands of archaeological sites, some dating back thousands of years, providing invaluable insights into the history of the Americas and its indigenous peoples. Furthermore, safeguarding Native American lands and resources is critical to the nation's environmental security (Coulthard, 2014). These lands contain some of the last remaining pristine ecosystems in the United States, serving as crucial habitats for numerous endangered species. The well-being and sustainability of these ecosystems are vital for the overall health of the planet and the future of humankind.

Thirdly, protecting Native American lands and resources is essential for the nation's cultural security. Native American culture is deeply intertwined with the nation's identity and heritage. By safeguarding Native American lands and resources, this rich culture can be preserved for future generations. Lastly, protecting Native American lands and resources holds significance for national security in a broader sense. The United States' relationship with Native American tribes is essential to its diplomacy with other nations. The manner in which the United States treats its indigenous peoples sends a powerful message to the world about its commitment to human rights and environmental protection. Protecting Native American lands and natural resources is vital for national security as it plays a crucial role in building trust between the government and the Native American community. For too long, the government has neglected the rights of Native Americans and failed to honor the treaties signed with them. By working towards the protection of Native American lands and natural resources, the government can begin to rebuild trust and strive for a more equitable relationship with Native American communities

(Bulltail, 2013). Additionally, protecting Native American lands and natural resources is critical for national security due to their pivotal role in the ecosystem. Native American lands are home to a diverse array of plant and animal species, many of which are threatened or endangered. Preserving these species and their habitats is essential for maintaining a healthy ecosystem, which is vital for human survival.

Furthermore, many Native American lands contain valuable natural resources such as oil, gas, and minerals. The responsible extraction and management of these resources can bring economic benefits to both Native American tribes and the nation as a whole. However, it is crucial to approach this endeavor in an environmentally sustainable manner that respects Native American cultural resources and traditions. The protection of Native American lands and natural resources is also vital for national security as it helps promote social stability and reduce conflict. When Native American tribes can safeguard their lands and natural resources, they can better preserve their cultural traditions and way of life. This, in turn, contributes to reducing tensions between Native American tribes and the larger society.

Regarding security, Native American lands and resources hold strategic importance to the United States, as previously discussed. Additionally, many Native American tribes possess unique knowledge and experience in security matters, including border security, counterterrorism, and emergency response. For instance, the Navajo Nation boasts a highly trained and experienced police force that ensures security not only within the Navajo Nation but also in neighboring communities (National Congress of American Indians, 2016).

When it comes to stability, Native American perspectives on this matter are deeply rooted in their cultural beliefs and traditions. Many tribes emphasize the importance of maintaining balance and harmony in all aspects of life, including social, economic, and environmental realms. This perspective can be applied to national security by promoting sustainable resource management, diplomatic practices, and conflict resolution strategies.

Furthermore, Native American societies are built upon complex social structures that prioritize community, cooperation, and mutual respect. These social orders provide a framework for addressing social and political issues, including those related to national security. An exemplary illustration of this is the Iroquois Confederacy, a confederation of six Native American tribes that developed a governance system emphasizing consensus-based decision-making and respect for individual rights, serving as a model for the United States Constitution.

In terms of beliefs, Native American convictions about the interconnectedness of all living things and the importance of maintaining a balance between humans and nature contribute to national security by promoting sustainable practices and conservation efforts.

Moreover, Native American beliefs regarding the significance of spiritual and cultural traditions can serve as a source of resilience and strength in times of crisis. Preserving cultural heritage is crucial for the well-being and way of life of Native American communities. Cultural practices and beliefs are not merely personal preferences for these communities but are intricately intertwined with their social, economic, and political well-being (National Congress of American Indians, 2016).

The preservation of Native American cultures is viewed as vital for maintaining community cohesion and well-being. Research conducted by the Indigenous Language Institute has revealed that the loss of Native American languages and cultures can significantly impact mental health and social cohesion. Consequently, it can lead to increased rates of substance abuse, domestic violence, and suicide among Native American communities.

Furthermore, as previously discussed, protecting Native American lands and resources is critical to national security, considering strategic, environmental, cultural, and diplomatic concerns. Native American perspectives on the importance of land preservation can also serve as a model for sustainable practices and environmental stewardship. Native American communities have always emphasized their relationship with the land, recognizing the protection of land and resources as essential for their survival and cultural preservation. This viewpoint is reflected in their concept of sovereignty, which encompasses political authority and control over their lands and resources.

A study conducted by the National Congress of American Indians (NCAI) (2014) highlights the significance of protecting tribal sovereignty and self-determination for the social, economic, and political well-being of Native American communities. The study also acknowledges that the actions of the U.S. government towards Native American communities, such as land seizures and forced relocations, have had significant and enduring adverse effects on Native American security and stability. In addition to physical protection, social and economic security are essential components of Indigenous peoples' security, as outlined by Native American beliefs. Coulthard (2014) states that preserving culture, language, and sovereignty is critical to Indigenous peoples' safety. The loss of cultural identity and heritage can erode social and economic systems within Native American communities.

As discussed in the previous analysis, Indigenous peoples' cultures and languages have been threatened by colonialism, assimilation, and globalization. These threats have resulted in the erosion of traditional knowledge systems and practices, which have economic and social implications for Native American communities. For instance, the loss of traditional ecological knowledge can impact the ability of Indigenous peoples to sustainably manage natural resources and engage in subsistence activities.

Similarly, the loss of Indigenous languages can hinder the transmission of cultural knowledge, impeding the social cohesion and resilience of Native American communities.
Indigenous sovereignty also plays a vital role in Native American security. As noted by Smith (2012), the history of American Indian policy has been characterized by the exertion of federal power over Native American lands and resources. This has resulted in the erosion of tribal sovereignty and the suppression of Indigenous

political systems. Restoring Indigenous sovereignty is crucial to the social, economic, and political security of Native American communities, as it enables them to exercise self-determination and govern their lands and resources. In order to address these issues, Indigenous peoples have developed various strategies to promote cultural, linguistic, and political revitalization.

For example, efforts aimed at language revitalization, such as immersion schools and community language programs, have successfully preserved and promoted Indigenous languages (Gonzales, 2010). Similarly, the reassertion of Indigenous political authority, exemplified by the establishment of tribal courts and the enactment of tribal laws, has been instrumental in advancing Indigenous sovereignty.

Briefly, Indigenous peoples' security encompasses more than physical protection and encompasses social and economic security, as well as the preservation of culture, language, and sovereignty. The loss of cultural identity and heritage has implications for the social and economic systems within Native American communities. Indigenous sovereignty is vital for Native American security, providing the opportunity for self-determination and the governance of lands and resources. Strategies aimed at promoting cultural, linguistic, and political revitalization are critical in ensuring the security and resilience of Indigenous peoples. In short, Native Americans' perspectives on security, stability, and land protection are national security matters. The protection of Native American lands and natural resources is crucial for the long-term sustainability of the environment and the nation as a whole.

Therefore, it is essential to collaborate with Native American tribes to develop strategies that safeguard their lands and natural resources while promoting economic growth, social stability, and environmental sustainability.

Native American's Reasons for War

Native Americans are generally peace-loving nations, but various factors contributed to conflicts and wars with other nations. While many Native American cultures indeed valued peace and diplomacy, it is important to acknowledge that intertribal conflicts and warfare were not uncommon. Additionally, Native American communities were not always the instigators of violence and often responded to threats from European settlers or other Native American groups. One contributing factor to Native American warfare was the competition for resources, including land and hunting grounds. As different tribes migrated and settled in new areas, conflicts often arose over access to these resources. Disputes over trade and tribute could also lead to conflict between tribes.

Another significant factor was the impact of European colonization on Native American societies. European settlers frequently encroached on Native American lands, appropriated resources, and forcibly displaced or assimilated Native American communities. This resulted in significant tension and violence between Native American groups and European colonizers. Furthermore, the introduction of European weapons and military tactics also played a role in Native American conflicts. Prior to European contact, Native American warfare primarily consisted of small-scale skirmishes and raids. However, the availability of firearms and advanced weaponry gave some tribes a substantial military advantage over others.

Land disputes were another common cause of Native American conflicts. European colonizers often claimed land that had been inhabited by Native American tribes for generations, leading to conflicts over land ownership and usage. For example, the Pequot War (1636-1638) in Connecticut was sparked by a land dispute between the Pequot tribe and English colonists. The colonists aimed to expand their settlements, but the Pequots refused to sell or share their land, resulting in a conflict that claimed the lives of hundreds of Pequot people.

Resource competition was also a significant factor. Native American tribes frequently clashed over resources such as food, water, and hunting grounds. With the arrival of European settlers, Native American tribes often found their traditional hunting grounds and fishing spots depleted or destroyed, leading to increased competition and conflict. For instance, the Blackfoot tribe in Montana and Alberta, Canada, often engaged in conflicts with other tribes over buffalo hunting grounds. Additionally, the introduction of firearms by European traders escalated the intensity and lethality of these conflicts.

Cultural differences and misunderstandings could also contribute to conflicts between Native American tribes or between Native Americans and Europeans. Europeans often had distinct customs, beliefs, and social structures that differed from those of Native American tribes, leading to misunderstandings and clashes. For instance, the Ghost Dance movement among the Sioux in the late 1800s was perceived as a threat by U.S. government officials, who feared it would incite a Native American uprising. The resulting conflict, known as the Wounded Knee Massacre, resulted in the deaths of over 200 Sioux men, women, and children.

Furthermore, conflicts could arise when European colonizers or the U.S. government violated treaties or agreements with Native American tribes. Many Native American tribes signed treaties with the U.S. government, which promised them land, resources, and protection in exchange for peace and cooperation. However, the government often disregarded or violated these treaties, leading to conflicts and eroding trust. The Sioux Wars in the late 1800s were particularly sparked by the U.S. government's violation of the Fort Laramie Treaty of 1868, which had granted the Sioux ownership of the Black Hills in South Dakota. When gold was discovered in the Black Hills, the U.S. government broke the treaty and forcibly removed the Sioux from the area, triggering a series of conflicts and battles.

In summary, it is crucial to recognize that Native American cultures were diverse and complex, and there is no singular explanation for the occurrence of conflicts. However, a combination of factors, including resource competition, European colonization, and the introduction of advanced weaponry, contributed to the prevalence of warfare among Native American communities.

Past And Recent Inquiries Of Native Americans In North America On Security

Native Americans' perspectives on security, stability, social order, beliefs, and land protection are crucial for their survival, stewardship, and well-being. Therefore, it holds cultural significance and plays a role in national security. The objective of this section is to review and highlight past and recent analyses of the Native American viewpoint on national security and land protection in North America. The Western world can gain valuable insights from these investigations into national security and territorial safeguarding.

LaDuke (2017) asserts that the Native American perspective on territorial protection is deeply rooted in the belief that humans are interconnected with the natural world and that the land is sacred. The research provides a comprehensive analysis of this perspective, underscoring its cultural foundations. According to LaDuke, Native Americans view their relationship with the land as reciprocal and symbiotic rather than exploitative. This viewpoint is reflected in their traditional practices and customs, emphasizing the importance of living in harmony with the environment. Native Americans have sought to protect their territorial rights through treaty agreements with the U.S. government, which were often negotiated to ensure the preservation of their lands, resources, and right to self-governance.

However, the U.S. government has repeatedly failed to honor these treaties, resulting in the displacement of Native American communities and the destruction of their cultural heritage. LaDuke also draws attention to the impact of environmental degradation on Native American communities. As custodians of the land, Native Americans have long been concerned about the consequences of industrialization and resource extraction on their territories.

Unfortunately, this has led to conflicts with the U.S. government and multinational corporations, who seek to exploit these resources for their own gain. In response, Native American communities have organized resistance movements and environmental campaigns to safeguard their territories and way of life.

The interconnectedness of human beings with the natural world is a fundamental aspect of Native American spirituality and culture. Native Americans believe that land, water, air, and all living things are interconnected, and human actions can have an impact on the natural world.

Therefore, protecting the environment is not merely about preserving natural resources; it also encompasses the preservation of the spiritual and cultural significance of the land. Moreover, the concept of sacred land holds central importance in Native American culture. The land is not just a physical space; it is also a spiritual and cultural realm intimately tied to the identity and well-being of Native American communities. This spiritual connection to the land makes territorial protection a matter of property rights and the duty to preserve cultural heritage and identity.

In short, LaDuke's analysis underscores the fundamental importance of the land in Native American culture and the ongoing struggle to protect their territorial rights. This perspective extends beyond land and resource protection to encompass the preservation of cultural identity and spiritual well-being. Understanding this viewpoint is essential for the development of effective policies that respect the cultural heritage, self-determination, and sovereignty of Native American communities. While treaty agreements and legal frameworks offer some protection, the persistent threats posed by environmental degradation and resource extraction demand ongoing activism and advocacy.

Ultimately, the safeguarding of Native American territorial rights is not solely a matter of property rights; it is vital for the preservation of their cultural heritage and way of life.

Moreover, Anderson (1996) asserts that the Native American perspective on territorial protection and security is intricately linked to their sovereignty as distinct nations. The research argues that sovereignty is fundamental to the Native American stance on territorial protection and security. Native Americans perceive themselves as unique nations with pre-existing political, cultural, and economic systems, and they consider their territories integral to their sovereignty.

According to Anderson, sovereignty refers to the ability to make decisions and govern one's affairs without external interference. Therefore, for Native Americans, territorial protection and security encompass the preservation of their sovereignty and the recognition of their political autonomy.

This perspective on sovereignty is grounded in centuries of history, including the treaties signed between Native American nations and the United States government. These treaties acknowledged the political autonomy and territorial rights of Native American tribes. However, they were often disregarded or violated by the U.S. government. This history of broken promises and forced assimilation has led many Native Americans to view sovereignty and territorial protection as essential for their survival and cultural preservation.

Furthermore, Anderson states that the concept of sovereignty is not merely a legal or political one but also a cultural one. Native American sovereignty is rooted in their spiritual beliefs and practices, which consider the land and natural resources as sacred and interconnected with human beings. Therefore, territorial protection and security for Native Americans also involve safeguarding their cultural and spiritual traditions, as well as their physical territories. In short, Anderson's analysis underscores the significance of sovereignty in the Native American perspective on territorial protection and security. This perspective is rooted in a history of treaties, broken promises, and forced assimilation, encompassing both legal and political concerns, as well as cultural and spiritual ones. Recognizing and respecting Native American sovereignty is crucial for developing effective and equitable policies for all parties involved.

Additionally, Coulthard (2014) argues that the Native American perspective on territorial protection and security is grounded in their resistance to colonialism and the politics of recognition.

According to Coulthard, colonialism is a process in which settler societies assert ownership over and exploit the lands and resources of Indigenous peoples, often through violence, dispossession, and displacement.

In response, Indigenous peoples have developed strategies of resistance, including struggles for territorial protection, cultural revitalization, and political self-determination.
Coulthard posits that the politics of recognition, which aims to assimilate Indigenous peoples into existing political systems and institutions, can be seen as a disguised form of colonialism.

Rather than challenging the underlying power dynamics between Indigenous peoples and settler societies, recognition often seeks to domesticate and co-opt Indigenous peoples, erasing their distinctiveness and reducing them to mere cultural identities. In contrast, Coulthard argues that Indigenous peoples' struggles for territorial protection and security are rooted in their inherent right to self-determination, which encompasses the ability to make decisions regarding their lands, resources, and political systems.

Furthermore, Coulthard emphasizes the importance of understanding Indigenous peoples' resistance as a response to colonialism and as a source of positive transformation and change. By asserting their sovereignty and autonomy, Indigenous peoples challenge the dominance of settler societies and create new forms of politics and culture based on Indigenous values and traditions. In this sense, Indigenous peoples' struggles for territorial protection and security are part of a broader movement for decolonization and social justice. In summary, Coulthard's analysis highlights the significance of comprehending the Native American perspective on territorial protection and security as a form of resistance to colonialism and the politics of recognition. By asserting their sovereignty and autonomy, Indigenous peoples defend their lands and cultures, while also forging new political and cultural paradigms that challenge prevailing norms and offer alternatives for a more just and sustainable future.

Additionally, a study by the National Congress of American Indians (NCAI) emphasizes that protecting tribal sovereignty and self-determination is crucial for the social, economic, and political well-being of Native American communities. The NCAI, a prominent organization advocating for the rights of Native American communities in the United States, conducted a recent study highlighting the importance of safeguarding tribal sovereignty and self-determination for the social, economic, and political well-being of these communities. This analysis will provide a concise overview of the study, including its key findings and implications.

The research conducted by the NCAI is titled "Tribal Sovereignty and Self-Determination: The Foundation of Native American Policy." It was published in 2019 and is available on the NCAI website. The study highlights the importance of tribal sovereignty and self-determination and how their protection can help Native American communities address their many challenges, including poverty, health disparities, and social inequality. According to the study, tribal sovereignty refers to the inherent right of Native American tribes to govern themselves, including the ability to make their laws, enforce them, and regulate their affairs. Self-determination, on the other hand, refers to the right of Native American tribes to determine their political status and shape their future.

The inquiry contends that protecting tribal sovereignty and self-determination is critical to the well-being of Native American communities. For example, it states that "tribal sovereignty is essential to the preservation of tribal culture, language, and traditions, which are important components of Native American identity and well-being" (NCAI, 2019, p. 3). The study also notes that the ability to make and enforce their respective laws is essential for tribes to protect their lands and natural resources, which are often threatened by outside interests. The examination further maintains that protecting tribal sovereignty and self-determination can also help Native American communities address their many challenges. For instance, it notes that "tribal governments are often better equipped to understand the needs of their communities and to design programs and policies that will be effective in meeting those needs" (NCAI, 2019, p. 4). Additionally, the study argues that by giving Native American tribes more control over their affairs, they can build robust and more resilient communities.

Regarding policy implications, the study recommends that the federal government work with Native American tribes to protect and enhance their sovereignty and self-determination. This could include increased funding for tribal programs and services, strengthening tribal consultation processes, and respecting tribal jurisdiction over their lands and resources. In short, the NCAI study highlights the importance of protecting tribal sovereignty and self-determination for the social, economic, and political well-being of Native American communities. It argues that these rights are essential for preserving tribal culture and identity, protecting tribal lands and resources, and addressing the many challenges faced by Native American communities.

Therefore, the study recommends that the federal government collaborate with tribes to enhance their sovereignty and self-determination and to respect their rights to govern themselves and shape their future.

Furthermore, the concept of security for Native Americans differs from the mainstream Western notion of national security. According to Deloria and Wilkins (1999), the Native American understanding of security is closely associated with protecting their land and resources. In their book, "Tribes, Treaties, and Constitutional Tribulations," the authors explain that for Native Americans, security is deeply connected to safeguarding their land and resources.

The authors argue that Native American communities have historically placed strong emphasis on the protection and preservation of their traditional lands and resources, which they view as central to their cultural and spiritual identity. They explain that for many Native American tribes, losing their lands and resources to outside interests has been one of the greatest threats to their security and well-being. Deloria and Wilkins further argue that the mainstream Western notion of national security, which prioritizes military strength and the protection of national borders, often conflicts with the Native American understanding of security. They point out that the U.S. government's efforts to safeguard national security have frequently come at the expense of Native American lands and resources, such as through the forced removal of tribes from their ancestral lands and the exploitation of natural resources on tribal lands.

The authors suggest that addressing the security concerns of Native American communities requires adopting a more inclusive and collaborative approach that recognizes and respects the unique perspectives and needs of these communities. They argue that this necessitates a shift from the traditional top-down approach to national security to a more bottom-up approach that emphasizes community involvement and participation.

In summary, Deloria and Wilkins' book provides a comprehensive and thought-provoking analysis of the challenges and opportunities facing Native American communities in the context of national security. The authors draw on various historical and contemporary examples to illustrate their arguments, and their analysis is supported by a plethora of primary and secondary sources.

In chapter four, we will focus on a different perspective on national security - Hinduism. We will examine the history of Hinduism and explore its viewpoints on national security, including its teachings on warfare, peace, and security. Learning about the Hindu perspectives on national security can broaden our views and understanding of the concept, which is especially crucial in today's interconnected world.

References:

Anderson, R. T. (1996). "The Significance of Sovereignty: Jurisdictional and Cultural Politics in the Treaty of Medicine Lodge." American Indian Quarterly, 20(4), 467-484.

"A Comprehensive National Cybersecurity Strategy: Challenges and Opportunities" The National Academies Press. https://www.nap.edu/read/25674/chapter/1

Bacevich, A. J. (2013). Breach of trust: How Americans failed their soldiers and their country. Metropolitan Books.

Barnes, T. G. (2016). A brief history of U.S. national security. Georgetown Security Studies Review, 4(2), 2-12.

Bulltail, J. R. (2013). The Impact of Indian Treaty Rights on National Security: The American Indian Perspective. American Indian Quarterly, 37(1/2), 27–47.

Buzan, B., Waever, O., & de Wilde, J. (2018). Security: A new framework for analysis. Routledge.

Calloway, Colin G. "Native American Warfare." Encyclopedia of American Military History, edited by Spencer C. Tucker, vol. 2, ABC-CLIO, 2013, pp. 976–980.

Carafano, J. J., & Ashford, E. (2021). The Future of National Security: Challenges and Opportunities for the Biden Administration. The Heritage Foundation.

9/11 Commission Report. National Commission on Terrorist Attacks Upon the United States, 2004.

Center for Native American Environmental Health Equity. (2021). Indigenous Environmental Health: From Local to Global.

Coulthard, G. S. (2014). Red skin, white masks: Rejecting the colonial politics of recognition. Minneapolis: University of Minnesota Press.

Deloria, V., & Wilkins, D. (1999). Tribes, Treaties, and Constitutional Tribulations. Austin: University of Texas Press.

Farley, Robert. "The Iraq War Was a Colossal Mistake and the United States Should Recognize It." The National Interest, 19.

Gonzales, L. (2010). Language revitalization and Indigenous education: Examining the role of language nests in Indigenous language and culture revitalization. Journal of Language, Identity, and Education, 9(5), 309–326.

Garamone, J. (2009). Project on National Security Reform Briefs Obama Team on Findings. U.S. Department of Defense. Retrieved from https://www.defense.gov/Explore/News/Article/Article/606197/project-on-national-security-reform-briefs-obama-team-on-findings/

Hämäläinen, Pekka. The Comanche Empire. Yale University Press, 2008.

Johansen, Bruce E., and Barry M. Pritzker. Encyclopedia of American Indian History, ABC- CLIO, 2016.

Johnson, J., & Masters, J. (2018). National Security Strategy: An Overview. Congressional Research Service.

Indigenous Language Institute. (2018). The Effects of Language Loss on Native American Health.

LaDuke, W. (2017). All our Relations: Native Struggles for Land and Life. Minneapolis: University of Minnesota Press.

Levinson-Waldman, R., & Verma, N. (2021). New Administration, New National Security Strategy. Lawfare.

Mueller, R. S. (2011). Reflections on the evolution of U.S. national security law. The American Journal of International Law, 105(2), 259-273.

National Commission on Terrorist Attacks upon the United States. (2004). The 9/11 Commission report. Washington, D.C.: National Commission on Terrorist Attacks upon the United States.

National Security Strategy of the United States, 2017. The White House. https://www.whitehouse.gov/wp-content/uploads/2017/12/NSS-Final-12-18-2017-0905.pdf

National Congress of American Indians. (2016). The Importance of Native American Lands and   Natural Resources to National Security. Retrieved from https://www.ncai.org/policy-research-center/research-data/prc-publications/The-Importance-of-Native-American-   Lands-and-Natural-Resources-to-National-Security.

National Congress of American Indians. (2014). Tribal Sovereignty and Self-Determination: A Basis for Resilience and Security in Native Communities.

National Congress of American Indians. (2019). Tribal sovereignty and self-determination: The foundation of Native American policy. Retrieved from https://www.ncai.org/policy-research-center/research-data/prc-publications/Tribal-Sovereignty-and-Self-Determination-The-Foundation-of-Native-American-Policy

Olsen, E. J. (2014). The evolution of U.S. national security strategy and policy. Journal of Strategic Security, 7(1), 1–21.

Powers, Jeanette. "Native American Governance and the U.S. Constitution." The Conversation, 13 Sept. 2017, theconversation.com/native-american-governance-and-the-us-constitution- 83192.

Prados, J. (2017). How the U.S. Government's Lies About the Pearl Harbor Attack Derailed Allied Strategy and Led to McCarthyism. The National Security Archive. Retrieved from https://nsarchive.gwu.edu/briefing-book/wwii/2017-12-07/how-us-governments-lies- about-pearl-harbor-attack-derailed-allied

Smith, A. D. (2012). Native Americans and the federal government: The struggle for sovereignty. University of Kansas Press.

U.S. Government Accountability Office. (2017). Native American Communities: Actions Needed to Improve Federal Response to Challenges Faced by Tribes.

U.S. Army: The National Defense Act of 1920. Retrieved from https://www.army.mil/article/103881/the_national_defense_act_of_1920

United States Congress. (1947). National Security Act of 1947. Retrieved from https://www.govinfo.gov/content/pkg/COMPS-218/pdf/COMPS-218.pdf

"The Constitution of the United States: A Transcription." National Archives and Records Administration, National Archives and Records Administration, June 25, 2018, www.archives.gov/founding-docs/constitution-transcript.

The White House. (2021). National Security Strategy of the United States of America. Retrieved from https://www.whitehouse.gov/wp-content/uploads/2021/03/NSC-1v2.pdf

Washington, G. (1796). George Washington's Farewell Address. United States Senate. https://www.senate.gov/artandhistory/history/resources/pdf/Washingtons_Farewell_Address.pdf

Wirtz, J. J., & Hoffman, F. G. (2017). American national security policy: authority, accountability, and the future of U.S. foreign policy. Routledge.

4

History of Hinduism and Its Standpoints On National Security

Hinduism Foundation on National Security

As one of the oldest religions in the world, Hinduism boasts a rich history of national security practices deeply ingrained in its religious texts and traditions. It has played a significant role in shaping the political and cultural landscape of the Indian subcontinent. Since ancient times, the concepts of national security and territorial protection have been intrinsic to Hinduism. The religious texts and practices of Hinduism offer valuable insights into national security, defense, and territorial safeguarding. The idea of national security in Hinduism is closely intertwined with the concept of Dharma, which encompasses duty, righteousness, and law. According to Hindu philosophy, every individual bears the responsibility of safeguarding their country and its people from external threats.

In Hindu tradition, everything in the universe is believed to have a specific dharma or purpose that must be fulfilled. This extends to human beings, who are bound to their particular societal roles and responsibilities. Dharma is thus intricately linked with duty and righteousness. Protecting Dharma equates to preserving the natural order of the universe and upholding moral and responsible principles. This duty is not limited to rulers or the military; it extends to every citizen of the country. Safeguarding one's land, people, and resources is considered a sacred duty and a responsibility towards society. Therefore, in addition to defending the kingdom from external threats, kings and rulers were expected to uphold Dharma by maintaining social order and justice within their realms (Trautmann, 2013).

Equally, the Rig Veda, one of the oldest Hindu texts, contains hymns that extol the significance of Dharma and the role of kings in upholding it. These hymns celebrate the king as the protector of Dharma and the defender of his people. In essence, the Rig Veda depicts the ideal king as someone who embodies the values of Dharma and wholeheartedly works to ensure that his kingdom is governed justly and compassionately. Furthermore, the king is portrayed as having the responsibility of protecting his people from enemies and maintaining social order within his domain (Pande, 2010).

Additionally, the Arthashastra, a treatise on statecraft and governance authored by the ancient Indian scholar Kautilya, underscores the importance of national security and the role of kings in safeguarding their kingdoms. The Arthashastra serves as an ancient Hindu guide to statecraft, highlighting the significance of maintaining law and order within the kingdom and outlining strategies to achieve this objective. Furthermore, the text delves into strategies for warfare, the maintenance of a formidable military, and the importance of alliances and diplomatic relations with neighboring states (Kangle, 1960).

The Manusmriti, an ancient Hindu legal code, offers further insight into the relationship between national security and Dharma. This text describes the duties of kings and rulers, which encompass the protection of their subjects and the preservation of social order. The king is expected to employ force, if necessary, to defend his kingdom from external threats and maintain law and order within his realm (Rocher, 2012). Moreover, the Mahabharata, an epic poem recounting a great war between two branches of a royal family, emphasizes the importance of upholding Dharma and protecting the kingdom from external threats. The war is portrayed as a struggle between good and evil, with the side fighting to uphold Dharma ultimately emerging victorious. This victory is regarded as a triumph for the natural order of the universe and a crucial step in ensuring the stability and continuity of society (Brockington, 2010).

One of the earliest illustrations of the connection between Dharma and the duties of rulers can be found in the Vedas, a collection of ancient Sanskrit hymns and texts. The Vedas depict Dharma as the universal principle that upholds the order of the universe, emphasizing the significance of upholding Dharma to ensure the well-being of society. This includes protecting the kingdom from external threats, as well as maintaining social order and justice (Ludwig, 2013). National security, within the context of Hinduism, is considered a pivotal aspect of safeguarding Dharma. This is because national security is directly tied to the well-being and stability of society. In Hindu philosophy, society is perceived as a web of interconnected relationships, and the well-being of each individual is interconnected with the well-being of the whole. Therefore, national security is viewed as an integral component of protecting the natural order of the universe, as it ensures the stability and continuity of society (Sharma, 2016).

The Bhagavad Gita, one of the most revered Hindu texts, contains several verses that underscore the importance of national security and defense. For example, in Chapter 2, Verse 31, Lord Krishna advises Arjuna, "Considering your specific duty as a Kshatriya, you should know that there is no better engagement for you than fighting on religious principles, so there is no need for hesitation." Thus, national security is seen as an essential component of protecting the natural order of the universe, as it ensures the stability and continuity of society.

Another instance can be found in Chapter 3, Verse 21, where Lord Krishna states, "Whatever action a great man performs, common people follow. Furthermore, all the world pursues whatever standards he sets by exemplary acts." This verse highlights the role and responsibility of leaders in setting the standards for their followers to protect their country and its people. Moreover, several stories in Hindu mythology exemplify the importance of national security and territorial protection. One such example is the story of Lord Rama, considered the embodiment of Dharma. In the epic Ramayana, Lord Rama engages in battle to defend his kingdom from the demon king Ravana, who had abducted his wife, Sita. Lord Rama's victory over Ravana symbolizes the triumph of righteousness over evil and serves as an inspiration for people to protect their country and its people from external threats.

Another instance can be found in the story of the Mahabharata, where the Pandavas, the rightful heirs to the kingdom, fight to reclaim their rightful place from the Kauravas. This story emphasizes the importance of safeguarding one's rightful territory and the duty to fight for what is just and righteous. The Mahabharata presents several examples of defending territories from external threats. The text narrates the story of King Janamejaya, who successfully defends his kingdom against the Nagas, a serpent race that posed a threat to his kingdom's security. This story highlights the significance of strategic planning, intelligence gathering, and the use of force to protect the kingdom from external threats.

In another example, the Ramayana depicts the god Rama and his allies fighting against the demon king Ravana to protect his kingdom from external threats. This story emphasizes the importance of alliances, diplomacy, and the use of force to safeguard the kingdom's sovereignty. Hindu religious texts also highlight the significance of individual security and self-defense. For instance, the Bhagavad Gita, one of the most sacred texts in Hinduism, teaches that a warrior must protect his people and defend his kingdom. This text encourages individuals to develop physical and mental strength to safeguard themselves and their communities.

One of the most prominent illustrations of territorial defense in Hindu texts is the story of the Mahabharata. The Mahabharata is an epic poem narrating a great war fought between two sets of cousins, the Pandavas and the Kauravas, over the kingdom of Hastinapur. The Pandavas emerged victorious, but the war caused widespread destruction and loss of life. In the Bhagavad Gita, a text within the Mahabharata, Lord Krishna advises Arjuna, one of the Pandava princes, on the importance of fulfilling one's duty and protecting one's territory. In chapter 2, verse 31, Lord Krishna states, "Considering your specific duty as a Kshatriya, you should know that there is no better engagement for you than fighting on religious principles, so there is no need for hesitation." Ultimately, the Pandavas defeated the Kauravas and restored peace to the kingdom. This story teaches us the importance of unity, strategy, and courage in defending one's territory. Additionally, this verse clarifies that defending one's territory is a sacred duty that must be performed without hesitation.

Another instance of territorial protection can be found in the Ramayana, another epic poem that recounts the story of Lord Rama and his quest to rescue his wife, Sita, from the demon king Ravana. Lord Rama, portrayed as the ideal king and protector, is depicted as a brave warrior willing to do whatever it takes to safeguard his people and kingdom. Rama and his army of monkeys and bears cross the ocean to reach Lanka, Ravana's kingdom. In the Ramayana, Lord Rama's army is shown to possess advanced weapons and strategies for defending their territory. For example, they construct a bridge across the ocean to reach Lanka, which is known as the Ram Setu. This bridge continues to be regarded as a marvel of engineering and a symbol of Hindu pride. After a fierce battle, Rama kills Ravana and rescues Sita. This story teaches us the importance of determination, perseverance, and strategic planning in defending one's territory.

In Chapter 18, Verse 44 of the Bhagavad Gita, Lord Krishna emphasizes the significance of one's duty, even if it is imperfectly performed, over another's duty performed well. Lord Krishna states, "One's own duty, even if imperfectly performed, is better than another's duty well performed. The duty prescribed for another is dangerous." This verse teaches us that it is the responsibility of every individual to fulfill their duty in protecting their land and people. The verse emphasizes the importance of individual responsibility in fulfilling one's duty towards national

security, rather than relying on others to execute it perfectly. It encourages individuals to take ownership of their responsibilities and strive to fulfill them to the best of their abilities, even if they sometimes fall short. This message is particularly relevant in national security, where each citizen has a role in safeguarding their country. It is essential to prioritize individual efforts over relying solely on external factors. The verse underscores the importance of individual responsibility and self-motivation in achieving success in any field, including national security.
Hinduism, the Concept of Dharma and Security

In the Vedas, the earliest and most sacred texts of Hinduism, several verses highlight the importance of protecting one's territory and the consequences of losing it. For instance, the Rigveda, Book 7, Hymn 6, Verse 3 states, "May our enemies be vanquished in battle, and may we enjoy the wealth of our foes. Let our heroes protect our borders, and our gods guard our land." In brief, Verse 3 expresses a desire for victory over enemies in battle and the hope of acquiring the wealth of those enemies. The hymn also seeks protection from heroes for their borders and the intervention of gods to safeguard their land. This verse reflects the prevailing beliefs and values of the time it was written, characterized by frequent warfare and the importance of acquiring wealth and protecting one's territory.

Similarly, in the Mahabharata, the epic describes the story of the Pandavas and their struggle to regain their kingdom from the Kauravas. The Pandavas were willing to go to war to protect their territory and safeguard their sovereignty. The Mahabharata, Book 6, Chapter 66, Verse 44 states, "For the protection of the earth, Arjuna has to kill his own kinsmen." This statement reflects the ethical and moral dilemmas faced by Arjuna in the war, where he finds himself pitted against his relatives and loved ones. Arjuna is torn between his duty as a warrior to protect the earth and his obligations as a family member to avoid harming his kin.

The verse also highlights the complex nature of the principle of Dharma or duty, which plays a central role in the Mahabharata. Arjuna is faced with conflicting duties, and he must make a difficult choice between them. Ultimately, he chooses to fulfill his duty as a warrior, even if it means killing his own relatives. The verse also raises important questions about the nature of violence, its justification, and its consequences. It underscores that violence can have far-reaching and tragic consequences, even if undertaken for what appears to be a just cause. The war between the Pandavas and Kauravas is presented as a struggle for the protection of Dharma, with the god Krishna advising the Pandava prince Arjuna to fight for what is right and just. Krishna says, "O Partha, happy are the Kshatriyas (warriors) to whom such a fight, which opens the door of heaven, comes of itself as an unsought opportunity" (Bhagavad Gita 2.32). In brief, this verse from the Mahabharata serves as a poignant reminder of the complexities and challenges of ethical decision-making, particularly when one's duty and obligations may conflict.

The concept of national security is also linked to the notion of Dharma-Yuddha, or righteous warfare. According to the Mahabharata, a sacred epic poem of Hinduism, a just war can be fought for the protection of Dharma, but only after all other means of resolving a conflict have been exhausted. The Mahabharata also emphasizes the importance of adhering to specific moral codes during warfare, such as not attacking unarmed or fleeing enemies. Overall, the concept of national security in Hinduism is closely linked to the protection of Dharma and the community, using force only as a last resort to defend what is right and just.

Several examples from Hindu mythology and history illustrate the importance of protecting Dharma to ensure national security. In the epic poem Mahabharata, for instance, the Pandavas fought a war against their cousins, the Kauravas, to uphold Dharma and protect the kingdom of Hastinapur. War is depicted as a struggle between good and evil, and the Pandavas emerge victorious because they are fighting to protect Dharma (Knott, 2016). Furthermore, Hinduism places great emphasis on diplomacy and strategic alliances in national security. The Mahabharata, for instance, describes the story of Krishna, who utilizes his diplomatic skills to form alliances and prevent a full-scale war. In the Mahabharata, Book 5, Chapter 83, Verse 12, it is stated, "Krishna is the master of diplomacy, and he knows how to form alliances and avoid unnecessary wars" (Ganguli, 2007).

Similarly, the concept of Rajdharma, or the duty of a ruler, is closely connected to the protection of Dharma and national security. Rajdharma is rooted in Hinduism and guides the behavior and actions of rulers. According to this principle, rulers must uphold the natural order of the universe and ensure the safety and security of their subjects. Fulfilling this duty is considered sacred, while neglecting it is seen as a violation of Dharma. Hindu philosophy dictates that rulers must uphold Dharma and the well-being of their subjects, including protecting the kingdom from external threats, maintaining law and order, and ensuring social justice. By fulfilling their Rajdharma, rulers uphold the natural order of the universe and ensure national security (Sharma, 2016). Rajdharma encompasses a broad range of responsibilities, including maintaining law and order, promoting social harmony, protecting the weak and vulnerable, and ensuring economic prosperity. By fulfilling their Rajdharma, rulers ensure the well-being of their subjects and contribute to the stability and progress of the nation.

Additionally, the concept of Rajdharma underscores the importance of ethical and moral leadership. Rulers are expected to lead by example, uphold the principles of Dharma, and act in the best interests of their subjects rather than pursuing personal gain or interests. The concept of Rajdharma is a vital aspect of traditional Hindu political philosophy, highlighting the importance of responsible and ethical leadership in ensuring the well-being and security of a nation.

Furthermore, the Manusmriti, an ancient Hindu legal code also known as the Laws of Manu, provides further insight into the relationship between national security and Dharma. The text describes the duties of kings and rulers, which include protecting their subjects and maintaining social order. These duties are integral to upholding Dharma, the natural law governing the universe. The Manusmriti emphasizes the importance of protecting the community from external threats, stating, "For, when a king protects his people duly, he prospers in this world and the next; but when he fails to protect them, he falls, with them, into hell" (Manusmriti 7.50).

According to the Manusmriti, the primary duty of a king is to protect his subjects from harm. This includes safeguarding the kingdom from external threats, such as invading armies or natural disasters. The text stresses the importance of maintaining a strong military to defend the kingdom, stating that "the king shall protect the kingdom from all dangers, with his army, which shall be strong and well-equipped" (Manusmriti 7.5). The Manusmriti highlights the significance of military might in ensuring the safety and security of the state.

In addition to protecting the kingdom from external threats, the Manusmriti emphasizes the importance of maintaining social order within the kingdom. The text delineates the duties of kings and rulers in upholding Dharma by promoting righteousness and punishing those who commit evil deeds. The king is expected to be a just ruler who ensures that all subjects are treated fairly, regardless of their social status or caste.

Furthermore, the Manusmriti emphasizes the significance of social order and hierarchy within the kingdom to maintain stability and harmony. The text outlines a detailed social structure with clear roles and responsibilities for each member of society, emphasizing the importance of fulfilling obligations and duties based on societal position. It promotes a system of social stratification and interdependence, aiming to maintain social order and balance within the kingdom.

The Manusmriti also provides guidelines for the conduct of warfare. The text emphasizes the importance of following ethical principles in warfare, stating that "one shall not kill the enemy who has surrendered, nor the one who has been defeated and is without arms, nor the one who is afflicted with sorrow or is fearful" (Manusmriti 7.91). These guidelines reflect the significance of upholding Dharma even in times of war. Ultimately, the Manusmriti provides further insight into the ancient Indian perspective on the relationship between national security and Dharma. It emphasizes the importance of protecting the kingdom from external threats and maintaining social order within the kingdom, both of which were considered integral to upholding Dharma, the natural law governing the universe.

From a Hinduism perspective, national security is not just about military strength, but also encompasses the protection of the environment, social and economic stability, and the overall well-being of the people. It is important to note that national security extends beyond a specific country or nation and encompasses the entire world and all its inhabitants. Hinduism's approach to national security emphasizes a multi-pronged approach, including strategic planning, intelligence gathering, alliances, diplomacy, and the use of force when necessary. It also emphasizes the significance of individual security and self-defense.

From a Hinduism stance, national security and territorial protection are essential for the survival and prosperity of a nation. Hindu texts teach us that protecting one's territory and sovereignty is a sacred duty that every citizen should fulfill. The texts also emphasize the importance of strong leaders who are willing to take decisive actions to safeguard the nation's security.

Additionally, in Hinduism, national security and territorial protection are seen as crucial for preserving a people's way of life and cultural identity. The emphasis on duty and responsibility, as seen in Lord Krishna's advice to Arjuna, is also central to the Hindu approach to national security. As mentioned earlier, national security is closely associated with Dharma, which includes protecting one's family, community, and country. Examples from Hindu religious texts demonstrate that defending territories and maintaining national security is essential to uphold Dharma and protect the sovereignty of the kingdom.

In modern times, the principles of territorial protection and national security outlined in Hindu texts can be integrated into national security strategies. For example, advanced technologies and innovative strategies can be employed to build bridges and other infrastructure that connect territories and secure borders. In addition, the emphasis on duty and responsibility can inspire leaders and citizens to work together to protect their country and way of life. Moreover, we can learn from these teachings and incorporate them into our national security strategies, prioritizing the protection of our citizens and territories, upholding international law and diplomacy, and drawing lessons from the teachings on governance and diplomacy found in the Arthashastra to develop effective national security policies.

In contemporary times, we can integrate these Hindu principles into our national security strategies by forging strong alliances with other nations and adopting a proactive approach to safeguard our territory and sovereignty. We can also learn from Hinduism the importance of strong leaders who are willing to take decisive actions to protect our nation's security.

Furthermore, the concept of national security in Hinduism has been associated with the idea of Hindutva or Hindu nationalism. This political ideology seeks to promote Hindu culture and values and considers the protection of the Hindu community as essential to national security. While some critics argue that this ideology is exclusionary and divisive, proponents argue that protecting Hindu culture and values is necessary against external threats.

Nowadays, the concept of national security in Hinduism has been tied to the sentiment of Hindutva or Hindu nationalism. This political ideology seeks to promote Hindu culture and values and sees the protection of the Hindu community as essential to national security. While some critics have argued that this ideology is exclusionary and divisive, proponents argue that protecting Hindu culture and values is necessary against external forces and threats. By integrating these principles into our modern national security strategies, we can better protect our territory and sovereignty and ensure the survival and prosperity of our nation.

In short, Hinduism provides valuable insights into the concept of national security and territorial protection. Hinduism emphasizes the importance of righteousness, duty, and leadership in defending the country and its people through its religious texts and practices. By integrating these insights into modern national security strategies, policymakers can promote a comprehensive approach to national security that upholds the values of justice, fairness, and respect for all people and nations. Additionally, Hindu religious texts and practices highlight the importance of protecting one's territory, people, and culture from external threats. The stories and verses in Hindu texts offer valuable lessons and insights that can be applied to modern national security strategies. By integrating these principles into national security planning and decision-making, countries can better protect their citizens and promote stability and prosperity.

The principle of Dharma played a central role in ancient Indian society, and the duties of kings and rulers were closely tied to the protection of the kingdom from external threats. The concept of Rajdharma emphasized the importance of upholding Dharma and protecting subjects. At the same time, the Ramayana provided an idealized portrayal of a king who upholds Dharma and protects his subjects. The Arthashastra emphasized the importance of maintaining law and order within the kingdom, highlighting the broader responsibilities of kings and rulers beyond protecting the kingdom from external threats. Kings and rulers were expected to uphold Dharma as part of their duties, which included the protection of their kingdoms from external threats. This can be seen through a historical analysis of Hindu texts and traditions such as the Rig Veda, Arthashastra, Manusmriti, and the Mahabharata. The importance of national security and the role of kings in protecting their kingdoms were emphasized in ancient Indian society and continue to be fundamental values in contemporary India.

As described in its religious texts and practices, Hinduism's rich history of national security practices can provide valuable insights into modern national security strategies. By studying these practices, we can learn the importance of a multi-pronged approach to national security, including strategic planning, alliances, diplomacy, and the use of force when necessary. We can also recognize the importance of individual security and self-defense in ensuring the security of our communities and nations. Hindu religious texts contain numerous examples and teachings on the importance of national security. These teachings emphasize the need to protect one's family, kingdom, and Dharma. By integrating these teachings into our modern national security strategies, we can ensure the safety and security of our citizens and territories.

Past And Current Studies of Hinduism On Security

As an ancient religion, Hinduism has exerted a tremendous influence on Indian culture and society for thousands of years. National security and territorial protection are significant concerns for India, and Hinduism's rich cultural heritage and philosophical traditions offer valuable insights in these areas. The aim of this section is to review and highlight past and current analyses of the Hinduism stance on national security and territorial protection, providing lessons that can be learned by the West and the world. Goel's (1993) study examines the historical perspective of Hinduism and national security. He argues that Hinduism has always emphasized the importance of national security and has faced threats from foreign invaders throughout history. To support his claim, Goel cites examples from Indian history, including the invasions of Mahmud of Ghazni and Timur, which he sees as attacks not only on Indian territory but also on Indian culture and religion.

According to Goel (1993), Hinduism has consistently stressed the security and protection of the nation, and repeated invasions have reinforced the concern for national security posed by foreign forces. Goel draws on various examples from Hindu mythology and history, such as the epic of Ramayana, to illustrate the struggle for national security and the need for a strong and just ruler who can defend the kingdom against external threats.

Goel also explores the role of Hinduism in contemporary Indian politics and national security. He contends that Hindu nationalism has emerged as a powerful force in recent years, partly in response to perceived threats to national security posed by terrorism and other external influences. Similarly, Goel cites the example of the Mughal invasions of India in the 16th and 17th centuries, which he argues posed significant threats to the security and sovereignty of Hindu kingdoms. He describes how Hindu kings and warriors bravely fought to defend their territories, and how this struggle became a symbol of national pride and identity for Hindus.

In agreement with Goel (1993), Hinduism has always been a religion that emphasizes the importance of protecting one's country and culture. Goel notes that this emphasis is rooted in the concept of dharma, which is seen as a guiding principle for individuals in Indian society.

Overall, Goel's study suggests that Hinduism has a long history of emphasizing the importance of national security, with this emphasis deeply rooted in the concept of dharma. He further argues that foreign invaders have constantly threatened Hinduism, and protecting India's territorial integrity and cultural heritage is essential for preserving the religion. Goel's evaluation provides a compelling argument for the close relationship between Hinduism and national security throughout history.

However, some scholars have criticized his work for its narrow focus on Hinduism and its failure to consider the complex and multifaceted nature of India's cultural and religious traditions. Ganguly (2002) also observes the impact of Hindu nationalism on India's security policies. He maintains that Hindu nationalism has been a significant factor in shaping India's approach to national security, particularly in relation to its relationship with Pakistan and its nuclear program. Ganguly notes that Hindu nationalists view national security as a critical issue and are primarily concerned with the threat of Islamic extremism and terrorism. He states that Hindu nationalist organizations have played an instrumental role in promoting a more aggressive foreign policy towards Pakistan and have shaped India's nuclear policy.

According to Ganguly (2002), Hindu nationalism has also influenced India's domestic security policies. He observes that Hindu nationalists have been involved in communal violence against religious minorities, particularly Muslims, and their activities have impacted India's internal security situation. In short, Ganguly's analysis suggests that Hindu nationalism has significantly shaped India's security policies, both domestically and internationally. He argues that Hindu nationalists consider national security a vital issue and have been instrumental in promoting a more aggressive approach towards Pakistan and shaping India's nuclear policy.

Additionally, the study "Hinduism and Security Studies: A Conceptual Framework" by Amit Gupta and Ayushi Singh (2019) offers a nuanced view of the relationship between Hinduism and security studies. The authors contend that Hinduism's stance on security and territorial protection is influenced by a range of factors, including its emphasis on dharma (righteousness), ahimsa (nonviolence), and karma (actions and their consequences). Furthermore, the authors highlight the diversity of Hinduism and its various interpretations by different sects, which can lead to differing attitudes towards security and warfare. The research also recognizes the impact of colonialism and modernization on Hindu thought and its perception of security.

From this analysis's perspective, the study presents a conceptual framework for analyzing Hinduism's approach to security studies, encompassing three elements: philosophical foundations, cultural practices, and political discourse. Understanding these elements can provide insights into how Hinduism's view of security has evolved over time. The study emphasizes the importance of comprehending Hinduism's approach to security studies, particularly in the context of India's strategic culture and foreign policy. The authors suggest that India's strategic culture is influenced by Hinduism's emphasis on dharma, which places a high value on upholding moral and ethical principles in domestic and international affairs.

In summary, this inquiry provides a comprehensive analysis of Hinduism and its relationship with security studies. The authors present a nuanced view of the subject, highlighting the diversity of Hindu thought and its impact on India's strategic culture and foreign policy. The analysis serves as a valuable resource for scholars of security studies and anyone interested in understanding the complexities of Hinduism and its influence on India's security policies.

Furthermore, in "Hinduism and Nationalism in India," edited by David Ludden (1996), the contributors delve into the connection between Hinduism and nationalism in India. The book argues that Hinduism has been a significant factor in shaping the Indian nationalist movement and explores this relationship from various viewpoints. This contribution to security studies is immense because it sheds light on how religious identities and nationalist movements interact and how they can lead to conflicts and security challenges. It also highlights how Hinduism has significantly shaped the Indian nationalist movement in the past and present, demonstrating how religious symbols and practices have been used to mobilize people around the cause of nationalism. This insight remains relevant today, as many conflicts worldwide have a religious dimension. For example, the ongoing conflict in the Middle East has religious undertones, and understanding the role of religion in shaping national identity is critical to resolving the conflict.

Hinduism has played a significant role in shaping the Indian nationalist movement, with both positive and negative consequences. On one hand, Hinduism has served as a unifying force, bringing people together based on a shared sense of identity, culture, and tradition. However, on the other hand, it has also been a source of division, leading to conflicts and tensions among different religious groups. The text explores this relationship through a series of articles that cover various aspects of the topic. For instance, one paper discusses how Hinduism has been used to legitimize political power and control in India, while another essay explores how Hindu nationalist groups have utilized religion to mobilize support for their political agenda. The manuscript also examines the role of Hinduism in the caste system, the impact of Hinduism on women's rights, and the connection between Hinduism and violence.

This book, "Hinduism and Nationalism in India," makes a significant contribution to security studies by shedding light on the complex relationship between religious identities and nationalist movements. This relationship has been explored in other countries as well, such as Israel, where Jewish nationalism has led to conflicts with Palestinians, and in the former Yugoslavia, where different religious groups fought for control of the region. In India, the relationship between Hinduism and nationalism has presented similar security challenges.

For example, the rise of Hindu nationalist groups like the Bharatiya Janata Party (BJP) has resulted in tensions and conflicts between Hindus and Muslims. The 2002 Gujarat riots, which claimed the lives of over a thousand people, were fueled by religious hatred and political tensions.

Furthermore, the book highlights the author's recognition of the dangers associated with religious nationalism. It demonstrates how the Hindu nationalist movement in India has led to the persecution of religious minorities, particularly Muslims. It emphasizes how religious nationalism can result in violence and conflict, posing a threat to the stability of a nation. This insight remains relevant today, as many countries worldwide are experiencing a rise in religious nationalism. The analysis provided in the text can assist policymakers in understanding the risks associated with religious nationalism and in developing strategies to mitigate its adverse effects.

Additionally, the book acknowledges the importance of inclusive nationalism. It argues that the Indian nationalist movement succeeded because it was able to create a broad-based national identity that encompassed people from different religions and castes. It demonstrates how nationalist leaders overcame religious and caste differences, uniting people around the cause of nationalism. This insight holds relevance today, as many countries struggle to forge inclusive national identities. The analysis in the text can aid policymakers in understanding the significance of inclusive nationalism and in formulating strategies to foster a more inclusive national identity.

Moreover, the writing sheds light on how religion can legitimize political power and control, thereby negatively impacting security. In India, Hindu nationalist groups have employed religion to garner support for their political agenda, leading to the marginalization of other religious groups and the erosion of democratic institutions.

Furthermore, the book's analysis of the caste system and its influence on Hinduism underscores the role of social inequality and exclusion in security challenges. The caste system has marginalized certain groups, such as Dalits, who have been excluded from mainstream society and denied fundamental rights and opportunities. This exclusion has contributed to social unrest and conflicts that threaten security and stability.

In a nutshell, "Hinduism and Nationalism in India" significantly contributes to security studies by illuminating the intricate relationship between religious identities and nationalist movements. The book provides a nuanced understanding of how Hinduism has influenced the nationalist movement in India and the diverse ways in which this influence has manifested. Additionally, in the article "Hinduism and the Ethics of War and Peace" by Sharma (2002), the role of Hinduism in shaping attitudes towards war and peace is explored. Sharma argues that Hinduism values nonviolence as a core principle, as reflected in the doctrine of ahimsa. However, Hinduism also recognizes the need for self-defense and protecting one's territory. In the Bhagavad Gita, Lord Krishna advises Arjuna to fight in the war against the Kauravas, emphasizing the duty of a warrior to protect the kingdom. Sharma contends that Hinduism acknowledges the necessity of self-defense and territorial protection but does not promote aggression or offensive war.

According to Sharma, Hinduism upholds the concept of dharma, which represents righteousness or duty. Dharma suggests that war is only justified when fought for a just cause, such as protecting one's territory, defending oneself or others from aggression, or upholding moral principles. Sharma highlights the importance of a valid reason for war in Hinduism, as it determines the legitimacy of engaging in armed conflict.

Sharma's article explores the role of Hinduism in shaping attitudes toward war and peace. According to Sharma, Hinduism values nonviolence as a core principle, which has played an essential role in shaping attitudes toward war and peace in India. However, Sharma argues that Hinduism also recognizes the need for self-defense and protecting one's territory. Sharma notes that the Hindu tradition recognizes the importance of dharma, which refers to righteous behavior or duty. Dharma is seen as a central principle of Hinduism, and it is believed that following dharma is essential for maintaining social order and harmony. Sharma asserts that the principle of dharma has played a critical role in shaping attitudes towards war and peace in Hinduism. Sharma notes that the practice of nonviolence is also a vital aspect of dharma. However, he says this principle is not absolute and must be balanced against the need for self-defense and protecting one's territory. As Sharma explains, the Hindu tradition recognizes that there are situations in which force is necessary to defend oneself and others.

What is more, Sharma analyzes the Hindu epics, the Mahabharata and the Ramayana, to illustrate Hinduism's complex and nuanced attitudes toward war and peace. He notes that while the Mahabharata contains extensive discussions on the ethics of war and the use of violence, the Ramayana portrays a more idealized vision of nonviolence. Sharma (2002) also discusses the role of the caste system in shaping attitudes towards war and peace in Hinduism. He observes that the warrior caste, or Kshatriyas, traditionally defended the community and protected the territory. However, Sharma argues that this responsibility was not unlimited and that strict ethical guidelines existed for using force.

Regarding implications for contemporary security challenges, Sharma's insights into the role of Hinduism in shaping attitudes towards war and peace can help us understand current security challenges in India. For example, India faces numerous security challenges, including terrorism, insurgency, and cross-border conflicts. Sharma's arguments suggest that India's approach to these challenges is likely influenced by dharma and the just cause of war. Sharma's assessment proposes that Hinduism values nonviolence as a core principle, which should be reflected in India's approach to security challenges. This means India's strategy should be based on nonviolence and the peaceful resolution of conflicts. However, if a just cause of war arises, then India's approach should be guided by the principles of dharma and the need for self-defense and protecting one's territory.

Briefly, Sharma's article offers valuable insights into the role of Hinduism in shaping attitudes towards war and peace. His arguments regarding the importance of the just cause of war and the recognition of the need for self-defense and protecting one's territory offer valuable insights into contemporary security challenges in India. Sharma's work suggests that India's approach to security challenges should be based on nonviolence, the peaceful resolution of conflicts, and the principles of dharma. The article highlights the need for a comprehensive understanding of the influence of religion and culture on security policy. Sharma's writing comprehensively analyzes Hinduism's stance on war and peace, explaining that although Hinduism values nonviolence as a core principle, it also recognizes the importance of self-defense and protecting one's community.

Additionally, Sharma's examination of the Hindu epics and the role of the caste system offers a nuanced understanding of the complex and diverse attitudes towards war and peace in Hinduism. Besides, in his article "Hinduism and National Security" (Sharma, 2013), Sharma explores the relationship between Hinduism and national security. He contends that Hinduism has always placed great importance on national security. Sharma notices that Hinduism has a long history of defending its territories and culture against foreign invaders. He cites several examples from Hindu mythology and history to support his claim, including the wars fought by the Pandavas in the Mahabharata and the resistance put up by the Marathas against the Mughal Empire. Sharma (2013) suggests that Hinduism's emphasis on national security is rooted in its belief in dharma, or duty. He notes that Hinduism greatly emphasizes fulfilling one's duties and responsibilities, including the obligation to protect one's homeland and culture. Altogether, Sharma's article suggests that Hinduism has always emphasized the importance of national security. Hindus view the protection of their homeland and culture as a sacred duty, and this belief has shaped how they approach national security challenges throughout their history.

Moreover, Sharma's (2013) writing maintains that Hinduism has always placed great importance on national security. He contends that Hinduism has a long history of defending its territories and culture against foreign invaders. Sharma notes that the Hindu tradition recognizes the importance of dharma, which refers to righteous behavior or duty. Dharma is seen as a central principle of Hinduism, and it is believed that following dharma is essential for maintaining social order and harmony.

Furthermore, the article contends that the principle of dharma has played an indispensable role in shaping attitudes toward national security in Hinduism. He notes that protecting one's territory and culture is seen as a duty that must be fulfilled to maintain social order and harmony. Sharma also notes that the principle of dharma has influenced the development of Hindu strategic thought. He holds that the principle of dharma has influenced Hindu strategic thinking by emphasizing the importance of understanding one's adversary and the need for proportionality in using force. Finally, he notes that the principle of dharma recognizes the importance of avoiding unnecessary harm and suffering and has influenced the development of Hindu strategic thought.

As for implications for contemporary security challenges, Sharma's insights into the relationship between Hinduism and national security can help us understand current security challenges in India. For example, India faces numerous security threats, including terrorism, insurgency, and cross-border conflicts. Sharma's arguments suggest that attitudes toward national security in India are likely to be shaped by the principle of dharma, which emphasizes the importance of righteous behavior and duty. Sharma's analysis also suggests that attitudes towards national security in India are likely to be shaped by recognizing the importance of understanding one's adversary and the need for proportionality in using force. This recognition is expected to be influenced by the principle of dharma, which emphasizes the importance of avoiding unnecessary harm and suffering.

Additionally, his arguments suggest that Hinduism's historical and cultural context is vital in shaping attitudes toward national security in India. The religion's history of defending its territories and culture against foreign invaders has created a strong national identity and pride among Hindus. This sense of identity and pride will likely play a paramount role in shaping attitudes toward national security in India, as it emphasizes the importance of defending the nation's sovereignty and territorial integrity.

In short, his article provides beneficial insights into the relationship between Hinduism and national security. His arguments regarding the role of dharma in shaping attitudes towards national security, the importance of understanding one's adversary, and the need for proportionality in the use of force offer practical understandings of recent security challenges in India. Broadly, Sharma's work highlights the need for a nuanced understanding of the role of religion and culture in shaping attitudes toward national security. Sharma's work emphasizes the need for a better understanding of the role of religion and culture in shaping attitudes toward national security.

Moreover, Bajoria and Xu (2019) examined the implications of Hindu nationalism for India's foreign policy. They claim that Hindu nationalism, which has become a significant political force in India in recent years, has shifted India's foreign policy priorities. Bajoria and Xu (2019) state that Hindu nationalism emphasizes the importance of national security and territorial protection. They note that Hindu nationalists view India's borders as sacrosanct and believe the country's territorial integrity must be protected at all costs. They argue that this emphasis on national security has led to a more assertive Indian foreign policy, particularly concerning its neighbors.

In their writing, they cite several examples to illustrate this point, including India's decision to conduct "surgical strikes" against militant groups in Pakistan in 2016 and its decision to withdraw from the South Asian Association for Regional Cooperation (SAARC) summit in 2016 after several member countries, including Pakistan, boycotted the event. Bajoria and Xu claim that Hindu nationalism's emphasis on national security has important implications for India's foreign policy. They suggest that India's foreign policy under Hindu nationalism is likely to be more assertive and focused on protecting India's territorial integrity, particularly in relation to its neighbors.

Furthermore, Shanthie Mariet D'Souza, in her 2016 study of "Hinduism and Security," argues that Hinduism offers a unique perspective on national security that emphasizes the importance of the individual. D'Souza contends that this perspective on security has important implications for contemporary security challenges in India. She begins by exploring the concept of dharma, which is a key principle in Hinduism.

She explains that dharma refers to a sense of duty and responsibility towards oneself and others. D'Souza states that this sense of responsibility is deeply ingrained in Hindu culture and has important implications for security.

She further discusses the role of the individual in Hinduism's perspective on security. She observes that Hinduism highly values individual freedom and autonomy, reflected in its emphasis on karma or the consequences of one's actions. D'Souza claims that this emphasis on personal responsibility means that individuals have an essential role in ensuring their security. D'Souza (2016) also explores the role of the state in Hinduism's perspective on security. She notes that while the state is responsible for providing security, it must also respect individual autonomy and freedom. D'Souza stipulates that this requires a balance between state power and individual rights.

In summary, D'Souza's writing offers a concise analysis of Hinduism's unique perspective on security. She argues that Hinduism's emphasis on individual responsibility and freedom has important implications for contemporary security challenges in India. Additionally, D'Souza's investigation of dharma and karma offers a nuanced understanding of how Hinduism's values can inform discussions on security.

Equally important, in his article, Bhatt (2019) examines the relationship between Hindu nationalism and India's foreign policy, focusing specifically on the case of Kashmir. Bhatt notes that some Hindu nationalists argue that India should take a more aggressive stance towards Pakistan and should use military force to reclaim the territory of Kashmir. Bhatt explains that these nationalists view the Kashmir issue as a matter of national pride and security. In addition, they see the presence of Pakistan-backed militants in Kashmir as a threat to India's territorial integrity and sovereignty. Therefore, they believe using force is necessary to reclaim the territory.

As reported by Bhatt (2019), these nationalists contend that India's current policy of restraint and dialogue with Pakistan has failed to produce results and that a more assertive approach is necessary. They also believe that the international community should support India's stance on Kashmir and that India should use its growing economic and military power to advance its interests in the region. In summary, Bhatt's article suggests that some Hindu nationalists advocate for a more aggressive foreign policy towards Pakistan, particularly regarding the issue of Kashmir. Furthermore, they believe using force is necessary to protect India's territorial integrity and sovereignty, and India should use its growing power and influence to advance its interests in the region.

Also, an evaluation conducted by Shastri (2008) examined the views of Kautilya, an ancient Indian statesman and philosopher, on the scope and method of intelligence gathering. Shastri noted that according to Kautilya, a ruler must ensure the security of his kingdom through a combination of military strength, diplomacy, and intelligence gathering. Shastri explained that Kautilya believed that intelligence gathering was an essential tool for ensuring the security of a kingdom. In addition, he found that Kautilya saw intelligence gathering as a way to gain information about potential threats to the kingdom and to develop strategies for countering those threats. Shastri's (2008) evaluation of Kautilya's views on collecting intelligence offers valuable insight into the scope and methodology of collecting intelligence in ancient India. This section will explore Shastri's arguments and their implications for contemporary security studies.

Shastri (2008) stated that Kautilya believed intelligence gathering should be conducted overtly and covertly. He observed that Kautilya saw diplomacy and espionage as complementary tools for intelligence gathering. In summary, Shastri's article suggests that, as articulated by Kautilya, a ruler must ensure the security of his kingdom through a combination of military strength, diplomacy, and intelligence gathering. Intelligence gathering is seen as an essential tool for countering potential threats and should be conducted through overt and covert means.

Shastri's evaluation focuses on Kautilya's views on intelligence gathering and how they can be applied to contemporary security studies. According to Shastri, Kautilya believed that a ruler must ensure the security of his kingdom through a combination of military strength, diplomacy, and intelligence gathering. Kautilya considered intelligence gathering critical for ensuring the kingdom's security. He emphasized the need for a well-organized intelligence system and believed that the ruler should be involved in intelligence gathering. Kautilya also recognized the importance of human intelligence and believed that spies and informants were critical for gathering information.

Moreover, Shastri says that Kautilya's views on intelligence gathering are relevant to contemporary security studies. He suggests that Kautilya's emphasis on a well-organized intelligence system and the involvement of the ruler in intelligence gathering can be applied to modern intelligence-gathering methods. Shastri also notes that Kautilya's recognition of the importance of human intelligence remains relevant today, and the use of spies and informants remains a critical aspect of intelligence gathering. Regarding implications for contemporary security studies, Shastri's evaluation of Kautilya's views on intelligence gathering has influenced recent security studies. The use of intelligence-gathering methods is crucial for ensuring the security of a state, and Kautilya's emphasis on a well-organized intelligence system and the involvement of the ruler in intelligence collection can be applied to modern intelligence-collection methods. Kautilya's recognition of the importance of human intelligence also has implications for contemporary security studies. Spies and informants are crucial for intelligence gathering, and modern intelligence agencies continue to rely on human intelligence to gather information.

In summary, Shastri's evaluation of Kautilya's views on intelligence gathering offers valuable insights into the scope and methods of intelligence gathering in ancient India. Kautilya's emphasis on a well-organized intelligence system and the involvement of the ruler in intelligence gathering can be applied to modern methods of intelligence collection. Additionally, Kautilya's recognition of the importance of human intelligence remains relevant today, and the use of spies and informants continues to be a critical aspect of intelligence gathering.

Moving on, Menon (2010), while writing about "The Mahabharata: A modern rendering," presents a contemporary interpretation of the ancient Indian epic, the Mahabharata. Menon notes that the text emphasizes the importance of loyalty and duty, particularly for warriors. Along with Menon, the Mahabharata suggests that warriors should fight not for personal gain but for the greater good of society. Warriors are expected to be loyal to their leaders and fulfill their duties, even if it means sacrificing their own lives. Menon's (2010) interpretation provides a modern understanding of the epic, highlighting its relevance to contemporary issues. Here, we will briefly explore Menon's arguments and their implications for today's security studies.

Menon asserts that this emphasis on loyalty and duty is rooted in the concept of dharma, which is a central theme in the Mahabharata. Dharma is often translated as "duty" or "righteousness" and is seen as a guiding principle for individuals in Indian society.

In summary, Menon's work suggests that the Mahabharata strongly emphasizes loyalty and duty, particularly for warriors. This emphasis is rooted in the concept of dharma, and it is seen as essential for maintaining order and stability in society.

Menon's (2010) writing underscores the significance of loyalty and duty, particularly for warriors. He notes that the text contains numerous examples of characters willing to sacrifice their interests for the community or the greater good. These characters demonstrate a strong sense of duty and loyalty, which is highly valued in Indian culture.

Furthermore, Menon reasons that focusing on dedication and commitment to the Mahabharata has significant implications for present-day security studies. He proposes that these values are critical for building strong, cohesive societies that can withstand external threats. Additionally, Menon notes that the text also showcases examples of the negative consequences of disloyalty and failing to fulfill one's duty.

In terms of implications for contemporary security studies, Menon's interpretation of the Mahabharata has had a profound impact on recent security studies. The emphasis on loyalty and duty highlights the importance of building solid and cohesive societies capable of withstanding external threats. In particular, Menon's focus on the importance of dedication and commitment for warriors has implications for military organizations and their role in national security. Loyalty and duty also influence the relationship between the army and civilian authorities. The Mahabharata emphasizes the importance of the military serving the broader interests of the community rather than pursuing their own interests. This suggests that the military must be subordinate to civilian authority and serve the larger interests of the community.

In brief, Menon's interpretation of the Mahabharata offers valuable insights into Indian culture and values, particularly regarding loyalty and duty. Moreover, his emphasis on the importance of these values for building stable and cohesive societies has significant implications for contemporary security studies. These values have implications for military organizations, their role in national security, and the relationship between the army and civilian authorities.

Additionally, in his study "National security and dharma: A Hindu perspective," Srivastava (2015) argues that Hinduism's conception of dharma provides a framework for understanding the ethical and moral dimensions of national security. Srivastava contends that dharma can guide policymakers in developing security policies that are both effective and ethical. Srivastava begins by explaining the concept of dharma, which refers to one's duty or responsibility in a given situation. He notes that dharma is a central principle in Hinduism and is closely tied to notions of morality and ethics. Srivastava suggests that dharma can provide a helpful framework for understanding the ethical dimensions of national security.

Srivastava (2015) then applies the concept of dharma to the context of national security. He argues that national security is a complex issue that requires policymakers to balance competing interests, such as security, human rights, and democracy. According to Srivastava, dharma can serve as a guide for policymakers in navigating these competing interests. He also discusses the role of the state in promoting national security from a Hindu perspective. Srivastava notes that the state is responsible for protecting its citizens and promoting their well-being, but it must do so in a manner consistent with dharma. He asserts that this requires the state to prioritize safeguarding human rights and democratic values.

In brief, Srivastava's analysis provides a comprehensive understanding of how Hinduism's concept of dharma can inform discussions on national security. He claims that dharma can offer a valuable framework for understanding the ethical and moral dimensions of national security and can guide policymakers in developing practical and ethical policies.

Similarly, Hinduism has a long history of political thought and engagement, including debates on the nature of governance, war, peace, and national security. Hinduism has traditionally emphasized the idea of dharma, which can be understood as a set of moral and ethical values that guide an individual's behavior in the world. Hindu thinkers and leaders have used the concept of dharma to articulate different positions on issues related to national security and territorial protection.

Firstly, Hinduism's emphasis on dharma (righteousness) can serve as a guiding principle for national security and land protection. Dharma encompasses the idea of moral duty, responsibility, and ethics. According to Hindu philosophy, everyone must uphold dharma and contribute to the greater good. Similarly, national security and land protection should be based on ethical principles and a sense of responsibility toward society and the environment's well-being.

Secondly, Hinduism's view of all beings' interconnectedness can help promote a holistic approach to national security and land protection. Hinduism recognizes that all beings are interconnected and interdependent, and that harm done to one can have far-reaching consequences. This philosophy can be applied to national security and land protection, where protecting one's land and people is intertwined with protecting others and the environment.

Thirdly, Hinduism's emphasis on ahimsa (nonviolence) can provide a valuable lesson for the West regarding national security and land protection. Ahimsa is the principle of nonviolence towards all living beings, and it is a critical component of Hindu ethics. By promoting peaceful conflict resolution and avoiding unnecessary violence, ahimsa can contribute to a more balanced and sustainable approach to national security and land protection.

In addition to these key lessons, Hinduism's cultural heritage and traditions offer valuable insights into the importance of spiritual and cultural preservation for national security and land protection. Hinduism's rich history and diverse cultural practices uniquely contribute to the world's cultural heritage. Preserving these traditions promotes a sense of cultural identity and national pride.

Similarly, some scholars maintain that Hinduism has a pacifist stance and emphasizes nonviolence, while others suggest it advocates for defensive war and protecting the homeland. In this treatise, we will succinctly examine past and contemporary studies on the topic, focusing on the main arguments and evidence presented.

One of the earliest studies on Hinduism and war is "The Hindu Concept of War" by K.M. de Silva (1979), which explores the historical and cultural roots of the Indian martial tradition. The author argues that Hinduism has a nuanced approach to warfare, reflecting the belief in karma, dharma, and ahimsa (nonviolence). According to de Silva, Hinduism recognizes that violence is sometimes necessary to defend oneself or others, but it should be used as a last resort and with restraint. He also highlights the role of caste and gender in Indian military culture, noting that the Kshatriya (warrior) caste and men were traditionally favored for combat roles.

Another influential investigation on Hinduism and security is "Hinduism and National Security" by David Frawley (2002), which examines India's contemporary challenges as a Hindu-majority nation. Frawley states that Hinduism provides a moral and spiritual foundation for national security based on the principles of unity, diversity, and self-defense. He contends that Hinduism supports the idea of a strong and independent India that can resist external threats and promote regional stability. Frawley also criticizes the Western view of Hinduism as passive or mystical and instead highlights the practical and pragmatic aspects of Hindu philosophy.

Security studies have been integral to the Hindu faith since ancient times and have been a subject of academic discourse for decades. Security is the central concern of states and societies, shaping political, economic, and social policies. India's experience with security has been unique due to its rich cultural heritage and diverse religious traditions. However, there has been a recent shift in the focus of security studies from the traditional Western-centric approach to a more diverse and inclusive perspective. In this context, Mitra's (2016) work "The Puzzle of India's Governance: Culture, Context, and Comparative Theory" makes a unique contribution to the field of security studies. Mitra argues that Hinduism offers a distinct perspective on security that emphasizes the importance of dharma (righteousness) and karma (action). In this analysis, we will examine Mitra's contribution to security studies and its relevance today.

Mitra's work is significant as it offers a new perspective on security studies rooted in Hinduism. According to Mitra, the Hindu philosophy of dharma and karma provides a unique approach to security that differs from the traditional Western-centric approach. Mitra argues that dharma, which refers to the righteous path, is the cornerstone of Hinduism and provides a framework for ethical conduct. The concept of dharma is central to the Hindu worldview, emphasizing the importance of individual and collective responsibility.

According to Mitra, dharma offers a distinct perspective on security by accentuating the implications of ethical behavior and responsible actions.

Similarly, Mitra also underscores the significance of karma in the Hindu security philosophy. Karma refers to actions and the consequences of those actions. According to Hinduism, every action has consequences, and individuals must take responsibility for their actions. Mitra argues that karma offers a unique perspective on security as it emphasizes the importance of responsible behavior and the consequences of actions. Mitra also explores the relationship between Hinduism and the state's role in providing security.

According to Mitra, Hinduism offers a unique perspective on the state's role in providing security. The Hindu philosophy emphasizes the importance of individual and collective responsibility, and the state ensures that individuals and communities fulfill their obligations.

According to Mitra, the state's role in providing security is to create an environment that enables individuals and communities to fulfill their responsibilities. Mitra contends that dharma and karma have significant implications for security in India. He maintains that pursuing dharma requires individuals to act according to their duties and responsibilities, which can lead to a sense of social harmony and order.

This, in turn, can contribute to better security by reducing the likelihood of conflict and disorder. Furthermore, Mitra claims that karma accentuates the essence of taking action to fulfill one's obligations, even if it requires sacrifice and hardship. This can inspire individuals to act courageously in the face of security threats, thereby contributing to greater security. Mitra also notes that Hinduism's emphasis on the interconnectedness of all living beings has security implications. Mitra expresses that this worldview can lead to greater empathy and compassion for others, contributing to more peaceful and harmonious community relations. Mitra argues that this can be particularly important in a diverse society like India, where daily communal tensions and conflicts occur.

Regarding the relevance of Mitra's contribution in today's world, Mitra's contribution to security studies is relevant as it offers a unique perspective on security that differs from the traditional Western-centric approach. The traditional Western-centric approach to security emphasizes military strength and the use of force to provide security. Mitra's approach, on the other hand, emphasizes ethical behavior, responsible actions, and individual and collective responsibility. In today's world, where the use of force is increasingly ineffective in providing security, Mitra's approach offers a fresh perspective that is relevant and practical.

Mitra's approach also has relevance in the context of non-state actors and terrorism. In recent years, non-state actors and terrorist organizations have emerged as significant threats to global security. Mitra's approach to security, which emphasizes ethical behavior and responsible actions, offers a unique perspective on countering non-state actors and terrorist organizations. Mitra argues that the state's role in providing security is to create an environment that enables individuals and communities to fulfill their responsibilities. In the context of non-state actors and terrorism, this approach is relevant as it emphasizes the importance of addressing the root causes of these issues and creating an environment that enables individuals and communities to fulfill their responsibilities.

Mitra's stress on the significance of dharma and karma can also be relevant to contemporary security challenges in India. In particular, India faces numerous security threats, including terrorism, insurgency, and cross-border conflicts. Mitra's arguments suggest that promoting a sense of duty and responsibility among citizens could be an essential step toward addressing these threats. This could involve promoting greater civic engagement, encouraging individuals to participate in community-building initiatives, and supporting programs promoting dharma and karma.

In short, Mitra's contribution to security studies offers a unique perspective that is different from the traditional Western-centric approach. His writing provides a unique perspective on security by examining the connections between Hinduism and security. His assessment regarding the importance of dharma and karma and the interconnectedness of all living beings offers helpful insights into present-day security challenges in India. Mitra's approach emphasizes ethical behavior, responsible actions, and individual and collective responsibility.

Mitra's work suggests that promoting empathy, compassion, and a sense of duty and responsibility among citizens could be necessary to address these challenges.

Furthermore, the study of security has been a crucial area of inquiry for scholars, policymakers, and practitioners. It has evolved and has been influenced by various cultural and religious traditions. India's experience with security has been unique due to its rich cultural heritage and diverse religious traditions. Here, we will investigate the contribution of Bajpai's (2015) study, "Karma and Nuclear Deterrence: India's Conception of Strategic Restraint," to today's security studies.

Specifically, we will focus on Bajpai's arguments regarding the influence of Hinduism's emphasis on karma on India's nuclear strategy and what we can learn from his insights. Specifically, we will focus on Bajpai's arguments regarding the importance of action and the consequences of one's actions in shaping India's nuclear strategy and how his insights can help us understand contemporary security challenges in India.

Bajpai's study argues that Hinduism's emphasis on karma has influenced India's nuclear strategy by highlighting the importance of action and the consequences of one's actions. According to Bajpai, Hinduism's concept of karma stresses the significance of action and its implications. It suggests that individuals must take responsibility for their actions and their effects on the world around them. This concept has influenced India's nuclear strategy by highlighting the importance of considering the consequences of nuclear weapons use and the responsibility of possessing such weapons.

Bajpai claims that India's nuclear strategy is based on the principles of restraint and responsibility, consistent with Hinduism's emphasis on karma.

First, he contends that India's nuclear doctrine is based on minimum deterrence, highlighting the use of nuclear weapons only in response to a nuclear attack. This approach is consistent with Hinduism's emphasis on responsibility and the consequences of one's actions.

Second, Bajpai notes that India's nuclear doctrine is founded on the concept of no first use, emphasizing the importance of restraint in nuclear weapons. This approach is consistent with Hinduism's emphasis on karma and the responsibility of possessing such weapons.

Finally, Bajpai asserts that India's approach to nuclear strategy reflects its commitment to the principles of accountability and restraint, which are consistent with Hinduism's emphasis on karma.

175

As for implications for contemporary security challenges, Bajpai's insights into the influence of Hinduism's emphasis on karma on India's nuclear strategy can help us understand current security challenges. In particular, the proliferation of nuclear weapons remains a critical security challenge today. Bajpai's arguments suggest that promoting a sense of responsibility and restraint among nuclear-armed states could be an essential step toward reducing the risks of nuclear conflict. This could involve promoting dialogue and cooperation between nuclear-armed states, supporting arms control and disarmament measures, and encouraging nuclear-armed states to adopt a minimum deterrence approach. Bajpai's insights into the influence of Hinduism's focus on karma on India's nuclear strategy can help us understand present-day security challenges in India. In particular, India faces numerous security threats, including terrorism, insurgency, and cross-border conflicts. Bajpai's arguments suggest that India's approach to these threats is likely to be influenced by the idea that actions have consequences and the importance of taking responsibility for those consequences.

Bajpai's analysis also indicates that India's approach to security is likely to be action-oriented. This means that India is expected to take a proactive approach to security threats rather than a reactive one. This proactive approach is founded on the idea that India must take action to protect its citizens and maintain its sovereignty. Bajpai's focus on the importance of restraint and responsibility is also relevant to contemporary security challenges, such as cybersecurity threats and the rise of non-state actors. Bajpai's arguments suggest that promoting responsibility and restraint among actors in the cyber domain and non-state actors could be an essential step toward reducing the risks of conflict and instability. This could involve promoting international norms and standards for cybersecurity, supporting initiatives that promote responsible behavior in cyberspace, and encouraging non-state actors to adopt a responsible approach to their actions.

In summary, Bajpai's work suggests that India's approach to security is likely influenced by the idea that actions have consequences and the importance of taking responsibility for those consequences. Bajpai's study highlights the need for a comprehensive understanding of the influence of culture and religion on security policy. Bajpai's inquiry emphasizes the influence of Hinduism's significance on karma on India's nuclear strategy. His examination regarding the importance of action and the consequences of one's actions in shaping India's approach to nuclear deterrence offers beneficial insights into current security challenges in India. His analysis proposes that promoting responsibility and restraint could be critical for addressing contemporary security challenges. Bajpai's work emphasizes the importance of considering the consequences of one's actions and the responsibility of possessing powerful weapons or engaging in activities that could have significant security implications.

Overall, Bajpai's study offers valuable insights into the role of culture and religion in shaping security policies and strategies.

Hindu Nationalism and Security

More recently, several scholars have analyzed the role of Hindu nationalism in shaping the discourse on security and territorial protection in India. For example, in "Hindutva and Security: The Rise of Hindu Nationalism in India" (2018), Riaz Hassan and his co-authors argue that Hindutva (Hindu nationalist ideology) has played a significant role in constructing a narrative of Hindu victimhood and Muslim aggression, which justifies a muscular and assertive approach to national security. Moreover, they contend that Hindutva advocates for a strong and centralized state that can protect Hindu identity and culture from perceived threats. However, they also note that this approach has led to communal tensions and polarization in Indian society.

In short, the studies examined here suggest that Hinduism has a complex and multifaceted stance on security and territorial protection, shaped by historical, cultural, and political factors. While some scholars emphasize Hindu philosophy's pacifist and nonviolent aspects, others highlight the role of defensive war and national defense in Hinduism.

Furthermore, the rise of Hindu nationalism in India has added a new dimension to the debate, with proponents and critics of Hindutva offering contrasting perspectives on security and identity. Further research is needed to explore these issues in greater depth and examine Hinduism's impact on security policy in India and beyond.

As evidenced above, in Hinduism, national security and territorial protection are considered sacred duties closely connected to preserving culture and tradition. Diplomacy and alliances are also crucial in maintaining national security, as evidenced by the Pandavas' efforts to gain support from other kingdoms in the Mahabharata. Additionally, self-defense and martial arts techniques are valuable skills that can be used to protect oneself and one's community. Another important text is the Manusmriti, which outlines the duties and responsibilities of various social classes within Hindu society, including the Kshatriya (warrior) class. The Manusmriti emphasizes the importance of protecting the community from external threats, stating, "For, when a king protects his people duly, he prospers in this world and the next; but when he fails to protect them, he falls, with them, into hell" (Manusmriti 7.50).

The illustrations from Hindu religious texts show that defending territories and maintaining national security is essential to uphold dharma and protect the kingdom's sovereignty. In Hinduism, national security is not just about military strength but also about safeguarding the environment, social and economic stability, and the overall well-being of the people. It is also important to note that national security is not limited to a particular country or nation but extends to the entire world and all its inhabitants. In Hinduism, national security and territorial protection are seen as essential for preserving a people's way of life and cultural identity. The emphasis on duty and responsibility, as seen in Lord Krishna's advice to Arjuna, is also central to the Hindu approach to national security.

In summary, past and current inquiries into Hinduism offer valuable lessons for the West and the world in relation to national security and land protection. Hinduism can contribute to a more sustainable and harmonious approach to these crucial issues by promoting ethical principles, holistic approaches, nonviolence, and cultural preservation. These insights into Hinduism's stance on national security and territorial protection reveal a complex relationship between the religion and these concepts. While some scholars argue that Hinduism emphasizes the importance of nonviolence and peaceful coexistence, others contend that foreign invaders have constantly threatened Hinduism and that self-defense is a central aspect of the religion's perspective on national security.

Equally, while some scholars maintain that Hinduism's stance on territorial protection is one of inclusivity and tolerance, others claim that Hindu nationalism's emphasis on solid borders and territorial defense has important implications for India's foreign policy.

Chapter four delved into the history of Hinduism and its viewpoints on national security, providing valuable insights into how one of the world's oldest religions has approached the issue of security over the centuries. In chapter five, we will shift our focus to another globally significant religion: Buddhism.

Specifically, we will explore Buddhism's stances on security and territorial protection. We will examine how Buddhist teachings and principles inform their approach to national security, including their views on conflict resolution, violence, and nonviolence. By comparing and contrasting the viewpoints of different religions on national security, we can gain a keen understanding of this complex issue and the various ways in which it can be approached.

References

Bajpai, K. (2015). Karma and Nuclear Deterrence: India's Conception of Strategic Restraint. The Nonproliferation Review, 22(1-2), 51

Bhagavad Gita. Translated by Eknath Easwaran, Nilgiri Press, 2007.

Bhatt, C. (2001). Hindu nationalism: Origins, ideologies, and modern myths. Oxford University Press.

Bhatt, C. (2019). Hindu nationalism and India's foreign policy: The case of Kashmir. Asian Journal of Political Science, 27(1), 1-17.

Brockington, J. (2010). The Sanskrit epics. BRILL.

Datta, S. K. (2014). Hinduism and national security: A conceptual framework. Journal of Defence Studies, 8(4), 89-104.

D'Souza, S. M. (2016). Hinduism and security. Strategic Analysis, 40(4), 275-288.

de Silva, K. M. (1979). The Hindu concept of war. Asian Survey, 19(6), 565-580.

Frawley, D. (2002). Hinduism and national security. Voice of India.

Hassan, R., Kennedy, D., & Riaz, S. (2018). Hindutva and security: The rise of Hindu nationalism in India. Journal of Muslim Minority Affairs, 38(1), 19-33.

Goel, S. R. (1993). Hinduism and national security: A historical perspective. Voice of India.

Ganguly, S. (2002). Hindu nationalism and the security of India. Asian Survey, 42(2), 286-304.

Ganguli, K. M. (2007). The Mahabharata of Krishna-Dwaipayana Vyasa. Sacred Books of the East, Volume.

Goldman, R. P. (2007). The Ramayana of Valmiki: An epic of ancient India. Princeton University Press.

Gupta, A., & Singh, A. (2019). Hinduism and security studies: A conceptual framework. Journal of Strategic Studies, 42(6), 821-845. doi 10.1080/01402390.2018.1525404.

Hardiman, D. (2003). Hinduism and the Freedom Movement: Some Explorations. In M. G. Wirsing, & R. L. Regan (Eds.), Hindu nationalism and governance (pp. 23-39). Routledge.

Kangle, R. P. (1960). The Kautilya Arthashastra. University of Bombay.

Knott, K. (2016). Hinduism: A very short introduction. Oxford University Press.

Kuruvilla, S. (2016). Hinduism and war: The military ethos in ancient India. Cambridge University Press.

Ludden, D. (Ed.). (1996). Hinduism and Nationalism in India. Indiana University Press.

Ludwig, T. M. (2013). The sacred paths of the East. Pearson.

Manusmriti. Translated by G. Buhler, The Sacred Books of the East, Volume 25, Oxford University Press, 1886

Manusmriti. (n.d.). In Ancient History Encyclopedia. Retrieved from https://www.ancient.eu/Manusmriti/

Mahabharata. Translated by Bibek Debroy, Penguin Books, 2015.

Menon, R. (2010). The Mahabharata: A modern rendering, Vol 1. North Point Press.

Mitra, S. K. (2016). The Puzzle of India's Governance: Culture, Context, and Comparative Theory. Routledge.

Olivelle, P. (2005). Manu's Code of Law: A Critical Edition and Translation of the Manava-Dharmasastra. Oxford University Press.

Pande, G. C. (2010). The Vedic Experience: Mantramanjari. Motilal Banarsidass Publishers.

Rocher, L. (2012). The Manusmriti. Oxford University Press.

Sharma, R. M. (2013). Hinduism and National Security. Journal of Defence Studies, 7(2), 47-63.

Sharma, A. (2002). Hinduism and the Ethics of War and Peace. Journal of Military Ethics, 1(2), 118-131.

Sharma, J. (2003). Hindutva: The Postmodern Turn in Indian Fundamentalism. In M. G. Wirsing, & R. L. Regan (Eds.), Hindu nationalism and governance (pp. 1-22). Routledge.

Sharma, A. (2016). Hinduism and national security. Journal of Defence Studies, 10(2), 1–14.

Shastri, A. (2008). Kautilya's views on intelligence gathering. Journal of the United Service Institution of India, 138(578), 385-393.

Srivastava, A. (2015). National security and dharma: A Hindu perspective. Journal of Defense Resources Management, 6(2), 25-33.

Trautmann, T. R. (2013). Arthashastra: The science of wealth. Penguin.

5

Buddhism's Stances on Security And Territorial Protection

Buddhism Foundation on Security

Buddhism, one of the world's major religions, originated in ancient India and spread across Asia. It is both a religion and a philosophy that emphasizes self-awareness, mindfulness, and compassion. Buddhism offers a unique perspective on security that is applicable to contemporary issues. Today, millions of people worldwide practice Buddhism, and its teachings have influenced various aspects of human life, including politics, economics, and security. The Buddhist approach to security highlights the interconnectedness of all beings, the significance of compassion and nonviolence, and the utilization of these values to promote territorial and human security. Siddhartha Gautama founded Buddhism, a religion and philosophy that underscores nonviolence and compassion toward all living beings. This section provides a comprehensive analysis of Buddhism's past and current history and perspectives on security and territorial protection.

The Buddha, the founder of Buddhism, lived in an era marked by violence and political instability. He witnessed wars and violence, and his teachings reflect a profound understanding of the human condition and the necessity of security and protection. In Buddhism, peace of mind and protection are closely tied to the concept of Dharma, meaning "the natural order of things" or "the way things are." The Buddha taught that individuals, communities, and nations can only flourish when they live in harmony with Dharma (Keown, 2003). This principle entails respecting each other's rights, practicing nonviolence, and working towards the greater good.

According to the Buddha, the ultimate goal of human life is to achieve enlightenment or Nirvana, the state of ultimate liberation from suffering. The Buddha also taught the Four Noble Truths, which encompass the truth of suffering, the cause of suffering, the cessation of suffering, and the path to the cessation of suffering. These teachings form the foundation of Buddhist philosophy and guide the way Buddhists live. Moreover, Buddhism emphasizes the importance of mindfulness—the practice of being aware of one's thoughts, feelings, and sensations in the present moment. This practice helps individuals become more attuned to their own suffering and the suffering of others, fostering greater compassion and understanding.

Buddhism has been associated with the security and protection of the land in various ways. One such way is through the practice of mindfulness, a critical component of Buddhist meditation. Mindfulness involves being fully present and aware of one's thoughts, feelings, and surroundings in the present moment. This practice has been proven to reduce stress, improve mental health, enhance decision-making, and promote more effective security measures. Buddhism also teaches nonviolence and compassion towards all living beings, including animals and the environment (Dalai Lama, 1999). This principle is reflected in the concept of ahimsa, which means non-harming or nonviolence. This philosophy has influenced many peace and social justice movements and has been applied to environmental protection and conservation efforts.

Buddhism and its relation to security highlight the belief that all beings are interconnected and that everything is impermanent. This understanding leads to the belief that individuals have a responsibility to contribute to the well-being of others and the environment. Buddhism also stresses nonviolence and the peaceful resolution of conflicts. In terms of security, Buddhism teaches that genuine security can only be achieved through inner peace and contentment. While external security measures like military power may offer temporary protection, they cannot guarantee long-term security. Additionally, Buddhism emphasizes the importance of safeguarding the environment and the natural world, as they are essential for the well-being of all beings (Lopez, 2008).

According to Buddhism, national security extends beyond military power and protection from external threats; it encompasses the creation of a just and peaceful society. Buddhism emphasizes social justice, equality, and compassion for all beings. A just and peaceful society ensures that individuals have access to basic needs such as food, shelter, and healthcare and are free from discrimination and oppression. Buddhism also underscores the significance of wise leadership in establishing a just and peaceful society. Leaders must be guided by principles of compassion, wisdom, and nonviolence, acting in the best interests of all beings.

Buddhism recognizes the need for security and territorial protection but advocates for a different approach compared to many other religions and ideologies. Instead of relying on violence and aggression, Buddhism promotes wisdom, compassion, and skillful means. This approach necessitates the use of intelligence, moral values, and strategic thinking by individuals, communities, and nations to protect themselves and their territories (Dalai Lama, 1999). Several verses and stories from Buddhist texts exemplify the importance of security and territorial protection. For instance, in the Dhammapada, a collection of the Buddha's sayings, there is a verse that states: "If a man finds a prudent companion who walks with him, is wise and lives soberly, he may walk with him, overcoming all dangers, happy but thoughtful." This verse underscores the significance of having wise and sober companions who can assist individuals in overcoming dangers and threats. Furthermore, it suggests that individuals should not face perils alone but should seek the support and guidance of others.

In another story from Buddhist texts, the Buddha advised a king facing an invasion from a neighboring kingdom. The Buddha suggested that the king should first and foremost attempt to negotiate a peaceful settlement and avoid violence if possible. Although interpretations may vary, some Buddhist texts contain stories and teachings relevant to these topics. One example of a story related to security and protection can be found in the Dhammapada, a collection of sayings of the Buddha. Verse 60 of the Dhammapada states:

"Victory breeds hatred,
  The defeated live in pain,
    Happily, the peaceful live,
      Giving up victory and defeat."

This verse teaches that conflict and competition can lead to hatred and suffering, highlighting the importance of striving for peace and nonviolence. It can be interpreted as a lesson in the futility of aggression and conquest and the significance of finding peaceful solutions to conflicts. Another example of teaching related to security can be found in the Sigalovada Sutta, a discourse in which the Buddha advises a young man named Sigala on how to live a virtuous life. In this discourse, the Buddha describes the four quarters, or directions, and assigns specific virtues to each one. He advises Sigala to honor and respect each direction and its corresponding virtue and to cultivate those virtues within himself (Rhys Davids & Stede, 1921). Although this discourse is not specifically about security or territorial protection, it can be interpreted as emphasizing the importance of respecting boundaries and living in harmony with one's surroundings.

As a religion, Buddhism does not have a specific stance on national security or territorial protection. However, Buddhism teaches principles that can be applied to these concepts. It emphasizes the importance of nonviolence and compassion toward all beings. The first precept in Buddhism is to abstain from taking the life of any living being. The Buddha taught that violence only leads to more violence and suffering. Thus, Buddhism does not support the use of violence for national security or territorial protection. However, Buddhism also teaches the importance of protecting oneself and others from harm. The Buddha taught his disciples to protect themselves from physical harm and danger.

In the Mahaparinibbana Sutta, the Buddha tells his disciple Ananda, "It is fitting for you, Ananda, to dwell with the Dharma as your island, with no other refuge. For the Dharma is the refuge of all, and none else" (DN 16). This verse suggests that one can protect oneself through the practice of the Dharma or the Buddhist teachings. Moreover, Buddhism teaches the importance of wise and just governance. The Buddha himself advised rulers on how to govern justly and with compassion. In the Cakkavatti Sutta, the Buddha describes the qualities of a righteous ruler who governs with compassion and wisdom. This ruler can maintain peace and stability in the kingdom, ensuring the security and well-being of its citizens.

History of Buddhists Defending Territories

In history, there are instances in which Buddhist practitioners defended their territories. For example, in the 16th century, the Buddhist monk Nichiren led a movement to defend Japan against foreign invasion. He argued that it was necessary to protect Japan to safeguard the Buddhist teachings and the Japanese people. While Nichiren's stance on violence has been debated, his movement demonstrates the importance of protecting one's homeland in Buddhism (Stone, 2009). In modern times, we can integrate the principles of nonviolence, compassion, and wise governance into national security strategies. Nonviolent approaches, such as diplomacy and conflict resolution, can be used to prevent conflicts and promote peace. Compassion can be integrated into policies and programs that prioritize the well-being and safety of all citizens, including marginalized groups. Finally, wise governance can be used to promote justice and stability, which are essential for national security.

According to Stone (2009), Nichiren believed that Japan was the "Land of the Buddha" and that it was the duty of the Japanese people to protect their land from foreign invasion. He encouraged his followers to arm themselves and defend their country. He even wrote a letter to Japan's military leaders, urging them to fight against the invading forces. Nichiren's movement became known as the "Honmon Butsuryu-shu," or the "True Buddhism Sect for the Protection of the Nation." The movement focused on defense against foreign invaders and promoting Buddhism as a means of protecting the Japanese from suffering and achieving enlightenment. While Nichiren's teachings and actions may contradict the principle of nonviolence in Buddhism, they demonstrate how religious beliefs can shape political and military actions. The case of Nichiren highlights the complex relationship between religion, philosophy, and politics in Buddhist history.

Despite this, instances in Buddhist texts where kings or rulers are portrayed as defending their territories and engaging in warfare are relatively rare. Buddhist texts primarily emphasize peaceful means to resolve conflicts. For example, the Dhammapada, a collection of sayings attributed to the Buddha, states: "Hatred does not cease by hatred, but only by love; this is the eternal rule" (Dhammapada 5:3). Similarly, the Anguttara Nikaya, another Buddhist scripture, teaches that "Victory breeds hatred. The defeated live in pain. Happily, the peaceful live giving up victory and defeat" (AN 5.62). What we can learn from Buddhism's stance on security and territorial protection is that violence should always be a last resort. Buddhist teachings emphasize that conflicts can be resolved peacefully and that war and violence only bring suffering and pain. As such, Buddhist values can inform modern national security strategies by prioritizing nonviolent means of conflict resolution, such as diplomatic negotiations and economic sanctions.

One example is the Dhammapada, a collection of sayings attributed to the Buddha. Verse 129 states, "All tremble at violence; all fear death. Putting oneself in the place of another, one should not kill nor cause another to kill." This verse emphasizes the importance of nonviolence and avoiding causing harm to others. Its teachings on respect, honesty, and ethical conduct can contribute to a sense of security and stability in personal and social relationships. However, it also acknowledges the reality of violence and the need to defend oneself and others.

Another example can be found in the Sutta Nipata, another collection of early Buddhist texts. In one story, the Buddha is approached by a group of people who ask him how they should defend themselves against invaders. The Buddha responds by saying, "If anyone should attack you, you should use all your skill to ward him off." This story illustrates that the Buddha recognized the need for self-defense and protection in certain situations. There are also examples in Buddhist history of defending territories. For example, in ancient India, the Mauryan Empire was ruled by King Ashoka, who converted to Buddhism after a ferocious war.

After his conversion, Ashoka adopted nonviolence, tolerance, and social justice policies, and he is credited with spreading Buddhism throughout India and beyond. However, he also defended his territories and waged wars when necessary. The Buddha taught that all beings have the right to live without fear or harm and that violence only leads to suffering. However, the Buddha also recognized that there are situations where violence may be necessary to protect oneself or others. In these situations, the Buddha advocated for using minimal force and avoiding harm to non-combatants.

One of the most well-known examples of the Buddhist approach to security and protection is the story of King Pasenadi and the Buddha. According to the story, King Pasenadi was concerned about the security of his kingdom and asked the Buddha for advice. The Buddha replied that the best way to ensure security was to cultivate a peaceful society based on ethical principles rather than relying on military might. In another story, the Buddha tells his disciples about a king facing an invasion by a neighboring kingdom. The king is advised to send emissaries to negotiate a peaceful solution, but he refuses and instead chooses to go to war. The Buddha comments that the king's refusal to negotiate shows a lack of wisdom and compassion and that the war will only bring suffering to both sides. Several verses in the Buddhist texts also address the issue of security and protection. For example, in the Dhammapada, verse 129, the Buddha teaches:

"All tremble at violence;
all fear death.
Putting oneself in the place of another,
one should not kill nor cause another to kill."

Regarding Buddhist texts on security and territorial protection, the Buddhist canon contains several examples of stories and verses related to security and territorial protection. One example is the story of King Pasenadi of Kosala, who asked the Buddha for advice on protecting his kingdom from external threats. The Buddha advised him to maintain a strong army and cultivate good relations with neighboring countries through diplomacy and peace. The Buddha also emphasized the importance of moral and spiritual strength in protecting the kingdom, saying, "The wise protectors of the land are those who live according to the Dhamma, who are virtuous, restrained, and just" (Dhammapada 227).

Another example is the story of King Dutthagamani, who fought a long and bloody war to reunite the island of Sri Lanka under his rule. In this story, the king is portrayed as a devout Buddhist who fought not for personal gain but to protect the Dhamma and the welfare of his people. The Buddhist text Mahavamsa describes him: "The king fought not for the sake of power, not for wealth, not for pleasure, but solely for the sake of the Dhamma and for the welfare and happiness of his people" (Mahavamsa 35:29). In ancient India, Buddhist monks were often called upon to protect the people against robbers and thieves. The Buddhist monasteries were also seen as places of refuge during war and conflict. Buddhist rulers, such as King Ashoka, were known for promoting peace and nonviolence in their territories. King Ashoka is also credited with spreading Buddhism beyond the borders of India. During the medieval period, Buddhism faced many challenges, including the invasion of India by Muslim armies. This led to the decline of Buddhism in India, although it continued to thrive in other parts of Asia, such as Sri Lanka, Thailand, and Cambodia.

The earliest teachings of Buddhism emphasized nonviolence and the rejection of all forms of violence. This was a response to the widespread violence and wars in ancient India. Furthermore, the Buddha taught that all beings are interconnected, and that violence and aggression only lead to more suffering. However, as Buddhism spread throughout Asia, it encountered different cultures and political systems that were sometimes only compatible with the pacifist teachings of the Buddha. One of the most famous examples of Buddhism's relationship with security and territorial protection is the story of Ashoka. Ashoka was an Indian emperor who ruled from 268 to 232 BCE. He was a ruthless conqueror who waged wars to expand his empire. However, after a fierce battle, Ashoka became disillusioned with violence and turned to Buddhism. He renounced violence and embraced the principles of nonviolence and compassion. He even went so far as to erect pillars throughout his empire with inscriptions promoting peace and nonviolence (Schumann, 2014).

The earliest teachings of Buddhism emphasized nonviolence and the rejection of all forms of violence. However, as Buddhism spread throughout Asia, it encountered different cultures and political systems that were sometimes only compatible with the pacifist teachings of the Buddha. For example, Ashoka, an Indian emperor who ruled from 268 to 232 BCE, was a ruthless conqueror who waged wars to expand his empire. However, after a fierce battle, he became disillusioned with violence and turned to Buddhism, embracing the principles of nonviolence and compassion (Lopez, 2008).

In China, Buddhism encountered a political system heavily influenced by Confucianism, which emphasized the importance of maintaining social order and stability, sometimes requiring the use of force. As a result, Chinese Buddhism developed a more nuanced view of violence and self-defense (Huntington, 1986). As a result, Chinese Buddhism developed a more nuanced view of violence and self-defense. Some past and modern Chinese Buddhist texts advocated using force in certain circumstances, such as defending oneself or others from harm (Deegalle, 2006).

In China, Buddhism ran into a political structure that occasionally necessitated the use of force to maintain social order. As a result, some Chinese Buddhist texts began to develop a more nuanced view of violence and self-defense. One example of this nuanced view can be found in the "Sutra of Bodhisattva Ksitigarbha's Fundamental Vows." This sutra teaches that while violence is generally discouraged in Buddhism, there are certain circumstances where force may be necessary. For example, if someone is attacking you or someone else, it may be necessary to defend yourself or others to prevent harm.

Another example of this nuanced view can be found in the "Sutra of the Wise and Foolish." This sutra teaches that while violence is generally discouraged in Buddhism, there are certain circumstances where it may be necessary to use force to prevent more significant harm. For example, if someone is about to harm a large group of people, it may be necessary to use force to stop them. Likewise, Sulak Sivaraksa, a Thai Buddhist activist, has advocated for a radical transformation of society based on Buddhist principles of nonviolence, interdependence, and compassion. He criticized the military-industrial complex and called for reducing military spending and abolishing nuclear weapons (Sivaraksa, 2013).

In the modern era, Buddhism continues to play a role in promoting peace and nonviolence. The Dalai Lama, the spiritual leader of Tibetan Buddhism, is a prominent advocate of nonviolence and has worked tirelessly to promote peace and understanding between different cultures and religions. There has been a growing interest in applying Buddhist principles to security and territorial protection issues in recent years. One example is the concept of "engaged Buddhism," which involves using Buddhist principles to promote social and political activism. Engaged Buddhism has been used to address various issues, including human rights, environmental protection, and conflict resolution.

Another significant development in the modern era is the emergence of "Buddhist nationalism." This refers to the idea that Buddhism is not just a religion but also a cultural and national identity. This has led to several conflicts, particularly in countries where Buddhism is the dominant religion, such as Sri Lanka and Myanmar. In some cases, Buddhist nationalists have used violence to defend their beliefs and protect their territories. Today, Buddhism has diverse perspectives on security and territorial protection. The Dalai Lama, the spiritual leader of Tibetan Buddhism, has been a vocal advocate for nonviolence and compassion. He has called for a shift from traditional military strategies toward a more holistic approach to security, including addressing the root causes of conflict and promoting dialogue and reconciliation (Dalai Lama, 2011).

Buddhism has several teachings that are relevant to national security. One of these is the concept of interdependence, which holds that all things are connected and that the actions of one individual or group can have far-reaching consequences for others. This principle is reflected in the Buddhist concept of dependent origination, which asserts that all things arise in dependence upon other things. Another relevant teaching is the concept of non-attachment, which holds that attachment to material possessions, power, or status can lead to suffering and conflict. This principle has been applied to political and economic systems, where greed and corruption can undermine security and stability.

While the early teachings emphasized nonviolence, Buddhism has encountered different cultures and political systems that sometimes-required force. Today, Buddhism has a diverse range of perspectives on security and territorial protection, ranging from strict adherence to the principles of nonviolence to a more nuanced view that recognizes the need for self-defense in certain circumstances. Ultimately, the challenge for Buddhists, wherever they may be, is to find a way to promote security and protect territorial boundaries without resorting to violence (Gethin, 1998). In short, Buddhism is not just a religion but also a philosophy emphasizing the importance of self-awareness, mindfulness, and compassion. Buddhism teaches that proper security can only be achieved through inner peace and contentment and that national security is not just about military power but also about creating a just and peaceful society. Buddhism's teachings on social justice, equality, and compassion can guide individuals and leaders in creating a more peaceful and just world.

Past And Present Studies of Buddhism On Security

Understanding past and current studies on Buddhism's perspectives on national security provides valuable insights into integrating these teachings into modern security studies. From a Buddhist viewpoint, security encompasses physical safety and psychological, social, and environmental factors that contribute to well-being and stability. Buddhism's emphasis on interconnectedness and compassion highlights the need to address the root causes of insecurity, such as poverty and environmental degradation, rather than relying solely on military or law enforcement solutions.

Buddhism's history offers examples of its influence on political and social movements worldwide. For instance, Buddhism played a significant role in peace movements in Vietnam, Sri Lanka, and Tibet, among other places. Understanding Buddhism's perspectives on national security allows for a more nuanced and holistic approach to addressing the complex challenges of the modern world. Integrating Buddhist teachings into modern security studies allows us to strive for a more peaceful, just, and sustainable future.

Toscano (2011) explores the relationship between Buddhist philosophy and national security ideology, arguing that Buddhist principles can offer a more balanced and holistic approach. He suggests that the traditional reliance on military force has failed to address the underlying causes of conflict, leading to more violence and suffering. Toscano proposes that Buddhist philosophy, emphasizing the Middle Way and interdependence, provides an alternative approach that addresses the root causes of conflict and promotes peace.

The Middle Way, according to Toscano, emphasizes finding a balanced and moderate approach to life. Applying this concept to national security involves balancing military force with diplomacy and humanitarian efforts and recognizing the interconnectedness of all nations and peoples. Interdependence, another key Buddhist principle, informs our understanding of national security by recognizing nations' and peoples' interconnected and interdependent nature. Moving away from a narrow focus on national self-interest, a global and cooperative approach to security becomes possible.

Toscano concludes by highlighting the importance of promoting peace and nonviolence as central components of a Buddhist-inspired approach to national security. This requires a fundamental shift from a military-based understanding of security to one grounded in cooperation, compassion, and the pursuit of the common good. Toscano's study offers a compelling argument for the relevance of Buddhist philosophy to contemporary debates on national security, presenting a more holistic and compassionate vision for the future.

Tanaka (2012) examines the notion of human security from a Buddhist perspective, arguing that compassion and the interconnectedness of all living beings can inform a human-centered approach to security. He outlines the principles of human security, emphasizing the need to protect individuals from various threats, including poverty, violence, and environmental degradation. Tanaka suggests that the Buddhist concept of compassion, recognizing the interconnectedness of all living beings, provides a foundation for a holistic and human-centered approach to security.

Tanaka also explores the importance of addressing the root causes of conflict, such as poverty and inequality, through nonviolent means. Buddhist philosophy, emphasizing nonviolence and the pursuit of the common good, offers valuable insights into addressing these underlying causes of insecurity. He emphasizes the significance of a collaborative and inclusive approach to security, recognizing the diversity of human experience and engaging all stakeholders in the pursuit of peace and well-being. The Buddhist concept of interconnectedness, emphasizing empathy and compassion, provides a robust framework for this collaborative and inclusive approach. Tanaka's writing presents a compelling argument for the relevance of Buddhist philosophy in contemporary discussions on human security, advocating for a human-centered and inclusive approach that addresses the root causes of conflict and promotes nonviolence and the common good.

De Silva (2016) explores the relevance of Buddhist teachings in promoting peace and security in the 21st century, advocating for a more nuanced understanding of national security beyond traditional notions of military power and state sovereignty. He argues that a holistic approach that addresses the root causes of conflict and promotes nonviolence and compassion is needed. De Silva examines the concept of security from a Buddhist perspective, emphasizing the importance of nonviolence and compassion as central components of a peaceful society. The Buddhist concept of interdependence, recognizing the interconnectedness of all living beings, provides a framework for this holistic approach to security.

De Silva emphasizes the need for a nuanced understanding of national security that acknowledges the complex interplay of social, economic, and environmental factors contributing to insecurity. A Buddhist-inspired approach to security would prioritize social justice, economic development, ecological sustainability, intercultural and interfaith dialogue, human rights, and dignity. Education and dialogue play crucial roles in fostering a deeper appreciation of Buddhist teachings and values, promoting a more compassionate and peaceful world. De Silva's inquiry offers a thought-provoking exploration of the relevance of Buddhist teachings in promoting peace and security in the 21st century, envisioning a more peaceful and compassionate world by drawing on essential Buddhist concepts such as compassion and interconnectedness.

Jerryson (2011) discusses the relationship between Buddhism and violence in the context of national security, asserting that Buddhism's emphasis on nonviolence and compassion can contribute to peace and stability in society. He examines the roots of Buddhist philosophy, which prioritizes nonviolence, compassion, and the pursuit of wisdom and enlightenment. These core principles form a foundation for a peaceful and harmonious society that values social justice, economic equality, and environmental sustainability. By promoting peace and stability, Buddhism challenges traditional notions of security based on military power and state sovereignty.

Understanding Buddhism's perspectives on national security allows for a more nuanced and comprehensive approach that recognizes the interdependence of all living beings and the importance of promoting social justice and environmental sustainability. Jerryson's work highlights the potential of Buddhist principles in promoting peace and stability, fostering a more harmonious and compassionate society.

Moreover, Jerryson explores how Buddhist teachings have influenced peace and security in various contexts, including conflict resolution, peacebuilding, and disarmament. He argues that by emphasizing compassion, empathy, and interdependence, Buddhist-inspired approaches to security can bridge diverse communities and foster a sense of shared humanity. Jerryson acknowledges the challenges and limitations of applying Buddhist principles to contemporary security issues, considering the persistence of violence and conflict globally. Nonetheless, he maintains that Buddhist-inspired approaches offer valuable insights into the importance of nonviolence, empathy, and compassion in promoting peace and stability.

In his book "Buddhist Warfare," Michael Jerryson examines the complex relationship between Buddhism and violence, particularly in the context of national security. He acknowledges that while Buddhism is often associated with nonviolence and compassion, historical evidence shows that Buddhist institutions and individuals have been involved in acts of violence and warfare. Jerryson explores how Buddhist teachings and practices have been used to justify and legitimize violence, including the concept of "righteous warfare" and the protection of Buddhist institutions and communities. Simultaneously, he investigates how Buddhist teachings have been invoked to promote nonviolence and compassion, highlighting the efforts of Buddhist activists and leaders advocating for peace and social justice.

Despite Buddhism's historical involvement in violence, Jerryson argues that the religion's emphasis on nonviolence and compassion can contribute to peace and stability in society. He contends that promoting Buddhist values such as compassion, empathy, and nonviolence can help create a more peaceful and just world. Jerryson's book provides a nuanced examination of the relationship between Buddhism and violence, shedding light on both the historical record and the potential of Buddhist teachings and practices to promote peace and security.

Furthermore, S. J. Thomas (2016) explores the intersection between Buddhist philosophy and contemporary security studies, underscoring the potential contributions of Buddhist perspectives on nonviolence and compassion. Thomas critiques traditional security studies approaches focusing solely on military power and state sovereignty, advocating for a more comprehensive understanding of security. He argues for recognizing the interconnectedness of all living beings and the importance of promoting social justice, economic development, and environmental sustainability in security discourse.

Thomas highlights how Buddhist philosophy and practice can enrich our understanding of security. He suggests that Buddhist teachings on nonviolence, compassion, and interdependence can provide insights into the root causes of insecurity and solutions for promoting peace and stability. By integrating Buddhist perspectives into security studies, a holistic and compassionate approach can be developed that prioritizes the well-being of all living beings, transcending the interests of the state or military power alone.

Thomas also discusses how Buddhist teachings and practices can promote peace and security at local, national, and international levels. He highlights the work of Buddhist activists and organizations, such as the International Network of Engaged Buddhists and the Sarvodaya Shramadana Movement in Sri Lanka, which has utilized Buddhist principles to drive nonviolent social change and community development. Ultimately, Thomas argues that integrating Buddhist perspectives on nonviolence and compassion into security studies can create a more inclusive and holistic approach that considers individuals' and communities' diverse needs and experiences. He underscores the importance of deepening our understanding of Buddhist philosophy and values to foster a more compassionate and peaceful world.

In short, Thomas's study offers a thought-provoking exploration of the potential contributions of Buddhist philosophy to security studies. By emphasizing nonviolence, compassion, and interdependence, Thomas suggests that Buddhist perspectives can counterbalance traditional security approaches and contribute to a more inclusive and compassionate approach to security that promotes peace and security for all.

John Negru (2019) examines the relationship between Buddhism and national security in Southeast Asia, with a particular focus on the role of Buddhist leaders and organizations in promoting peace and reconciliation in the region. Negru provides a brief historical overview of the relationship between Buddhism and Southeast Asian society, emphasizing the profound influence of Buddhism on culture and politics in the region. He then delves into the contributions of Buddhist leaders and organizations to peace and reconciliation efforts in Southeast Asia, citing specific examples from countries such as Cambodia, Thailand, and Myanmar.

Negru argues that Buddhist leaders and organizations have played a crucial role in promoting peace and reconciliation in Southeast Asia by emphasizing nonviolence, compassion, and interdependence. He suggests that these principles can serve as a framework for conflict resolution and foster greater understanding and cooperation among diverse groups. However, he acknowledges the challenges faced by Buddhist leaders and organizations, including political instability, ethnic and religious conflicts, and the spread of extremist ideologies. Negru emphasizes the need for collaborative efforts among Buddhist leaders and organizations to address these challenges and promote regional peace and stability. In conclusion, he asserts that Buddhism can significantly promote national security in Southeast Asia through peace and reconciliation efforts. He underscores the ongoing necessity for Buddhist leaders and organizations to address the complex challenges in the region and foster understanding and cooperation among different groups.

In addition, Ritu Verma and Anand Kumar Jaiswal (2018) investigate the role of Buddhism in promoting peace and security in South Asia, focusing on the contributions of Buddhist leaders and organizations to conflict resolution and peacebuilding. They begin by providing an overview of Buddhism's historical and cultural significance in South Asia, emphasizing its influence on the region's social, cultural, and political landscape. The authors then delve into the involvement of Buddhist leaders and organizations in conflict resolution and peacebuilding, highlighting the significance of nonviolence, compassion, and interdependence in these endeavors.

Verma and Jaiswal highlight the work of influential Buddhist leaders such as the Dalai Lama and Thich Nhat Hanh, who have actively advocated for peace and nonviolence in the region. They also discuss the contributions of organizations like the Buddhist Peace Fellowship and the Sarvodaya Shramadana Movement, which have utilized Buddhist principles to promote peacebuilding and community development in South Asia.

According to Verma and Jaiswal, integrating Buddhist teachings and practices can foster a more comprehensive and inclusive approach to conflict resolution and peacebuilding in the region. They argue that by promoting a deeper understanding of

Buddhist philosophy and values, South Asian societies can cultivate greater compassion and peaceful coexistence. The research conducted by Verma and Jaiswal offers a captivating analysis of Buddhism's role in promoting peace and security in South Asia. By highlighting the contributions of Buddhist leaders and organizations to conflict resolution and peacebuilding efforts, they suggest that Buddhist principles can serve as a valuable resource for creating a more peaceful and just society.

Buddhism Contributions to Modern Security Studies

The research on Buddhism's perspectives and contributions to national security has encompassed various fields, including philosophy, history, and psychology. Scholars have explored how Buddhist security and territorial protection concepts can be incorporated into modern strategies. While Buddhist texts do not directly reference national security, their perspectives and teachings offer concepts that can be translated into contemporary security strategies.

Firstly, Buddhism's emphasis on nonviolence and compassion serves as a foundation for building a peaceful and secure society. Nonviolence practices can prevent conflicts and foster harmonious coexistence between nations, thereby contributing to national security. Buddhism's emphasis on compassion also encourages empathy and community, promoting cooperation and mutual understanding among people and nations.

Secondly, Buddhism's teachings on impermanence can be applied to national security. The philosophy emphasizes that everything is constantly changing and interconnected. This understanding helps us recognize that security threats are not permanent and necessitate a flexible approach. Additionally, it highlights the interconnectedness of nations, calling for global cooperation in addressing security challenges.

Thirdly, Buddhism's teachings on mindfulness can contribute to national security. By cultivating awareness and being present in the moment, mindfulness helps identify potential security threats and respond appropriately. It also aids in making informed decisions by fostering a fully present and aware mindset.

Lastly, Buddhism's teachings on detachment offer insights into national security. Detachment encourages individuals to let go of attachments and desires that can lead to conflict and aggression. By embracing detachment, unnecessary disputes can be avoided, enabling a focus on achieving national security goals peacefully.

Past studies have primarily focused on the role of Buddhist principles in promoting peace and reconciliation. Scholars argue that Buddhist teachings emphasize nonviolence, compassion, and tolerance, which contribute to a more peaceful and secure society. For example, the concept of ahimsa or nonviolence in Buddhism is viewed as a means to prevent conflict and encourage peaceful dispute resolution. Recent studies have explored the potential of Buddhist concepts of security and territorial protection in modern national security strategies. One such concept is dharma-buddha, or just war, which emphasizes using force only as a last resort to protect innocent lives.

Moreover, Buddhism's promotion of peaceful coexistence and nonviolent conflict resolution has been studied extensively. Buddhist teachings emphasize compassion, empathy, and mindfulness, facilitating peaceful resolutions to disputes. The emphasis on self-restraint and non-attachment to material possessions helps reduce greed, corruption, and other forms of violence that can jeopardize national security.

Additionally, scholars suggest that Buddhist concepts of interdependence and interconnectedness can inform contemporary approaches to national security. Recognizing that the security of one nation is intricately linked to others and the environment, a comprehensive security approach should consider the interconnections between different actors and systems. This perspective encourages mutual benefits and sustainable outcomes through global cooperation.

Furthermore, Buddhism can contribute to national security by promoting social cohesion and resilience. Its teachings emphasize community and social harmony, mitigating social unrest and conflict. Policymakers and practitioners can integrate Buddhist teachings and practices into security strategies in several ways:

1. Incorporating mindfulness and empathy training into security and defense programs to promote nonviolent conflict resolution and reduce the risk of violence.
2. Promoting regional cooperation and mutual understanding by applying Buddhist concepts of interdependence and interconnectedness.
3. Building strong and resilient communities by fostering social cohesion and addressing underlying social and economic factors contributing to insecurity.

In summary, Buddhism offers unique perspectives and contributions to national security, informing modern security and territorial protection strategies. Policymakers can work towards a more peaceful and secure society by drawing on Buddhist concepts of nonviolence, compassion, and responsible governance. Additionally, incorporating mindfulness and meditation practices can promote mental health and resilience, fostering stability and safety. Buddhism's perspectives on national security emphasize nonviolence, interdependence, inner peace, compassion, and responsible resource management. By integrating these values into national security policies, a more peaceful and stable world can be fostered. Also, in the next chapter, we will examine Confucius and Sun Tzu's Perspectives on Territorial Protection and their contributions and relevance to modern-day security studies.

References:

Dalai Lama. (1999). Ethics for the new millennium. New York: Riverhead Books.

Dalai Lama. (2011). A human approach to world peace. Shambhala Publications

De Silva, P. (2016). Buddhist teachings for peace and security in the 21st century: A review article. Contemporary Buddhism, 17(1), 151-170. doi: 10.1080/14639947.2016.1151017.

Gethin, R. (1998). The foundations of Buddhism. Oxford University Press.

Huntington, C. W. (1986). The human potential for peace: An anthropological challenge to assumptions about war and violence. Routledge.

Jerryson, M. (2011). Buddhist contributions to peace and security theory and practice. Journal of Global Buddhism, 12, 1-24.

Keown, D. (2003). Buddhism: A very short introduction. Oxford: Oxford University Press.

Lopez, D. S. (2008). Buddhism and science: A guide for the perplexed. University of Chicago Press.

Negru, J. (2019). Buddhism and national security in Southeast Asia: The role of Buddhist leaders and organizations in promoting peace and reconciliation. International Journal of Asian Studies, 16(2), 171-191.

Rhys Davids, T. W., & Stede, W. (Eds.). (1921). The Pali Text Society's Pali-English dictionary. Pali Text Society.

Tanaka, Y. (2012). Buddhist philosophy and the concept of human security. Journal of Human Security Studies, 1(1), 1-15. doi: 10.7575/aiac.ijhss.v.1n.1p.1

Sivaraksa, S. (2013). Engaged Buddhism: The Dalai Lama's worldview. Parallax Press.

Thomas, S. J. (2016). Buddhism and security studies. Journal of Global Buddhism, 17, 69-81.

Toscano, G. (2011). Buddhism and national security: A conceptual exploration. Journal of Global Ethics, 7(1), 75-89. doi: 10.1080/17449626.2011.550563

Stone, J. (2009). The Nichirenshu and National Defense. In C. Queen & R. King (Eds.), Engaged Buddhism: Buddhist liberation movements in Asia (pp. 23–36). SUNY Press.

Verma, R., & Jaiswal, A. K. (2018). Buddhism and peacebuilding in South Asia. Journal of Asian and African Studies, 53(6), 880-895.

6

Confucius and Sun Tzu's Perspectives on Territorial Protection

Confucius, a Chinese philosopher, and teacher who lived in the 5th century BCE, firmly focused on ethics, morality, and social order. When it came to protecting one's nation against internal and external threats, Confucius emphasized the cultivation of ethical leadership and the creation of a just and harmonious society. According to Confucius, safeguarding a nation involves developing virtue and moral character in individuals and promoting social harmony and good governance. He believed that the key to protecting a nation from internal and external threats was establishing a stable and just society where individuals were motivated by a sense of duty and responsibility rather than fear or force.

Regarding internal security, Confucius greatly emphasized cultivating moral character in individuals. He believed that virtuous and ethical individuals would naturally act in the best interests of their society and refrain from actions that would harm it. In the Analects, Confucius states, "The man of virtue makes the difficulty to be overcome his first business, and success only a subsequent consideration; this may be called perfect virtue" (7.6). This passage suggests that a virtuous individual prioritizes the greater good of the nation over personal interests and works to overcome difficulties in achieving this goal.

One of Confucius' central ideas was the concept of Ren, which can be translated as "humaneness," "benevolence," or "compassion." Ren involves treating others with kindness, respect, and empathy, and it is considered a critical virtue for individuals and leaders. Confucius believed that leaders who practice Ren would govern their people more effectively and maintain social stability. He also stressed the importance of creating a just and harmonious society by promoting social order and ethical behavior. According to Confucius, individuals must behave virtuously and contribute to the well-being of their communities, which helps prevent social unrest and maintain stability within the nation.

Regarding external security, Confucius believed in the significance of strong and just governance. He emphasized the importance of diplomacy and peaceful relations with other countries. Confucius advocated for the avoidance of war and violence whenever possible, urging nations to resolve conflicts through negotiation and compromise. He believed that a just ruler, governing with wisdom and compassion, would earn the loyalty and respect of their subjects, creating a strong and unified society capable of withstanding external threats. In the Analects, Confucius states, "When the prince's personal conduct is correct, his government is effective without issuing orders. If his conduct is not correct, he may issue orders, but they will not be followed" (13.6). This passage suggests that a ruler who sets a good example and governs with moral authority will be able to lead their nation effectively without resorting to force or coercion.

Confucius believed protecting one's nation against internal and external threats was essential for creating a stable and harmonious society. He emphasized the importance of cultivating moral character and promoting good governance as the foundation for maintaining social order and protecting the nation. Internally, Confucius identified poverty, corruption, and social unrest as critical threats to a nation's stability (Wong, 2008). He believed these issues could be addressed through effective governance and cultivating virtue among the people. Therefore, Confucius advocated for leaders to set an excellent example by embodying the principles of decency, sincerity, and benevolence in their conduct and promoting these values throughout society. In the

Analects, Confucius stated, "Lead the people with administrative injunctions and put them in their place with penal law, and they will avoid punishments but will be without a sense of shame. Lead them with excellence and put them in their place through roles and positions, and in addition to avoiding punishments, they will have a sense of shame." This passage highlights the importance of leading by example and cultivating moral character to promote social order.

Externally, Confucius viewed invasion and warfare as the primary threats to a nation's stability. He believed that a government could protect itself from external threats through military preparedness, alliances with other countries, and diplomatic negotiations. However, Confucius also emphasized the importance of avoiding war whenever possible, believing that diplomacy and peaceful coexistence were preferable to conflict. In the Analects, Confucius stated, "It is better to recapture an army than to destroy it; better to capture a regiment than to destroy it. Better to take a man alive than to kill him. There is no excellence in killing men." This passage highlights Confucius' belief in the value of human life and his preference for peaceful solutions to conflicts (Wong, 2008).

To put it briefly, Confucius maintained that protecting one's nation involved cultivating virtue and moral character in individuals and promoting social harmony and good governance. By creating a just and stable society, individuals would be motivated to act in the best interests of their nation, creating a strong and resilient society capable of withstanding both internal and external threats. Confucius' perspective on protecting one's nation against internal and external threats involved promoting ethical leadership, creating a just and harmonious society, and avoiding war and violence through diplomacy and negotiation. Confucius believed in leading by example and prioritizing peaceful solutions whenever possible, emphasizing the value of peaceful resolutions and the avoidance of conflict.

The Military Strategist Sun Tzu's Viewpoints on National Security

Sun Tzu, one of the most acclaimed war strategists, had an obscure religious upbringing, and there is much debate among scholars regarding the influence of Taoism on his philosophical and strategic approach to warfare. Some assert that Sun Tzu's strategy was heavily influenced by Taoism, a Chinese philosophy emphasizing the harmony and balance of nature. Others argue that his approach was more pragmatic and focused on practical matters rather than philosophical or religious beliefs. However, it is commonly believed that Sun Tzu was influenced by the teachings of Confucianism and Taoism, two major philosophical and religious traditions in ancient China, given that he lived during the Eastern Zhou period. Lionel Giles, a scholar who has studied Sun Tzu's work and its philosophical underpinnings, contends that Sun Tzu's approach to warfare reflects Taoist principles of balance and harmony. Giles suggests that Sun Tzu "understands warfare as a form of natural conflict, and he sees the principles of warfare as emerging from the principles of nature" (Giles, 2005, p. 43).

Despite Giles' interpretation, other scholars have contested this view and proposed that Sun Tzu's outlook on warfare was more practical than philosophical. While some, like Lionel Giles, interpret "The Art of War" as having a philosophical outlook on warfare, others argue that Sun Tzu's perspective was primarily practical. They suggest that Sun Tzu's main concern was providing practical advice and strategies for achieving victory in battle. According to this interpretation, Sun Tzu's emphasis on terrain, tactics, spies, and deception indicates a pragmatic approach to warfare. Furthermore, his focus on preparation and training highlights a realistic stance. Historian Victor Davis Hanson, for instance, asserts that Sun Tzu's emphasis on deception and surprise in war reflects a realistic awareness of human psychology and military maneuvers rather than a philosophical commitment to Taoism (Hanson, 2001).

In short, while Sun Tzu's work has had a significant impact on military strategy and philosophy, there is little concrete information available about his religious beliefs and upbringing, and scholars hold conflicting opinions on the subject. Some argue that his approach to warfare reflects Taoist principles, while others see it as more practical and focused on practical matters. Although Sun Tzu's religious beliefs are not well-documented, it is evident that his thinking was influenced by the Taoist concept of Wu Wei, or "effortless action." According to Taoist philosophy, the most effective action is one taken without effort or force, and success depends on aligning oneself with the natural flow of the universe.

Sun Tzu extensively wrote on national security in his influential book, "The Art of War." He emphasized the importance of understanding and preparing for potential threats to maintain national security. Although not a comprehensive treatise on national security, it contains many insights into the nature of security and how it can be achieved. One of Sun Tzu's crucial insights is that genuine security does not come from brute force or overwhelming military strength, but from the ability to anticipate and prevent potential threats before they arise. Sun Tzu writes, "The supreme art of war is to subdue the enemy without fighting... To win one hundred victories in one hundred battles is not the acme of skill. To subdue the enemy without fighting is the acme of skill." This notion of winning without fighting reflects Sun Tzu's belief that true security arises not from defeating enemies on the battlefield but from outmaneuvering them and preventing conflicts from arising in the first place.

A key element of Sun Tzu's approach to national security was the careful assessment of one's military strengths and weaknesses and those of potential adversaries. He wrote, "If you know the enemy and know yourself, you need not fear the result of a hundred battles." This suggests that a thorough understanding of one's capabilities and those of the enemy is critical to achieving victory in battle and maintaining national security. Sun Tzu believed that genuine protection stems not only from superior military power but also from a deep understanding of one's strengths and weaknesses, as well as those of opponents.

Sun Tzu also emphasized the importance of flexibility and adaptability in achieving security. For instance, he wrote, "In war, the way is to avoid what is strong and to strike at what is weak." This idea of flexibility and adaptability reflects Sun Tzu's belief that true security arises not only from having a fixed plan but also from adapting to changing circumstances on the battlefield. Another critical element of Sun Tzu's approach to national security was the use of deception and strategic planning to gain an advantage over the enemy. He wrote, "All warfare is based on deception. Hence, when able to attack, we must seem unable; when using our forces, we must seem inactive; when we are near, we must make the enemy believe we are far away." This approach suggests that strategic deception can effectively achieve military objectives and maintain national security.

Additionally, Sun Tzu emphasized the importance of maintaining discipline and order within one's military. He wrote, "Regard your soldiers as your children, and they will follow you into the deepest valleys; look upon them as your beloved sons, and they will stand by you even unto death." This idea suggests that a well-trained and disciplined military is essential for maintaining national security. Sun Tzu's perspectives on national security offer valuable insights into the nature of security and how it can be achieved. His approach emphasizes the importance of understanding one's strengths and weaknesses, as well as those of potential adversaries and developing strategies to prevent conflicts from arising in the first place. Adopting Sun Tzu's principles can improve our ability to manage risks and respond proactively and effectively to threats.

Sun Tzu's perspectives on national security provide valuable insights into achieving security and preventing conflicts. One of the most important lessons we can learn from Sun Tzu is the significance of understanding oneself and one's opponents. By comprehending our strengths and weaknesses, as well as those of our adversaries, we can make better decisions and avoid costly mistakes. Another critical lesson from Sun Tzu's perspective on national security is the importance of adaptability. Sun Tzu emphasizes the need to be flexible and responsive to changing circumstances rather than relying on a fixed plan. This approach allows leaders to adjust their strategies based on evolving threats and opportunities, keeping them ahead of potential adversaries.

Another vital lesson from Sun Tzu's perspective is the value of intelligence and understanding. Sun Tzu stresses the importance of understanding one's strengths, weaknesses, and those of potential adversaries. This understanding requires leaders to invest in intelligence gathering and analysis and develop a deep understanding of the geopolitical landscape in which they operate. By doing so, they can identify potential threats and opportunities and develop effective strategies to manage them. Another crucial lesson from Sun Tzu is anticipating and preventing potential threats before they arise. Instead of relying solely on military power, absolute security comes from outmaneuvering opponents and avoiding conflicts altogether. This approach necessitates a profound understanding of the political, economic, and social factors that drive conflicts and the ability to develop strategies to prevent them.

Sun Tzu also emphasizes the importance of flexibility and adaptability in achieving security. This means adapting to changing circumstances and being prepared to change strategies when necessary. This is particularly important in an era of rapidly evolving technology and globalization, where new threats can emerge quickly and require new approaches to security. Finally, Sun Tzu's perspectives on national security emphasize the importance of prevention. Instead of relying on military power to defeat adversaries, Sun Tzu advocates for a proactive approach that seeks to prevent conflicts from arising in the first place. This requires leaders to develop strategies to deter potential adversaries and manage risks before they escalate into full-blown disputes. Sun Tzu's approach to national security was multifaceted and focused on various strategic considerations, from assessing one's capabilities and those of the enemy to using deception and maintaining discipline within one's military. His insights on national security continue to be studied and applied by military strategists and policymakers worldwide.

Sun Tzu's perspectives on national security provide valuable insights into achieving security in an ever-changing world. By adopting Sun Tzu's adaptability, intelligence, and prevention principles, leaders can improve their ability to achieve security and stability in a rapidly changing geopolitical landscape. By emphasizing the importance of understanding oneself and one's opponents, anticipating and preventing potential threats, and being flexible and adaptable, effective strategies can be developed to achieve security and avoid conflicts. Succinctly, Sun Tzu's teachings on national security emphasize the importance of intelligence gathering, adaptability, and proactive measures. By understanding the nature of the enemy and being flexible in response to changing circumstances, nations can maintain their security without necessarily resorting to military conflict.

Sun Tzu's Strategic Wisdom: Understanding Powers, Terrain, and Tactics for Victory and Their Relationship with National Security

This section aims to comprehensively analyze Sun Tzu's strategic wisdom, focusing on understanding powers, terrain, tactics, and their crucial relationship with national security. Realistic examples will be provided to illustrate the practical applicability of Sun Tzu's teachings. Sun Tzu emphasized the importance of understanding one's power and adversaries. Recognizing one's strengths and weaknesses allows for effective resource allocation and exploiting vulnerabilities in the opponent. This principle is equally applicable in the realm of national security. This understanding allows for effective resource allocation and exploitation of vulnerabilities, similarly beneficial in national security. This section explores the importance of comprehending powers in the context of national security and provides insights into resource allocation and exploiting adversary weaknesses.

Understanding One's Power: To effectively allocate resources and plan strategies, nations must comprehensively appreciate their power. This means assessing military capabilities, economic strength, technological advancements, diplomatic influence, and national resilience. By recognizing their strengths and weaknesses, nations can leverage their advantages and mitigate vulnerabilities, ensuring optimal resource allocation and strategic decision-making.

Self-Assessment: Sun Tzu highlighted the importance of self-assessment in understanding power. It involves profoundly and honestly evaluating a nation's strengths and weaknesses, military capabilities, economic resources, technological advancements, and societal resilience. By objectively analyzing these factors, a government can understand its power and make informed decisions about resource allocation, strategy formulation, and defense planning. It can leverage its strengths while mitigating its weaknesses.

Resource Allocation and Strategy: Understanding one's power enables effective resource allocation, ensuring that available resources are directed towards areas of strategic importance. For example, a nation with advanced technological capabilities may prioritize research and development in defense technologies and intelligence assets. In contrast, a nation with limited military strength may focus on diplomatic initiatives to foster alliances and partnerships. By aligning resources with areas of comparative advantage, countries can enhance their national security posture and optimize their strategic plans. Proper resource allocation based on a clear understanding of power maximizes national security preparedness. By understanding the quantity and quality of available resources, decision-makers can effectively allocate them to achieve desired national security objectives.

Resource Allocation from Sun Tzu's Viewpoint:

1. Assessing Resources: Sun Tzu stressed the importance of evaluating available resources accurately. This involves comprehensively assessing a nation's military capabilities, economic strength, technological advancements, intelligence assets, and diplomatic influence. By understanding the quantity and quality of available resources, decision-makers can effectively allocate them to achieve desired national security objectives.
2. Prioritizing Objectives: Sun Tzu advocated for prioritizing objectives based on available resources. In the face of limited resources, it is crucial to identify and prioritize critical objectives that align with national security interests. This requires a clear understanding of the strategic landscape, potential threats, and long-term goals. By focusing resources on critical areas, nations can maximize their impact and efficiently utilize limited resources.
3. Flexibility in Resource Allocation: Sun Tzu emphasized the importance of flexibility in resource allocation. As the strategic environment evolves, the distribution of resources may need to be adjusted accordingly. This requires ongoing evaluation and adaptation to ensure optimal resource utilization. Flexibility enables nations to respond to emerging threats, exploit new opportunities, and adapt strategies to changing circumstances, enhancing their national security posture.

Understanding power allows for strategic decision-making in national security. By recognizing their respective strength and those of the adversary, nations can make informed choices regarding defense priorities, resource allocation, and diplomatic engagements. This understanding informs the development of comprehensive strategies that leverage strengths, mitigate weaknesses, and exploit adversary vulnerabilities, enhancing the likelihood of achieving national security objectives.

Relevance to Modern-Day National Security:

Resource Allocation: Understanding power is essential for effective resource allocation in modern-day national security. With limited resources, nations must allocate them judiciously based on their comparative advantages and strategic priorities. This understanding enables optimal utilization of resources, whether in military hardware, intelligence capabilities, cybersecurity, or diplomatic engagements, thereby enhancing national security preparedness.

Asymmetric Warfare: In an era of asymmetric warfare, understanding power becomes even more critical. Non-state actors, such as terrorist organizations or cybercriminal networks, possess different forms of power that cannot be solely measured in conventional terms. National security entities must comprehend these actors' power dynamics and motivations to counter their threats effectively. By understanding their power sources, capabilities, and tactics, nations can develop appropriate countermeasures and respond effectively to asymmetric challenges.

Deterrence and Diplomacy: Understanding power is crucial in deterrence and diplomacy. By comprehending the power dynamics between nations, states can gauge the intentions and capabilities of potential adversaries. This understanding informs diplomatic negotiations, alliance building, and deterrence strategies, ultimately enhancing national security. It also aids in managing geopolitical relationships and resolving conflicts through peaceful means, contributing to global stability.

Knowledge of the Adversary: Sun Tzu emphasized the need to understand the adversary's power. This involves gathering intelligence, studying their military capabilities, analyzing their tactics and strategies, and assessing their strengths and weaknesses. In addition to understanding one's power, recognizing the adversary's strengths and weaknesses is crucial for national security. This assessment helps identify vulnerabilities that can be exploited to gain an advantage. By analyzing the adversary's military capabilities, defensive strategies, historical patterns, and potential weaknesses, nations can develop strategies to exploit those vulnerabilities effectively. This could involve targeting weak points in an adversary's defense, disrupting their supply chains, or undermining their alliances. By comprehending the adversary's power, a nation can effectively anticipate its moves, exploit vulnerabilities, and develop countermeasures to neutralize potential threats.

Analyzing the adversary's military capabilities, defensive strategies, historical patterns, and potential weaknesses enables nations to develop strategies to exploit those vulnerabilities effectively. This may involve leveraging technological superiority to neutralize an adversary's defenses or utilizing diplomatic means to exploit divisions within their alliances. Using adversary vulnerabilities allows for a more strategic and advantageous approach to national security.

Realistic Examples:

1. Cold War: The United States and the Soviet Union: Throughout the Cold War, both the United States and the Soviet Union recognized the importance of understanding each other's power dynamics. By closely monitoring the adversary's military capabilities, nuclear advancements, and global influence, both powers could allocate resources effectively and develop strategies that maintained a balance of power. This understanding influenced arms race strategies, diplomatic negotiations, and intelligence operations, all vital elements of national security during that era.
2. Terrorism and Counterterrorism: In the fight against terrorism, understanding the power dynamics is crucial. Nations must comprehend the strengths and weaknesses of terrorist organizations to counter them effectively. This understanding allows for targeted

intelligence gathering, disruption of funding networks, and exploitation of ideological divisions within terrorist groups. By comprehending the adversary's power, nations can implement counterterrorism strategies that weaken terrorist organizations and enhance national security.
3. The Falklands War (1982): During the Falklands War between Argentina and the United Kingdom, understanding powers played a critical role. In the Falklands War, understanding the powers at play was crucial in shaping the outcome. The United Kingdom recognized its outstanding naval power and strategically employed it to deploy a task force to retake the Falkland Islands from Argentina. The United Kingdom, recognizing its advantage in naval capabilities, deployed a daunting task force comprised of aircraft carriers, surface ships, and submarines. This force projected power and allowed the UK to quickly muster and embark on amphibious operations to retake the Falkland Islands. The British naval dominance gave them a considerable advantage in logistics, air support, and overall operational agility. The task force's command to project force across the vast South Atlantic Ocean exemplified the essence of understanding and leveraging one's power in military operations (Middlebrook, 2011). On the other hand, Argentina underestimated the U.K.'s capabilities and needed to anticipate their response. By comprehending their respective powers, the U.K. exploited Argentina's lack of naval strength and vulnerability in defending the remote islands, resulting in a successful military operation.
4. Cybersecurity: In the digital age, understanding powers is vital in cybersecurity. Nation-states and malicious actors constantly assess their cyber capabilities and those of their adversaries. This understanding allows them to identify vulnerabilities in their opponent's digital infrastructure, exploit weaknesses, and launch

cyberattacks. For instance, a nation with advanced offensive cyber capabilities may target an adversary's critical infrastructure to disrupt its operations or steal sensitive information.

Additionally, the United States and the Soviet Union during the Cold War During the Cold War, both the United States and the Soviet Union recognized the importance of understanding each other's military capabilities by closely monitoring the enemy's nuclear capabilities, troop movements, and technological advancements, both powers aimed to maintain strategic balance and avoid a catastrophic conflict. This understanding of powers influenced national security policies, arms race strategies, and diplomatic negotiations.

Understanding Terrain: Sun Tzu emphasized the significance of terrain and its impact on military operations. Terrain analysis involves studying geographical features, climate, infrastructure, and the socio-political environment. Such knowledge enables commanders to choose favorable battlegrounds and exploit natural advantages, increasing the likelihood of victory.

Understanding Terrain and Environmental Factors:

1. Geographical Features: Sun Tzu stressed the importance of understanding and utilizing geographical features in military strategy. Different types of terrain, such as mountains, rivers, forests, or urban areas, can provide advantages or pose challenges to forces engaged in conflict. Understanding the characteristics of the terrain allows commanders to plan tactics and maneuvers that exploit natural cover, provide defensive positions, or facilitate surprise attacks.
2. Weather Conditions: Sun Tzu recognized the impact of weather conditions on warfare. Factors such as rain, snow, fog, or extreme temperatures can significantly influence the effectiveness of military operations. Weather conditions can affect visibility, mobility, communication, and logistics. Understanding the local

climate and adapting tactics accordingly enable forces to exploit weather-related advantages or mitigate its adverse effects.
3. Environmental Considerations: Sun Tzu also emphasized the importance of ecological factors in military strategy. These include factors such as the availability of resources, vegetation, animal habitats, or infrastructure. Utilizing resources from the environment, such as water sources or local materials, can enhance the sustainability and effectiveness of military operations. Furthermore, understanding the local climate enables forces to blend in with the surroundings and conduct stealthy operations.

Impact on Military Strategy:

1. Terrain-Based Tactics: Understanding terrain allows commanders to develop tactics that leverage advantageous positions and neutralize the enemy's strengths derived from the environment. For example, controlling high ground in mountainous regions provides strategic advantages, such as better visibility, commanding firing positions, and denying the enemy access. Similarly, urban warfare requires specific tactics to navigate and exploit the complex terrain of cities.
2. Weather-Driven Operations: Weather conditions significantly impact military operations. Understanding weather patterns and adapting tactics allow forces to exploit weather-related advantages or mitigate challenges. For instance, foggy conditions can launch surprise attacks or create confusion, while extreme temperatures may require special equipment or adjusted operational timelines.
3. Environmental Adaptation: Understanding the local environment helps forces adapt tactics to blend in with the surroundings and minimize their footprint. This includes camouflage techniques, minimizing environmental impact, and utilizing local resources for

sustenance and logistics. By assimilating into the environment, forces can gain an element of surprise and reduce vulnerability to detection.

Practical Examples:

1. Battle of Stalingrad (1942-1943): The Battle of Stalingrad during World War II showcased the impact of terrain on military strategy. The urban landscape of Stalingrad provided natural defensive positions, making it difficult for the attacking German forces. The city's urban configuration and the existence of buildings, factories, and infrastructure offered natural defensive positions to the defending Soviet forces. This terrain favored close-quarter fighting and effective counterattacks, impeding the German forces' ability to operate their armored and mechanized units. The street-to-street fighting and fortified structures turned the battle into a brutal and prolonged engagement, ultimately favoring the defenders (Beevor, 1999).
2. Operation Neptune Spear (2011): The raid on Osama bin Laden's compound in Abbottabad, Pakistan, demonstrated the importance of environmental considerations. U.S. special forces used terrain analysis to plan their approach, considering building layout, vegetation cover, and nearby structures. This understanding enabled them to execute a successful mission with minimal detection and maximize the element of surprise.

Additionally, the case of Afghanistan presents a complex terrain to navigate. The country's rugged and mountainous terrain and intricate cave networks have proven challenging for foreign forces throughout history. The Soviet Union's failed invasion in the 1980s and the subsequent difficulties faced by the United States and its coalition partners highlight the importance of understanding and adapting to the complexities of the Afghan terrain.

Sun Tzu's teachings on terrain and environmental factors underscore their importance in military strategy. Understanding and adapting to geographical features, weather conditions, and other environmental considerations are essential in optimizing military operations. Practical examples, such as the Battle of Stalingrad and Operation Neptune Spear, highlight the practical applicability of Sun Tzu's teachings. By leveraging terrain and environmental factors, forces can exploit advantages, neutralize the enemy's strengths, and enhance their chances of victory in modern warfare.

In brief, Sun Tzu's wisdom on understanding powers holds significant relevance in national security. Comprehending one's perspective strength and that of the adversary enables effective resource allocation, strategic decision-making, and the exploitation of vulnerabilities. By assessing strengths and weaknesses, nations can optimize their defense capabilities and enhance their overall security. Realistic examples, such as the Cold War and counterterrorism efforts, highlight the practical application of this principle. By embracing the lessons of Sun Tzu, nations can strengthen their national security posture and effectively navigate the complexities of an ever-changing global landscape.

Choosing Effective Tactics and Techniques: Sun Tzu's Approach to Flexibility, Adaptability, and Deception.

This section focuses on the selection of tactics and techniques. It highlights Sun Tzu's emphasis on flexibility, adaptability, and deception. By understanding the strengths and weaknesses of different approaches, a commander can deploy the most suitable tactics to exploit vulnerabilities and achieve victory. Sun Tzu stressed the importance of choosing effective tactics and techniques in warfare. This section explores Sun Tzu's emphasis on flexibility, adaptability, and deception when selecting tactics. By understanding the strengths and weaknesses of different approaches, commanders can deploy the most suitable tactics to exploit vulnerabilities and achieve victory. This comprehensive analysis provides insights into Sun Tzu's teachings, focusing on practical examples.

Flexibility and Adaptability in Tactics:

1. Contextual Analysis: Sun Tzu emphasized the need for commanders to analyze the specific context of each situation. This includes factors such as terrain, available resources, weather conditions, and the strengths and weaknesses of both sides. By conducting a comprehensive assessment, commanders can determine the most appropriate tactics and adapt them to the unique circumstances of the battlefield.
2. Maneuver Warfare: Sun Tzu advocated for maneuver warfare, which involves utilizing mobility, speed, and surprise to outmaneuver and outflank the enemy. This tactic enables forces to disrupt the enemy's defensive positions, exploit vulnerabilities, and gain advantageous positions. Maneuver warfare requires flexibility and adaptability to adjust tactics dynamically in response to changing circumstances on the battlefield.
3. Timing and Opportunism: Sun Tzu stressed the importance of timing and opportunism in tactics. Recognizing favorable opportunities, such as distractions or weaknesses in the enemy's defense, allows commanders to launch decisive attacks or retreat strategically. This approach relies on a commander's ability to adapt tactics quickly and seize the right moment to achieve maximum impact.

Deception in Tactics:

1. Psychological Operations: Sun Tzu stressed the importance of psychological operations (PSYOPS) in warfare. Deceptive tactics, such as misinformation, propaganda, or pretend movements, can confuse and demoralize the enemy. Commanders can create psychological effects that undermine the enemy's morale

and decision-making by utilizing misinformation, propaganda, and feigned movements. Delivering false information or propaganda can sow confusion and doubt within the enemy ranks. By manipulating their perceptions and expectations, commanders can disrupt their decision-making processes and create advantages for their forces. Sun Tzu acknowledged the psychological aspect of warfare and the power of deception in exploiting and affecting the enemy's behavior. Commanders can gain the upper hand and create strategic advantages by using the enemy's vulnerabilities and weaknesses through psychological operations (Griffith, 1971). By manipulating their perceptions and expectations, commanders can create advantages, disrupt the enemy's decision-making process, and gain the element of surprise.

2. Pretend Weakness and Strength: Sun Tzu advocated strategically using pretend weakness and strength. Presenting a facade of weakness can lure the enemy into complacency, making them underestimate the true capabilities of one's forces. Conversely, projecting a false sense of strength can intimidate adversaries, potentially deterring aggression or influencing their strategic calculations. Skillful manipulation of perceptions through deception allows commanders to control the tempo and direction of the conflict.

3. Ambush and Strategic Misdirection: Sun Tzu highlighted the effectiveness of ambushes and strategic misdirection as deception tactics. Commanders can create advantageous scenarios by setting traps, concealing forces, or diverting the enemy's attention. Ambushes catch the enemy off guard, disrupt their formations, and inflict significant damage. Strategic misdirection can lead the enemy to make erroneous assumptions or commit resources to the wrong areas, creating opportunities for exploitation.

Realistic Examples:

1. Battle of Cannae (216 BC): During the Battle of Cannae, Hannibal Barca, a Carthaginian general, employed a tactical envelopment strategy against the Roman Republic forces. Hannibal's forces, though outnumbered, utilized flexible tactics, luring the Roman legions into a central position. Once the Romans were fully engaged, Hannibal executed a classic double envelopment, encircling and annihilating the enemy forces. This flexible and deceptive tactic demonstrated the effectiveness of maneuver warfare and strategic deception. The Battle of Cannae demonstrates Hannibal Barca's tactical, intellectual, and strategic envelopment approach utilized by the Carthaginian troops against the Roman Republic. Despite being outnumbered, Hannibal's adaptable tactics and strategic maneuvers led to a mighty victory. Hannibal's approach at Cannae involved beguiling the Roman legions into a central position by forming a concave formation. This formation permitted the Carthaginians to encircle and trap the Roman forces. By drawing the Roman army into the center, Hannibal maximized the strength of his cavalry and flanking infantry units. The Carthaginian forces utilized their superior cavalry to outsmart the Roman cavalry, enveloping and isolating the Roman infantry in the center. This tactical envelopment profoundly weakened the Roman army's capability to operate and engage accordingly, leading to substantial losses (Lazenby, 1998).
2. Operation Fortitude (1944): In World War II, Operation Fortitude was a large-scale deception plan implemented by the Allies. The goal was to mislead the Germans about the location and timing of the D-Day invasion. Through various deceptive measures, including fake radio traffic, dummy equipment, and false intelligence leaks, the Allies successfully convinced the Germans that the main attack would occur in the Pas-de-Calais

region, diverting attention from the actual landing sites in Normandy. This tactical deception played a crucial role in the success of the D-Day invasion.

In short, Sun Tzu's teachings on choosing effective tactics and techniques emphasize flexibility, adaptability, and deception. Commanders can exploit vulnerabilities and gain strategic advantages by analyzing the context, utilizing maneuver warfare, capitalizing on timing and opportunism, and employing psychological operations. Realistic examples, such as the Battle of Cannae and Operation Fortitude, illustrate the practical applicability of Sun Tzu's teachings. Understanding and engaging these principles in modern warfare enable commanders to outmaneuver adversaries, control the narrative, and increase the chances of achieving victory.

Also, as an example: The Taiwan Strait Conflict Scenario as tensions rise between China and Taiwan, Sun Tzu's teachings can inform the strategies employed by both parties. The Chinese government, aware of its growing military capabilities, must understand the strength and capabilities of the Taiwanese military. They should also consider the complex terrain of the Taiwan Strait and strategically plan their tactics to exploit vulnerabilities and achieve their objectives. Conversely, Taiwan must comprehensively understand China's powers, terrain advantages, and potential tactics to devise a robust defense strategy and maintain national security.

Sun Tzu's strategic wisdom continues to offer valuable insights into national security in the modern era. Understanding powers, terrain, and tactics provides a foundation for effective decision-making, resource allocation, and strategic planning. Realistic examples, such as the Cold War arms race, the conflict in Afghanistan, and cyber warfare, highlight the practical applicability of Sun Tzu's teachings. By embracing these principles, nations can enhance their security, deter adversaries, and achieve favorable outcomes in an ever-evolving global landscape.

In essence, Sun Tzu's teachings on choosing effective tactics and techniques emphasize flexibility, adaptability, and deception. Commanders can exploit vulnerabilities and gain strategic advantages by analyzing the context, utilizing maneuver warfare, capitalizing on timing and opportunism, and employing psychological operations. Realistic examples, such as the Battle of Cannae and Operation Fortitude, illustrate the practical applicability of Sun Tzu's teachings. Understanding and engaging these principles in modern warfare enable commanders to outmaneuver adversaries, control the narrative, and increase the chances of achieving victory.

Historical and Contemporary Examples: Applying Sun Tzu's Teachings

This section examines historical and contemporary examples to illustrate the application of Sun Tzu's teachings. By analyzing renowned battles and modern conflicts, we can observe how understanding strengths, weaknesses, and environmental factors played crucial roles in determining outcomes. This comprehensive analysis demonstrates Sun Tzu's principles' continued relevance in historical and contemporary operational environments.

Historical Examples:

1. Battle of Thermopylae (480 BC): The Battle of Thermopylae provides an example of how understanding strengths, weaknesses, and environmental factors influenced outcomes. The Greek forces, led by King Leonidas I, recognized their numerical disadvantage against the massive Persian army. They chose to exploit the narrow pass of Thermopylae, effectively negating the Persian numerical advantage. By understanding the terrain and employing strategic tactics, the Greeks could hold off the Persian forces for several days, inflicting heavy losses and buying time for the Greek city-states to prepare a more substantial defense.

2. Battle of Waterloo (1815): The Battle of Waterloo demonstrates the importance of understanding strengths and weaknesses. With his seasoned and battle-hardened troops, Napoleon Bonaparte faced a coalition force led by the Duke of Wellington. While Napoleon possessed a formidable army, he underestimated the strategic capabilities and determination of the coalition forces. Wellington positioned his troops on advantageous terrain, maximizing their defensive capabilities and exploiting Napoleon's weaknesses. This understanding of the strengths and weaknesses of both sides ultimately led to Napoleon's defeat.

Contemporary Examples:

1. Vietnam War (1955-1975): The Vietnam War is a notable example where understanding environmental factors played a significant role. Vietnam's dense jungles and intricate tunnel systems provided the Viet Cong guerrilla fighters and North Vietnamese Army with advantages in mobility, concealment, and surprise.
2. The Vietnam War, which lasted from 1955 to 1975, symbolizes the consequential impact of understanding environmental challenges on military operations. Vietnam's overgrown jungles and complex tunnel systems gave the Viet Cong guerrilla fighters and North Vietnamese Army advantages. The lush jungles gave the Viet Cong and North Vietnamese Army ideal cover and concealment. They could move through the thick vegetation, avoiding detection and ambushing unsuspecting enemy forces. The dense foliage limited visibility and hindered the effectiveness of conventional warfare tactics, as it was difficult to spot enemy positions or movements (Tucker, 1999).
3. The elaborate tunnel systems, such as the Cu Chi tunnels, were vital lifelines for the Viet Cong. These tunnels provided hidden transportation routes, supply lines, and hideouts, allowing them to sustain a

networked guerrilla uprising. The tunnels allowed the Viet Cong to launch surprise incursions, disappear quickly, and regroup underground, confounding the conventional forces.
4. The advantages achieved from understanding the ecological characteristics in Vietnam presented substantial challenges for the United States and its allies. Traditional military techniques were often impractical in this complex and combative setting, as the overgrown jungles and tunnel systems negated some of their strengths. The U.S. forces faced challenges adapting to this environment, leading to strategic difficulties and costly engagements. The ability of the Vietnamese forces to understand and exploit the environmental factors contributed to their resilience and ultimately influenced the war's outcome (Tucker, 1999).
5. Asymmetric Warfare: In contemporary conflicts characterized by asymmetric warfare, understanding strengths, weaknesses, and environmental factors remains critical. Insurgent groups or non-state actors often utilize unconventional tactics and terrain to offset the superior military power of conventional forces. Understanding the strengths and weaknesses of both sides enables effective counterinsurgency strategies that adapt to the local environment, engage with the population, and neutralize the advantages of the insurgent groups.
6. Cyber Warfare: In cyber warfare, understanding strengths, weaknesses, and environmental factors is crucial. Nation-states and malicious actors exploit vulnerabilities in computer networks, systems, and infrastructure. Understanding the strengths and weaknesses of defensive and offensive cyber capabilities allows governments and organizations to prioritize investments in cybersecurity measures, develop robust defenses, and effectively anticipate and counter cyber threats.

In a nutshell, the historical examples of the Battle of Thermopylae and the Battle of Waterloo highlight the importance of understanding strengths, weaknesses, and environmental factors. These principles remain relevant in contemporary conflicts, such as the Vietnam War, asymmetric warfare, and cyber warfare. By comprehending these elements, military strategists and decision-makers can adapt tactics, exploit vulnerabilities, and increase the chances of success in complex operational environments. Sun Tzu's teachings continue to provide valuable insights for understanding and navigating the intricacies of warfare throughout history and in the modern era.

Leveraging Technological Advancements: Sun Tzu's Teachings and Their Application

Leveraging Technological Advancements: This portion discusses the importance of comprehending the technological strengths and weaknesses of one's armies. It highlights Sun Tzu's teachings on evaluating the availability and effectiveness of weaponry, communication systems, intelligence capabilities, and other technological advancements. By harnessing these strengths and addressing any deficiencies, commanders can optimize the utilization of technology on the battlefield. Also, it explores the importance of comprehending the technological strengths and weaknesses of one's armies, as well as Sun Tzu's teachings on evaluating and leveraging technological advancements. By understanding the availability and effectiveness of weaponry, communication systems, intelligence capabilities, and other technological factors, commanders can optimize the utilization of technology on the battlefield. This comprehensive analysis provides insights into the application of Sun Tzu's teachings, with historical and realistic examples.

Understanding Technological Strengths and Weaknesses:

1. Assessment of Available Technology: Sun Tzu emphasized the importance of accurately assessing the technological capabilities at one's disposal. This includes understanding the range, accuracy, firepower, and other capabilities of weapons systems. It also involves evaluating the effectiveness and reliability of communication systems, intelligence-gathering tools, and other technological advancements. By understanding the available technology, commanders can identify strengths and address any weaknesses or deficiencies.
2. Integration and Interoperability: Sun Tzu recognized the need for technology integration and interoperability. Commanders must evaluate how various technological components can work cohesively to enhance operational effectiveness. This includes ensuring compatibility between weapon systems, communication devices, and intelligence platforms. Integrating technology seamlessly enables commanders to leverage their full potential on the battlefield.

Leveraging Technological Advancements:

1. Enhancing Battlefield Awareness: Technological advancements, such as surveillance systems, unmanned aerial vehicles (UAVs), and satellite imagery, provide commanders with enhanced battlefield awareness. By leveraging these capabilities, commanders can gather real-time information about enemy movements, terrain features, and potential threats. This information enhances situational awareness and enables commanders to make informed decisions and adjust tactics accordingly.

2. Precision Strikes and Force Multipliers: Technological advancements, such as precision-guided munitions and advanced targeting systems, offer increased accuracy and effectiveness in striking enemy targets. By leveraging these capabilities, commanders can execute precise and decisive attacks, minimizing collateral damage and maximizing the impact of military operations. Additionally, technology can serve as force multipliers, allowing smaller forces to project greater power and influence on the battlefield.
3. Communication and Coordination: Effective communication is crucial in warfare, and technological advancements provide commanders with advanced communication systems to facilitate coordination and synchronization. Secure radio systems, encrypted networks, and real-time information-sharing platforms enable seamless communication and coordination between units. This fosters unity of effort enhances command and control and allows rapid decision-making in dynamic environments.

Historical and Realistic Examples:

1. Battle of Midway (1942): During World War II, the Battle of Midway showcased the importance of technological advantages. The United States Navy, through superior intelligence capabilities and effective use of code-breaking technology, was able to decipher Japanese plans and gain a significant advantage. This intelligence allowed them to exploit weaknesses in the Japanese fleet's positioning, leading to a decisive victory for the United States. Before the Battle of Midway, the United States had successfully intercepted and decrypted Japanese communications, particularly their naval codes. This breakthrough allowed the U.S. Navy to gain valuable insights into the Japanese plans and intentions, including their target and the timeframe of the attack. This intelligence advantage provided by

advanced code-breaking technology enabled the U.S. commanders to formulate effective strategies and allocate their resources accordingly. The United States' knowledge of the Japanese plans allowed them to position their forces strategically and ambush the Japanese fleet. They launched a devastating airstrike against the Japanese carriers, sinking four of them while losing only one of their carriers. This decisive victory shifted the balance of power in the Pacific theater and marked a turning point in World War II. The Battle of Midway demonstrated the significance of technological advantages, such as superior intelligence capabilities and code-breaking technology. The United States' ability to decipher the enemy's plans gave them a critical edge, enabling effective decision-making and precise targeting. This example highlights how technological advancements can significantly impact the outcome of a battle, emphasizing the importance of investing in intelligence capabilities and leveraging technological superiority in military operations.
2. Modern Cyber Warfare: Cyber warfare provides a realistic example of leveraging technological advancements. Nation-states and malicious actors exploit computer network and system vulnerabilities to conduct cyberattacks. Understanding offensive and defensive cyber capabilities allows governments and organizations to develop robust defenses, identify threats, and respond effectively to cyber incidents.

In brief, Sun Tzu's teachings on understanding and leveraging technological advancements remain relevant in modern warfare. By comprehending the technical strengths and weaknesses of one's armies, commanders can optimize the utilization of technology on the battlefield. Historical examples, such as the Battle of Midway, demonstrate the impact of technological advantages. Realistic illustrations, such as cyber warfare, highlight the ongoing relevance of Sun Tzu's teachings. By embracing and integrating technological advancements, commanders can enhance situational awareness, achieve precision strikes, improve communication and coordination, and ultimately increase the effectiveness of military operations.

Mitigating Vulnerabilities: Sun Tzu's Guidance and Strategies for Strengthening Armies

Mitigating Vulnerabilities: This section addresses Sun Tzu's guidance on identifying and mitigating weaknesses within one's armies. It explores the importance of recognizing vulnerabilities such as logistical limitations, gaps in training or equipment, or internal conflicts. By acknowledging these weaknesses, commanders can devise strategies to minimize their impact and develop plans to strengthen those areas over time. This concise analysis provides insights into Sun Tzu's teachings and offers real practical examples to illustrate effective strategies for mitigating vulnerabilities.

Identifying Vulnerabilities:

1. Logistical Limitations: Sun Tzu recognized the critical role of logistics in military operations. It is crucial to Identify logistical weaknesses, such as supply chain inefficiencies, insufficient transport capabilities, or limited resource access. By understanding these vulnerabilities, commanders can address them through improved planning, resource allocation, and coordination to ensure the sustained support of their forces.
2. Training and Equipment Gaps: Sun Tzu emphasized identifying training and equipment gaps within one's armies. Recognizing deficiencies in skill sets, outdated technology, or inadequate equipment allows commanders to prioritize training programs, upgrade resources, or seek external assistance to bridge the gaps. Addressing these weaknesses enhances

operational effectiveness and increases the chances of success on the battlefield.
3. Internal Conflicts: Sun Tzu acknowledged the detrimental impact of internal conflicts on military effectiveness. Identifying and addressing an army's internal divisions, rivalries, or leadership challenges is vital. By fostering unity, encouraging teamwork, and resolving conflicts through effective leadership, commanders can build more effective, resilient fighting forces capable of confronting external threats.

Strategies for Mitigating Vulnerabilities:

1. Comprehensive Training Programs: Developing comprehensive training programs tailored to address identified weaknesses is essential. By focusing on specific skills, tactics, and technologies, commanders can enhance the capabilities of their forces. Regular training exercises, simulations, and evaluations enable continuous improvement, fostering a culture of learning and adaptability within the military.
2. Partnerships and Alliances: Establishing partnerships and alliances can mitigate vulnerabilities. Collaborating with friendly nations or international organizations allows for resource-sharing, joint training exercises, and knowledge exchange. By leveraging the strengths and expertise of partner nations, commanders can fill capability gaps, enhance interoperability, and strengthen their armies collectively.
3. Innovation and Technological Advancements: Sun Tzu's teachings encourage embracing innovation and leveraging technological advancements to address vulnerabilities. Identifying emerging technologies or techniques relevant to military operations enables commanders to enhance capabilities, improve efficiency, and gain advantages over adversaries. Commanders can encourage the development and adoption of cutting-edge solutions by fostering a culture of innovation.

Real Practical Examples:
1. The British Army's Transformation (2000s): The British Army has struggled to define its role in the post-Cold War world, with a significant focus on counterinsurgency campaigns in Iraq and Afghanistan. The state of obsolescence in its armored vehicle capability and the challenges faced in introducing new vehicles or upgrading existing ones have left the army vulnerable. Addressing these vulnerabilities and investing in modernizing armored vehicle capabilities should be a priority to ensure the army remains effective and prepared for future challenges. As a result, the British Army recognized weaknesses in its capability to conduct expeditionary operations in the early 2000s. In response, they implemented a comprehensive transformation plan to improve rapid deployability, enhance equipment, and emphasize joint operations with international partners (Fisher, 2020). This strategy enabled the British Army to mitigate vulnerabilities, strengthen operational effectiveness, and successfully carry out complex operations in subsequent conflicts.
2. U.S. Army's Lessons Learned Program: The U.S. Army's Lessons Learned Program serves as a practical example of mitigating vulnerabilities. By analyzing and disseminating lessons from previous conflicts, commanders can identify weaknesses and develop strategies for improvement. This ongoing process allows the U.S. Army to adapt to evolving threats, refine tactics, and enhance operational readiness.

Concisely, Sun Tzu's teachings on mitigating vulnerabilities provide valuable guidance for commanders. By identifying weaknesses in logistics, training, equipment, and internal cohesion, commanders can develop strategies to address these vulnerabilities. Practical examples, such as the British Army's transformation and the U.S. Army's Lessons Learned Program, demonstrate pragmatic approaches to mitigating weaknesses. By implementing comprehensive training programs, forging partnerships, fostering innovation, and prioritizing continuous improvement, commanders can strengthen their armies, enhance operational effectiveness, and increase their chances of success in military operations.

Sun Tzu Focus Practical Contributing Factors

According to Sun Tzu, strategic planning, tactics, and winning in war depend on five contributing factors: the Moral Law, Heaven, Earth, the Commander, and Method and Discipline (Sun Tzu, 1910). This section will concisely analyze these factors and their significance in winning battles. The Moral Law refers to the ethical and moral principles that guide a commander's and his soldiers' actions. Sun Tzu argues that soldiers with a strong sense of morality and duty to their country and leader are likelier to fight harder and win battles (Sun Tzu, 1910). In other words, a commander must have the support of his soldiers, and they must be willing to follow him into battle. This factor emphasizes the importance of leadership and its effect on troop morale.

From Sun Tzu's viewpoint, the Moral Law is essential to the success of any military campaign. He believed that a leader must act with integrity and moral purpose to gain the trust and loyalty of his troops. Sun Tzu emphasizes the significance of treating soldiers with respect and fairness and avoiding unnecessary violence and cruelty. He contends that a successful military campaign hinges on strategic planning and tactical maneuvers and the ability to inspire and motivate troops through moral leadership. Sun Tzu states that a leader must lead by example, demonstrating a commitment to the moral principles he champions. He supposes that a leader who acts with integrity and treats his troops with respect will be able to inspire them to act with bravery and courage, even in the face of great adversity.

To sum up, from Sun Tzu's viewpoint, the Moral Law is an essential component of successful military leadership. A leader must act with integrity and moral purpose to gain the trust and loyalty of his troops while also using deception and tactical maneuvering to gain an advantage in battle (Giles, 2005). Simultaneously, Sun Tzu realized the necessity of deception and tactical maneuvering in warfare. He maintains that a practical leader must be able to adapt to changing circumstances and use deception and misdirection to gain the upper hand in battle. Heaven and Earth are the natural factors that influence the outcome of battles. Heaven refers to the weather, which can be used to gain an advantage over the enemy. For example, Sun Tzu advises that attacking during a storm can disorient the enemy and make it easier to achieve victory. Earth refers to the battlefield's terrain, which can be used to one's advantage. For example, a commander familiar with the landscape can use it to outmaneuver the enemy and gain a strategic advantage. Sun Tzu accentuates the essence of discerning and utilizing natural factors, such as Heaven and Earth, to gain an advantage in battle.

Heaven refers to the weather, which can significantly impact the outcome of a battle. Sun Tzu argues that a skilled commander can use the weather to his advantage, such as by choosing a time and place for fighting that is advantageous based on the weather conditions. To illustrate this point, a commander may choose to attack during a rainstorm, making the ground muddy and challenging for the enemy to maneuver. Moreover, Sun Tzu stresses the essence of familiarizing with the cycles of the seasons and how they impact warfare. In particular, winter may be a good time to attack an enemy unprepared for the harsh conditions, while summer may be better suited for defensive war. Furthermore, Sun Tzu argues that a commander must be prepared for unexpected changes in the weather, such as sudden storms or changes in wind direction. Therefore, he underlines the implication of adaptability and flexibility in response to changing weather conditions.

To end, Sun Tzu's focus on the natural characteristics of Heaven and Earth stresses the essence of familiarity and utilizing the environment to attain an advantage in battle. A skilled commander must be able to adapt to changing weather conditions and use them to his advantage, as well as understand the seasonal cycles and how they can affect warfare.

The Commander is the person responsible for leading his troops into battle. Sun Tzu argues that a successful commander must possess certain qualities, such as intelligence, courage, and the ability to inspire and motivate his troops (Sun Tzu, 1910). He must also be able to adapt to changing situations and come up with innovative strategies to defeat the enemy. Sun Tzu accentuates that a successful commander must possess several essential qualities to lead his troops into battle effectively. These qualities include intelligence, courage, and the ability to inspire and motivate troops.

Intelligence is a crucial characteristic of a successful commander. A commander must be able to analyze and understand the battlefield, including the terrain, weather, and the enemy's strengths and weaknesses. The commander must also be able to adapt his strategy based on changing circumstances and make quick decisions under pressure. Courage is another essential quality of a successful commander. The commander must be willing to take risks and make difficult decisions, even in the face of danger or uncertainty. A commander who lacks courage may hesitate or make poor decisions, leading to a defeat on the battlefield. The ability to inspire and motivate troops is also critical. A commander must be able to communicate his vision and goals to his forces, instilling confidence, and a sense of purpose. He must also be able to lead by example, showing his troops that he is willing to share in their hardships and risks. In addition to these essential qualities, Sun Tzu emphasizes the importance of strategy and tactics. A successful commander must be able to devise a sound plan and adjust it as necessary based on the situation on the battlefield. He must also be skilled in tactics, such as feints and ambushes, to gain an advantage over the enemy (Sawyer, 1996).

Also, Sun Tzu underscores the significance of a comprehensive approach to leadership in battle. A successful commander must possess intelligence, courage, the ability to inspire and motivate troops, and skill in strategy and tactics. By cultivating these qualities, a commander can lead his troops to victory on the battlefield. Method and discipline refer to the tactics and techniques used in battle. Sun Tzu argues that a commander must be flexible and adaptable and use various tactics depending on the situation. He must also ensure that his soldiers are well-disciplined and can follow his orders without hesitation. Sun Tzu underscores the implication of a commander's method and discipline, which relates to the tactics and techniques employed in battle. He asserts that an adept commander must be flexible and adaptable, utilizing diverse tactics depending on the situation.

Moreover, Sun Tzu stresses the necessity of comprehending the strengths and weaknesses of both one's armies and the enemy, as well as the terrain and other environmental factors. Based on this understanding, a commander must be able to choose the most effective tactics and techniques to achieve victory. Additionally, Sun Tzu stresses the importance of deception and surprise in warfare. He advocates for the use of tactics such as feints, ambushes, and the use of spies to gain an advantage over the enemy (Giles, 2005). He also emphasizes the importance of being able to quickly change tactics and strategies if the situation on the battlefield changes.

Furthermore, Sun Tzu argues that a commander must be disciplined and maintain control over his forces while fostering unity and teamwork. He underlines the significance of exercise, preparation, good organization, and logistics. In brief, Sun Tzu's focus on a commander's method and discipline underscores the importance of flexibility, adaptability, and a profound awareness of the situation on the battlefield. A competent commander must choose the most effective tactics and techniques based on the circumstances while maintaining discipline and control over his armies.

In a nutshell, Sun Tzu's five factors for winning the war provide a comprehensive framework for military strategy. The Moral Law emphasizes the importance of leadership and morale, while Heaven and Earth refer to the natural factors that can be used to gain an advantage. In addition, the commander must possess certain qualities and adapt to changing situations, while Method and Discipline refer to the tactics and techniques used in battle. A successful commander must consider all of these factors and use them to achieve victory in battle.

Also, in the next chapter, we will examine the history of Jewish security, including the challenges and threats they faced over the centuries. By studying the evolution of Jewish security perspectives, we can better understand the cultural and historical factors influencing national security policies across different regions and religions.

References:

Beevor, A. (1999). Stalingrad: The Fateful Siege: 1942-1943. Penguin Books.

Confucius. (2006). The Analects. Penguin Classics.

Garver, J. W. (1996). Sun Tzu and the art of modern warfare. Comparative Strategy, 15(1), 51-66.

Giles, L. (2005). Sun Tzu on the art of war: The oldest military treatise in the world. Courier Corporation.

Griffith, S. B. (1963). Sun Tzu: The Art of War. Oxford University Press.

Griffith, S. B. (1971). The Art of War: Sun Zi's Military Methods. Columbia University Press.

Hanson, V. D. (2001). The Western way of war: Infantry battle in classical Greece. University of California Press.

Ji, Z. (2017). National Security in the Era of the Silk Road: A Comparative Study of Sun Tzu and Clausewitz. Journal of Conflict and Security Law, 22(3), 449-464.

Jullien, F. (1995). The Propensity of Things: Toward a History of Efficacy in China. Zone Books.

Lai, H. S. (2011). Chinese strategic culture and foreign policy decision-making: Confucianism, leadership, and war. Routledge.

Lambert, A. (2011, February 17). The Battle of Midway. BBC.

Lazenby, J. F. (1998). Hannibal's War: A Military History of the Second Punic War. University of Oklahoma Press.

McNeilly, M. (2001). Sun Tzu and the Art of Modern Warfare. Oxford University Press.

Middlebrook, M. (2011). The Falklands War. Penguin.

National WWII Museum. (n.d.). The Battle of Midway. Retrieved from https://www.nationalww2museum.org/war/articles/battle-midway

Sawyer, R. D. (1993). Sun Tzu's Art of War: The Modern Chinese Interpretation. Westview Press.

Sawyer, R. D. (1996). The Seven Military Classics of Ancient China. Basic Books.

Sun Tzu. (1910). The Art of War. (L. Giles, Trans.). Project Gutenberg. (Original work published 5th century BCE)

Sun Tzu. (2003). The Art of War. Shambhala Publications

Tucker, S. C. (1999). Vietnam. In Encyclopedia of the Vietnam War: A Political, Social, and Military History (pp. 1097–1106). ABC-CLIO.

Wong, D. B. (2008). Confucian ethics in the age of globalization. SUNY Press.

7

History Of Ancient Judaism's Stances On Security

Judaism Foundation on National Security

This section provides a comprehensive analysis of the history of ancient Judaism as it relates to its national security. Throughout its history, Judaism has had a complex relationship with national security.

The Biblical Period: The earliest period of Judaism is the Biblical period, which covers the time from the world's creation to the end of the Second Temple era. During this time, the Jewish people faced numerous threats to their national security, including invasion, conquest, and exile. However, they also experienced periods of relative peace and prosperity.

One of the earliest examples of a threat to Jewish national security in the Bible is the story of the Exodus. According to the biblical account, the Jewish people were enslaved in Egypt and faced brutal treatment at the hands of the Egyptian Pharaoh. Moses led the Jewish people out of Egypt but faced numerous challenges in the desert, including attacks from neighboring tribes. However, God protected them and eventually led them to the Promised Land.

During the Judges period, the Jewish people faced numerous threats from neighboring tribes, including the Philistines and the Ammonites. The period of the United Monarchy, under King David and King Solomon, was a time of relative peace and prosperity for the Jewish people. However, after the kingdom split into the northern kingdom of Israel and the southern kingdom of Judah, both kingdoms faced threats from neighboring empires, including Assyria and Babylon.

The Second Temple Period: The Second Temple period covers the time from the rebuilding of the Temple in Jerusalem in 515 BCE to its destruction by the Romans in 70 CE. During this time, the Jewish people faced numerous threats to their national security, including the conquests of Alexander the Great, the Seleucid Empire, and the Roman Empire.

In addition, the Maccabean Revolt, which took place in the 2nd century BCE, was a crucial event in Jewish history that demonstrated the Jewish people's commitment to their national security. The Seleucid Empire, which controlled Judea, attempted to suppress Jewish religious practices and force the Jewish people to assimilate into Hellenistic culture. The Maccabees, led by Judah Maccabee, rebelled against the Seleucids and eventually established an independent Jewish state.

However, the Jewish state was short-lived, and the Romans eventually conquered Judea and destroyed the Second Temple in 70 CE. The Roman conquest significantly impacted Jewish national security, as it led to the dispersion of the Jewish people throughout the Roman Empire and the loss of their homeland.

To maintain cultural and religious security, the Jewish people established laws and customs to distinguish themselves from other cultures. These included dietary laws, circumcision, and observing the Sabbath. The Jewish people also found a system of education to pass on their religious and cultural traditions from generation to generation.

Furthermore, the concept of national security in ancient Judaism was primarily focused on protecting the Jewish people and their way of life. This approach included physical security from external threats such as invading armies and cultural and religious security from internal threats such as idol worship and assimilation. To illustrate this point, in Deuteronomy 20:1-4, Moses instructs the Israelites that when going to war, they should not be afraid of their enemies, for the Lord their God is with them and will fight for them. This passage illustrates the importance of divine protection in securing the nation.

Moreover, the construction and fortification of cities were also crucial for national security. For instance, King David fortified Jerusalem and made it the capital of Israel (2 Samuel 5:6-10), and King Solomon built the Temple and other important structures (1 Kings 5-7). The fortified walls and structures protected the city and its inhabitants physically.

Additionally, the Book of Exodus describes the Israelites escaping from slavery in Egypt and facing a military threat from the Egyptian army pursuing them. Further, the Book of Judges explains the Israelites being attacked by neighboring nations such as the Philistines and the Ammonites.

One of the critical institutions in ancient Judaism was the monarchy. The monarchy played a vital role in the political and military affairs of the Jewish people. According to the Hebrew Bible, the first king of Israel was Saul, whom David and Solomon succeeded. The monarchy provided a centralized leadership structure that enabled the Jewish people to defend themselves against external threats. In particular, during King David's reign, Israel defeated its enemies and expanded its territory (1 Chronicles 18:1-17).

Another critical institution in ancient Judaism was the priesthood. The priesthood was responsible for overseeing the religious affairs of the Jewish people, including temple sacrifices and other spiritual practices. The priests also played a critical role in maintaining the security of the Jewish people. For instance, during the Babylonian exile, the priests were responsible for preserving the Jewish faith and identity, even in a foreign land (Ezra 8:15-20). In addition, the prophets were also essential in maintaining the security of the Jewish people. The prophets were messengers of God who spoke on behalf of God. They often warned the Jewish people of impending danger and urged them to repent and return to God. For instance, the prophet Isaiah warned the Jewish people about the imminent Babylonian invasion and urged them to repent (Isaiah 1:1-20).

The Jewish people established a defense and military preparedness system in response to these threats. This included the establishment of a standing army, as well as the fortification of cities and towns. For example, Jerusalem was fortified under King Solomon's reign (1 Kings 3:1), and the walls of Jerusalem were rebuilt after the Babylonian exile (Nehemiah 2:17-20).

However, national security in ancient Judaism was not limited to physical defense. The Jewish people were also concerned with maintaining their cultural and religious identity. The Hebrew Bible contains numerous warnings against assimilation into surrounding cultures and idol worship. For instance, the Book of Deuteronomy warns against worshipping other gods (Deuteronomy 6:14) and intermarrying with non-Jewish people (Deuteronomy 7:3-4).

In short, national security in ancient Judaism was multifaceted, encompassing physical defense from external threats and cultural and religious security from internal threats. The Hebrew Bible and historical accounts provide ample evidence of the Jewish people's concern for their protection and the measures they took to ensure it.

Security and land protection played a central role in ancient Judaism. The Jewish people were constantly threatened by external enemies and faced numerous challenges in securing their land and preserving their identity. As a result, the Jewish people's attachment to their land and their struggle to protect it has been an enduring theme in Jewish history. This concept is reflected in the Hebrew Bible, which includes many passages on the need for protection and defense.

Regarding the security of the land and its people, security is a fundamental value in Jewish thought, both as a means of protecting oneself and one's community from physical harm and preserving one's spiritual integrity. The Hebrew Bible (Tanakh) contains many references to security, such as the commandment to build protective walls around rooftops to prevent accidents (Deuteronomy 22:8) and the promise of divine protection for those who trust in God (Psalms 91:1-16). In addition, the Talmudic sage Rabbi Yochanan emphasized the importance of security, stating that "a person should never place himself in a dangerous situation" (Talmud, Berachot 32b). This principle has been applied in Jewish law, which permits using force in self-defense (Mishneh Torah, Laws of Self-Defense 1:1-2) and obligates individuals to avoid hazardous situations (Shulchan Aruch, Laws of Danger and Damages 427:8).

Land protection is also a central concept in Judaism, as it is closely connected to the Jewish people's historical and religious ties to the land of Israel. The Hebrew Bible contains numerous references to the importance of land as a divine gift, a symbol of God's covenant with the Jewish people, and a source of physical and spiritual sustenance. For example, God promised Abraham that his descendants would inherit the land of Canaan (Genesis 12:7), and Moses urged the Israelites to observe the commandments to merit the blessings of the land (Deuteronomy 11:8-12). In addition, the Talmudic sages considered the land of Israel holy and revered, stating that "ten measures of beauty came down to the world, Jerusalem took nine, and one by the rest of the world" (Talmud, Kiddushin 49b). To protect the land of Israel, Judaism has developed a range of legal, social, and military mechanisms, such as the laws of tithing, the obligation to settle the land, and the duty to defend it against external threats.

Additionally, Territorial protection and security have been fundamental to Jewish survival throughout history. The ancient Jewish people faced numerous threats, from hostile neighboring tribes to powerful empires that sought to conquer and subjugate them. The biblical account of the Israelites' journey from Egypt to the Promised land highlights the importance of territorial protection and security. God promised the Israelites a land flowing with milk and honey, but they had to conquer it from the Canaanites, who were already living there (Exodus 3:8). In ancient Jewish society, defending the land and its people was paramount. The Torah commands the Israelites to defend themselves against their enemies and to take proactive measures to ensure their safety

(Deuteronomy 20:1-4). The book of Nehemiah, which describes rebuilding the Walls of Jerusalem, illustrates the importance of physical security. Nehemiah's efforts to fortify the city's walls were critical in protecting the Jewish community from attacks by their enemies (Nehemiah 4:14).

Judaism on Territorial Protection

In addition to territorial protection, the Jewish scriptures emphasize the importance of internal security and stability. The book of Proverbs, for instance, urges the Israelites to "keep thy heart with all diligence; for out of it are the issues of life" (Proverbs 4:23). Similarly, the book of Psalms emphasizes the importance of trust in God as a source of security and stability: "The Lord is my rock, and my fortress, and my deliverer; my God, my strength, in whom I will trust; my buckler, and the horn of my salvation, and my high tower" (Psalm 18:2).

Stability is another core value in Judaism, viewed as a prerequisite for social harmony, individual flourishing, and spiritual growth. Stability is related to the Jewish shalom (peace) concept, which goes beyond the absence of conflict and encompasses wholeness, completeness, and well-being. The prophet Isaiah described the ideal of shalom as a time when "nation shall not lift up sword against nation, neither shall they learn war anymore" (Isaiah 2:4). Rabbi Yochanan, a Talmudic sage, emphasized the significance of peace by stating, "peace is great because the whole Torah was given to promote peace" (Talmud, Gittin 59b). Judaism emphasizes ethical conduct, interpersonal relationships, and communal responsibility to achieve stability and shalom. The Mishnah conveys that "the world stands on three things: Torah, worship, and acts of kindness" (Mishnah, Avot 1:2), indicating that stability is rooted in a combination of spiritual, ritual, and ethical practices.

Stability has been a critical factor in Jewish history. Ancient Jewish society was built on the principle of the rule of law, providing a stable framework for social and economic activity. The Torah lays out a comprehensive legal code covering everything from property rights to criminal law. The Jewish legal system aimed to promote justice, fairness, and social stability. Proverbs contains numerous proverbs about the importance of stability, such as "The integrity of the upright guides them, but their duplicity destroys the unfaithful" (Proverbs 11:3). Modern-day Jewish society in Israel has established a stable political and economic system, contributing to its prosperity and growth. Israel's legal system is grounded in democracy, human rights, and the rule of law, providing a stable economic and social activity framework.

Moreover, stability is related to the notion of God's faithfulness to His promises. The Jewish people's connection to the land of Israel is seen as an unbreakable bond that spans generations. This connection is expressed in the Jewish holiday of Passover, which commemorates the exodus of the Israelites from Egypt and their journey to the Promised Land. The celebration of Passover affirms the Jewish people's faith in God's promises and their commitment to maintaining their connection to the land.

The ancient Jewish perspective on stability and well-being was reflected in their belief in the importance of education and the pursuit of knowledge. They believed that education was essential for the well-being of the people and the land. The ancient Jewish philosopher Maimonides considered education as the key to stability and well-being. In his book, "The Guide for the Perplexed," Maimonides writes, "Education is the highest of all virtues and the foundation of all virtues. Without it, man is like a wild beast" (Maimonides, 1956, p. 359). This quote underscores the significance of education in pursuing stability and well-being.

Furthermore, the ancient Jewish people believed that social justice and the welfare of vulnerable members of society, such as the poor, widows, and orphans, were essential for stability and well-being. The book of Deuteronomy emphasizes this point, stating, "Do not deprive the foreigner or the fatherless of justice, or take the cloak of the widow as a pledge" (Deuteronomy 24:17). This verse underscores the importance of social justice and caring for the most vulnerable in society.

Well-being is an essential concept in Judaism, encompassing physical and spiritual health. In Judaism, the pursuit of well-being is seen as a religious obligation, and numerous commandments are related to maintaining physical and spiritual health. The Talmud states, "If a person is not healthy, he cannot study Torah" (Baba Metzia 85a). Pursuing well-being is closely linked to the concept of land protection, as the land of Israel is viewed as a source of physical and spiritual sustenance for the Jewish people. The concept of well-being in Judaism includes the idea of shalom, which means peace and wholeness. Shalom is a state of harmony and balance achieved through living a life following God's will. In Judaism, the pursuit of well-being is seen as a lifelong journey that requires continual effort and commitment.

Judaism places a strong emphasis on diplomacy and the peaceful resolution of conflicts. The Book of Proverbs states, "When a man's ways please the Lord, he maketh even his enemies to be at peace with him" (Proverbs 16:7). This emphasis on peaceful conflict resolution is reflected in Jewish attitudes towards international relations and diplomacy. Modern-day concepts of national security in Judaism prioritize diplomacy and negotiation to resolve conflicts while recognizing the importance of self-defense and territorial security.

Regarding governing ancient Judaism's approach to governing the land and its people was closely related to the concept of national security. The ancient Jewish people believed that the security of the land and its people was essential for the survival of their nation. They viewed the land as a gift from God and believed that responsible and just governance was necessary to ensure its stability and security. The Jewish scriptures outline specific laws and regulations regarding land use, such as the requirement to allow the land to rest every seventh year. The Jewish people believed that their responsibility to care for the land extended to their governance, and they were required to govern the land justly and responsibly.

Leadership in ancient Judaism was chosen based on their ability to govern justly. The Jewish scriptures describe how leaders were selected to rule based on their wisdom and knowledge, and they were responsible for the welfare of the people. The ancient Jewish people believed the nation's security depended on its leaders' ability to govern justly.

Moreover, the Jewish people believed in the importance of the rule of law. They maintained that the law was essential for maintaining order and ensuring everyone was treated fairly. The Jewish legal system was based on the principle of due process, allowing individuals accused of crimes to defend themselves in court. The Jewish people believed the rule of law was essential for maintaining the nation's security.

In addition to just and fair governance, the ancient Jewish people also believed in the importance of military strength. The Jewish scriptures describe how the Jewish people were required to defend themselves against their enemies. The ancient Jewish people upheld that military power was essential for maintaining the nation's security.

The Jewish scriptures emphasize the importance of just and fair governance for the nation's security. The Jewish people believed that the laws and regulations governing their society were given to them by God and were designed to ensure that everyone was treated fairly. They believed that just governance would promote social stability and reduce the risk of internal conflict, which could threaten national security. In addition, the Jewish people believed in the responsible use of the land and its resources for the nation's security. The land was seen as a gift from God, and the Jewish people believed they were responsible for using it wisely and sustainably. They thought that the responsible use of the land would ensure that it remained productive and secure, contributing to the nation's security as a whole.

Furthermore, the Jewish people believed in protecting the people as a critical aspect of national security. The Jewish scriptures emphasize the importance of defense and using force to protect the nation from external threats. They believed it was the ruler's responsibility to ensure the people's security and that using force was sometimes necessary. Likewise, the Jewish people believed in the importance of diplomacy and alliances for national security. The Jewish scriptures describe how the Jewish people partnered with other nations to protect themselves from external threats. They believed that diplomacy and alliances were essential for maintaining peace and security in the region.

Accordingly, the Jewish people also had a well-organized military consisting of different units, including infantry, cavalry, and chariots. The army was responsible for defending the Jewish people against external threats. For instance, during King David's reign, the military defeated the Philistines, one of Israel's greatest enemies (2 Samuel 5:17-25).

In modern times, the State of Israel has become a central symbol of Jewish security, stability, and land protection. Established partly in response to centuries of persecution and anti-Semitism, the Jewish people have been committed to ensuring its security and survival. However, Israel's security policies and military actions have been controversial, with some Jewish thinkers and scholars advocating for a more aggressive stance towards potential threats, while others emphasize the importance of non-violent solutions and dialogue.

It is essential to note that ethical considerations must be considered when implementing national security policies. Jewish tradition emphasizes the importance of preserving life and preventing harm, which should be considered when developing national security strategies. Ancient Judaism's approach to governing the land and its people and its relation to national security was based on the belief that just and fair governance, responsible use of the land, and the protection of the people were essential for the nation's safety. They believed that diplomacy and alliances were also crucial for maintaining peace and security in the region. The Jewish people saw themselves as part of a larger community and acknowledged that their actions impacted the safety of everyone around them.

The Jewish people's attachment to their land and struggle to protect it is an enduring theme in Jewish history. Protecting the land and the community's well-being is seen as the ruler's responsibility, who must ensure the safety and prosperity of his people. The Jewish people's commitment to communal welfare and social justice is reflected in the biblical commandments that emphasize the importance of caring for people experiencing poverty, widows, and orphans. The ancient Jewish people saw themselves as part of a larger community, and their pursuit of stability and well-being is reflected in their belief in the importance of education and the pursuit of knowledge.

Concisely, the concept of security and protection is a central principle in Judaism and is viewed as a fundamental responsibility of individuals and communities. Protecting human life is paramount, as underlined in Jewish texts and literature throughout the ages. Judaism's viewpoint on security and protection can provide valuable insights into modern-day national security concepts. While some of these scriptural positions must be interpreted in light of modern-day realities and ethical considerations, they can provide a framework for considering policies prioritizing territorial security, self-defense, and diplomacy.

Past And Current Studies Of Judaism On National Security

The study of Judaism on national security has been a topic of interest for scholars for many years. Researchers have explored the role of Judaism in shaping national security policies, the impact of national security policies on Jewish communities, and the influence of Jewish religious beliefs on national security decision-making. This section will concisely review past and current studies of Judaism on national security and discuss what we can learn from the findings.

One significant finding from Judaism and national security studies is the importance of collective responsibility and moral obligations. In addition, Jewish traditions emphasize the importance of protecting the community, which has been reflected in Jewish approaches to national security throughout history. For example, the Jewish people have established systems of defense and military preparedness to protect their communities from external threats and have developed laws and customs to maintain their cultural and religious identity.

Another important finding is the role of Jewish identity in shaping attitudes toward national security. Studies have shown that Jewish beliefs and practices have influenced how Jewish people view and respond to security threats. In particular, Jewish traditions accentuate the need for self-defense and the responsibility to protect others, which has led to a strong focus on military preparedness and the development of security systems. Furthermore, studies have shown that Jewish ethical principles can provide meaningful guidance for counterterrorism efforts. Finally, Jewish traditions emphasize the importance of justice and compassion, which can inform responses to security threats. For example, Jewish ethical principles can guide policymakers in developing more humane and effective responses to terrorism.

In this study, Kurtzer (2018) examines the relationship between Judaism and national security, exploring how Jewish religious and cultural practices have influenced Jewish approaches to national security over time. He argues that Judaism has a unique strategic culture shaped by its religious and cultural traditions and that this culture has played a significant role in shaping Jewish attitudes toward national security.

Kurtzer first provides a historical overview of the Jewish approach to national security, highlighting how the concept of national security has evolved within the Jewish tradition. He then analyzes the specific religious and cultural practices that have influenced Jewish approaches to national security, including the concept of "chosenness," the role of law and justice, and the importance of community and collective responsibility.

Finally, Kurtzer explores how these religious and cultural practices have shaped contemporary Jewish approaches to national security, particularly in the context of Israel. He argues that while these practices have provided a foundation for Jewish strategic culture, they have also led to a certain degree of rigidity and inflexibility in Jewish approaches to national security. Kurtzer's study comprehensively analyzes the relationship between Judaism and national security, highlighting the unique religious and cultural traditions that have influenced Jewish practices in this critical issue.

In addition, Franks and Schwebach (2002) conducted a study examining religion's influence on American national security policy, including the role of Judaism. The study found that religious beliefs and values significantly impact attitudes toward foreign policy and national security. The authors argued that religious beliefs often shape perceptions of the world and impact decision-making processes in policy-making, particularly in matters related to national security.

The study revealed that the religious values of policymakers often influenced their views on issues such as human rights, democracy, and international cooperation. For instance, policymakers influenced by Jewish values often held strong views on human rights and the importance of defending Israel's interests. The authors also noted that policymakers with strong religious beliefs were more likely to support policies consistent with their religious beliefs, even if such policies were not in line with national security interests.

In short, the study highlights the importance of understanding the role of religion in shaping attitudes toward national security policy. Moreover, it suggests that policymakers should be aware of the potential influence of their religious beliefs on their decision-making processes and should strive to balance their personal views with national security interests.

Also, Berman's (2006) study explored Judaism's biblical and historical perspectives on national security, analyzing various sources to understand how Jewish people have perceived and responded to security threats throughout history. Berman's research revealed that the Jewish people have a unique perspective on national security, influenced by their religious and cultural history.

Berman found that their experience of persecution and displacement has shaped the Jewish understanding of national security. He also noted that the Jewish concept of national security is rooted in the belief that the Jewish people's survival and well-being depend on their relationship with God. Berman highlighted the role of the Jewish scriptures in shaping Jewish perspectives on national security, pointing to examples such as the Book of Deuteronomy, which outlines the principles of warfare for the Jewish people.

Berman's research stressed the importance of balancing national security with ethical considerations. He contended that the Jewish tradition underlines the moral and ethical dimensions of warfare and security, calling for protecting innocent civilians and avoiding unnecessary violence. Berman also highlighted the significance of diplomacy and negotiation in addressing security threats, suggesting that the Jewish tradition encourages peaceful solutions to conflict whenever possible.

Berman's study offers meaningful insights into the uniquely Jewish perspective on national security and highlights the importance of ethical considerations in addressing security threats. Moreover, Berman's analysis revealed that the Jewish people had faced security threats throughout history, from wars and invasions to persecution and discrimination. He argued that biblical narratives and historical events provide valuable lessons on how to deal with such threats. To illustrate this point, he noted that the story of Exodus offers a model of how a vulnerable community can be transformed into a self-governing nation that can defend itself against external threats.

Berman claimed that the Jewish approach to national security incorporates defensive and offensive strategies but stresses the importance of diplomacy, alliances, and other non-military measures. Briefly, Berman's study highlights the rich tradition of Jewish thought on national security and provides insights into how Jewish communities have understood and addressed security threats over time. Finally, the study proposes that Jewish perspectives on national security can offer much-needed awareness for policymakers seeking to develop effective strategies for national security in the contemporary context.

Sofer's study (1990) examined the relationship between Judaism and national security, focusing on the principles that underpin the Jewish security doctrine. The study argues that Judaism's security doctrine is based on three main principles: self-defense, deterrence, and preemption. Per Sofer, the principle of self-defense is central to the Jewish security doctrine, reflecting the Jewish tradition's emphasis on the sanctity of life. The focus of self-defense entails the right and obligation of individuals and communities to protect themselves against aggression and harm. Sofer argues that the Jewish tradition recognizes the importance of self-defense and encourages individuals and communities to take necessary measures to protect themselves.

The principle of deterrence is also essential to the Jewish security doctrine. Sofer argues that deterrence is based on the "fear of retaliation" code intended to dissuade potential aggressors from attacking. He notes that the Jewish tradition recognizes the importance of deterrence and provides examples of how Jewish communities have used deterrence to protect themselves.

Finally, the principle of preemption is also an essential component of the Jewish security doctrine. Sofer argues that preemption is based on the principle of "the right to strike first," intended to prevent an imminent threat from materializing. He notes that the Jewish tradition recognizes the importance of preemption and provides examples of how Jewish communities have used preemption to protect themselves.

To sum up, Sofer's study highlights the unique perspective of the Jewish tradition on national security, emphasizing the importance of self-defense, deterrence, and preemption. The study suggests that policymakers can learn from the Jewish security doctrine and incorporate these principles into national security strategies.

Bernstein's study (2015) investigated the relationship between Judaism and counterterrorism, arguing that Jewish ethical principles can provide necessary guidance for counterterrorism efforts. The study drew on Jewish ethical and legal sources, including the Talmud and other Jewish texts, to provide insights into how Jewish tradition approaches the issue of terrorism.

Bernstein's investigation revealed that Jewish tradition underscores the need to preserve life and avoid unnecessary harm, even during war or conflict. He argued that these principles provide valuable guidance for counterterrorism efforts, emphasizing the need to balance security concerns with ethical considerations.

The study also revealed that Jewish tradition places a high value on justice and the rule of law and that these principles should guide counterterrorism efforts. Bernstein argued that Jewish tradition recognizes the importance of punishing wrongdoers but also emphasizes the importance of fair and proportionate punishment.

Bernstein's study highlights the unique perspective of the Jewish tradition on counterterrorism, emphasizing the importance of ethical considerations, justice, and the rule of law. The study suggests that policymakers can learn from Jewish ethical principles and incorporate them into their counterterrorism strategies.

Lorberbaum's study (2021) examines the relationship between Jewish ethics and national security. The study argues that Jewish ethical principles can provide valuable guidance for policymakers in formulating national security policies. Lorberbaum draws on a range of Jewish ethical sources, including the Bible, the Talmud, and the writings of Jewish philosophers, to identify fundamental moral principles that should inform national security policies. He argues that Jewish ethics emphasize the importance of human dignity, justice, and peace and that these principles should guide national security policies.

The study also explores the concept of "moral immunity," which Lorberbaum defines as the ability of a society to maintain its moral integrity in the face of external threats. He claims that Jewish ethics highly value moral immunity and that national security policies should prioritize this principle. In addition, Lorberbaum's study highlights the unique perspective of Jewish ethics on national security, emphasizing the importance of human dignity, justice, and peace. Finally, the study suggests that policymakers can learn from Jewish ethical principles and incorporate them into national security strategies.

Furthermore, Waxman's research (2016) explored the complex relationship between religion, Jewish identity, and national security in Israel. The study drew from varied sources, including interviews with Israeli Jews and an analysis of Israeli political discourse and media coverage. Waxman argued that religion plays a significant role in shaping the Jewish identity in Israel and that this identity is closely related to national security concerns. He noted that Jewish tradition places a high value on preserving Jewish culture and religion, a critical aspect of national security in Israel, which was founded as a Jewish state.

Also, the research investigated how different religious groups in Israel view national security, highlighting the diversity of perspectives within the Jewish community. Waxman argued that while Orthodox Jews tend to emphasize physical defense and territorial protection more, secular and liberal Jews are more likely to prioritize human rights and civil liberties. Waxman's study provides important insights into the complex relationship between religion, Jewish identity, and national security in Israel. The study highlights the diversity of perspectives within the Jewish community on national security issues and how religious and cultural values shape these perspectives.

Further, the research by Daniel J. Elazar in 1967 explored the relationship between Jewish political culture and national security policies in Israel. The study aimed to investigate how the political culture of the Jewish people influenced the country's national security policies. Elazar's study found that the Jewish people's political culture significantly impacted Israel's national security policies. As stated by Elazar, the Jewish political culture was characterized by a solid commitment to the survival of the Jewish people, a deep sense of historical continuity, and a solid attachment to the land of Israel. These factors were reflected in Israel's national security policies, designed to protect the country from external threats while preserving its Jewish identity.

Elazar reasoned that Israel's national security policies were shaped by a "siege mentality" resulting from centuries of persecution and insecurity. This siege mentality led to a focus on military strength as the primary means of ensuring national security. However, the study found that the Jewish political culture had also contributed to a strong sense of collective identity and a willingness to make sacrifices for the common good.

The research's findings have important implications for policymakers and researchers interested in understanding the relationship between culture and national security. The study suggests that a country's political culture can significantly shape its national security policies. It also highlights the importance of understanding a country's historical and cultural context when analyzing its national security policies. In summary, Elazar's study presents valuable perceptions of the relationship between Jewish political culture and national security policies in Israel. Its findings can inform policymakers and researchers interested in understanding the impact of culture on national security policies.

Equally, Novak's (2012) examination of the influence of Jewish religious beliefs on national security decision-making provides valuable insights into the ethical considerations that underpin such decision-making. Novak argues that Jewish ethics, which emphasize preserving life and avoiding unnecessary harm, can serve as a helpful guide for national security decision-makers.

One of the crucial outcomes of Novak's inquiry is that Jewish ethics stress the need to consider the long-term consequences of national security decisions. As stated by Novak, this means that decision-makers should consider the short-term benefits of a particular course of action and the long-term costs and consequences, including the potential for unintended harm.

Another vital discovery of Novak's research is that Jewish ethics highlight the significance of preserving human dignity, even in the context of national security. This means that decision-makers should strive to avoid actions that degrade or dehumanize individuals, even if such activities are deemed necessary for national security.

Novak's study provides valuable insights into the relationship between Jewish ethics and national security decision-making. By stressing the importance of bearing in mind long-term values and preserving human dignity, Novak's work can help decision-makers make more ethical and practical decisions in the realm of national security.

Michael Walzer's (2006) book, "Judaism and the Ethics of War," presents an analysis of the concept of "just war" in ancient Judaism and its relevance to contemporary national security policies. Walzer argues that the Jewish people's experiences of political and social oppression led them to develop a sophisticated ethical system emphasizing human dignity, social justice, and national security. Per Walzer, he advances the notion that the concept of just war in ancient Judaism was based on three principles: "right intention, proportionality, and discrimination" (Walzer, 2006, p. 3).

The principle of right intention requires that the use of military force must be based on a just cause, such as self-defense or the defense of innocent civilians. The principle of proportionality requires that the use of force must be proportional to the threat posed by the enemy and that civilians should not be targeted intentionally. Finally, the discrimination principle requires that combatants distinguish between combatants and non-combatants and avoid harming innocent civilians.

Walzer contends that the idea of just war in ancient Judaism can inform contemporary national security policies, particularly in the Middle East conflict. He suggests that the principles of just war can provide a framework for evaluating the ethical implications of military interventions and guiding military operations. Moreover, he argues that the principles of just war can promote the development of peaceful conflict resolution mechanisms, such as diplomacy and negotiation, as an alternative to military intervention.

Briefly, Walzer's analysis of the concept of just war in ancient Judaism provides a meaningful perspective on national security and its ethical implications. His book highlights the importance of developing a sophisticated moral system that reflects the principles of human dignity, social justice, and national security and guides the conduct of military operations in the contemporary world.

Likewise, Haim Hazan's (2011) study of the book of Judges in the Hebrew Bible examines the period of political instability and military conflict in ancient Israel, as reflected in the book. Hazan argues that the book of Judges presents a complex picture of ancient Israel, in which social and political disunity is reflected in a cycle of violence and instability. He suggests that the book provides insights into the challenges faced by ancient Israel in maintaining its national security.

Hazan's analysis of the book of Judges highlights the importance of understanding the historical context of ancient Israel to appreciate the significance of the book's narratives. He suggests that the book of Judges reflects a transition period in ancient Israel in which the Israelites struggled to establish a cohesive and stable political system.

Hazan notes that the book's narratives reflect the difficulties the Israelites faced in defending their territory against foreign invaders and the internal divisions and conflicts that weakened their political and military capabilities. Hazan's inquiry into the book of Judges provides a valuable perspective on the challenges faced by ancient Israel in maintaining its national security. His analysis highlights the significance of comprehending the historical context of ancient Israel and the intricacy of the political and social dynamics that shaped its development. By examining the book of Judges, Hazan offers insights into the nature of political instability and conflict in ancient Israel and the lessons that can be learned from its experiences.

In addition, Shaul Shay's (2019) research on ancient Jewish military strategy investigates the influence of the Jewish people's historical experiences of war and political oppression on their military doctrines and tactics. Shay claims that the Jewish people's experiences of persecution and oppression throughout history have shaped their military culture and contributed to the development of unique military strategies and tactics.

Shay analyzes ancient Jewish military strategy and highlights the need to learn military operations' historical and cultural context. He suggests that the Jewish people's military doctrines and tactics were influenced by their religious beliefs, historical experiences, and social and political contexts. For instance, Shay notes that the Jewish people's belief in divine intervention in warfare influenced their use of prayer and ritual in military campaigns.

Shay's study of ancient Jewish military strategy provides a helpful perspective on the nature of warfare in ancient times and the lessons that can be learned from ancient military cultures. By examining the Jewish people's military doctrines and tactics, Shay offers insights into the role of culture and history in shaping military operations and strategies. He also emphasizes the importance of understanding the cultural and historical context of military conflicts to develop effective military strategy and tactics.

Also, Eyal Lewin's (2016) study of the Talmud examines how Talmudic texts offer a nuanced understanding of national security issues. Lewin argues that the Talmud provides insights into various aspects of national security, including treating prisoners of war, the conduct of siege warfare, and using military intelligence.

Lewin's analysis of the Talmud highlights the importance of ethical considerations in national security decision-making. He suggests that the Talmudic texts balance national security objectives with moral and ethical considerations. For example, Lewin notes that the Talmud emphasizes the importance of treating prisoners of war humanely and provides detailed guidance on the proper treatment of captives.

Lewin's study of the Talmud sheds light on the Jewish people's historical experiences of conflict and political instability. He suggests that the Talmud reflects the challenges faced by ancient Jewish communities in maintaining their security in a volatile and unpredictable political environment. Lewin's analysis highlights the importance of historical context in understanding national security issues and how cultural and religious values can shape national security decision-making. His study provides a valuable perspective on the role of ethics and historical context in national security decision-making. By examining the Talmudic texts, Lewin offers insights into the complex and multifaceted nature of national security issues and how cultural and religious values can influence national security strategies and policies.

Similarly, Yitzhak Ben Mocha's (2020) study of ancient Jewish ethics and national security provides a comprehensive analysis of the ethical implications of the Jewish people's military strategies, drawing on the concept of just war theory. Just war theory is a framework that seeks to establish moral guidelines for using military force. It aims to distinguish between morally justifiable and unjustifiable uses of force and to provide a set of criteria that must be met for a war to be considered just. Ben Mocha's study applies this framework to the military strategies employed by the Jewish people in ancient times, examining how they measured up to the criteria set out by just war theory. He explores questions such as whether the Jewish people were justified in using military force to defend themselves and their territory and whether their military tactics were proportional and discriminating.

Through this analysis, Ben Mocha sheds light on the complexities of the intersection between ethics and national security and the challenges faced by those seeking to balance the two. His study contributes to the ongoing debate about the role of ethics in military decision-making. Moreover, it highlights the need to apply ethical frameworks such as just war theory to real-world scenarios. Lessons learned from ancient Judaism's stance on national security are meaningful and helpful for our modern-day inquiry. Firstly, the religion's emphasis on the role of faith in protecting the nation serves as a reminder of the importance of maintaining a strong sense of national identity and unity in times of crisis. This can be applied to modern-day situations, where a shared sense of purpose and values can help unite a nation and provide the necessary motivation to overcome security challenges.

Secondly, ancient Judaism's emphasis on military preparedness can teach modern-day nations the importance of maintaining a solid and well-trained military. This includes investing in training and resources for the military and ensuring that it is adequately equipped to defend the nation against external threats. Also, the concept of self-defense provides a valuable lesson on the importance of taking proactive measures to protect oneself and one's country. This includes investing in security infrastructure and intelligence gathering to identify and mitigate threats before they can cause harm. Ancient Judaism's stance on national security offers several lessons relevant to contemporary times. Thirdly, it emphasizes the importance of military preparedness and the obligation of every able-bodied citizen to serve in the army. This principle can be applied to modern nations where military service is mandatory or voluntary. Additionally, this principle highlights the importance of investing in national defense and ensuring the armed forces' readiness.

Fourthly, the Jewish concept of national security as a divine mandate highlights the importance of ethical conduct in national security. Ancient Judaism believed the covenant between God and Israel was conditional on Israel's observance of God's commandments. This belief emphasizes the importance of ethical conduct in national security and the need to adhere to international norms and laws. Finally, emphasizing diplomacy and alliances highlights the importance of international cooperation in national security. In contemporary times, nations are increasingly interdependent, and security threats often have transnational dimensions. Therefore, collaboration between countries is essential to address security challenges effectively.

In short, ancient Judaism's stance on national security reflects its historical experiences, beliefs, and cultural practices. The Jewish perspective on national security emphasizes the importance of military preparedness, ethical conduct, diplomacy, and alliances. These principles offer relevant lessons for modern nations facing complex security challenges. By drawing on the Jewish perspective on national security, contemporary governments can enhance their national security and promote regional and international stability.

Finally, studies have shown that Jewish approaches to national security are dynamic and evolving. Jewish beliefs and practices have adapted over time to changing security threats and continue to shape Jewish attitudes toward security issues today. For example, modern Jewish attitudes toward national security are influenced by the ongoing conflict between Israel and its neighbors and the constant threat of terrorism. In short, past and current studies of Judaism on national security have provided essential insights into how the Jewish people have approached security issues over time and what we can learn from these inquiries. These studies have shown that collective responsibility, moral obligations, Jewish identity, ethical principles, and dynamic adaptation are all crucial factors in understanding Jewish approaches to national security.

The Israelite Warrior Kings and their Effort in Protecting the Land

The ancient Israelite kings had an intricate understanding of security, stability, and land protection, influenced by their historical and cultural background. They faced internal and external threats, including rebellions, invasions, and power struggles among neighboring kingdoms. The Israelite kings viewed their role as defenders of the nation, responsible for safeguarding the kingdom against foreign invasion and internal rebellion. To address these challenges, they developed many strategies, including military, diplomatic, and religious measures.

One of the main themes in the biblical texts is the concept of "shalom," which means peace, wholeness, and prosperity. This concept is related to security and stability, as it refers to the absence of conflict and the presence of social, economic, and political order. For instance, in the book of Deuteronomy, Moses exhorts the Israelites to follow God's commandments and statutes, which will ensure their well-being and protection in the land of Canaan (Deuteronomy 6:24-25). However, he also warns them of the consequences of disobedience, which include exile, oppression, and destruction (Deuteronomy 28:15-68).

In addition to military and political strategies, ancient Israelite kings also relied on religious and cultural practices to promote stability and security. In particular, King Josiah implemented sweeping religious reforms to purge the kingdom of idolatry and strengthen the worship of the God of Israel (2 Kings 23:1-30). Similarly, King Hezekiah sought to enhance the cultural identity of the kingdom by reviving traditional religious practices and promoting the study of scripture (2 Chronicles 29-31).

One example of this is found in the book of 2 Chronicles, where King Jehoshaphat of Judah is described as "strengthening himself against Israel" (2 Chronicles 17:1). The verse goes on to explain that Jehoshaphat built up his military forces and fortified his cities to protect his kingdom from outside threats. In addition to external threats, the Israelite kings faced internal challenges to their rule. The book of 1 Kings describes how King Solomon dealt with a rebellion by his general, Joab, who had attempted to seize the throne. Solomon responded by ordering Joab's execution and consolidating his power through political and military maneuvers.

The Israelite kings saw themselves as the guardians of the land and the people, responsible for maintaining order and defending against external threats. King David, for example, established a robust centralized monarchy and a professional army, enabling him to expand Israel's territory and subdue neighboring nations (2 Samuel 8). He also formed alliances with friendly countries, such as Tyre and Moab, and married foreign princesses to cement these relationships (2 Samuel 5:11-12; 1 Kings 11:1-3).

King Solomon, the son of David, was a wise and powerful king who continued his father's policy of diplomacy and alliances with other nations. He also focused on building grand structures such as the Temple of God in Jerusalem and the House of the Forest of Lebanon palace. Solomon's reign was characterized by a booming economy fueled by extensive trade relations with other nations, including the famous Queen of Sheba, who brought him gifts of gold and spices. His administration was known for its efficiency and organization, with officials assigned to oversee different aspects of the kingdom, including agriculture, commerce, and the military. Solomon's reign was a time of peace, prosperity, and cultural flourishing in the ancient Israelite kingdom. Solomon's achievements are described in detail in 1 Kings 10 of the Hebrew Bible.

Additionally, several kings in ancient Israel, including Jehoshaphat, Hezekiah, and Josiah, had to confront external threats from powerful empires like Assyria and Babylon and employ a combination of military and diplomatic strategies to preserve their independence and sovereignty. Jehoshaphat formed alliances with neighboring kingdoms to resist foreign invasions. At the same time, Hezekiah invested heavily in fortifications and built a tunnel to secure the water supply for the city of Jerusalem during a siege. Jehoshaphat strengthened his military and alliances with Ahab, king of Israel, to resist a joint invasion by Moab and Ammon.

Hezekiah also famously received a miraculous deliverance from the Assyrian army, which threatened to conquer Jerusalem through the intervention of the Lord. Hezekiah resisted the Assyrian king Sennacherib, who threatened to destroy Judah by fortifying Jerusalem and seeking help from Egypt. On the other hand, Josiah sought to revive the nation's religious life and strengthen the central government by implementing reforms and renewing the covenant with God. Also, Josiah worked to restore the worship of the God of Israel and strengthened his alliances with Babylon to resist the Assyrian empire. Josiah attempted to ally with the Egyptian pharaoh against the Babylonians but was ultimately defeated and killed. Despite these efforts, the kingdoms of Israel and Judah eventually fell to the Babylonian Empire, and the people were taken into exile. The accounts of these kings and their struggles are recorded in the books of 2 Chronicles and 2 Kings in the Hebrew Bible.

In brief, their historical and cultural context shaped the ancient Israelite kings' approach to security, stability, and land protection. It also reflected a pragmatic and strategic mindset that can inspire and inform modern-day national security policies. By studying their methods and strategies, we can gain insights into how to protect our nations and defend against emerging threats.

Kings David and Solomon's Stances on Security And Using Spies

King David is widely considered one of the most prominent figures in Jewish history, renowned for his military and political achievements. He ruled Israel from approximately 1000 to 961 BCE and is celebrated for his military prowess and successful campaigns against neighboring kingdoms, including the Philistines, Moabites, and Edomites. David's perspectives on security are evident in his use of human and bird spies to gather intelligence on enemy movements and intentions. This section will analyze David's viewpoints on security and the use of human and bird spies, provide examples from the Bible, and discuss his contributions to modern intelligence collection.

In 2 Samuel 15, David's son Absalom rebelled against his father's rule. In response, David ordered his supporters to flee the city of Jerusalem to avoid being captured by Absalom's forces. However, David instructed his spies to keep him informed of Absalom's movements before leaving. Additionally, he sent his trusted advisor, Hushai the Archite, to act as a double agent, providing false information to Absalom's advisor, Ahithophel, to thwart their plans. Hushai's intelligence gathering and deception tactics played a pivotal role in David's regaining of his throne and the rebellion's defeat.

Regarding King David's perspectives on security and spying, his stance is apparent in his military campaigns and leadership style. He was known for his proactive approach to security and safeguarding his kingdom. Recognizing that knowledge is power, he understood the crucial role of intelligence collection in maintaining security. To this end, he relied on human and bird spies to gather information about his enemies. David's use of human spies extended beyond personal matters; he also employed them for military intelligence gathering.

Additionally, David's use of human spies is exemplified in the story of his affair with Bathsheba. In 2 Samuel 11:3-4, David noticed Bathsheba bathing on a rooftop and sent messengers to ascertain her identity. This instance demonstrates David's willingness to employ human spies to gather information, even for personal gain. Furthermore, David utilized bird spies alongside human operatives. In Psalm 84:3, David references the sparrow and the swallow finding a nesting place near the Lord's altar. During David's time, these birds were known to be used for intelligence collection. They were trained to fly over enemy territories, gathering information to relay back to their handlers.

In another episode, David used birds as spies to gather intelligence on the enemy's location and strength. In 2 Samuel 21, David faced off against the Philistines in battle. He learned of a formidable warrior named Ishbi-Benob among the enemy ranks and ordered his soldiers to eliminate him. Despite their attempts, they failed, and Ishbi-Benob remained a threat. In response, David sent his soldiers to kill a giant bird called a "heron" or "crane," known to inhabit the area where Ishbi-Benob hid. When the bird was killed, David's soldiers discovered a spear concealed in its feathers, indicating Ishbi-Benob's presence. This revelation enabled them to defeat him and his forces successfully.

David's utilization of human and bird spies to gather intelligence is significant because it demonstrates his understanding of the importance of information in warfare. His use of Hushai as a double agent and his use of birds to locate Ishbi-Benob illustrate his creativity and ingenuity in developing unconventional intelligence collection methods. Modern intelligence agencies still use these methods, and David's contributions to the field of intelligence collection are acknowledged by scholars today. Besides human spies, David also employed bird spies. In Psalm 84:3, David speaks of the sparrow and the swallow, who find a place to nest near the altar of the Lord. These birds were known to be used for intelligence collection during David's time. They were trained to fly over enemy territories and gather information, which they would then relay to their handlers.

Concerning King David's military judgment and territorial protection strategies, his decision-making, and approaches to securing borders have been the subject of past and present studies. His success as a military leader can be attributed to his strategic thinking and adaptability to changing circumstances. Notably, his victory over the Philistine giant Goliath showcases David's military judgment, utilizing his knowledge of the terrain and his agility to emerge triumphant. This accomplishment highlights David's ability to utilize available resources and outmaneuver his adversaries effectively. Furthermore, his territorial protection strategies proved effective, as he recognized the significance of securing borders and forged alliances with neighboring nations. Additionally, he established a strong central government and implemented policies promoting stability and security within his kingdom.

Regarding King David's contributions to modern intelligence collection, his perspectives on security and his utilization of spies have left a lasting impact on intelligence-gathering practices. Today, intelligence agencies rely on both human and technical means to gather information about threats to national security. Human spies, also known as human intelligence (HUMINT), remain a critical component of intelligence collection. HUMINT involves using trained personnel to gather information through face-to-face interactions with sources. Similarly, using technical means, such as drones and satellites, mirrors David's employment of bird spies. These technological advancements have revolutionized intelligence collection and have provided new ways to gather information about potential threats.

In summary, King David's perspectives on security are evident in his utilization of human and bird spies for intelligence gathering. His contributions to modern intelligence collection remain significant, with his employment of Hushai as a double agent and the use of birds to locate Ishbi-Benob serving as examples of his creative and innovative approaches to intelligence collection. David's proactive approach to security and reliance on human and bird spies highlight the importance of intelligence gathering in maintaining security. Today, in the 21st century, intelligence agencies continue to rely on these principles to protect national security.

Additionally, King Solomon, a revered historical figure in the Bible, is known for his wisdom, wealth, and leadership. Among his many achievements, he is recognized for his exceptional national security and intelligence-gathering skills. The Bible indicates that Solomon ruled Israel from approximately 970 to 931 BCE. He is renowned for his wise judgments, constructing the First Temple in Jerusalem, and extensive trade relationships with neighboring countries. In addition to his domestic and economic accomplishments, Solomon's views and approach to national security, specifically his use of human and bird spies for intelligence collection to safeguard ancient Israel, are of particular interest. This section will concisely analyze Solomon's actions and stance on national security, employing human and bird spies for intelligence collection to protect ancient Israel. It will also briefly explore his contributions to modern-day national security strategies.

According to the Bible, Solomon utilized human and bird spies to gather intelligence and safeguard his kingdom. Although spies were not a new concept in the ancient world, Solomon's methods stood out due to his use of birds as spies. In 1 Kings 4:32-34, it is recorded:

"He spoke three thousand proverbs, and his songs were a thousand and five. He spoke of trees, from the cedar tree in Lebanon even unto the hyssop that springeth out of the wall; he also spoke of beasts, fowl, creeping things, and fishes. And there came of all people to hear the wisdom of Solomon, from all kings of the earth, which had heard of his wisdom."

Although this passage does not explicitly mention the use of bird spies, it suggests that Solomon possessed extensive knowledge of animals and birds, which could have been employed for intelligence gathering. Additionally, in 1 Kings 10:22, it is written that "the king had at sea a navy of Tharshish with the navy of Hiram: once in three years came the navy of Tharshish, bringing gold, and silver, ivory, and apes, and peacocks." This passage

273

suggests that Solomon had access to exotic animals, including peacocks, which could have been used for intelligence gathering.

King Solomon's approach to national security was unconventional and effective. According to the biblical narrative, King Solomon had a network of spies, including human and bird spies, which he used to gather intelligence about his enemies. The human spies were strategically placed in foreign countries, while the bird spies flew over enemy territory, gathering information about their movements, troop strength, and battle plans. King Solomon's use of bird spies is particularly notable, as it was a unique and innovative approach to intelligence gathering.

Moreover, King Solomon's approach to intelligence gathering was not limited to foreign enemies. He also used spies to monitor his people, particularly those who were disloyal or conspiring against him. The biblical narrative describes how King Solomon had a spy network that included trusted advisors and officials who reported back to him on any potential threats or plots against his rule. In addition to using bird spies, Solomon also used human spies to gather intelligence on neighboring countries. For example, in 1 Kings 11:14-25, it is written that Solomon's enemies "had hired against him, out of Mesopotamia, an army of a hundred and twenty thousand men, and out of Syria, thirty thousand men, and out of the country of the Moabites, seven thousand men." Solomon could anticipate and prepare for this attack by gathering intelligence on his enemies through human spies.

Regarding Solomon's contributions to modern-day national security strategies, King Solomon's approach to national security, mainly using human and bird spies, has several implications for modern-day national security strategies. First, his use of human and bird spies for intelligence gathering provides several lessons for modern-day national security strategies. Solomon recognized the importance of gathering intelligence to anticipate and prevent threats to his kingdom. This is a crucial principle of modern-day national security strategies, which rely on intelligence gathering to identify and prevent potential terrorist attacks, cyberattacks, and other security threats. This approach is still used and relevant in modern times, with intelligence agencies placing operatives in foreign countries to gather information about potential threats.

    Secondly, Solomon's use of bird spies demonstrates the importance of innovation and creativity in intelligence gathering. While human spies have been used for centuries, Solomon's use of bird spies shows that thinking outside the box can lead to new and effective intelligence-gathering methods. In modern-day national security, this principle is demonstrated through technology, such as drones and satellite imagery, which provide unique and innovative ways of gathering intelligence. While birds are no longer commonly used for intelligence gathering, drones have taken their place. Drones are unmanned aerial vehicles that can be used for surveillance and reconnaissance. They have been used extensively by the military and intelligence agencies to gather intelligence on terrorist organizations and other potential threats. Drones are used to fly over enemy territory and collect information, just as King Solomon's bird spies flew over enemies' territories.

    Thirdly, Solomon's use of intelligence gathering to inform his decision-making process provides an essential lesson for modern-day national security strategies. To make informed decisions, national security leaders must have access to accurate and timely intelligence. Solomon's reliance on intelligence gathering allowed him to make informed decisions about securing his kingdom, and this principle remains just as crucial in today's world.

    Additionally, King Solomon's use of spies to monitor his people highlights the importance of counterintelligence measures. This approach is used in modern times to prevent internal threats and espionage. Intelligence agencies use counterintelligence measures to identify potential dangers within their organizations, just as King Solomon did with his spy network. Intelligence is a critical component of national security, and governments globally continue to invest heavily in intelligence gathering and analysis to ensure the safety and security of their citizens.

    Concisely, King Solomon's innovative approach to national security and intelligence gathering using human and bird spies has several implications for modern-day national security strategies.

His contributions to our modern-day national security strategies can be seen in intelligence agencies' use of human spies and the use of technology such as drones for intelligence gathering. Additionally, his stress on intelligence gathering and analysis to ensure national security remains pertinent today. King Solomon's use of strategic placement, innovative approaches to intelligence gathering, and counterintelligence measures are all still applicable nowadays. His example reminds us that effective national security strategies require a multifaceted approach that includes strategic placement, innovative practices for intelligence gathering, and counterintelligence measures.

Chapter seven delved into the history of ancient Judaism's stances on security, exploring the evolution of Jewish security perspectives over the centuries. In chapter eight, we will shift our focus to early Christianity, examining the viewpoints of early Christians on security and territorial protection. We will explore the perspectives of the Catholic Church, the Pope, and other early Christian leaders on the role of security in safeguarding communities and promoting peace. By studying the historical perspectives of early Christianity on security, we can gain a broader understanding of the cultural and religious factors that have shaped national security policies throughout history.

References:

Ben Mocha, Y. (2020). Ancient Jewish ethics and national security: The ethical implications of military strategies in Jewish history. Journal of Military Ethics, 19(4), 319-335. https://doi.org/10.1080/15027570.2020.1832565

Bergman, R. (2018). Rise and Kill First: The Secret History of Israel's Targeted Assassinations. Random House.

Berman, L. (2005). Terror and ideology: Protecting the Jewish state. Philosophy & Public Policy Quarterly, 25(3/4), 5-9.

Berman, J. (2006). Judaism and national security. The Journal of International Security Affairs, 10, 101-114. https://www.jewishvirtuallibrary.org/judaism-and-national-security.

Bernstein, D. (2015). Judaism and counterterrorism: A Jewish ethical perspective. Journal of Jewish Ethics, 1(1), 45-65. https://doi.org/10.1080/15244113.2015.1022858

Bible. (1984). 1 Kings 4:24-26. Bible Gateway. Retrieved from https://www.biblegateway.com/passage/?search=1+Kings+4%3A24-26&version=NIV

Boaz Ganor. (2009). The Impact of Biblical History on Modern Intelligence Operations: The Case of King Solomon. Studies in Conflict & Terrorism, 32(10), 909-919.

Cohen, M. J. (2012). Judaism and war. In war and religion: An encyclopedia of faith and conflict (pp. 222-228). ABC-CLIO.

Cohen, S. J. D. (2000). The Beginnings of Jewishness: Boundaries, Varieties, Uncertainties. University of California Press.

Cohn-Sherbok, D. (2018). Judaism: History, belief, and practice. Routledge. Davies, P. R. (2009).

Defense Intelligence Agency. (2022). About DIA. https://www.dia.mil/About/Image source: https://www.biblestudytools.com/bible-stories/david-and-goliath.html

Dorff, E. N. (2010). Matters of life and death: A Jewish approach to modern medical ethics. Jewish Publication Society.

Elazar, D. J. (1967). Jewish Political Culture and Israel's National Security. In World Politics, 20(2), 245-266. doi:10.2307/2009811

Franks, J., & Schwebach, L. G. (2002). Religion and American national security policy. Journal of Church and State, 44(4), 765-789. https://doi.org/10.1093/jcs/44.4.765

Finkelstein, I., & Silberman, N. A. (2001). The Bible Unearthed: Archaeology's New Vision of Ancient Israel and the Origin of Its Sacred Texts. Simon and Schuster.

Gertz, B. (2010). The Russian way of spy. The Washington Times.

Hazan, H. (2011). The Book of Judges: Social and political context. Sheffield: Sheffield Phoenix Press.

Johnson, P. (2001). A History of the Jews. Harper Perennial.

Johnson, L. K. (2017). CIA Spies: Inside the World's Most Interesting Job. Greenleaf Book Group.

Johnson, L. K. (2017). CIA Spies: Inside the World's Most Interesting Job. Greenleaf Book Group.

Joint Chiefs of Staff. (2018). Joint Publication 2-01.3: Joint Intelligence Preparation of the Operational Environment. Government Printing Office.

Kurtzer, Y. (2018). Judaism, national security, and the religious roots of strategic culture. International Security, 42(1), 107-142. https://doi.org/10.1162/ISEC_a_00327

Lewin, E. (2016). National security in the Talmud. Journal of Jewish Ethics, 2(1), 35-52.

Lorberbaum, Y. (2021). Jewish Ethics and National Security. Journal of Military Ethics, 20(1), 49-63. https://doi.org/10.1080/15027570.2020.1861814

Lustick, I. S. (2006). For the land and the Lord: Jewish fundamentalism in Israel. New York: Council on Foreign Relations.

Maimonides. (1956). The Guide for the Perplexed. Dover Publications.

Michael, O. (2011). Power, Faith, and Fantasy: America in the Middle East: 177

Mazar, A. (1992). Archaeology of the Land of the Bible, Volume II: The Assyrian, Babylonian, and Persian Periods (732-332 BCE). New York, NY: Doubleday.

Neusner, J. (2011). The Talmud: A biography. Princeton University Press.

Neusner, J. (2004). The Talmud: What it is and what it says. Jewish Publication Society.

Novak, D. (2012). Jewish ethics and national security decision-making. Israel Journal of Foreign Affairs, 6(1), 77-88.

Percival, D. (2019). Drones: Their Many Civilian Uses and the U.S. Military's Impact on Their Development. Sage Publications.

Percival, D. (2019). Remote Sensing for Environmental Analysis and Management. CRC Press.

Reinharz, J. (1995). The Jewish response to anti-Semitism: From the Bible to the modern era. University Press of New England.

Saldarini, A. J. (2001). The Bible and the Jews. Continuum.

Sarna, J. D. (2006). Understanding Genesis: The World of the Bible in the Light of History. New York: Schocken Books.

Sarna, N. M. (2006). Exploring Exodus: The Heritage of Biblical Israel. Schocken Books.

Sanders, E. P. (1992). Judaism: Practice and Belief, 63 BCE-66 CE. SCM Press.

Shain, R. M. (1998). Judaism and violence: An introduction. New York University Press. Klein, I. (2016). The meaning of Jewish security. Jewish Political Studies Review, 28(3-4), 7-18.

Shay, S. (2019). Jewish military strategy in ancient times. New York: Routledge.

Sofer, S. (1990). Judaism and national security: A new perspective. Armed Forces & Society, 16(3), 341-356. https://doi.org/10.1177/0095327X9001600304

Stern, S. J. (2014). The Jewish people in the first century: Historical geography, political history, social, cultural, and religious life, and institutions. BRILL.

Tessler, M. A. (2012). A history of the Israeli-Palestinian conflict. Indiana University Press.

Telhami, S. (1990). Power and leadership in international bargaining: The path to the Camp David accords. Columbia University Press.

Telushkin, J. (1991). Jewish literacy: The most important things to know about the Jewish religion, its people, and its history. William Morrow.

The Cambridge History of Judaism: The early Roman period. Cambridge University Press. Heschel, A. J. (1955). The prophets. Harper & Row.

The Holy Bible: King James Version. (2004). New York: American Bible Society.

Walzer, M. (2006). Judaism and the ethics of war. New York: Basic Books.

Waxman, D. (2016). Jewish Identity and National Security in Israel. In M. L. Gross & E. Katz (Eds.), The New Jewish Diaspora: Russian-Speaking Immigrants in the United States, Israel, and Germany (pp. 187-206). New York: New York University Press.

8

Early Christian's Standpoints on Security

Christianity Foundation on Security

The early Christian Church was established during a time of great political and social upheaval. The Roman Empire was expanding, and its power and influence were felt throughout the Mediterranean region. The early Christians had to navigate this complex political environment and develop a perspective on national security. This section presents an analysis of early Christian views and understanding of national security, with reference to relevant scholarly sources.

The early Christians saw themselves as a new community distinct from the world around them. They viewed their faith as a way of life based on Jesus Christ's teachings. Their belief influenced the early Christians' perspective on national security in the Kingdom of God. They believed that God's Kingdom was not of this world and that their ultimate allegiance was to God and not to any earthly power (Harnack, 1908).

Early Christian writings, such as the New Testament, provide insights into the early Christians' understanding of national security. For example, in his letter to the Romans, the Apostle Paul wrote that Christians should "live peaceably with all" (Romans 12:18, New International Version). This view suggests that the early Christians saw themselves as peacemakers and that their approach to national security was non-violence and reconciliation.

Another critical aspect of early Christian perspectives on national security was their view of the state. The early Christians were wary of the state's power and saw it as a potential source of oppression. This was evident in their refusal to participate in the worship of the Roman Emperor, which was seen as a way of affirming the state's power (Pliny the Younger, 112 AD). Instead, the early Christians saw themselves as citizens of a higher Kingdom, and their loyalty was to God rather than any earthly power (Harnack, 1908).

Early Christian perspectives and understanding of national security were shaped by their belief in the Kingdom of God, their commitment to non-violence and reconciliation, and their suspicion of the state's power. These perspectives are evident in early Christian writings such as the New Testament and provide insights into how early Christians navigated the complex political environment of their time. Therefore, understanding the early Christian perspective on national security is crucial in developing effective policies and strategies that promote peace and justice while upholding Christian values and principles.

Besides, the early Christians also had their perspectives on national security shaped by their religious beliefs, the New Testament, traditions, and circumstances of their time. It offers a wealth of insight into ancient Christians' perspectives on national security. Early Christians navigated various political contexts throughout the Gospels and Epistles, including the Roman Empire's hegemony over much of the Mediterranean world. The New Testament is a collection of Christian Bible books containing Jesus Christ's and his disciples' teachings. Also, these texts can shed light on how ancient Christians viewed national security.

Early Christians' notion of security and territorial protection in the New Testament is primarily related to the spiritual realm rather than the physical. The New Testament emphasizes the need for individuals to secure their souls and protect themselves from spiritual threats, such as sin and evil. However, there are also physical protection and security examples in the New Testament and early traditions. In this section, we will concisely analyze the ancient Christians' perspectives on national security from the New Testament and early Christian writings and traditions and what we can learn and benefit from their contributions to contemporary debates and practices in these areas.

The early Christian writers were primarily concerned with protecting their communities from external threats such as persecution, invasion, and oppression. For instance, Tertullian, one of the earliest Christian writers, argues that Christians must defend their community against attacks. He writes, "We are not ashamed of the walls that protect our homes, nor of the gates that defend them, nor of the armies that protect our borders" (Tertullian, Apology, 42). Tertullian's argument highlights the importance of protecting one's community against external threats as an essential aspect of national security.

Likewise, early Christians' views on these issues can be traced back to the New Testament, where Jesus and his disciples faced political and social turmoil in the Roman Empire. The New Testament emphasizes the need for Christians to respect and obey secular authorities, as they are appointed by God (Romans 13:1-7). Nevertheless, it also stresses the importance of loyalty to God over commitment to earthly powers (Matthew 22:21). This tension between submission to authority and faithfulness to God would continue to shape Christians' views on national security and territorial protection throughout history.

In the early Christian tradition, theologians such as Augustine of Hippo and Thomas Aquinas contributed significantly to developing the just war theory. This theory aimed to provide ethical guidelines for when it is acceptable for a state to use military force. Just war theory requires the war to be for a just cause, have a reasonable chance of success, and use proportional means to achieve its goals. Additionally, it stressed the need for minimizing harm to civilians and prisoners of war. These principles remain relevant today in debates about using force and military intervention in conflicts. Likewise, in his work, City of God, Augustine maintains that the state is responsible for protecting its citizens from external aggression. He writes, "It is not a matter of shedding blood, but of safeguarding peace, which is not possible without military discipline" (Augustine, City of God, 19.7). Augustine's argument highlights the need for the state to use military force to maintain peace and security, and he sees the military as a necessary means to that end.

Furthermore, early Christians' perspectives on national security were predisposed by their understanding of the nature of human conflict and the need for reconciliation. Jesus' teachings underlined the essence of forgiveness and reconciliation, and early Christians saw these as essential components of peacemaking. As a result, the early Christian Church practiced forgiveness and reconciliation, even in cases of severe conflict, as demonstrated in the example of the Church in Corinth (2 Corinthians 2:5-11). These practices have influenced contemporary approaches to conflict resolution and reconciliation.

The early Christians believed that God was sovereign over all things, including national security. They understood that the safety and security of a nation ultimately depended on God's providence and protection. In this regard, Tertullian, a leading Christian theologian, claimed that the Roman Empire's security depended on its faithfulness to God. He believed Rome's military strength alone could not guarantee its safety if it lacked moral integrity and faith in God (Tertullian, 1953). Similarly, Augustine of Hippo, another dominant Christian thinker, reasoned that a just government must seek to promote the common good and protect its citizens from external threats. Nevertheless, he also maintained that, ultimately, the safety and security of a nation rested in God's hands (Augustine, 1998).

Early Christians believed the government had a God-given responsibility to maintain law and order and protect its citizens from harm. Nonetheless, they also recognized that the government's authority was limited and should be exercised following God's laws. In particular, Origen, an early Christian theologian, contended that government officials were accountable to God for their actions and must use their power justly and for the common good (Origen, 1989). Equally, Ambrose of Milan, a prominent Christian bishop, highlighted the significance of the government's role in ensuring social stability and security. However, he also maintained that the government's power must be balanced with individual liberties and human rights (Ambrose, 1989).

The relationship between Christians and the state was also crucial in influencing early Christians' views on national security. While they recognized the need for the government's role in maintaining security, they also believed Christians' ultimate allegiance was to God. Consequently, they were wary of the state's potential to abuse its power and infringe on Christians' religious liberties. Tertullian, for example, said that Christians should not serve in the military or participate in warfare because it conflicted with their commitment to Christ's teachings of non-violence (Tertullian, 1953). Similarly, Augustine argued that Christians should obey the government's laws as long as they do not conflict with God's laws. He also maintained that Christians should be willing to suffer persecution for their faith rather than compromise their commitment to Christ (Augustine, 1998).

In addition to external threats, early Christian writers were also concerned with internal threats to the community's security, such as heresy, corruption, and moral decay. For instance, Clement of Alexandria, another early Christian writer, maintains that moral decay within a society can significantly threaten national security. He writes, "The ruin of a state comes when those who are in it are corrupt and careless" (Clement of Alexandria, Stromata, 7.16). Clement's argument highlights the essence of moral values and ethics in maintaining the security of a community.

Additionally, the early Christian tradition accentuates the importance of peace and reconciliation as essential components of national security. The concept of forgiveness and reconciliation was central to the teachings of Jesus Christ, and early Christians believed that these values could be transformative in resolving conflicts and maintaining peace. For instance, the Apostle Paul writes, "If it is possible, as far as it depends on you, live at peace with everyone" (Romans 12:18). This teaching emphasizes the importance of pursuing peace and reconciliation with others as an essential aspect of national security. According to the early Christians, God is the ultimate source of security, and national security is contingent on God's protection. For example, the book of Psalms affirms that "unless the Lord watches over the city, the watchman stays awake in vain" (Psalm 127:1). Therefore, the early Christians believed that national security is not solely dependent on military might but also on faith in God's protection.

Furthermore, unlike the modern conception of the state as the ultimate authority, the early Christians viewed the state as a secondary authority that should submit to God's authority. For instance, the Apostle Paul wrote in Romans 13:1-7 that "there is no authority except from God, and God has instituted those that exist." Therefore, the state's responsibility was to uphold God's justice and provide a conducive environment for the Christian community to fulfill its mission. Moreover, the early Christians' perspectives on national security were shaped by their mission to spread the gospel to all nations. They believed the Christian community's primary allegiance was to God's kingdom rather than any earthly kingdom. Therefore, the early Christians viewed national security as a means to an end, which was the fulfillment of their mission. To give you an idea, Tertullian, an early Christian writer, wrote that "we offer prayer for the safety of our princes to the eternal, the true, the living God, whose favor, beyond all others, they must themselves desire" (Tertullian, Apology, 30). This implies that the early Christians viewed national security as a means to an end, which was the spread of the gospel, rather than an end in itself.

The early Christians' perspectives offer beneficial insights into contemporary times. First, their emphasis on God's sovereignty and protection challenges the modern notion that national security depends solely on military might. It calls for a renewed focus on faith in God's protection as an essential aspect of national security. Second, their understanding of the state's role challenges the modern conception of the state as the ultimate authority. It calls for a renewed focus on the state's responsibility to uphold God's justice and provide a conducive environment for the Christian community to fulfill its mission.

Also, one key aspect of ancient Christians' perspectives on national security is their emphasis on non-violence and peace. For example, Jesus taught his disciples to love their enemies, turn the other cheek, and pray for those who persecute them (Matthew 5:44). He also warned that those who live by the sword would die by the sword (Matthew 26:52) and instructed his followers to put away their swords during his arrest (Matthew 26:52-54). Similarly, the Apostle Paul urged Christians to live at peace with everyone as far as it depends on them (Romans 12:18) and to overcome evil with good (Romans 12:21). These teachings suggest that ancient Christians valued peace and non-violence to promote national security.

Another aspect of ancient Christians' perspectives on national security is their belief in divine protection. The New Testament portrays God as a protector of his people and a defender against their enemies (Psalm 91:1-2; Isaiah 54:17). The Apostle Paul asserted that nothing could separate believers from the love of God, including persecution, famine, or danger (Romans 8:35-39). This belief in divine protection may have given ancient Christians a sense of security even in the face of external threats.

In addition, ancient Christians' perspectives on national security were shaped by their view of the world as a temporary dwelling place. They believed that their true citizenship was in heaven and that they were strangers and exiles on the earth (Hebrews 11:13; Philippians 3:20). This perspective may have led them to prioritize eternal security over temporal security and to be less concerned with national security issues.

Despite these seemingly conflicting messages, ancient Christians developed a nuanced approach to national security that balanced the need for protection with a commitment to peace and non-violence. One way they did this was by emphasizing the importance of just war theory, which holds that wars are only justifiable when they meet specific criteria, such as being waged in self-defense or responding to an unjust attack.

The early church fathers also recognized the limits of political power and the need for spiritual transformation to address underlying conflicts. For example, in his Letter to Diognetus, a second-century Christian apologist writes that Christians "are not distinguished from other people by country, language, or customs...they dwell in their own countries but simply as sojourners" (Chapter 5). This emphasis on the transience of earthly political allegiances reflects a broader commitment to the idea that ultimate security can only be found in God rather than in any human institution.

Firstly, ancient Christians had a strong belief in the power of prayer as a means of achieving peace and security. In Philippians 4:6-7, the apostle Paul encouraged Christians to "not be anxious about anything, but in every situation, by prayer and petition, with thanksgiving, present your requests to God. Moreover, the peace of God, which transcends all understanding, will guard your hearts and minds in Christ Jesus" (New International Version). This passage emphasizes the importance of seeking God's help and protection in times of trouble and how it can bring peace to individuals and communities. This principle can be applied to modern-day concerns about national security by encouraging people to turn to prayer to promote peace and security in their country.

Secondly, ancient Christians believed in treating others with love and respect, even in conflict. Notably, in Matthew 5:44, Jesus taught his followers to "love your enemies and pray for those who persecute you" (NIV). This teaching emphasizes the importance of showing compassion and forgiveness towards those who may threaten national security. Therefore, even in conflict, treating others with love and respect can help reduce tensions and promote peaceful coexistence.

Thirdly, ancient Christians valued the importance of justice and fairness in society. In Romans 13:1-7, Paul taught that governing authorities are established by God and are responsible for maintaining order and promoting justice. This teaching emphasizes the importance of respecting the rule of law and upholding the principles of justice and fairness in society. This principle can be applied to modern-day concerns about national security by encouraging governments to respect human rights and the rule of law to maintain security and protect their citizens.

The perspectives of ancient Christians on national security provide several benefits for contemporary society. First, their commitment to non-violence and concern for the well-being of others can inspire contemporary debates about the use of military force and the treatment of refugees and immigrants. Second, their emphasis on justice can encourage contemporary debates about the role of government in promoting social and economic equality.

The ancient Christians believed that national security was essential for the nation's and its people's well-being. For example, in the New Testament, Paul, one of the apostles of Jesus Christ, wrote to the Romans, "Let every person be subject to the governing authorities. For there is no authority except God and those that exist have been instituted by God" (Romans 13:1, English Standard Version). This verse emphasizes the importance of submitting to the authorities because God appoints them. Therefore, the ancient Christians believed that obeying the laws of the land and respecting the authorities was crucial for national security.

Besides, ancient Christians believed that national security should be maintained without compromising their faith. The New Testament teaches Christians not to compromise their faith for national security. For example, in the book of Daniel, Daniel and his friends refused to worship the idol of King Nebuchadnezzar, even though it was required by law. As a result, they were thrown into a fiery furnace but were miraculously saved by God (Daniel 3). This story shows that the ancient Christians believed their faith should not be compromised, even if it meant facing persecution or death.

Ancient Christians also believed in the power of prayer for national security. The New Testament teaches that Christians should pray for their leaders and authorities. Paul wrote to Timothy, "I urge that supplications, prayers, intercessions, and thanksgivings be made for all people, for kings and all who are in high positions, that we may lead a peaceful and quiet life, godly and dignified in every way" (1 Timothy 2:1-2, ESV). This verse emphasizes the importance of praying for those in authority so that they may govern the nation in a way that promotes peace and security.

Likewise, the ancient Christians believed that national security was not just a physical but spiritual issue. For example, the New Testament teaches that Christians should not fear those who can harm the body but fear God, who has the power to destroy both body and soul in hell (Matthew 10:28). This verse emphasizes that national security is not just about protecting the physical body but also about protecting the soul. Therefore, the ancient Christians believed that national security should also involve promoting moral and spiritual values in society.

The New Testament teaches that individuals can achieve spiritual security through faith in Jesus Christ. In John 10:27-28, Jesus states, "My sheep listen to my voice; I know them, and they follow me. I give them eternal life, and they shall never perish; no one can snatch them out of my hand." This passage emphasizes the idea that believers in Christ are secure in their salvation and that nothing can take that security away from them. Jesus Christ is often referred to as a "shepherd" who cares for and protects his flock. In John 10:11, Jesus states, "I am the good shepherd. The good shepherd lays down his life for the sheep."

Furthermore, many early Christian writers, such as Tertullian and Origen, believed Christians should not participate in military service or take up arms against others. They argued that violence was incompatible with Jesus' teachings on love and forgiveness and that Christians should instead seek to emulate Jesus' example of non-violence. This perspective is reflected in the early Christian text known as the Didache, which instructs Christians not to engage in "wars, strife, or dissensions" (Didache 2:2) and to "love your enemies and pray for those who persecute you" (Didache 1:3).

Another aspect of early Christians' perspectives on national security was their ambivalent attitude toward the state. While some early Christian writers, such as Augustine, saw the state as a necessary institution for maintaining order and protecting citizens, others, such as Tertullian, viewed the state as inherently corrupt and opposed to Christian values. They saw the state as promoting violence, war, and idolatry and believed Christians should distance themselves from it as much as possible. This perspective is reflected in the early Christian text known as The Martyrdom of Polycarp, which portrays the Roman authorities as persecutors of Christians and Polycarp as a faithful witness to the truth.

Besides, their eschatological beliefs shaped early Christians' perspectives on national security. They believed that the world's end was imminent, and that Jesus would return to establish his earthly kingdom. This belief led some early Christians to prioritize spiritual preparation over material security and to view suffering and persecution as signs of the coming kingdom. This perspective is reflected in the early Christian text, The Shepherd of Hermas, which encourages Christians to endure suffering with patience and trust in God's ultimate victory over evil.

Moreover, the Apostle Paul speaks about Christians' spiritual protection in Christ in Ephesians 6:10-18. He describes the "armor of God" that Christians should put on to protect themselves against spiritual attacks, including the belt of truth, the breastplate of righteousness, the shoes of the gospel of peace, the shield of faith, the helmet of salvation, and the sword of the Spirit, which is the word of God.

As for the Old Testament, one of the critical examples of security and protection is the story of the exodus from Egypt. In this story, God provides protection and security to the Israelites as they escape from slavery in Egypt and journey to the Promised Land. In Exodus 14:19-20, God protects the Israelites by going before them in a pillar of cloud by day and a pillar of fire by night, a physical barrier between the Israelites and the pursuing Egyptian army. Another example of God's protection in the Old Testament is found in Psalm 91, which speaks of God's faithfulness in protecting those who trust him. The psalm states, "He who dwells in the shelter of the Highest will abide in the shadow of the Almighty. I will say to the Lord, 'My refuge and my fortress, my God, in whom I trust'" (Psalm 91:1-2).

Contemporary discussions on national security can benefit from these insights in several ways. First, by emphasizing the importance of just war theory, contemporary policymakers can ensure that military force is only used when necessary and in ways consistent with international law and human rights norms. Second, by recognizing the limits of political power and the need for spiritual transformation, contemporary policymakers can work towards addressing underlying conflicts rather than simply relying on military force to maintain security. In addition to spiritual security, the New Testament provides examples of physical protection and security. For example, in Luke 22:36, Jesus instructs his disciples to carry swords for protection, saying, "But now if you have a purse, take it, and also a bag; and if you do not have a sword, sell your cloak and buy one." This passage shows that even Jesus, who preached peace and non-violence, recognized the need for physical protection in a dangerous world. Another example of physical protection in the New Testament can be found in Acts 23:12-24. In this passage, a group of Jews conspires to kill the apostle Paul, but Paul is protected by Roman soldiers stationed nearby. This example shows that even in the early Christian Church, physical protection was sometimes necessary to ensure the safety of believers.

The Influence of Faith on Christians' Views on Security and Protection

Early Christians' perspectives on national security were significantly influenced by their faith, love, justice, and peace. Their worldview saw national security as part of God's will for humanity, aiming to create a just and peaceful world. Their writings reflected this view, emphasizing the importance of justice and peace as fundamental values in creating a secure and prosperous society. For instance, the New Testament writers urged Christians to seek peace with all people and to pursue justice as the foundation of social stability and security (Romans 12:18, Micah 6:8). Similarly, the early Christian theologians such as Augustine of Hippo, Ambrose of Milan, and Thomas Aquinas emphasized the importance of peace and justice in the context of national security (Berkowitz, 2016).

They were also influenced by their eschatology, which held that God's ultimate purpose for humanity was to create a new heaven and earth where justice and peace would reign. Therefore, they saw national security as a means to an end, a necessary precondition for fulfilling God's purpose. In this view, national security was not an end but a means to create a peaceful society that reflected God's will. The early Christians also emphasized the importance of morality and ethics in national security. They believed that national security must be grounded in ethical principles that reflect the dignity and worth of every human being. Therefore, they opposed any form of violence or injustice that would undermine the moral foundations of society. For instance, the early Christians rejected violence in resolving conflicts and instead advocated for peaceful means of conflict resolution (Matthew 5:9). Moreover, their views on the relationship between the state and the Church influenced the early Christians' standpoints on national security. They believed that the state was responsible for maintaining law and order and protecting its citizens from external threats. However, they also believed that the Church had a role in shaping society's ethical foundations and promoting peace and justice. Therefore, they advocated for a partnership between the state and the Church, where the Church would provide moral guidance and the state would provide security and protection.

Equally, the story of Cornelius, a Roman centurion who converted to Christianity after meeting the apostle Peter, is one of early Christians' most significant examples of territorial protection. According to the book of Acts in the Bible, Cornelius was a devout man who feared God and gave generously to the poor, but he was not a Jew and had not been circumcised. Then, one day, an angel appeared and told him to send for Peter, who stayed in Joppa. Meanwhile, Peter was on the rooftop of a house in Joppa, praying, when he had a vision of a sheet descending from heaven containing all kinds of clean and unclean animals and heard a voice telling him to kill and eat. Peter refused, saying that he had never eaten anything unclean. The voice responded, "What God has cleansed, you must not call common." This happened three times, and then the sheet was taken back up into heaven.

As Peter tried to make sense of this vision, the messengers from Cornelius arrived and asked him to come to Caesarea. Peter went with them, and when he arrived, Cornelius fell at his feet and worshipped him. Peter told him to get up, saying, "I myself am also a man." Then Cornelius explained how an angel had visited him and told him to send for Peter. Peter realized that God had shown him in the vision that he should not call anyone common or unclean. He then preached the gospel to Cornelius and his household; they all believed and were baptized. This was a significant event in the early Church because it showed that God was not just the God of the Jews but also of the Gentiles. It also showed that God was breaking down the barriers between different peoples and nations and that all were welcome in his kingdom.

In short, the story of Cornelius is a powerful example of how territorial protection among early Christians was challenged and ultimately overcome. Through Peter and Cornelius's actions, the gospel's message was spread to people of all nations and cultures, and the boundaries between them were broken down. This story inspires and challenges Christians today to be open to people from all backgrounds and share God's love with everyone.

Regarding the relevance of ancient Christians' standpoints on national security today, their emphasis on peace and justice as fundamental values for creating a secure and prosperous society resonates with contemporary calls for social justice and human rights. National security cannot be achieved at the expense of justice and human dignity; it must be grounded in ethical principles that uphold human rights and dignity. Moreover, their emphasis on the importance of morality and ethics in national security is particularly relevant today, given the increasing complexity of global security threats. As societies face new and emerging threats, ensuring that national security policies are guided by ethical principles that promote human dignity and respect for human rights is critical.

The early Christians also believed in the concept of just war. Just war theory is the idea that certain conditions must be met before a war can be considered just. These conditions include just cause, proper authority, right intention, probability of success, proportionality, and last resort. The early Christians believed that if these conditions were met, a government was permissible to engage in warfare. Their beliefs about God and humanity also shaped their stance on territorial protection. They believed that all human beings were equal in the eyes of God and that all people had the right to live in peace and security. This meant that the early Christians opposed any aggression or violence directed at innocent people.

However, the early Christians also believed that protecting their communities from external threats was essential. Therefore, they believed that if a neighboring community threatened their community, it was permissible to take defensive measures to protect themselves. This belief was based on the idea that human life is sacred, and that the government is responsible for protecting its citizens.

The early Christians' contributions to the discussion of national security and territorial protection are significant. They believed in the sanctity of human life and the responsibility of governments to protect their citizens. They also believed in just war and the importance of exhausting all diplomatic measures before taking military action. These contributions are relevant today because they offer a framework for thinking about these issues morally and ethically. The early Christians' beliefs about the sanctity of human life and the responsibility of governments to protect their citizens are still critical today. They offer a basis for evaluating governments' actions and holding them accountable for their actions.

It should be noted that national security and territorial protection have been significant concerns of societies throughout history, and early Christians were not exempted from these concerns. Instead, the prevailing ancient Christians' viewpoints on national security and territorial protection were shaped by their religious beliefs, political context, and cultural values. These perspectives are still relevant today, and we can learn and benefit from them by applying them in our lives and societies. By doing so, we can contribute to the well-being and security of our nations and promote peace and prosperity for all.

In a nutshell, the prevailing ancient Christians' standpoints on national security were shaped by their understanding of God's sovereignty, the role of government, and the relationship between Christians and the state. They believed that the safety and security of a nation ultimately depended on God's providence and protection. They also recognized the government's God-given responsibility to maintain law and order and protect its citizens from harm. However, they were wary of the state's potential to abuse its power and infringe on Christians' religious liberties. We can learn from their contributions that national security must be pursued in a manner that is consistent with God's laws and promotes the common good. We can also benefit from their insights on balancing government power with individual liberties and human rights.

Early Christian Rulers and Their Stance On Security

Constantine the Great, also known as Saint Constantine, was a Roman Emperor who ruled from 306 to 337 CE. He is renowned for his contributions to the spread and establishment of Christianity as a legitimate religion within the Roman Empire. In his letters, Constantine frequently emphasized his military campaigns as a way to protect and expand the Christian empire, as seen in his letter to the bishops of the East in 325 CE.

In this letter, Constantine addressed the bishops' concerns about the persecution of Christians in the East and sought to assure them of his support for the Christian faith. He stated that his military campaigns were necessary to protect the peace and unity of the empire, which he believed was essential to safeguarding the Church. Constantine also expressed his view that anyone who sought to destroy the empire's unity or disturb the Church's peace was fighting against God and would meet with divine punishment (Constantine, Letter to the Bishops of the East, 325 CE).

Constantine's letter reflects his belief that the Christian faith was integral to the Roman Empire's security and prosperity. He saw Christianity as a unifying force that could bring together the diverse peoples of the empire and provide a shared sense of purpose and identity. Constantine's military campaigns, in his view, were not simply a means of expanding the empire's borders but were also a way to spread and protect the Christian faith. Furthermore, Constantine's letter shows his use of religious rhetoric to legitimize his military actions. He presented his campaigns as a divine mission to protect the Church and the empire, justifying the use of force to pursue these goals. Constantine's religious language and imagery were intended to persuade his Christian audience of his cause's righteousness and inspire them to support his efforts.

One notable example of an ancient Christian ruler's approach to territorial protection is Emperor Constantine, who famously converted to Christianity in the early 4th century. Constantine's policies reflected a belief that God's protection was necessary for the survival of the Roman Empire, and he saw himself as an instrument of divine providence. Emperor Constantine's approach to territorial protection was shaped by his belief in the importance of divine providence and his conviction that God's protection was necessary for the survival of the Roman Empire. As a result, Constantine's policies reflected a deep commitment to Christianity and a desire to promote the faith throughout his realm.

His Christian faith and belief deeply influenced Emperor Constantine's approach to territorial protection in divine providence. As Cameron (2011) notes, Constantine saw himself as an instrument of God's will and believed that God's protection was necessary for the survival of the Roman Empire. One of the most significant examples of Constantine's approach to territorial protection was his issuance of the Edict of Milan in 313 CE, which granted religious tolerance to all inhabitants of the Roman Empire. This edict was a major turning point in the history of Christianity, as it marked the first time that the religion was officially recognized and protected by the state (Drake, 2000).

One of the most significant examples of Constantine's approach to territorial protection was his decision to issue the Edict of Milan in 313 CE, which granted religious tolerance to all inhabitants of the Roman Empire. This edict was a major turning point in the history of Christianity, as it marked the first time that the religion was officially recognized and protected by the state. Another important aspect of Constantine's approach to territorial protection was his use of Christian symbolism and rhetoric to promote unity and loyalty among his subjects. For example, Constantine adopted the Chi-Rho symbol, representing the first two letters of Christ's name in Greek, as his emblem and used it in his military standards. He also referred to himself as a "soldier of Christ" and emphasized the importance of Christian virtue and piety in his public speeches and proclamations.

To put it briefly, Constantine the Great's letter to the bishops of the East in 325 CE reflects his belief that the Christian faith was essential to the Roman Empire's security and unity. His military campaigns were portrayed as a means of protecting and expanding the Christian empire, and his use of religious rhetoric was intended to legitimize his actions and inspire support from his Christian audience. Constantine's policies reflected a deep commitment to Christianity and a belief that God's protection was necessary for the survival of the Roman Empire. A combination of religious tolerance, Christian symbolism, rhetoric, and a strong sense of divine providence characterized his approach to territorial protection.

In brief, Constantine's approach to territorial protection was characterized by a combination of religious tolerance, Christian symbolism and rhetoric, and a strong sense of divine providence. His policies reflected his commitment to Christianity and his belief that God's protection was necessary for the survival of the Roman Empire. Constantine the Great's military campaigns were motivated by a variety of factors, including his desire to protect the Christian faith from external threats. He saw himself as a defender of the faith against pagans and heretics and took action to ensure the survival and growth of the Church. However, his military campaigns were also driven by political considerations, as he sought to solidify his authority and gain support from a growing Christian constituency within the empire.

Another example is Emperor Justinian I, who ruled the Byzantine Empire in the 6th century. Justinian saw himself as the defender of Christianity and the protector of the Roman Empire's eastern borders. He ordered the construction of fortifications and defensive walls, such as the famous Walls of Constantinople, to protect the empire from external threats. Justinian also codified Roman law, including the concept of just war, which allowed for defensive military action in certain circumstances. Emperor Justinian I was a prominent ruler of the Byzantine Empire who reigned from 527 CE to 565 CE. He was renowned for his efforts to safeguard the Eastern Roman Empire from external threats, particularly from the Persians and barbarian invaders. Several notable achievements, including constructing fortified walls, codifying Roman law, and promoting Christianity, marked Justinian's reigns in Christianity.

Justinian's primary concern was to defend the Byzantine Empire from external threats. He commissioned the construction of the famous Walls of Constantinople, a series of fortifications that encircled the city and provided a formidable defense against potential invaders. The walls were constructed with a height of 40 feet and a thickness of 20 feet, and they featured towers and gates strategically placed to control access to the city (Treadgold, 1997). The Walls of Constantinople protected the city against many attacks by the Persians, Avars, and Slavs during Justinian's reign.

In addition to fortifying the Byzantine Empire's borders, Justinian also sought to codify Roman law. He commissioned a team of legal experts to compile and organize the existing legal code, resulting in the Corpus Juris Civilis, a comprehensive set of legal codes that became the foundation of civil law in Western Europe (Kelly, 2008). Justinian's codification of Roman law significantly impacted the development of legal systems in Europe. It provided a common legal framework facilitating trade and commerce across the continent.

Justinian's reign was also marked by his efforts to promote Christianity. He saw himself as a defender of the faith and actively promoted the spread of Christianity throughout the Byzantine Empire. Justinian built several churches, including the Hagia Sophia, which remains one of the most significant architectural achievements of the Byzantine Empire. The emperor also took an active role in the theological debates of his time and convened several councils to resolve doctrinal disputes within the Church (Meyendorff, 1989).

Justinian saw the Byzantine Empire as a continuation of the Roman Empire and believed it was his responsibility to defend its borders and territories. Accordingly, he launched numerous military campaigns to expand and defend the empire, most notably against the Goths, Vandals, and Persians. He saw these campaigns as part of a larger struggle to defend Christian civilization from outside threats. Justinian I, also known as Justinian the Great, ruled the Byzantine Empire from 527 to 565 CE. He saw himself as the inheritor of the Roman Empire's legacy and believed his duty was to defend and expand its territories. He launched numerous military campaigns against enemies, including the Goths, Vandals, and Persians.

One of Justinian's most significant military campaigns was against the Goths, who had established a powerful kingdom in Italy. In 535 CE, Justinian sent his general Belisarius to Italy with a large army to reclaim the territory for the Byzantine Empire. The campaign was long and difficult but ultimately successful, and the Byzantine Empire regained control over much of Italy. This campaign continued the Roman Empire's efforts to maintain control over Italy. Justinian saw it as a way to reassert Byzantine power and influence in the region. Justinian also launched a campaign against the Vandals, who had established a powerful kingdom in North Africa. In 533 CE, he sent a fleet and army to North Africa, and after a short campaign, the Byzantine Empire regained control over the region. Again, this campaign was a way to restore Roman control over North Africa, which had been lost to the Vandals in the fifth century.

Justinian's campaigns against the Persians were less successful, but he still saw them as an important part of his defense of Christian civilization. The Byzantine Empire and the Persian Empire had a long history of conflict, and Justinian sought to protect the empire's eastern borders by launching campaigns against the Persians. While these campaigns were ultimately unsuccessful in reclaiming territory, they helped to maintain a balance of power between the two empires. Procopius, a Byzantine historian and Justinian's contemporary stated that the emperor believed he was duty-bound to defend the Roman Empire's borders and territories. He saw himself as the defender of the Roman Empire's legacy and was committed to upholding the empire's traditions and values (Procopius, Wars 1.17.1).

Emperor Justinian believed the Byzantine Empire was a continuation of the Roman Empire. Therefore, he saw his role as the emperor of the Byzantines as one of preserving the empire's unity and strength (Haldon, 2016). Justinian's military campaigns were essential to his vision of defending the Byzantine Empire. He launched a series of campaigns to expand and defend the empire's borders and territories, most notably against the Goths, Vandals, and Persians. In addition, Justinian's campaigns were motivated by a desire to protect the empire from outside threats and spread Christian civilization (Haldon, 2016).

Emperor Justinian's campaigns against the Goths and Vandals were particularly successful. In 533 CE, he launched a campaign against the Vandal Kingdom in North Africa, culminating in capturing the Vandal capital of Carthage (Procopius, Wars 3.10.1). The campaign was partly motivated by a desire to protect the empire's Mediterranean trade routes and, in part, to spread Christianity (Heather, 2018). Justinian's campaign against the Gothic Kingdom of Italy was similarly successful. He launched a campaign in 535 CE, ultimately capturing Ravenna, the Gothic capital (Procopius, Wars 4.28.1). Justinian's campaign against the Goths was motivated by a desire to reunite the Western and Eastern Roman Empires and restore the Roman Empire's unity (Heather, 2018). Justinian's campaigns against the Persians were less successful but were nevertheless motivated by a desire to protect the empire's eastern borders and prevent them from expanding their territory (Haldon, 2016).

Regarding territorial protection, Justinian oversaw the construction of numerous fortresses, walls, and other defensive structures throughout the empire. One of his most famous projects was the construction of the Theodosian Walls around Constantinople, which helped to protect the city from attack for centuries. Justinian's national security and territorial protection legacy can teach us several valuable lessons today:

1. His focus on defending the empire against external threats reminds us of the importance of maintaining strong borders and a robust national defense. In an era of globalization and transnational threats, it is easy to overlook the importance of securing our territory and protecting our citizens.
2. Justinian's belief in the duty of rulers to protect their people can inspire us to prioritize the safety and security of our citizens in our policy decisions. Protecting human life and defending the common good should always be the highest priority of any government.

3. Justinian's example can teach us the importance of investing in long-term infrastructure and defensive structures.

The Theodosian Walls, for example, protected Constantinople for centuries and served as a testament to the importance of long-term planning and investment in national security.

Emperor Justinian I was a remarkable ruler who significantly contributed to the Byzantine Empire's security, legal system, and religious culture. Justinian's efforts to fortify the empire's borders with the construction of the Walls of Constantinople, his codification of Roman law in the Corpus Juris Civilis, and his promotion of Christianity through the construction of churches and theological debates left an enduring legacy that continues to influence the world today. Justinian's vision of defending the Byzantine Empire was motivated by a desire to uphold the empire's traditions and values and to protect the empire from external threats.

Catholic Church and its Position on Territorial Protection

The Catholic Church has had a complex relationship with national security and territorial protection. While the Bible does not provide specific guidance on these matters, the Church has often been called upon to provide moral and spiritual guidance on issues related to war, peace, and the protection of human life. In general, the Catholic Church has stressed the essence of just war theory, which sets out criteria for when it is morally acceptable to use military force.

According to this theory, military action is only justifiable when it meets certain conditions, such as being a last resort, having a just cause, and being proportionate to preventing harm. The Catholic Church has also underscored protecting human life and dignity during war. This has led the Church to advocate for the protection of noncombatants and the humane treatment of prisoners of war. Additionally, the Church has spoken out against using weapons of mass destruction and other indiscriminate warfare.

Regarding territorial protection, the Catholic Church has traditionally supported the idea of territorial sovereignty and the importance of maintaining secure borders. This is reflected in the Church's teachings on immigration, which emphasize the rights of nations to regulate the movement of people across their borders. However, the Church also emphasizes the importance of treating immigrants and refugees with dignity and respect and has spoken out against policies that dehumanize or discriminate against vulnerable populations.

Today, we can benefit from the Catholic Church's contributions by reflecting on the ethical dimensions of national security and territorial protection. The Church's emphasis on just war theory and the protection of human life can help us think critically about when and how military force should be used and how we can ensure that society's most vulnerable members do not disproportionately bear the costs of war. Additionally, the Church's teachings on immigration can help us to balance the need for secure borders with our obligations to treat all people with dignity and respect. Finally, the ancient Popes remind us that wars should only be fought when all other options have been exhausted and that even amid conflict, we must strive to protect the most vulnerable members of society.

The Church's emphasis on moral principles and social justice can help us think critically about contemporary national security and territorial protection issues. For example, the Church's teachings on the responsibility of rulers to act justly and under Christian principles can provide a framework for evaluating the actions of contemporary political leaders. While their views may have been shaped by their time's political and social realities, their insights into just war theory and the importance of peaceful solutions to conflicts remain relevant today. Similarly, the Church's teachings on the importance of promoting and defending the Christian faith can help us understand religion's role in contemporary conflicts.

In summary, the views of ancient Popes on national security and territorial protection were shaped by the religious texts and traditions of the Catholic Church. Their contributions to the Church's teachings on these issues provide helpful knowledge into contemporary political and social realities. Also, various Popes had to navigate the complex political realities of their time while upholding the Church's teachings on ethical principles and human dignity. One significant illustration of the ancient Popes' views on security is their approach to the barbarian invasions of the Roman Empire in the 4th and 5th centuries.

Pope Leo the Great, for example, was instrumental in negotiating with Attila the Hun to spare Rome from destruction. In addition, he accentuated the need to safeguard innocent civilians and preserve the cultural heritage of Rome while also recognizing the military realities of the time.

Pope Leo the Great was a significant figure in the early Christian Church who served as the bishop of Rome from 440 to 461 AD. Also known as Saint Leo I, he was crucial in negotiating with Attila the Hun to spare Rome from destruction in 452 AD. Attila had already ravaged many cities in Italy and was marching towards Rome with his army, causing panic among the citizens. However, when Leo went to meet Attila in person, the Hun leader was so impressed by him that he agreed to spare the city and withdraw his troops. This event is regarded as one of the most significant moments in the history of the early Christian Church and has been extensively studied by scholars.

The negotiation between Pope Leo the Great and Attila the Hun is widely regarded as one of the most significant diplomatic triumphs in the history of the early Christian Church. Accordingly, scholars have extensively analyzed it and have attempted to understand the factors that led to its success. Some have argued that the pope's intervention was motivated by a desire to preserve the Christian faith, while others have suggested that he may have used diplomatic channels to communicate with Attila before the negotiation.

Historian Richard Krautheimer states that Leo's successful negotiation with Attila resulted from his "personal qualities, the prestige of his office, and the spiritual and moral authority that he represented" (Krautheimer, 1980, p. 42). Krautheimer also notes that Leo's "tactical skills in handling a difficult situation" were evident when he convinced Attila to spare Rome without concessions or tribute (p. 42). Leo's negotiation with Attila is considered a pivotal moment in the history of Rome and the Catholic Church, as it demonstrated the power of the papacy and the importance of diplomacy in international relations. Historian Thomas F. X. Noble notes, "Leo's actions provided a foundation for the idea that the pope was not only the spiritual leader of the Christian church but also a political force to be reckoned with" (Noble, 2012, p. 36).

Furthermore, historian John Julius Norwich, in his book Byzantium: The Early Centuries, suggests that Pope Leo the Great's success in negotiating with Attila was due to his extraordinary personal charisma and forceful personality (Norwich, 1988). Norwich notes that the pope's approach was firm and conciliatory, allowing him to convince Attila to spare Rome without resorting to military force. Historian John Julius Norwich's analysis of Pope Leo the Great's negotiation with Attila the Hun provides insight into the factors that contributed to its success. According to Norwich, Pope Leo's extraordinary personal charisma and forceful personality played a crucial role in convincing Attila to spare Rome (Norwich, 1988).

Norwich suggests that the pope's approach was firm and conciliatory, allowing him to negotiate with Attila without resorting to military force. This approach was possible because of the pope's persuasive powers and his ability to communicate effectively with Attila. Norwich notes, "Leo's forceful and persuasive personality allowed him to communicate with Attila in a language that the Hun could understand" (Norwich, 1988, p. 135). In addition, Norwich's analysis is supported by other scholars who have studied the negotiation between Pope Leo and Attila. In particular, historian Richard Landes suggests that the pope's success in negotiating with Attila was due to his ability to represent a higher power (Landes, 2011). Landes said the pope's spiritual authority allowed him to persuade Attila to spare Rome without violence.

The pope's firmness and determination helped him to stand his ground in the face of Attila's aggression. In contrast, his conciliatory approach helped him to find common ground with the Hun leader. These qualities allowed Pope Leo the Great to establish a rapport with Attila, which enabled him to persuade the Hun leader to spare Rome. Moreover, Norwich's analysis suggests that Pope Leo the Great may have used diplomatic channels to communicate with Attila before the negotiation. This could have helped the pope establish a rapport with Attila and gain his trust, which would have made the negotiation easier.

In short, historian John Julius Norwich's analysis of Pope Leo the Great's negotiation with Attila the Hun highlights the role of the pope's personal charisma and forceful personality in convincing Attila to spare Rome. Norwich's analysis is supported by other scholars who suggest that the pope's ability to communicate effectively with Attila and his spiritual authority were crucial factors in the negotiation's success. Pope Leo the Great's negotiation was a remarkable achievement that demonstrated his personal qualities, tactical skills, and the papacy's power. This event played a significant role in shaping the history of Rome and the Catholic Church, and it continues to be studied and admired by historians and scholars today.

Christians Past and Current Inquiries on National Security

Christian perspectives on national security have been extensively studied and continue to be of interest in modern times. Past studies focused on Christianity's role in shaping national security policies, its relationship with power, war, and peace, and the connection between Christian ethics and national security decision-making.

Recent studies, however, have shifted the focus towards the role of Christian leaders and organizations in promoting peace and reconciliation, as well as the impact of Christian beliefs on individuals' perceptions of national security threats. Additionally, there is a growing interest in exploring how Christianity intersects with other religious traditions in promoting global security. Christian perspectives on national security are multifaceted and have practical and theoretical implications. These studies provide insights into how Christian beliefs and values influence national security decision-making and how they can be used to promote peace, justice, and equality. Understanding the Christian perspective on national security is crucial in developing effective policies and strategies that encourage security while upholding Christian values.

In his book "The Irony of American History," Niebuhr argues that Christians should exercise caution when it comes to security and territorial protection. He believes pursuing power and security could lead to arrogance and hubris, ultimately undermining national security (Niebuhr, 2008). This section analyzes Niebuhr's rationale and discusses its relevance in the current political security climate.

Niebuhr argues that pursuing power and security can lead to arrogance and hubris, which in turn can undermine national security. He asserts that nations must balance power and humility to avoid the pitfalls of hubris. Niebuhr believes that Christians, in particular, should be cautious in their approach to power and security because the Christian faith values humility and rejects arrogance. According to Niebuhr, "The Christian faith, like all great religions, insists upon the virtue of humility, which is the virtue of men who are not in a hurry" (Niebuhr, 2008, p. 34). He contends that pursuing power and security can lead to a distorted view of reality, where nations become so focused on their security that they fail to see the larger picture. Niebuhr writes, "The pursuit of security is not only a myth but a distortion of reality. The fact is that the world is insecure, and the attempts by any one nation to achieve security by itself are doomed to failure" (Niebuhr, 2008, p.

50). He believes that nations must work together to achieve security and that pursuing security should not be the primary goal of foreign policy.

Niebuhr's justification is still relevant in the current political climate. In recent years, there has been a growing trend towards nationalism and protectionism in many countries. This trend is often driven by a desire for security and the belief that a nation can best protect its citizens by limiting its engagement with the outside world. Nevertheless, Niebuhr would argue that this approach needs to be reconsidered and could ultimately lead to greater insecurity. Moreover, Niebuhr's argument is relevant in the context of ongoing conflicts in the Middle East, where many countries have become entangled in the conflict, and there is a growing sense that military force is the only solution to the region's problems. However, Niebuhr would contend that military force alone cannot solve the region's problems and that a more nuanced approach is required. In brief, Niebuhr's argument that Christians should be cautious in their approach to power and security is still relevant today. His belief that seeking power and security can lead to arrogance and hubris is particularly relevant in the current political climate, where nationalism and protectionism are on the rise. Niebuhr's rationale serves as a reminder that nations must strike a balance between power and humility and that seeking security should not be the sole focus of foreign policy.

Similarly, Stanley Hauerwas, a theologian, argued in the late 20th century that Christians should embrace a radical approach to security that rejects violence and emphasizes reconciliation and forgiveness (Hauerwas, 1991). Here, we examine Hauerwas's rationale and discuss what we can learn and benefit from its findings.

Hauerwas argues that Christians should embrace a radical approach to security that rejects violence and emphasizes reconciliation and forgiveness. He believes that Christians must reject the idea that violence can solve problems and that non-violence is the only viable option for Christians. According to Hauerwas, "Non-violence is not an optional add-on for the

Christian; it is an integral part of Christian discipleship" (Hauerwas, 1991, p. 1).

Additionally, Hauerwas maintains that pursuing security through violence ultimately undermines security itself. He believes that violence creates a cycle of violence that can never be broken. Instead, Hauerwas writes, "Violence begets violence, and its spiraling momentum can lead to the total destruction of both parties involved" (Hauerwas, 1991, p. 19). He says that the cycle of violence can only be broken, and true security can be achieved by rejecting violence and embracing reconciliation and forgiveness.

Hauerwas's justification is still relevant in the current political climate. There has been a growing trend towards violence and aggression in many parts of the world in recent years. This trend is often driven by the belief that violence is necessary to achieve security. However, Hauerwas would argue that this approach is misguided, and that violence only begets more violence. Furthermore, Hauerwas's rationale is relevant in the context of ongoing conflicts in the Middle East, where many countries have become entangled in the conflict, and violence has been extensively used to solve the region's problems. Nevertheless, Hauerwas would contend that violence is not the answer and that only through reconciliation and forgiveness can valid security be achieved.

Hauerwas's explanation reminds us that violence is not the answer to our problems. It is easy to believe that violence is necessary to achieve security, but Hauerwas's argument challenges us to think differently. His stress on reconciliation and forgiveness reminds us that proper security can only be achieved peacefully. Also, Hauerwas's assessment highlights the need for non-violence in Christian discipleship. As Christians, we are called to follow the example of Christ, who rejected violence and embraced love and forgiveness. Hauerwas's logic challenges us to live out this calling daily and reject the idea that violence can solve problems.

Hauerwas's thinking that Christians should embrace a radical approach to security that rejects violence and emphasizes reconciliation and forgiveness is still relevant today. His reminder that violence only begets more violence challenges us to think differently about how we approach security in our daily lives and the larger political context. As Christians, Hauerwas's justification prompts us to recognize the need for non-violence in our discipleship and our pursuit of proper security.

Moreover, in his book "Just War Reconsidered," Mark Allman argues that Christians should re-examine the concept of the "just war" and consider alternative approaches to promoting security and peace (Allman, 2016). Here, we explore Allman's rationale and discuss what we can learn and benefit from its findings.

Allman contends that Christians should be more skeptical of using military force and more willing to embrace nonviolent strategies. He argues that the traditional criteria of a "just war," such as cause, proportionality, and discrimination, have become increasingly challenging in modern warfare. As a result, Christians should be more willing to explore alternative approaches to promoting security and peace.

Allman also maintains that Christians should embrace a more holistic view of security beyond the traditional focus on military force. He believes that proper security and peace can only be achieved through political, economic, and social measures rooted in justice, compassion, and non-violence.

Allman's rationalization is principally relevant in the current political climate, where conflicts and tensions between nations continue to escalate. Military force is a common approach to dealing with these conflicts despite the risks and uncertainties involved. Allman's argument challenges us to think more critically about this approach's effectiveness and consider alternative strategies for promoting security and peace. Moreover, Allman's justification prompts us to realize that military force should not be taken lightly and should be subject to scrutiny. The traditional criteria of a "just war" may not always be applicable or sufficient in modern warfare, and Christians should be more willing to explore alternative approaches to promoting security and peace.

In addition, Allman's focus on a more holistic view of security reminds us that absolute security and peace are not solely dependent on military strength. Political, economic, and social factors are necessary for creating a stable and just society. By embracing these principles, Christians can work towards promoting security and peace more comprehensively and effectively.

In short, Allman's rationale that Christians should re-examine the "just war" concept and consider alternative approaches to promoting security and peace is particularly relevant in the current political climate. His stress on a more holistic view of security and the necessity of exploring alternative strategies challenges us to think more critically about our approach to security and peace. By embracing these principles, Christians can work towards promoting security and peace more comprehensively and effectively.

In her writing "Security and Development in Global Politics," Rita Abrahamsen explores the role of Christian NGOs in promoting security and development in conflict-affected areas (Abrahamsen, 2017). In this segment, we study Abrahamsen's explanation and discuss what we can learn and benefit from its findings.

Abrahamsen maintains that Christian NGOs promote security and development in conflict-affected areas. She contends that these organizations are uniquely positioned to provide aid and support to vulnerable communities, and a solid commitment to principles of justice and compassion guides their work.

Also, Abrahamsen argues that Christian NGOs are often more effective than other organizations in promoting long-term, sustainable development. This is because they are more willing to engage with local communities and build partnerships based on trust and mutual respect. Christian NGOs can help create more resilient and self-sufficient communities that can better withstand future conflicts and crises by working in this way. Abrahamsen's justification is mainly germane in the current political climate, where conflicts and crises continue to threaten the security and well-being of vulnerable communities around the world. Christian NGOs have a long history of providing aid and support in these contexts, and their work is increasingly important in promoting security and development.

Abrahamsen's rationale highlights the significant role that Christian NGOs play in promoting security and development in conflict-affected areas. These organizations are often better equipped to provide aid and support to vulnerable communities, and a solid commitment to principles of justice and compassion guides their work. Besides, Abrahamsen's focus on building partnerships based on trust and mutual respect informs us that effective development work requires a long-term and collaborative approach. By working closely with local communities and building partnerships based on trust and mutual respect, Christian NGOs can help promote sustainable and long-term development that is more resilient to future conflicts and crises. To sum up, Abrahamsen's argument that Christian NGOs play a vital role in promoting security and development in conflict-affected areas is particularly relevant in the current political climate. Furthermore, her stress on building partnerships based on trust and mutual respect reminds us of the need for a long-term and collaborative approach to development work. By embracing these principles, Christian NGOs can continue to play a vital role in promoting security and development worldwide.

Furthermore, in their study, Francis and Kanyoro (2012) examined the role of Christian churches in promoting peace and security in Africa. They maintain that Christian churches have played a significant role in promoting peace and security in Africa. They contend that churches have been instrumental in promoting reconciliation and conflict resolution in conflict-affected areas. Additionally, the authors claim that churches are uniquely positioned to promote peace and security in Africa because they have a strong presence in local communities and are often trusted by local people. This allows them to serve as mediators and facilitators in conflict resolution efforts. Churches also often provide social services to their communities, such as education and healthcare, which can help address some of the underlying causes of conflict.

The authors also underline the need for interfaith dialogue and cooperation to promote African peace and security. They claim that churches have played a key role in fostering interfaith dialogue and cooperation, which has helped reduce tensions and promote understanding between different religious groups. Francis and Kanyoro's justification is still applicable in the current political climate, where conflicts and crises threaten African communities' peace and security. The inquiry emphasizes the crucial role that churches can play in sponsoring peace and reconciliation in these contexts. Moreover, their research informs us of the critical role that churches can play in fostering peace and security in Africa.

Their analysis suggests that churches are uniquely positioned to serve as mediators and facilitators in conflict resolution efforts and can help address some of the underlying causes of conflict by providing social services to their communities. The authors' focus on the relevance of interfaith dialogue and cooperation also reminds us of the need for a collaborative and inclusive approach to promoting African peace and security. By fostering understanding and cooperation between different religious groups, churches can help reduce tensions and promote lasting peace. Lastly, these findings are essential for policymakers, development practitioners, and other stakeholders involved in peacebuilding initiatives. They suggest that Christian churches can be vital in sponsoring peace and security in conflict-affected areas. Their involvement can help ensure more inclusive, sustainable, and effective peacebuilding efforts.

Succinctly, Francis and Kanyoro's study highlights the critical role that churches can play in promoting peace and security in Africa. Their analysis suggests that churches are uniquely positioned to serve as mediators and facilitators in conflict resolution efforts and can help address some of the underlying causes of conflict by providing social services to their communities. By embracing these principles and promoting interfaith dialogue and cooperation, churches can continue to play a vital role in promoting peace and security in Africa.

Equally, Moltmann's (1993) inquiry into the relationship between Christian theology and security highlights the importance of hope in redefining our understanding of security. Moltmann argues that the Christian concept of hope, rooted in the belief in the resurrection, offers a new perspective on security. Here, we explore Moltmann's rationale and discuss the potential benefits of his findings. Moltmann contends that traditional understandings of security must be revised in dealing with the challenges of the modern world. He argues that the dominant concept of security is based on fear and the desire for control, which results in the exclusion of those deemed to be a threat. Moltmann claims that the Christian concept of hope provides an alternative to this understanding of security. He contends that hope is not about control or exclusion but the possibility of new beginnings and transformation. According to Moltmann, hope is not just a psychological state, but a theological virtue grounded in the belief in the resurrection.

Additionally, Moltmann's (1993) research has several implications for our understanding of security:

1. It highlights the limitations of the dominant security concept based on fear and control. Moltmann claims that this understanding of security is not only ineffective but can also be harmful. The focus on control and exclusion can lead to the marginalization of certain groups and perpetuate violence and conflict.
2. Moltmann's inquiry suggests that hope provides an alternative to this understanding of security. Hope is not just a psychological state grounded in a theological belief in the resurrection. This understanding of hope emphasizes the possibility of transformation and new beginnings, providing a basis for a more inclusive and peaceful security framework.
3. Moltmann's rationale has practical implications for policymakers and practitioners.

A more inclusive and peaceful security framework can be built by focusing on hope and transformation rather than fear and control. This can be achieved by promoting policies and practices that prioritize inclusion, dialogue, and reconciliation.

In short, Moltmann's (1993) undertaking stresses the essence of having hope in redefining our understanding of security. His research proposes that hope provides an alternative to the dominant understanding of security based on fear and control. This alternative framework, grounded in the belief in the resurrection, emphasizes the possibility of transformation and new beginnings. This understanding of hope can provide a basis for a more inclusive and peaceful security framework, promoting inclusion, dialogue, and reconciliation.

As we finish discussing early Christianity's security and territorial protection standpoints, we now focus on the Islamic religion. In the following chapter, we will delve into the viewpoints of Quranic texts and Prophet Muhammad's teachings on national security and territorial protection, exploring its teachings and insights on the subject matter. By investigating another major world religion's stances on national security, we hope to comprehend better how faith shapes and informs our sense of security.

References:

Abrahamsen, R. (2017). Security and development in global politics: A critical comparison. Polity.

Allman, M. T. (2016). Just war reconsidered: Strategy, ethics, and theory. Georgetown University Press.

Ambrose. (1989). Concerning the Duties of the Clergy. In P. Schaff & H. Wace (Eds.), A Select Library of the Nicene and Post-Nicene

Aquinas, T. (2002). On Law, Morality and Politics (R. Regan, Ed.). Indianapolis: Hackett.

Augustine. (1984). The City of God. (H. Bettenson, Trans.). Penguin Classics.

Borg, M. J. (2004). Jesus: Uncovering the life, teachings, and relevance of a religious revolutionary. HarperCollins.

Cameron, A. (2011). The emperor and the Christian God. Harvard University Press.

Constantine. (325 CE). Letter to the Bishops of the East. Retrieved from https://www.newadvent.org/fathers/3202040.htm

Compendium of the Social Doctrine of the Church. (2004). Vatican City: Pontifical Council for Justice and Peace.

Clement of Alexandria. (1885). Stromata. (Rev. William Wilson, Trans.). T. & T. Clark.

Drake, H. A. (2000). Constantine and the bishops: The politics of intolerance. The Johns Hopkins University Press.

Duffy, E. (1997). Saints and Sinners: A History of the Popes. Yale University Press.

Francis, D. J., & Kanyoro, R. W. (2012). Religion, conflict, and peacebuilding in Africa: A case for Catholic and evangelical church partnership. Journal of Ecumenical Studies, 47(2), 221-238.

Frend, W. H. C. (1984). The rise of Christianity. Fortress Press.

Hauerwas, S. (1991). A community of character: Toward a constructive Christian social ethic. University of Notre Dame Press.

Hays, R. B. (2011). The moral vision of the New Testament: A contemporary introduction to New Testament ethics. HarperCollins.

Haldon, J. (2016). The Empire That Would Not Die: The Paradox of Eastern Roman Survival, 640–740. Harvard University Press.

Harnack, A. (1908). Militia Christi: The Christian religion and the military in the first three centuries. Putnam.

Hauerwas, S. (1984). Should Christians fight? Reflections on war and nonviolence. Brazos Press.

Heather, P. (2018). The Restoration of Rome: Barbarian Popes and Imperial Pretenders. Oxford University.

Gonzalez, J. L. (2010). The Story of Christianity: The early church to the present day. HarperOne.

Jones, A. H. M. (1971). Constantine and the conversion of Europe. University of Toronto Press.

Kelly, C. (2008). The Oxford Dictionary of Byzantium (Vol. 1). Oxford University Press.

Keener, C. S. (2012). Acts: An Exegetical Commentary: Volume 3: 15:1-23:35. Baker Academic.

Krautheimer, R. (1980). Rome: Profile of a city, 312-1308. Princeton University Press.

Landes, R. (2011). Heaven on Earth: The Varieties of the Millennial Experience. Oxford University Press.

Meyendorff, J. (1989). Imperial unity and Christian divisions: The Church 450-680 AD St Vladimir's Seminary Press.

Moltmann, J. (1993). Theology of hope: On the ground and the implications of a Christian eschatology. Augsburg Fortress Publishers.

Mounce, R. H. (2007). The New International Commentary on the New Testament: The Book of Revelation. William B. Eerdmans Publishing Company.

New International Version. (2011). Philippians 4:6-7. Bible Gateway. https://www.biblegateway.com/passage/?search=Philippians%204%3A6-7&version=NIV

New International Version. (2011). Matthew 5:44. Bible Gateway. https://www.biblegateway.com/passage/?search=Matthew%205%3A44&version=NIV

New International Version. (2011). Romans 13:1-7. Bible Gateway. https://www.biblegateway.com/passage/?search=Romans%2013%3A1-7&version=NIV

Niebuhr, R. (2008). The irony of American history. University of Chicago Press.

Noble, T. F. X. (2012). Western civilization: Beyond boundaries. Cengage Learning.

Norwich, J. J. (1988). Byzantium: The early centuries. Alfred A. Knopf, Inc.

Norwich, J. J. (1997). A Short History of Byzantium. Vintage.

The Apostolic Fathers: Greek texts and English translations (3rd ed.). (2007). Baker Academic.

Tertullian. (1972). Apology. (T. R. Glover, Trans.). Loeb Classical Library.

The Holy Bible: New International Version. (2011). Biblica.

Tierney, B. (1999). The Crisis of Church and State 1050-1300. University of Toronto Press.

Treadgold, W. (1997). A history of the Byzantine state and society. Stanford University Press.

9

Quranic Texts' Viewpoints on National Security

The evolution of Islam and the teachings of its Prophet, Muhammad, played a significant role in framing the concept of national security during the early Islamic era. The Quran, as the primary holy text of Islam, provides guidance on various aspects of life, including stability, territorial protection, and national security. Throughout history, Muslims have looked to the Quran for direction in establishing stable societies and protecting their territories.

Islam emerged in the 7th century in the Arabian Peninsula, facing countless challenges and threats to its security, and foreign invasions were common. The early Muslims were persecuted by the ruling Meccan tribes, which led to their migration (Hijra) to Medina in 622 CE. Muhammad established the first Islamic state in Medina and faced numerous military campaigns against the Meccan tribes and other hostile groups. As a result, the religion has developed a set of principles and practices that promote peace, justice, and security.

The Islamic notion of national security is primarily connected to the idea of the Ummah, which means community or nation. Shared values, beliefs, and practices define the Ummah, and it includes Muslims from all over the world. Therefore, Islam's perspectives on national security are not limited to a particular country or region but encompass the entire Muslim community. In this context, the Quranic message emphasized the importance of social order, justice, territorial protection, and defensive force when necessary.

The Quranic injunctions significantly shaped the concept of national security during Muhammad's time. The Quran underlines the importance of self-defense and protecting oneself and others from harm. For instance, Surah al-Hajj, chapter 22 states: "Permission [to fight] has been given to those who are being fought because they were wronged. And indeed, Allah is competent to give them victory" (22:39). Moreover, Muhammad also recognized the importance of intelligence gathering and information security, which helped him to anticipate and counter potential threats to the Islamic state. He established a network of spies and informants to gather information about the enemies and their plans, which proved critical in several military campaigns.

This underscores the Islamic belief that social stability is a prerequisite for a just and prosperous society. The Quran states that justice is essential for the stability of society and that Muslims must uphold it. In addition, the Quran underscores the implication of justice, saying, "O you who have believed, be persistently standing firm in justice, witnesses for Allah, even if it be against yourselves or parents and relatives" (4:135). In terms of territorial protection, the Quran emphasizes the importance of defending one's homeland against external threats. The Quran states that Muslims must protect their land and resist those who seek to harm them (Quran 22:39-40). This duty extends to all Muslims, regardless of their social status or societal position. This highlights the importance of fairness and impartiality in maintaining stability and order. The concept of justice in Islam encompasses not only the distribution of wealth and resources but also the treatment of individuals and the establishment of laws and regulations that promote equality and fairness (Ghafar, 2017).

At its core, Islam teaches that individuals and societies must be protected from internal and external threats. The Quran states that "Allah does not love those who cause corruption and mischief" (2:205), emphasizing the importance of security and stability. Islam also recognizes the need for collective security, where nations work together to ensure the safety and prosperity of their citizens. The Prophet Muhammad established a treaty with the Jewish community in Medina, known as the Constitution of Medina, which provided for the mutual defense of all parties in the event of an attack.

Islam's perspectives on national security have also evolved. During the medieval period, Islamic scholars developed the concept of jihad, which means struggle or striving. Jihad has two forms: the greater jihad, which refers to the individual's internal struggle against sin and temptation, and the lesser jihad, which refers to the defense of the Muslim community against external threats. The principle of jihad has been controversial in modern times, as some groups have wrongfully used it to justify violent actions. Nevertheless, the Prophet's teaching and directives stress that jihad is only defensive and should only be used preemptively as a last resort to stop looming threats. The Quran states, "Fight in the way of Allah those who fight you but do not transgress. Indeed. Allah does not like transgressors" (Quran 2:190).

The Quran also emphasizes the importance of territorial protection and self-defense. This verse accentuates the obligation of Muslims to defend themselves against aggression. It also accentuates the essence of conducting warfare with justice and fairness, showing restraint, and avoiding excessive force. The Quran encourages Muslims to seek peace and reconciliation whenever possible. Allah says in Surah Al-Anfal, Verse 61: "And if they incline to peace, then incline to it and trust in Allah. Indeed, it is He who is the Hearing, the Knowing." This verse emphasizes the importance of seeking peace and reconciliation whenever possible rather than resorting to violence.

Protecting life and property is greatly emphasized in the Quran. It is stated in Surah Al-Ma'idah (Chapter 5) Verse 32: "On that account, We ordained for the Children of Israel that if anyone killed a person not in retaliation of murder, or (and) to spread mischief in the land - it would be as if he killed all mankind, and if anyone saved a life, it would be as if he saved the life of all mankind." This verse highlights the importance of protecting human life and the severe consequences of taking it unjustly. Protecting property is also essential in maintaining stability and preventing chaos in society.

In the early years of Islam, the Muslim community faced significant threats to its territorial integrity and security. The pagan tribes of Mecca, which controlled the commercial and strategic hub of the Arabian Peninsula, opposed the Muslim community, and launched several military campaigns against them. In response, the Quranic message emphasized the importance of self-defense and territorial protection. For example, in Chapter 22, Verse 39, the Quran states, "Permission to fight is given to those against whom war is made because they have been wronged" (22:39). This verse pinpoints the Islamic belief that defensive warfare is justified in response to aggression and injustice.

The Quran also addresses national security, particularly in war and conflict. The Quran emphasizes the importance of self-defense and encourages Muslims to prepare for battle if necessary (Quran 8:60). However, the Quran also emphasizes the importance of peace and urges Muslims to seek peaceful solutions to conflicts whenever possible (Quran 8:61). Historically, Muslims have relied on the Quranic teachings regarding stability, territorial protection, and national security to establish and maintain stable societies. In particular, during the time of the Prophet Muhammad, Muslims established a stable society in Medina by adhering to the Quranic principles of justice, equality, and fairness (Asad, 2003). Similarly, during the Ottoman Empire, Muslims maintained control of their territories by adhering to the Quranic principles of self-defense and territorial protection (Khalidi, 2010).

In addition, the Quran also emphasizes the importance of territorial protection. For instance, Surah Al-Anfal (Chapter 8) verse 60 states, "And prepare against them whatever you are able of power and of steeds of war by which you may terrify the enemy of Allah and your enemy and others besides them whom you do not know [but] whom Allah knows. And whatever you spend in the cause of Allah will be fully repaid to you, and you will not be wronged." This verse underscores the need to be prepared for military defense, including acquiring military equipment and training, to protect oneself and one's people from potential enemies. In addition to military preparedness, the Prophet Muhammad also emphasized the importance of diplomacy in national security (Esposito, 2002). He established diplomatic relations with neighboring tribes and countries and negotiated treaties that ensured peace and security for the Ummah.

The Prophet Muhammad recognized the need for peaceful relations with neighboring countries and tribes and believed diplomacy was essential to achieving national security. Correspondingly, the notion of jihad, often misunderstood as a call for violence, is rooted in defending one's faith and homeland. Jihad is a concept that includes, first and foremost, striving internally, non-military, and, as a last resort, maybe exerting physical efforts to protect people, the land, and resources, uphold justice, protect the weak, and defend the Islamic community from external threats.

As the Muslim community expanded and faced new threats, such as the Byzantine and Sassanid empires, the Quranic message accentuated the importance of territorial protection and self-defense. The Quran also emphasized the value of alliances and diplomacy to ensure territorial and national security. For example, in Chapter 8, Verse 61, the Quran states, "And if they incline to peace, then incline to it [also] and rely upon Allah" (8:61). This verse highlights the Islamic belief in the necessity of peaceful resolution of conflicts and the use of diplomacy to ensure territorial and national security.

The Prophet Muhammad's teachings stressed the essence of protecting the Ummah from external threats and internal conflicts. He recognized that a strong and cohesive community was essential for national security, and internal conflicts could weaken the Ummah's ability to defend itself. The Prophet also emphasized the importance of preparedness and training for military defense, noting that "the best of people are those who are most beneficial to people" (Hadith Sahih Bukhari, Book 73, Hadith 41). The hadith, which are the sayings and actions of the Prophet Muhammad (peace be upon him), also provide guidance on security and territorial protection. In particular, the Prophet (peace be upon him) is reported to have said, "Whoever kills a non-Muslim under Muslim protection shall not smell the fragrance of Paradise." The concept of territorial protection is also underlined in the hadith. The Prophet (peace be upon him) is reported to have said, "The land belongs to Allah and His Messenger, and I do not wish to prevent you from leaving it if you wish."

The hadith, which are the recorded sayings and actions of the Prophet Muhammad, also accentuate the significance of stability, territorial protection, and national security. For instance, in one hadith, the Prophet Muhammad said, "The one who fights for the sake of Allah and gets killed, or attains victory, will be rewarded with paradise" (Bukhari 52:46). This Hadith highlights the importance of defending one's land and religion. The Prophet Muhammad also emphasized the importance of justice and mercy in warfare, stating, "Do not kill a child, a woman, or an old person. Do not harm trees, crops, or livestock" (Abu Dawud 2635).

The early Islamic community saw itself as a distinct entity with religious beliefs, cultural practices, and political aspirations. The concept of national security during this period was closely tied to the Ummah's survival and growth, as the Muslims faced opposition from their pagan and Jewish neighbors. The Battle of Badr in 624 CE was a significant event in Islamic history, as it marked the first military victory of the Muslims over the Meccan forces. This victory was seen as a divine intervention and reinforced the Muslims' belief in their mission to establish an Islamic state (Klein, 2004). The Sunnah, the practices and examples set by the Prophet Muhammad, also guide stability, territorial protection, and national security. The Prophet Muhammad was involved in numerous defensive battles to protect the Muslim community from aggression.

Furthermore, Islam's perspectives on national security are based on several fundamental principles, including the sanctity of life, the importance of justice, and the need for cooperation and collaboration. These principles are reflected in the Islamic concept of "siyasa shar'iyya," Islamic politics, which emphasizes the importance of maintaining order and stability while upholding Islamic law principles. In addition, Islamic scholars and leaders have emphasized the importance of maintaining strong relationships with neighboring countries and promoting cooperation and collaboration among nations. They have also stressed the need for effective communication and dialogue between nations to resolve conflicts and prevent the escalation of violence. Islam also focuses on the implication of individual and community preparedness for emergencies and disasters. The concept of "tawakkul," which means trust in God, encourages individuals and communities to take practical measures to ensure their safety and security while relying on God for guidance and protection (Abdelnasser, 2015).

Historically, Muslim dynasties, starting with the Rashidun Caliphate (632-661 CE) and continuing through the Umayyad (661-750 CE), Abbasid (750-1258 CE), and Ottoman Empires (1299-1922 CE), faced various security challenges, including external invasions, internal rebellions, and sectarian conflicts. The early Muslim community faced significant security challenges, including the Ridda Wars, a series of military campaigns to suppress rebellions against the first caliph, Abu Bakr (Esposito, 1998). The caliphate's security policy aimed to protect the nascent Muslim community's unity and territorial integrity. The Quran and Sunnah guided the caliphate's security policy, emphasizing the importance of maintaining justice, protecting life and property, and avoiding aggression.

During the Umayyad Dynasty, which ruled from 661 to 750 CE, the issue of national security became more formalized. They also established a professional army and intelligence system to ensure the state's security. The Umayyad dynasty succeeded the Rashidun Caliphate and faced external threats from the Byzantine and Sassanian Empires and internal rebellions by non-Arab Muslims. The Umayyads' security policy aimed to consolidate their political power, expand the caliphate's territory, and suppress internal dissent (Tabatabai, 1987). The Umayyad caliphs relied on a centralized military and administrative system, including Arab tribal armies and Persian and Byzantine bureaucrats.

In contrast, the Abbasid Dynasty overthrew the Umayyads and ruled from 750 to 1258 CE, focusing more on the internal aspects of national security. The Abbasid caliphs emphasized the importance of maintaining social stability and order within the Islamic state. They also established a solid bureaucracy to ensure the efficient functioning of the state and prevent corruption and abuse of power. It faced security challenges from external enemies, including the Byzantine and Tang Empires, and internal uprisings by various groups, including the Kharijites and Shiites. The Abbasids' security policy emphasized the need for a strong military and intelligence apparatus to defend the caliphate's borders and suppress internal dissent. The Abbasids also relied on a decentralized administrative system, including local governors and tax collectors (Abdul-Majid, 2015).

Furthermore, during the early Islamic period, the concern of national security was primarily focused on protecting the Islamic community or Ummah. The Prophet Muhammad established the Islamic community in Medina, and his successors, the Rashidun caliphs, continued to expand the Islamic empire through military conquests. During this period, many jurists formulated the concept based on the idea of Dar al-Islam (the abode of Islam) and Dar al-Harb (the abode of war), where Muslims were required to defend themselves and expand the Islamic empire (Abdul-Majid, 2015). It should be noted that the concepts of Dar al-Islam and Dar al-Harb are neither Quranic nor in the teachings of Prophet Muhammad. Instead, the Muslims reacted to the circumstances of their time, using it as a protective mechanism to discourage Muslims from traveling to unfriendly territory that could cause war with the Muslim community. The early Islamic period also saw the development of the concept of jihad, which was seen as a defensive or offensive struggle to protect the Islamic community from external threats (Esposito, 1998). The concept of national security during this period was thus closely linked to Islamic identity and the protection of the Islamic community.

Moreover, during the Umayyad and Abbasid dynasties, the concept of national security became more complex as Muslim territories expanded and the Islamic empire became more diverse. The Islamic empire was no longer confined to the Arabian Peninsula but extended to North Africa, Spain, Persia, and Central Asia. In addition, the Umayyad and Abbasid caliphs had to deal with various internal and external threats, including the Byzantine and Sassanian empires, the Mongol invasions, and internal revolts. During this period, the concept of national security focused on protecting the Islamic empire from these threats and maintaining political stability and social order. The concept of jihad also evolved from a primarily military concept to a more spiritual and moral one (Ali, 2016).

During the Ottoman Empire, the concept of national security became more centralized and bureaucratic. The empire was vast and diverse, and the sultans had to balance the interests of various ethnic and religious groups. Additionally, they faced numerous external threats from European powers, particularly during the 19th century. To counter these threats, the Ottomans modernized their military and political institutions. During this period, the concept of national security focused on protecting the empire from external threats, maintaining territorial integrity, and preserving Ottoman identity and culture (Abdul-Majid, 2015).

In terms of the Prophet's teachings on governance, they have significant implications for contemporary security challenges. He emphasized the importance of justice, compassion, consultation, and non-violence in creating a stable and secure society. The principle of justice in governance is particularly relevant in contemporary security challenges, where the abuse of power by government officials can lead to widespread discontent and radicalization. Additionally, the Prophet emphasized the need for rulers to treat their subjects fairly, regardless of their religion or social status.

The Prophet Muhammad's teachings on governance emphasized the principles of justice, fairness, and consultation. He recognized that a strong and cohesive community was essential for national security, and internal conflicts could weaken the community's ability to defend itself. Therefore, the Prophet established a system of governance that included consultation with all members of the community and emphasized the importance of justice and fairness for all, regardless of background or beliefs. This approach ensured that decisions were made in the community's best interests and that all members of society had a voice.

The Prophet also established a governance system based on Islamic principles, including the importance of protecting the weak and vulnerable, ensuring the accountability of leaders, and upholding the rule of law. He accentuated the importance of good governance and recognized that a corrupt or unjust government could threaten national security. He also realized the need for military preparedness and training for national defense. The Prophet emphasized the significance of seeking peaceful solutions to conflicts and negotiating treaties with neighboring tribes and empires, providing a framework for peaceful coexistence and reducing the risk of conflict.

Regarding the implications of Prophet Muhammad's teachings for contemporary security challenges, his contributions to modern security studies are significant. His teachings on governance provide valuable insights into contemporary security challenges, particularly in areas such as democracy, human rights, and accountability. The emphasis on consultation and community involvement in decision-making processes is highly relevant in democratic societies, ensuring that policies and decisions reflect the community's best interests.

The emphasis on justice and fairness is also relevant to contemporary security challenges, including terrorism and social unrest, often arising from perceived injustice and inequality. Furthermore, the focus on accountability and the rule of law is highly relevant to contemporary security challenges, such as corruption and human rights abuses, which can weaken states and threaten national security.

The Prophet's emphasis on consultation and peaceful conflict resolution provides an essential framework for addressing contemporary security challenges, including cyber warfare and international conflicts. Finally, his recognition of the importance of military preparedness and training is relevant to contemporary security challenges, such as the proliferation of weapons of mass destruction and the rise of non-state actors.

Contextualizing National Security in Islam

In terms of contextualizing national security in Islam, the challenges faced by the Ummah during Prophet Muhammad's time influenced the concept of national security in several ways. The early Islamic concept of national security recognizes the importance of religious ideology in shaping state security policies and emphasizes the need for the Ummah to be united in the face of threats. The Prophet Muhammad encouraged Muslims to form alliances and work together to overcome their enemies, capitalizing on the necessity of maintaining unity and cooperation among different societal groups. Additionally, this concept provides a valuable framework for promoting international peace and security, relevant in many Muslim countries today where religion plays a significant role in politics.

Secondly, the early Islamic concept of national security highlights the importance of a strong sense of identity and belonging in shaping security policies. The early Muslims saw themselves as a distinct community with unique beliefs, practices, and aspirations. This relevance to modern security studies requires states to consider the role of identity in shaping security policies. It also emphasizes the essence of military power in protecting the Ummah, with the Prophet Muhammad and his companions recognizing the importance of military strength to defend against external threats. Furthermore, it accentuates justice and fairness, ensuring that security measures respect human rights and promote social justice. In contemporary times, this translates to the need for modernizing and strengthening the military to protect against external threats.

Thirdly, the early Islamic concept of national security provides insights into the role of military power in shaping security policies. Early Muslims recognized the significance of military strength in protecting the Ummah and establishing an Islamic state, offering relevance in modern security studies, where states must consider the role of military power in defending against external threats. The concept also stresses the significance of religious and moral values in national security. The Prophet Muhammad taught Muslims to behave ethically and justly, even in the face of aggression. Additionally, it emphasizes the importance of individual and community preparedness to build resilience and reduce vulnerability during emergencies and disasters. In modern times, this emphasizes the need for governments to uphold human rights and democratic values in their security policies.

In modern times, Islam's perspectives on national security have been shaped by various factors, including colonialism, globalization, and terrorism. Many Muslim-majority countries have experienced significant instability and conflict in recent decades, leading to an increased emphasis on national security. For example, Saudi Arabia has faced numerous challenges to its national security, including terrorist attacks by Al-Qaeda and ISIS and the ongoing conflict in Yemen. In response, Saudi Arabia has heavily invested in its military and intelligence capabilities and worked closely with its Gulf Cooperation Council (GCC) allies to counter external threats.

In present times, the concept of national security in Muslim countries has been influenced by both Western and Islamic ideas. Muslim countries have been exposed to Western concepts of national security, particularly during the Cold War, when they were caught in the crossfire between the US and the USSR. Consequently, many Muslim countries have adopted Western-style political institutions and security structures, such as intelligence agencies and national security councils. However, they have also sought to reconcile Western national security ideas with Islamic principles, particularly protecting Islamic identity and the Ummah.

The evolution of the concept of national security in Islam has several lessons for modern security studies:

1. The Islamic concept of national security is related to Islamic identity and the protection of the Ummah, making Muslim countries prioritize the protection of Islamic identity and values over other security concerns.
2. The idea of jihad in Islam has evolved to primarily involve internal struggle and enlightenment, although some people project it as a military offensive. As a result, Muslim countries may prioritize non-military means of achieving national security, such as economic development and social welfare.
3. The Ottoman centralized and bureaucratic national security model may offer some insights into how Muslim countries can approach national security in modern times.

In recent decades, Islam's perspectives on national security have been influenced by several factors, including colonialism, globalization, and terrorism. Additionally, many Muslim-majority countries have experienced significant instability and conflict, leading to an increased emphasis on national security. This essay explores how Islam views national security, the factors shaping its perspectives, and the challenges facing Muslim-majority countries today. Islam places a high value on security and stability at the individual and collective levels, with the Quran emphasizing justice, peace, and security and encouraging Muslims to strive for a society embodying these values (Kamrava, 2006). Sharia, the Islamic law, provides a framework for promoting security and order, including using force when necessary to protect public safety. The concept of Ummah, or the Muslim community, also reinforces the importance of collective security and mutual protection among Muslims.

Colonialism significantly impacted the Muslim world's understanding of national security, as Muslim-majority countries were often subject to political, economic, and cultural domination by Western powers during the colonial period, leading to a sense of vulnerability and insecurity. This experience has deeply influenced the Muslim world's perspective on national security, with many countries prioritizing the protection of their independence and sovereignty (Riaz, 2012). While globalization has brought economic growth and development opportunities, it has also created new challenges and risks. For instance, it facilitated the spread of extremist ideologies and made it easier for terrorist groups to operate across borders. Moreover, economic globalization has generated new inequalities and social tensions, contributing to instability and conflict.

Terrorism has had a profound impact on Muslim-majority countries in recent decades, with groups like Al Qaeda, ISIS, and other groups attacking civilians and government institutions, causing widespread fear and disruption. While these groups justify their actions in the name of Islam, Muslim scholars and leaders widely condemn their tactics. As a result, Muslim-majority countries must balance security measures with respect for human rights and the rule of law. Terrorism's impact extends beyond physical damage, affecting the mental health of individuals who experience such attacks or fear them (Kamrava, 2006).

The rise of terrorist groups like Al Qaeda and ISIS is associated with various factors, including geopolitical instability, economic inequality, and political oppression. These groups exploit the grievances of marginalized communities, presenting themselves as defenders of Islam and an alternative to corrupt and oppressive governments. Social media has enabled them to spread their ideology and recruit followers worldwide. Additionally, the US-led wars in Afghanistan and Iraq have provided fertile ground for these groups to gain support and establish a foothold in the region (Riaz, 2012).

Governments in Muslim-majority countries have implemented various measures to combat terrorism, ranging from military operations against terrorist groups to counter-terrorism laws and strategies. However, these measures have not always been effective, and in some cases, they have led to human rights abuses and further alienation of marginalized communities. Addressing the root causes of terrorism, such as economic inequality and political oppression, is essential for achieving long-term solutions. Also, recognizing that most Muslims reject terrorism and that Islam does not condone violence, the fight against terrorism must be a collective effort involving governments, civil society, and religious leaders working together to promote peace and stability.

Prophet Muhammad's Position on Stability and Territorial Protection

Maintaining stability and territorial protection is essential for the survival and prosperity of any nation, and early Muslims during Prophet Muhammad's time are no exception. A country's stability depends on its government's ability to control and manage the various factors that affect its economy, social structures, and political landscape. On the other hand, territorial protection refers to safeguarding a country's borders from external threats, such as foreign military invasion, terrorist attacks, or smuggling. A country's borders are its first line of defense against external threats. Without proper territorial protection, a country is vulnerable to invasion, terrorism, and smuggling.

The Prophet Muhammad's teachings regarding good governance and national security are essential to Islamic history and remain relevant today. He recognized the significance of effective governance and its role in maintaining national security. He believed that a corrupt or unjust government could pose a significant threat to the security of a nation. In his teachings, the Prophet accentuated the essence of sound and impartial leadership and the need for leaders to be accountable to their people. Also, he stressed the idea of Shura, or mutual consultation, which means that leaders should consult with their people and consider their views. As the Quran states, "And consult them in the matter. And when you have decided, then rely upon Allah" (Quran 3:159). The Prophet himself was known for his consultation with his companions and the importance he placed on their advice.

These teachings highlight the importance of good governance and the need for leaders to be just and consultative in their decision-making. They also emphasize the importance of the rule of law and the need to uphold justice, which is essential for maintaining national security. These teachings remain relevant in contemporary times, as corrupt or unjust governments can lead to political instability, social unrest, and even conflict. He said, "The best of rulers are those whom you love and who love you, who pray for you, and you pray for them. The worst of rulers are those whom you hate and who hate you and whom you curse and who curse you" (Al-Tirmidhi, 1352). This statement emphasizes the importance of leaders having a close relationship with their people and working towards their best interests.

The Prophet Muhammad also stressed the need for leaders to be transparent in their decision-making processes and consult with their people before making significant decisions. He said, "Consult your people in governance matters, and they will love and support you" (Al-Tirmidhi, 1352). This statement highlights the essence of leaders collaborating with their people to achieve a common goal. The Prophet also realized the need for military preparedness and training for community defense. He underlines the implication of having a well-trained and equipped army to protect the nation against external threats. He encouraged his followers to prepare for defense and acquire the necessary military skills. As stated in the Quran, "And prepare against them whatever you are able of power and of steeds of war by which you may terrify the enemy of Allah and your enemy and others besides them whom you do not know [but] whom Allah knows" (Quran 8:60). He was known to have said, "The strong believer is better and more beloved to Allah than the weak believer, although both are good. Strive for what will benefit you, seek help from Allah, and do not despair. If a misfortune befalls you, know that what has befallen you was not going to miss you, and what has missed you will not befall you."

Furthermore, He said, "Oppression will be darkness on the Day of Judgment" (Muslim, 2578). This statement emphasizes the importance of leaders being just and fair in their decisions to prevent any form of oppression or injustice that could lead to unrest or violence. The Prophet Muhammad also recognized the need for military preparedness and training for national defense. He said, "Preparation for war is a means of peace" (Bukhari, 2993). This statement highlights the importance of being prepared for any eventuality that could threaten national security.

Also, Prophet Muhammad underlined the significance of ethical behavior in all aspects of life, including interactions with others. He taught that Muslims should be just, kind, and merciful, even to their enemies. As mentioned in the Quran, "And do not let the hatred of a people for having obstructed you from al-Masjid al-Haram lead you to transgress. And cooperate in righteousness and piety, but do not cooperate in sin and aggression" (Quran 5:2). This verse highlights the importance of ethical behavior, even in the face of aggression, and the need to cooperate in righteousness and piety. Moreover, he stressed the need for unity and cooperation among Muslims for security and defense. Consequently, he established a strong sense of community and brotherhood among his followers, facilitating military cooperation and preparedness. This emphasis on military preparedness and unity remains relevant today, as nations must be prepared to defend themselves against potential threats and safeguard their national security.

His teachings on ethics and justice remain relevant in modern-day as policymakers seek to promote peace and stability in their countries. His teachings emphasize the importance of ethical behavior and the need to be just and fair in all matters, including those related to territorial protection. By behaving ethically and justly, policymakers can build trust and cooperation with their neighbors, which can contribute to maintaining territorial protection and stability.

In addition to protecting individuals, Islam also emphasizes the importance of preserving social harmony. The Quran states: "Indeed, Allah orders justice and good conduct and giving to relatives and forbids immorality and bad conduct and oppression. He admonishes you that perhaps you will be reminded" (16:90). This verse highlights the importance of justice and good conduct in maintaining social harmony and warns against immorality, immoral conduct, and oppression, which can disrupt societal stability.

Islam also emphasizes protecting individual rights, including the right to life, liberty, and property. In particular, the Quran states: "Whoever kills a soul unless for a soul or corruption [done] in the land - it is as if he had slain mankind entirely. And whoever saves one - it is as if he had saved mankind entirely" (5:32). This verse highlights the sanctity of human life and emphasizes the importance of protecting it. Similarly, the Quran states: "And do not consume one another's wealth unjustly or send it [in bribery] to the rulers in order that [they might aid] you [to] consume a portion of the wealth of the people in sin, while you know [it is unlawful]" (2:188). This verse emphasizes the importance of protecting individual property rights and highlights the negative consequences of violating them.

In addition to military preparedness, the Prophet emphasized the importance of diplomacy and the peaceful resolution of conflicts. He encouraged his followers to seek peaceful solutions to disputes and treat others respectfully and with dignity.

The Prophet's teachings on good governance and national security have had a lasting impact on Islamic history. His emphasis on just leadership, consultation, military preparedness, and diplomacy is still relevant today. Many Muslim countries today strive to implement these principles in their governance, although there is always room for improvement. Furthermore, he recognized that a unified community is crucial for national security, and he encouraged his companions to work together to defend themselves against potential threats. His teachings on unity and cooperation remain relevant in the modern-day, as nations must be prepared to defend themselves against potential threats and safeguard their national security.

Islam's perspectives on national security have been shaped by colonialism, globalization, and terrorism. Consequently, Muslim-majority countries face significant challenges in maintaining security and stability in the face of political, economic, and social upheaval. However, the values of justice, peace, and security central to Islamic tradition offer a framework for promoting stability and order. By working together to address common challenges and promoting mutual understanding and cooperation, Muslim-majority countries can build a more secure and prosperous future for their citizens.

In essence, the Prophet Muhammad's perspectives on good governance and national security were based on the principles of justice, accountability, military preparedness, and peaceful resolution of conflicts. These teachings remain relevant today and can provide valuable insights for contemporary leaders seeking to promote national security and good governance. He capitalizes on the importance of leaders being just and fair in their decision-making processes to prevent any form of oppression or injustice. He recognized that a corrupt or unjust government could pose a significant threat to national security and that military preparedness and training were essential for defense. His teachings are still relevant today, and leaders can draw inspiration from them to promote good governance and ensure national security. His perspectives on security and territorial protection remain relevant in contemporary times. His focus on good governance, justice, and military preparedness highpoints the need for sustaining a strong and just government while ensuring that nations are sufficiently prepared and equipped to defend themselves against potential threats. By contextualizing his teachings, we can better understand the importance of national security and the steps that must be taken to safeguard it.

Past and Current Inquiries about Islamic Stance on National Security

Muslim scholars have extensively considered the notion of national security in Islamic thought over the years, both in the past and present. Today, the Islamic stance on national security remains a subject of interest and debate, especially in modern-day security challenges. One of the critical issues investigated in Islamic studies is the relationship between Islam and national security. This issue is particularly relevant in the contemporary world, given the prevalence of conflicts rooted in religious differences. In addition, Islam has a rich tradition of political and strategic thought, providing insights into the Islamic stance on national security and its contributions to modern-day security.

Historically, Islamic scholars have placed significant focus on the implications of national security. They believed that the protection of the state was paramount, and it was the ruler's responsibility to ensure the safety and well-being of the citizens. Islamic law, or Sharia, provides guidelines for the protection of national security, developed over time to address the changing needs of society. In the modern era, Islamic scholars continue to examine the Islamic stance on national security and its relevance to contemporary security challenges. For instance, scholars have explored the role of Islamic law in regulating modern forms of warfare, including cyberwarfare and drone strikes. They have also analyzed the impact of globalization and terrorism on national security and the challenges these pose for Muslim-majority states.

Traditionally, Islamic civilization was renowned for its sophisticated security infrastructure and military organization, with a strong emphasis on justice and the protection of civilians. This legacy continues to influence modern-day security practices in Muslim-majority countries, where the role of religion and traditional values in national security policy remains significant. In recent years, scholars have explored how Islamic teachings and values can contribute to modern-day security challenges, such as terrorism, extremism, and insurgency. A deeper understanding of Islamic principles and history can provide insights into the root causes of these issues and help develop more effective strategies to counter them.

One of the earliest and most influential contributions to the Islamic concept of national security was made by the 14th-century Islamic scholar Ibn Khaldun. In his masterpiece "Muqaddimah," he laid out a theory of social and political organization that emphasized the importance of unity and solidarity among citizens for the security and stability of a nation. Ibn Khaldun was a 14th-century Islamic scholar from North Africa who enormously contributed to political and social theory (Khaldun, 1958).

One of Ibn Khaldun's key ideas was the concept of 'asabiyyah,' referring to the social cohesion and sense of community that binds people together. According to Ibn Khaldun, a nation's strength and security depend on the soundness of its 'asabiyyah.' He asserted that 'asabiyyah' is strongest among tribes and families and that their sense of unity and solidarity weakens as these groups unite to form larger communities and nations. This weakening of 'asabiyyah' makes the country vulnerable to external threats and internal divisions.

Another significant contribution of Ibn Khaldun's ideas is the recognition of the role of education in promoting national security. Ibn Khaldun stressed the significance of religious and secular education in fostering unity and purpose among citizens. This has been echoed in present-day debates on national security, where education is often seen as a key component of efforts to promote social cohesion and combat extremism.

Furthermore, Ibn Khaldun's theory of 'asabiyyah' has also influenced modern security studies. The notion of 'asabiyyah' refers to the social cohesion and sense of community that binds people together. This has been used to analyze modern-day social and political dynamics in the Islamic world. Many scholars claim that the weakening of 'asabiyyah' has contributed to social and political instability. Also, Ibn Khaldun's emphasis on the role of education in fostering social cohesion and unity has also contributed to contemporary debates on education policy and its impact on national security. Scholars have argued that education can be a powerful tool for promoting citizenship, civic engagement, and social integration, which are essential for national security.

To counteract this trend, Ibn Khaldun argued that leaders must foster community and shared identity among citizens. He stressed the importance of religious and secular education to promote unity and instill a sense of purpose and direction in the nation's citizens

(Smith, 1991). He also believed that effective governance and justice were essential for maintaining social order and security. Ibn Khaldun's ideas have had a lasting impact on Islamic political and social thought. His emphasis on the importance of social cohesion and the role of education in fostering unity and purpose continues to influence contemporary debates on national security in the Islamic world.

In summary, Ibn Khaldun's contributions to the Islamic concept of national security in his book "Muqaddimah" have immensely impacted the field of political and social theory. In addition, his ideas about the importance of unity and solidarity among citizens, the strength of 'asabiyyah,' and the role of education in promoting social cohesion have continued to shape Islamic political and social thought. His ideas in promoting social cohesion and the significance of social capital and civic nationalism in fostering collective action and mobilization continue to shape contemporary national security discourse.

Besides, Arshad Alam and Aparajita Biswas (2015) conducted a study that examined the concept of national security in Islamic political thought. The authors shed light on how the Islamic concept of national security prioritizes the protection of the Ummah and its values, in contrast to Western conceptions that focus on protecting state institutions and national interests. The study offers a comprehensive analysis of the critical contributions made by Alam and Biswas in their study and their implications for contemporary political discourse.

Alam and Biswas begin their investigation by accentuating the historical context in which the concept of national security emerged in Islamic political thought. They argue that national security was central to Islamic political discourse in the post-colonial era when newly independent Muslim-majority countries sought to establish their national identities. Before this, Islamic political thought was primarily concerned with protecting the Ummah and its religious values.

The authors then explore the Islamic concept of national security in greater depth:

1. They contend that the Islamic concept of national security prioritizes the protection of the Ummah and its religious values rather than the protection of the state. This priority on the Ummah reflects the Islamic belief that Muslims are a single community with shared values and beliefs.
2. The authors argue that the Islamic concept of national security goes beyond the physical protection of the Ummah to include the security of its cultural and religious values. Per Alam and Biswas, this focus on the Ummah echoes the Islamic belief that Muslims are a single community with shared values and beliefs.
3. The authors argue that the Islamic concept of national security extends beyond the physical protection of the Ummah to include the protection of its cultural and religious values.

In this sense, national security is not just about safeguarding the physical well-being of the Ummah but also about preserving its spiritual and cultural identity.

Alam and Biswas's contributions are significant as they challenge the dominant Western discourse on national security, which prioritizes the protection of state institutions and national interests over the well-being of communities and their values. In addition, the authors highlight the importance of recognizing and respecting the cultural and religious identities of minority communities, particularly in the context of Muslim-majority countries. The study's insights are particularly relevant in contemporary political discourse, where national security and cultural identity issues remain hotly debated. The implications of these examinations are significant for modern political discourse. Firstly, they challenge the dominant Western discourse on national security, which prioritizes the protection of state institutions and national interests over the well-being of communities and their values. Secondly, they highlight the importance of recognizing and respecting the cultural and religious identities of minority communities, particularly in the context of Muslim-majority countries.

In short, Arshad Alam and Aparajita Biswas's (2015) study provides a valuable analysis of the concept of national security in Islamic political thought. Their research highlights the importance of protecting the Ummah and its values. It challenges the Western discourse on national security that prioritizes protecting state institutions and national interests. Their contributions have significant implications for contemporary political discourse, particularly in terms of recognizing and respecting the cultural and religious identities of minority communities.

Additionally, a study by Mehmet Akif Okur (2015) analyzed the Islamic perspective on territorial protection. The author argued that territorial protection is an important aspect of Islamic statecraft and that Islamic principles, such as the concept of the Ummah and defensive jihad, can be used to justify territorial defense. Okur's study on the Islamic perspective on territorial protection provides valuable insights that can contribute to modern-day security studies. The study highlights the importance of understanding the historical and cultural contexts in which Islamic political thought developed and the relevance of these concepts in contemporary political contexts.

One essential contribution of Okur's study is emphasizing the concept of defensive jihad. This concept is vital in Islamic political thought as it provides a framework for regulating defensive warfare and justifies using force to defend the Ummah or Muslim community. In modern-day security studies, defensive action is relevant in the context of state and non-state actors' use of force in self-defense against external threats. Another contribution of Okur's study is the discussion of the concept of the Ummah. The Ummah represents the global community of Muslims, and protecting the Ummah is seen as a fundamental duty of Islamic political leaders. The concept of the Ummah is relevant to modern-day security studies in the context of transnational threats such as terrorism and extremism, as it highlights the importance of promoting cooperation and unity among Muslim-majority countries.

Mehmet Akif Okur's study on the Islamic perspective on territorial protection makes essential contributions to understanding Islam's role in national security policy. By analyzing Islamic principles such as the concept of the Ummah and the notion of defensive jihad, Okur demonstrates how these ideas can be used to justify territorial defense and provide a framework for developing effective security policies. One key takeaway from Okur's study is the importance of historical examples of Islamic territorial defense in shaping contemporary perspectives on national security. By examining events such as the Battle of Badr and the Siege of Vienna, we can gain insights into how Islamic principles have been applied to real-world security challenges.

Also, a significant contribution of Okur's study is its emphasis on the role of religion in shaping national security policy. Okur challenges the notion that religion should be completely separated from politics and security by highlighting the importance of Islamic principles in guiding territorial defense. Lastly, Okur's study provides a nuanced analysis of the Islamic perspective on territorial protection and highlights the importance of understanding the complexities of Islamic political thought. The study's contributions to modern-day security studies lie in its emphasis on defensive jihad and Ummah and their relevance to contemporary security challenges.

Additionally, a study by Fawaz A. Gerges (2015) focused on the Islamic State of Iraq and Syria (ISIS) and its interpretation of the concept of national security in Islam. The author argued that ISIS' notion of national security is based on a distorted understanding of Islamic texts and is used to justify its violent actions. The Islamic State of Iraq and Syria (ISIS) has become a significant threat to national security in the Middle East and beyond. Fawaz A. Gerges (2015) conducted a study on ISIS and its interpretation of the concept of national security in Islam. He argued that the group's understanding of national security is distorted and used to justify its violent actions. This section concisely analyzes Gerges' study and its contributions to security studies.

Gerges (2015) argued that ISIS' notion of national security is based on a selective and narrow interpretation of Islamic texts, particularly those related to the concept of "takfir." Takfir is the practice of declaring someone an apostate or unbeliever, a severe accusation in Islam. ISIS uses this concept to justify violence against other Muslims who do not subscribe to its extreme interpretation of Islam. Gerges maintained that this distorted interpretation of takfir is the cornerstone of ISIS' national security strategy. Gerges (2015) also underscored the role of historical grievances and political factors in shaping ISIS' notion of national security. The author argued that the group's violent actions are not solely based on its distorted interpretation of Islamic texts but are also motivated by political factors such as the exclusion of Sunni Muslims from power in Iraq and Syria. The historical grievances of Sunni Muslims in the region, particularly the marginalization of their communities, have also contributed to the rise of ISIS.

Gerges's study has made several contributions to security studies:
1. It highlights the importance of understanding the role of religion in shaping national security strategies. Religious beliefs and interpretations can significantly impact how groups perceive and respond to threats.
2. The study emphasizes the need to consider political and historical factors when analyzing security issues. Conflicts and grievances based on political exclusion can fuel violent extremism.
3. The study illustrates the dangers of selective and narrow interpretations of religious texts.

Such interpretations can be used to justify violence and extremism.

In summary, Fawaz A. Gerges' (2015) study on ISIS and its distorted interpretation of national security in Islam provides important insights for security studies. The study highlights the role of religious beliefs, political factors, and historical grievances in shaping security strategies. Security analysts must consider these factors when analyzing security threats in the Middle East and beyond.

Furthermore, research by Ahmed Fekry Ibrahim (2017) explored the concept of territorial protection in the Islamic tradition. The author argued that Islamic law provides a framework for regulating territorial disputes and warfare and that the idea of territorial integrity is rooted in Islamic political thought. The author conducted a study on the concept of territorial protection in the Islamic tradition. The study explores the Islamic legal framework for regulating territorial disputes and warfare and argues that territorial integrity is rooted in Islamic political thought. This section concisely surveys Ibrahim's study and its contributions to security studies.

Ibrahim (2017) argued that the concept of territorial integrity in Islam is rooted in the Quranic injunction to maintain peace and justice. The author noted that the Quran emphasizes the importance of resolving disputes peacefully and encourages Muslims to avoid violence whenever possible.

The Islamic tradition also guides how to conduct warfare and ethically. The author maintained that the Islamic legal framework for war is designed to protect innocent civilians and avoid unnecessary destruction. Further, he highlighted the role of Islamic political thought in shaping the concept of territorial protection. The author argued that the Islamic tradition emphasizes the importance of a just ruler responsible for maintaining his subjects' security and well-being. The concept of territorial integrity is, therefore, closely correlated to political sovereignty. The author claimed that Islamic political thought provides a framework for regulating territorial disputes and ensuring that rulers respect the power of other states.

Ibrahim's inquiry has several contributions to security studies:

1. It highlights the importance of understanding the role of religion in shaping concepts of territorial protection. Islamic law provides a rich framework for regulating territorial disputes and warfare, and understanding this framework is crucial for developing effective security policies in Muslim-majority countries.
2. The study emphasizes the importance of a just ruler responsible for protecting his subjects and maintaining the security of his state. This concept can also be applied to non-Muslim-majority countries, as a rightful ruler is essential for maintaining stability and security in any state.
3. The study provides insights into how Islamic political thought can be used to regulate interstate relations and ensure respect for sovereignty.

In short, Ahmed Fekry Ibrahim's (2017) study on territorial protection in the Islamic tradition offers essential perspicuity for security studies. The study highlights the role of religion in shaping concepts of territorial protection. It underscores the implication of a just ruler responsible for maintaining the security and well-being of his subjects. The study also spotlights the relevance of Islamic political thought in regulating interstate relations and ensuring respect for sovereignty.

Similarly, research by Farid Abdel-Nour (2019) analyzed the concept of national security in Islamic political thought from a comparative perspective. The author compared the Islamic idea of national security with Western and Chinese views and argued that Islamic political thought emphasizes the importance of social harmony and justice in promoting national security. In recent years, the study of national security in Islamic political thought has gained significant attention from scholars interested in understanding the Islamic concept of national security and its implications for security studies. This section investigates Farid Abdel-Nour's (2019) national security analysis in Islamic political thought and its contributions to security studies.

Islamic Concept of National Security Abdel-Nour's study (2019) analyzed the Islamic concept of national security from a comparative perspective, comparing it with Western and Chinese views. The author argued that Islamic political thought emphasizes the importance of social harmony and justice in promoting national security.

According to Abdel-Nour, the Islamic concept of national security is based on three main principles:

1. The preservation of the Islamic faith
2. The protection of the Islamic community
3. The promotion of social justice and harmony

Preserving the Islamic faith is the first principle of the Islamic concept of national security. Therefore, the state should protect the Islamic faith from external and internal threats. The protection of the Islamic community is the second principle, which means that the state should ensure the security of the Muslim community from external aggression and internal conflict. Finally, promoting social justice and harmony is the third principle, which means that the state should ensure social justice and balance to promote national security.

Comparative Perspective Abdel-Nour's study (2019) compared the Islamic concept of national security with Western and Chinese perspectives. According to the author, Western perspectives on national security focus mainly on military and economic power, while Chinese perspectives focus on maintaining social stability and economic development. However, the Islamic concept of national security emphasizes social harmony and justice as the key factors in promoting national security.

Contributions to Security Studies Abdel-Nour's study (2019) significantly contributes to security studies by highlighting the importance of social harmony and justice in promoting national security. The study challenges the dominant Western perspective on national security, focusing mainly on military and economic power. The Islamic concept of national security emphasizes the importance of social justice and harmony as critical factors in promoting national security. Therefore, Abdel-Nour's study calls for a more holistic approach to national security, considering social, economic, and cultural factors.

In brief, Abdel-Nour's study (2019) provides an insightful analysis of the Islamic concept of national security and its contributions to security studies. The study highlights the importance of social harmony and justice in promoting national security, challenging the dominant Western perspective that primarily focuses on military and economic power. Therefore, Abdel-Nour's study calls for a more comprehensive approach to national security, considering social, economic, and cultural factors. This study is essential for scholars interested in understanding the Islamic concept of national security and its implications for security studies.

A study by Md. Saidul Islam and Md. Tarikul Islam (2021) analyzed the concept of territorial protection in Islamic political thought. Muhammad Saidul Islam and Md. Tarikul Islam conducted one such analysis. Here, we survey the contributions of their study to security studies and how it can enhance our understanding of territorial protection. The authors contended that territorial protection is a fundamental concept in Islamic political thought and closely related to sovereignty. According to their analysis, territorial protection in Islamic political thought is based on the principle of al-Wilayah al-'Imamiyyah, which refers to the general guardianship of the Islamic community. This principle stresses the need to protect the Islamic community's territorial boundaries and preserve its sovereignty.

Their study provides several contributions to security studies. First, it highlights the significance of territorial protection as a core security element. Territorial integrity is essential for any state to function and maintain its sovereignty. The concept of al-Wilayah al-'Imamiyyah underlines the essence of territorial protection and authority in Islamic political thought, providing a unique perspective. Secondly, Islam and Islam (2021) emphasized the state's role in delivering territorial protection. They argued that the state is primarily responsible for safeguarding its territorial boundaries and ensuring the safety of its citizens. The state's failure to provide adequate territorial protection can lead to instability and conflict, threatening its sovereignty and the security of its citizens.

Thirdly, their study provides insights into the Islamic approach to security, which is distinct from the Western system. Islamic political thought considers security a holistic concept, encompassing physical, social, and moral security. This approach emphasizes the importance of maintaining social stability, ensuring justice, and protecting the moral fabric of society alongside physical security. Furthermore, their study provides insights into the Islamic concept of just war, based on the principles of self-defense and protection of the Islamic community. According to their analysis, just war is permissible in Islamic political thought only under specific conditions, such as when the Islamic community is threatened or when there is a clear and present danger to its sovereignty.

Finally, the study by Islam and Islam (2021) provides valuable contributions to security studies. Their analysis highlights the importance of territorial protection as a fundamental element of security, the role of the state in delivering territorial defense, the Islamic approach to security, and the concept of just war in Islamic political thought. These insights can enhance our understanding of security and provide a unique perspective on the subject.

Jawad Anani's (2021) study examined the role of Islamic principles in promoting stability and national security in the Middle East. The author argued that Islamic values such as justice, tolerance, and cooperation could help address the root causes of instability in the region. The Middle East has long been associated with instability, conflict, and violence, and the search for solutions to these problems has been ongoing for many years.

Jawad Anani's 2021 study examined the role of Islamic principles in promoting stability and national security in the region. This essay will critically analyze the contributions of the inquiry and how it can enhance our understanding of the role of Islamic principles in addressing the root causes of instability. Anani's inquiry highlights the significance of Islamic principles in promoting stability and national security in the Middle East. He argued that Islam fosters values such as justice, tolerance, and cooperation that can help address the root causes of regional instability and conflict. According to Anani, these values are central to Islamic teachings and can serve as a foundation for promoting stability and security in the region. One of the significant contributions of Anani's study is the focus on the implication of Islamic principles in addressing the root causes of instability. He argued that many of the region's problems, such as poverty, unemployment, and corruption, result from the lack of adherence to Islamic principles. Therefore, he suggested that Islamic values can be used to address these issues and promote stability and security in the region.

Furthermore, Anani's study provides valuable insights into the role of Islamic principles in promoting cooperation and collaboration in the region. He asserted that Islamic teachings accentuate the significance of cooperation and collaboration among individuals and groups. These values can be used to promote regional cooperation and partnership in addressing common problems such as poverty and terrorism. However, one of the significant challenges of Anani's study is the need for clear strategies or solutions for implementing Islamic principles to promote stability and security in the region. While the study highlights the importance of the Islamic tenets, it needs to provide a comprehensive framework or approach for implementing these principles practically.

Another challenge is the potential for different interpretations of Islamic principles, which could lead to conflicts and misunderstandings. In addition, the understanding of Islamic principles can vary widely among other groups, and this could lead to disagreements and disputes. In short, Anani's study provides valuable contributions to our understanding of the role of Islamic principles in promoting stability and national security in the Middle East. His emphasis on the importance of Islamic values such as justice, tolerance, and cooperation highlights the potential for using these principles to address the root causes of regional instability. However, further research is needed to develop practical strategies for implementing these principles and to overcome the potential challenges of different interpretations of Islamic principles.

Recent studies by Khan (2021) focused on the role of Islamic finance in promoting stability, national security, and territorial protection. Islamic finance has become an increasingly significant aspect of the global financial system. Recent studies, such as the one conducted by Khan (2021), highlight the potential of Islamic finance in promoting stability, national security, and territorial protection. This critical, comprehensive essay will analyze Khan's study and discuss what we can learn from it. Khan's analysis focused on the role of Islamic finance in promoting stability, national security, and territorial protection. The study argues Islamic finance can contribute to the financial system's resilience by promoting ethical and socially responsible behavior. Furthermore, Islamic finance can contribute to national security and territorial protection by providing financing compliant with Islamic principles and values.

One of the main strengths of Khan's study is how it highlights the unique features of Islamic finance that contribute to stability and security. Islamic finance is based on principles that promote ethical behavior and social responsibility, such as the prohibition of interest and speculation. These principles create a financial system that is more stable and less prone to the kinds of risks and vulnerabilities that have contributed to financial crises in the past. Moreover, Islamic finance is built on the foundation of risk-sharing, which means that investors and financiers share the risks and rewards of investments. This promotes a more equitable distribution of risks and rewards and reduces the likelihood of financial instability.

Additionally, Islamic finance delivers financing compliant with Islamic principles and values, which can promote national security and territorial protection by reducing reliance on foreign funding. While the study presents a convincing theoretical argument for the potential benefits of Islamic finance, there is a need for empirical research to test these claims and provide concrete evidence of the impact of Islamic finance on stability, security, and protection. Another drawback of Khan's study is the need for more attention to the challenges and limitations of Islamic finance. While the study acknowledges some of the challenges facing Islamic finance, such as the lack of standardization and regulation, it needs to provide a comprehensive analysis of these challenges and their potential impact on the effectiveness of Islamic finance in promoting stability, security, and protection. Finally, Khan's study contributes to the literature on Islamic finance and its potential role in promoting stability, national security, and territorial protection. However, there is a need for further empirical research to test the claims made in the study and provide concrete evidence of the impact of Islamic finance on these outcomes. Furthermore, a more comprehensive analysis of Islamic finance's challenges and limitations is necessary to understand its potential impact fully.

Also, "Ancient Religions, Modern Politics: The Islamic Case in Comparative Perspective" by Michael Cook (2016) is an insightful and thought-provoking analysis of the role of religion in modern politics, with a particular focus on Islam. The book offers valuable insights into modern security studies, highlighting the complex relationship between religion, politics, and security in the contemporary world. One of the main benefits of the book for modern security studies is its focus on comparative analysis. Cook explores the role of religion in modern politics by comparing and contrasting the Islamic case with other cases from different religious traditions, including Hinduism, Buddhism, and Christianity. This comparative approach is vital for modern security studies, as it helps to provide a broader and more nuanced understanding of the complex relationship between religion and politics.

Moreover, Cook's (2016) analysis highlights the diversity and complexity of the Islamic tradition. He explores how different Islamic movements and ideologies have responded to modern political challenges, from the rise of nationalism to the global war on terror. This diversity is critical for modern security studies, as it challenges simplistic and essentialist narratives about Islam and the Muslim world that can fuel conflict and misunderstanding. Another benefit of the book for modern security studies is its emphasis on historical context. Cook provides a rich and detailed analysis of the historical forces that have shaped the Islamic world's relationship between religion and politics. In particular, he explores the legacy of colonialism, the emergence of modern nation-states, and the impact of global economic and political trends. By exploring these historical forces in-depth, Cook offers a more nuanced understanding of the Muslim world's contemporary challenges.

The writing challenges the assumption that religion should be completely separated from politics and security and instead argues that faith can significantly shape national security policy. One of the critical contributions of Cook's research to security studies is its analysis of how Islamic principles and historical examples have influenced modern-day security challenges. For instance, Cook examines the concept of jihad and shows how its historical and religious roots have been interpreted and applied in modern-day conflicts. Cook's analysis also sheds light on the complex relationship between religion and politics in Islamic societies. It underlines the need for a more nuanced understanding of the role of religion in shaping national security policy. The book demonstrates how religion can promote and undermine security, depending on how it is interpreted and applied.

Moreover, the writing's emphasis on comparative analysis may need to be more relevant for security studies focused on specific regions or countries. Despite these limitations, "Ancient Religions, Modern Politics" offers valuable insights for modern security studies. Its focus on comparative analysis, diversity, and historical context can help challenge simplistic narratives about the Muslim world and provide a more nuanced understanding of the complex relationship between religion, politics, and security. As such, the research is a valuable resource for scholars, policymakers, and practitioners in security studies. By promoting a deeper understanding of the complex relationship between religion and security, policymakers and scholars can work towards developing more effective and inclusive security policies that benefit all members of society.

Additionally, Kennedy's (2004) writing "The Prophet and the Age of the Caliphates: The Islamic Near East from the 6th to the 11th Century" provides a comprehensive historical analysis of the early Islamic period, examining the political, social, and cultural dynamics of the region. While the book focuses primarily on the first five Islamic centuries, it offers valuable insights for modern security studies. One key benefit of the book for modern security studies is its examination of the role of religion in politics. Kennedy explores how Islam emerged as a political force in the early Islamic period and how political leaders sought to justify their rule through religious authority. This analysis is relevant to contemporary discussions about the role of religion in politics, particularly in Muslim-majority countries.

Another benefit of the study is its focus on the dynamics of power and authority. Kennedy examines the relationships between political leaders, religious scholars, and other influential figures in the early Islamic period. He explores how these dynamics shaped political decision-making and how different factions vied for power and influence. This analysis is relevant to contemporary security studies, accentuating the essence of understanding power dynamics in other regions and conflicts. Finally, Kennedy's book offers insights into the development of Islamic legal and ethical systems. He explores the emergence of Islamic law and how it was applied in different contexts. This analysis is essential for modern security studies, as it provides insights into the role of law and ethics in shaping political decisions and conflicts. In summary,

"The Prophet and the Age of the Caliphates" offers valuable insights for modern security studies.

Kennedy's analysis of the role of religion in politics, the dynamics of power and authority, and the development of Islamic legal and ethical systems presents a nuanced understanding of the early Islamic period and its relevance to contemporary issues. As such, the writing is a necessary resource for scholars, policymakers, and practitioners in security studies.

These inquiries seek to understand the Islamic perspective on national security, its foundations, and its implications for modern security studies. One of the key contributions of the Islamic concept to modern security studies is its emphasis on the importance of safeguarding the welfare and security of the entire community, both domestically and internationally. In Islamic thought, national security protects the Islamic community, or Ummah, against internal and external threats that may undermine its stability and well-being.

This concept of national security is closely linked to the principles of justice, equality, and social welfare, which are central to Islamic ethics and morality. Therefore, in Islamic thought, national security is not limited to military defense but includes economic development, social justice, and political stability. Another significant contribution of the Islamic concept to modern security studies is its emphasis on the importance of moral and ethical considerations in security policy. Islamic ethics and morality provide a framework for evaluating the legitimacy of various security practices, including using force, surveillance, and detention.

Islamic scholars have also made significant contributions to the development of security studies by analyzing the historical experiences of Islamic societies and their security challenges. These studies have shed light on the various strategies Islamic societies have used to address security threats, such as forming alliances, diplomacy, and military preparedness. In short, the Islamic concept of national security offers a unique perspective on security studies, emphasizing the importance of justice, equality, and social welfare and the role of ethical and moral considerations in security policy. Islamic scholars and experts continue to contribute to the ongoing debates on security studies, enriching our understanding of the challenges and opportunities facing modern societies in the field of security.

Islamic standpoints on territorial protection and national security are rooted in the Quran's teachings and the Prophet Muhammad's traditions (peace be upon him). Islam stresses the priority of protecting one's homeland and defending it against any internal or external threat but also acknowledges the need for diplomacy and peaceful resolution of conflicts. Islamic scholars, jurists, and leaders have contributed significantly to modern security studies by accentuating the implication of sound and ethical governance, respect for human rights, and rejection of extremism and terrorism. They have also called for the advancement of peace and the avoidance of violence.

In summary, Islamic standpoints on territorial protection and national security provide a comprehensive framework for understanding the role of defense, diplomacy, and ethical governance in promoting peace and security. Drawing on Quranic texts and traditions, Islamic scholars and leaders have emphasized the importance of territorial integrity and the homeland's defense while recognizing the need for peaceful resolution of conflicts. The Quranic instructions and Islamic traditions are noteworthy for modern security studies and can inform policy and practice in nurturing peace and security. Islamic teachings can create a more stable and peaceful world by stressing the need for sound and ethical governance, respect for human rights, and peaceful resolution of conflicts.

As we conclude the exploration of ancient civilizations, religious texts, and their outlooks on national security, we have seen how the ancient civilizations and their religious beliefs have contributed to the evolution of security studies. From the early cultures of the world to modern times, we have examined how each religion has shaped the views of its followers on national security, territorial protection, and conflict resolution. The subsequent final chapter summarizes each civilization and religion's essential findings and contributions and how they have influenced the modern-day security discourse. We also explore how these civilizations and religious texts can continue to inform our understanding of national security in the future.

References:

Abdul-Majid, M. A. (2015). Islamic perspectives on security. Journal of International Affairs, 68(2), 215-227.

Abdel-Nour, F. (2019). The Concept of National Security in Islamic Political Thought: A Comparative Perspective. Journal of Muslim Minority Affairs, 39(2), 178-193 https://doi.org/10.1080/13602004.2018.1547786

Alam, A., & Biswas, A. (2015). National security in Islamic political thought. Journal of Muslim Minority Affairs, 35(2), 219-233. doi: 10.1080/13602004.2015.1056239.

Ali, A. Y. (2016). Islam and national security: Beyond classical paradigms. Journal of Muslim Minority Affairs, 36(1), 1–19.

Al-Bukhari, M. I. (2021). Sahih al-Bukhari [Online]. Available: https://sunnah.com/bukhari

Ahmed, A. (2009). The Islamic concept of national security. Strategic Studies Quarterly, 3(2), 124–145.

Al-Tirmidhi. (1352). Book 36, Hadith 19. Retrieved from https://sunnah.com/tirmidhi/36/19

Asad, M. (2003). The Message of the Quran. The Book Foundation.

Abdelnasser, W. (2015). The concept of national security in Islamic political thought. Journal of Islamic State Practices in International Law, 11(1), 4-18.

Bukhari, M. (n.d.). Sahih Bukhari. Retrieved from https://sunnah.com/bukhari

Cook, M. (2016). Ancient religions, modern politics: The Islamic case in comparative perspective. Princeton University Press.

Coulson, N. J. (2004). A history of Islamic law. Aldine Transaction.

Esposito, J. L. (1998). Islam and politics. Syracuse University Press.

Esposito, J. L. (2002). The Oxford Dictionary of Islam. Oxford University Press.

Esposito, J. L. (2011). The Oxford Handbook of Islam and Politics. Oxford University Press.

Gerges, F. A. (2015). The ideology of ISIS and its distortion of Islamic texts. Perspectives on Terrorism, 9(4), 91-101.

Ghafar, A. (2017). Islamic Concept of Justice and Its Implications for Muslim Societies. Journal of Social Sciences and Humanities Review, 8(2), 52–63.

Ibn Mājah, Muḥammad ibn Yazīd. (2018). Sunan Ibn Mājah. Maktabat al-Maʻārif.

Ibrahim, S. (2017). Islamic perspectives on national security. Georgetown Journal of International Affairs, 18(2), 106–114.

Ibrahim, A. F. (2017). Territorial protection in Islamic law and tradition. Journal of Islamic Studies, 28(1), 51-70.

Islam, M. S., & Islam, M. T. (2021). Territorial protection in Islamic political thought. Journal of Muslim Minority Affairs, 41(1), 1-16. doi: 10.1080/13602004.2021.1874646

Kamali, M. H. (2008). Shari'ah law: An introduction. Oneworld Publications.

Kamrava, M. (2006). The modern Middle East: A political history since the First World War. The University of California Press.

Kaya, Y. (2021). History and evolution of Islam's concept of national security during Muslim dynasties. Retrieved from https://www.academia.edu/49860134/History_and_Evolution_of_Islams_Concept_of_National_Security_During_Muslim_Dynasties

Kennedy, H. (2004). The Prophet and the Age of the Caliphates: The Islamic Near East from the 6th to the 11th Century (Vol. 2). Pearson Education.

Khalidi, T. (2010). The Muslim Empires of the Ottomans, Safavids, and Mughals. Cambridge University Press.

Khan, M. A. (2021). The Role of Islamic Finance in Promoting Stability, National Security and Territorial Protection. Journal of Islamic Banking and Finance, 38(1), 1-18.

Khaldun, I. (1958). The Muqaddimah: An introduction to history. Translated by Franz Rosenthal. Princeton: Princeton University Press.

Klein, A. (2004). Islam and international relations: perspectives and prospects. Palgrave Macmillan.

Klein, M. (2015). The evolution of Islam's perspectives on national security. Journal of Strategic Security, 8(3), 1–20.

Muslim, I. (2019). Sahih Muslim [Online]. Available: https://sunnah.com/muslim

Nasr, V. (2016). The Islamic State and the challenge of national security. Current History, 115(780), 213–218.

Okur, M. A. (2015). Islamic perspective on territorial protection: a conceptual analysis. Journal of Religion and Politics, 8(2), 341-355. doi: 10.5772/61117.

Sachedina, A. A. (2009). Islam and the Challenge of Human Rights. Oxford University Press.

Razvi, S. M. A. (2003). The Prophet's concept of human rights and social welfare. Journal of Islamic Research, 1(1), 9-23.

Rapoport, D. C. (2004). The four waves of modern terrorism. In A. Silke (Ed.), Researching terrorism: Trends, achievements, failures (pp. 11-24). Routledge.

Riaz, A. (2012). Islam and Pakistan's national security. The Round Table, 101(4), 333–346.

Roy, O. (1994). The failure of political Islam. Harvard University Press.

Tabatabai, M. H. (1987). Shia Islam. State University of New York Press.

Siddiqui, M. Z. (2011). Islam and contemporary international relations. Routledge.

Smith, A. D. (1991). National identity. University of Nevada Press.

Waines, D. (1992). An introduction to Islam. Cambridge University Press.

Friedmann, J. (1991). Towards a non-Eurocentric IR: Islam and the study of international relations. Millennium, 20(3), 463-484. doi: 10.1177/030582989102000307

Kamali, M. H. (2006). War and peace in Islam: The uses and abuses of jihad. The Islamic Texts Society.

Zaman, M. Q. (1997). Religion and politics under the early Abbasids: The emergence of the proto-Sunni elite. Brill.

10

Summary

Lessons Learned from Past Civilizations and Religious Texts

Today, as we grapple with modern security challenges, we can learn from the wisdom and insights of these religious texts and ancient civilizations. Ancient civilizations had different positions on stability and territorial protection, and their teachings have contributed to modern security studies. For illustration, the Mesopotamians believed in a strong central authority to preserve peace and relied on a powerful army to protect their territory. On the other hand, the Egyptians focused on a strong ruler who was viewed as a god, and they used diplomacy and military might to maintain their borders. The Greeks valued individualism and democracy, which contributed to their military dexterity and enabled them to repel external threats. The Romans believed in the rule of law and used a well-organized military to conquer and sustain their vast empire. In China, stability was achieved through Confucianism's teachings, which stressed the essence of moral values, education, and social harmony. The Chinese also built the Great Wall to protect themselves from external threats.

Lessons from these ancient civilizations show that stability and territorial protection require strong leadership, organized military and diplomacy, and a law and justice system. In addition, the implications of culture, religion, and moral values must be addressed to achieve lasting security. Furthermore, the contributions of these ancient civilizations to security studies include the development of military tactics and technology. They also utilized intelligence collection and diplomacy and building alliances to preserve peace. Modern security organizations and policymakers have adapted these contributions to address recent security challenges. In brief, the positions and teachings of ancient civilizations on stability and territorial protection and the lessons and contributions derived from them are vital to modern security studies. They provide a historical perspective and a wealth of knowledge that policymakers can use to develop effective security policies that ensure enduring peace and stability. Besides, the need to protect citizens and sustain stability has shaped political and military strategies from ancient empires to modern nation-states.

One fascinating perspective on national security can be found in religious texts and the practices of ancient civilizations. The wisdom and insights of these texts and practices offer meaningful lessons that can inform our modern understanding of security challenges. By investigating these perspectives, we can gain a deeper appreciation for the complexities of national security and develop new approaches to meeting current security threats. We have learned that ancient civilizations placed a great deal of emphasis on the protection of their territory and often developed sophisticated security systems and military strategies. These systems were constantly informed by religious beliefs and practices, closely intertwined with the society's political and military structures. One notable instance is the ancient Israelites, who placed a great deal of focus on the protection of their homeland. The Hebrew Bible contains numerous accounts of wars and battles, and their religious beliefs informed many of the Israelites' military strategies. To illustrate the point, the Israelites believed that their God Yahweh had promised them the land of Canaan. This belief played a substantial role in their military campaigns to conquer and secure the territory.

Likewise, the "Mandate of Heaven" concept was crucial in developing the country's military and security systems in ancient

China. The Mandate of Heaven was a belief that the ruler of China had the divine right to rule. This belief shaped the country's military strategies and the development of its security systems. In particular, during the Qin dynasty, the first emperor of China ordered the construction of the Great Wall to protect the country from invasion by foreign powers. Also, we have learned that ancient civilizations such as the Greeks, Romans, and Egyptians were concerned with security and territorial protection. The Greeks, for instance, built walls around their cities to protect them from invaders. To give you an idea, the famous Acropolis in Athens was protected by the Long Walls, which were built to connect the city to the harbor of Piraeus (Hornblower, 2014).

Equally, the Romans built fortifications such as Hadrian's Wall to protect their territory from invaders. The Egyptians also built fortresses and walls to protect their land from neighboring tribes and enemies (Hagen, 2016). These instances reveal how ancient civilizations approached security and territorial protection and the influence of their strategies on modern security. These teachings have given us a better understanding of the implications of sustaining reliable defensive capabilities, the dangers of overreaching and over-extension, and the role of diplomacy in promoting peace and stability. One of the critical lessons that we have learned from the past is the importance of keeping strong defensive abilities. The ancient Greeks, for illustration, could defend their territories against invading armies by developing a sophisticated system of defensive walls and military tactics. Similarly, the ancient Romans upheld control over vast territories for centuries by developing a powerful military and a sophisticated system of governance.

The Correlations Between Sacred Texts, Ancient Civilizations, And Their Contributions

The correlations between sacred texts, ancient civilizations, and their contributions to modern security are significant, as holy texts often contain historical narratives and principles that have shaped the security practices of ancient civilizations. These principles, rooted in religious and ethical values, continue to influence contemporary security approaches. Here is a compelling review analysis with realistic examples of contemporary challenges:

1. Sacred Texts and Historical Narratives: Sacred texts, such as the Quran, the Bible, and the Vedas, contain historical narratives of ancient civilizations that faced security challenges and contributed to their defense and stability. These stories offer valuable insights into the strategies and principles employed by ancient societies to address security threats.
2. Religious and Ethical Values in Ancient Civilizations: Ancient civilizations often derived their ethical and moral values from sacred texts. These religious and ethical principles influenced their decision-making, emphasizing the protection of vulnerable populations and promoting justice and fairness.
3. Resilience and Enduring Stability: Ancient civilizations' focus on cultural preservation and national identity fostered resilience and enduring stability. In contemporary security, preserving cultural heritage and promoting national identity can unite communities and enhance societal cohesion, contributing to long-term stability.
4. Collective Security and Alliances: Ancient civilizations formed alliances and coalitions for mutual defense, reflecting the concept of collective security. In modern security, organizations like NATO, the UN, and regional security partnerships demonstrate the significance of collective defense against common threats.
5. Tactfulness and Strategic Thinking: The stories of ancient leaders, such as King Harsha, Prophet David, Solomon, and Muhammad, exemplify the significance of diplomacy and strategic thinking in navigating

complicated security challenges. These traits remain valuable in modern diplomatic and security efforts.
6. Cultural Sensitivity in Conflict Resolution: Ancient civilizations often respected religious and cultural sensitivities during conflict resolution. Understanding and respecting cultural differences in contemporary security can promote peaceful negotiations and prevent escalation.
7. Adapting Ancient Wisdom to Modern Challenges: The principles from sacred texts and ancient civilizations offer timeless wisdom that can be adapted to address modern security challenges. For instance, capitalizing on robust leadership and decisive action remains crucial in responding to emerging threats like cyber warfare and terrorism.
8. Humanitarian and Human Rights Considerations: The sacred texts of various faiths emphasize humanitarian and human rights values, guiding ancient civilizations in treating prisoners of war and the vulnerable. In modern security, upholding human rights in conflict zones and during intelligence operations is critical for ethical conduct.

The preservation of cultural heritage in conflict zones, as inspired by ancient civilizations' focus on cultural preservation, is exemplified by UNESCO's efforts to protect world heritage sites like Palmyra in Syria and Timbuktu in Mali during times of conflict. In short, understanding the correlations between sacred texts, ancient civilizations, and their contributions to modern security provides practical wisdom for addressing co-occurring challenges. The ethical and moral principles from these ancient societies, rooted in religious values, continue to influence current security practices, stressing resilience, cultural preservation, collective security, strategic thinking, and humanitarian considerations. Drawing on these historical examples, modern-day security can be guided by timeless wisdom while navigating the complexities of the contemporary world and safeguarding global peace and stability.

Regarding correlations between sacred texts, ancient civilizations, and modern security, this book has shown that the relationships between sacred texts, ancient civilizations, and modern security can be seen in using walls and fortifications to protect territories. Like ancient civilizations, modern states build walls and fortifications to protect their borders from invaders. For illustration, the United States built a wall along its southern border with Mexico to prevent illegal immigration and drug trafficking (Hanson, 2020). Likewise, in the Middle East, Israel also built a wall along its border with the West Bank to control the movement of Palestinians entering Israel and simultaneously prevent terrorist attacks (Brinkley, 2021). These examples reveal the influence of ancient civilizations' approach to security on modern security.

Ancient Civilizations and Religious Texts' Contributions to Modern Security

Ancient civilizations have significantly contributed to current national and global security studies through their methods and insights. Their principles of decisive leadership, a strong military, tactfulness, cultural preservation, religious values, and ethical considerations remain applicable in modern security practices. Here is how modern security studies can benefit from these practical examples of intelligence gathering:

1. Decisive Leadership: Ancient civilizations recognized the importance of decisive leadership in times of crisis. Modern security studies can benefit from this by emphasizing strong leadership that can make swift and effective decisions to address emerging threats and challenges.
2. Strong Military and Defense: Ancient civilizations understood the need for a robust military and well-structured defense systems to protect their territories. In contemporary security, a well-trained and strong

military remains a cornerstone for safeguarding national interests.
3. Tactfulness and Strategic Thinking: Ancient civilizations employed strategic thinking and tactfulness to handle conflicts and negotiations. In modern security studies, strategic planning and diplomatic skills are essential for navigating complex geopolitical landscapes and resolving disputes peacefully.
4. Cultural Preservation and National Identity: Ancient civilizations recognized that preserving their cultural heritage and national identity is vital for enduring stability. In modern security, efforts to protect cultural sites and preserve national identity foster resilience and unity among citizens.
5. Religious and Ethical Values: Ancient civilizations valued religious and ethical principles that guided their decision-making and actions. Modern security studies can benefit from incorporating ethical considerations and respecting religious beliefs to promote trust and cooperation among diverse communities.
6. Collaboration and Alliances: Ancient civilizations formed alliances and coalitions to strengthen their defenses. In contemporary security, international cooperation and partnerships among nations play a crucial role in addressing global challenges, such as terrorism and climate change.
7. Long-Term Vision: Ancient civilizations understood the implications of long-term planning for the sustainability and security of their respective nations. Modern security studies can benefit from adopting a forward-looking approach that considers future challenges and opportunities.

The concept of collective security, as seen in ancient civilizations forming alliances for mutual defense, parallels modern security with organizations such as NATO (North Atlantic

Treaty Organization), where member nations commit to collective defense against threats.

In brief, ancient civilizations' contributions to current national and global security studies lie in their principles of decisive leadership, a strong military, diplomacy, cultural preservation, religious values, ethical considerations, collaboration, and long-term vision. By drawing wisdom from their methods and knowledge, modern security practices can improve their efficacy in addressing contemporary challenges and ensuring enduring stability and security. Ancient lessons continue to provide valuable guidance in navigating the complexities of the modern world and safeguarding national and global interests.

In terms of benefiting from their contributions to present-day security studies, we can benefit from ancient civilizations and sacred texts' contributions to security studies by adopting and enhancing their strategies and approaches. For instance, modern states can adopt ancient civilizations' approach to building fortifications and walls to protect their territories. By incorporating these lessons into modern security, states can develop more effective strategies to protect their citizens and territories. Several correlations exist between ancient civilizations' security systems and modern security practices. To illustrate this point, using walls and fortifications to protect territory is a strategy that has been employed throughout history, from ancient China's Great Wall to the modern-day Israeli security barrier. In the same fashion, using religious beliefs to motivate and inspire soldiers has been a common practice throughout history, and it continues to be used in some modern conflicts.

Nonetheless, the lessons from the past also warn us about the dangers of overreaching and over-extension. The Persian Empire, for instance, was vast and powerful, but it ultimately collapsed due to its inability to sustain its vast territories and its failure to adapt to changing circumstances. Besides, the downfall of the Roman Empire illustrates the dangers of over-reliance on military power and the neglect of other vital aspects of governance, such as economics and social cohesion. Another lesson we have learned from the past is the importance of diplomacy in sponsoring peace and stability. Religious texts such as the Quran and the Bible underline the essence of justice, fairness, and non-violent conflict resolution.

Moreover, ancient civilizations like the Greeks and Romans cherished diplomacy and negotiation to avoid conflict and maintain peace. This research indicates that studying ancient civilizations' security and territorial protection perspectives can provide helpful outlooks into present-day security studies. Additionally, by reviewing how religion and politics were intertwined in ancient societies, we can learn how religion and politics continue to intersect in modern conflicts.

Hinduism's Contributions to Intelligence Collection

The contributions of King Harsha of Kanauj to contemporary national and global security studies reside in his establishment of a sophisticated intelligence collection network. By drawing lessons from his approach, modern security can benefit in several ways. Here is a succinct and compelling analysis with practical examples:

1. Emphasis on Intelligence Gathering: King Harsha's recognition of the importance of intelligence gathering underscores its significance in contemporary security studies. Creating a robust intelligence collection system enables informed decision-making and proactive threat assessment.
2. Utilization of Local Networks: King Harsha's network of spies and concerned citizens illustrates the value of leveraging local communities and resources for intelligence collection. In modern security, involving local populations in community policing and information sharing can aid in identifying potential threats and criminal activities.

3. Adapting to Geopolitical Challenges: King Harsha's approach demonstrates adaptability to changing geopolitical challenges. In contemporary security, staying responsive to emerging threats, such as cyber warfare or transnational terrorism, is crucial.
4. Proactive Risk Mitigation: King Harsha's use of intelligence to foresee potential threats allowed him to take proactive measures. In modern security studies, intelligence-driven policies enable preemptive actions against potential risks, enhancing overall security.
5. Combining Human Intelligence and Technology: King Harsha's network blended human intelligence with concerned citizens. Integrating traditional human intelligence with advanced technological tools, such as surveillance systems and data analytics, optimizes intelligence collection in modern security.
6. Protection of Borders and Territories: King Harsha's efforts to safeguard his kingdom highlight the importance of securing national borders and territories. In contemporary security, border surveillance and protection are critical to prevent illicit activities and intrusions.
7. Public Safety and Well-Being: King Harsha's intelligence network aimed to ensure the safety and well-being of his subjects. In modern security, a focus on public safety through intelligence-led initiatives fosters trust between citizens and security agencies.

Establishing community watch programs and anonymous tip lines by law enforcement agencies in various countries draws inspiration from King Harsha's network of concerned citizens and spies. These modern initiatives encourage citizens to participate in intelligence gathering to enhance security actively. In short, the contributions of King Harsha of Kanauj to contemporary national and global security studies lie in his emphasis on intelligence gathering, utilization of local networks, adaptability to geopolitical challenges, proactive risk mitigation, blending human intelligence with technology, protection of borders and territories, and prioritizing public safety. By learning from his approach, modern security can optimize intelligence collection, foster collaboration with local communities, and implement intelligence-driven policies to strengthen national and global security. King Harsha's historical benchmark is valuable for effectively addressing modern security challenges.

Further, the Hindu and Buddhist sacred texts provide valuable insights into security and territorial protection concepts, which remain relevant today. These texts are replete with hands-on examples and strategies for preserving order and safety in ancient societies. The relevance of these texts to present-day security lies in their focus on the need for extensive security measures that encompass physical and spiritual dimensions. These texts recognize that security is not just about protecting oneself against external threats but also about creating an inner sense of peace and harmony that can prevent conflict from arising. From past and current Hindu and Buddhist studies on security, we have learned that security is not just a matter of military might or technological superiority but also depends on a society's moral and ethical values. The principles of nonviolence, compassion, and respect for human dignity that underpin these religions are essential for building a secure and stable society. Furthermore, these texts stress understanding the root causes of conflict and addressing them through dialogue and diplomacy rather than resorting to violence. This approach requires a deep understanding of the complexities of human nature and the social, cultural, and economic factors that contribute to conflict.

Concerning intelligence collection and the employment of spies in Hindu texts and traditions, there are numerous examples of kings, princes, and warriors utilizing intelligence collection and spies to protect their communities and people from external threats. Their contributions to modern security studies lie in recognizing the importance of intelligence gathering and using spies for territorial protection. One such example is the story of King Harsha of Kanauj, as described in the 7th-century text,

Harshacharita. King Harsha employed a vast network of spies and informants to gather information about his enemies and potential threats to his kingdom. His spies would collect information on enemy troop movements, alliances, and even the personal habits of enemy commanders. This information enabled King Harsha to plan his military campaigns more effectively and outmaneuver his opponents.

Another example is the story of Arjuna in the epic Mahabharata. Arjuna, one of the Pandava brothers, was tasked with gathering information about the Kaurava army before the start of the great war. So, Arjuna disguised himself as a wandering ascetic and infiltrated the Kaurava army camp, collecting valuable intelligence on their troop strength, deployment, and battle plans. This information allowed the Pandava brothers to gain an advantage and judiciously plan their military strategy more effectively, ultimately leading to victory.

The Hindu texts suggest that intelligence collection and the use of spies were seen as essential components of statecraft in ancient India. They recognized that knowledge was power and that gathering information about the enemy's strengths, weaknesses, and intentions could give a state a strategic advantage in times of war. The insights from the Hindu texts on intelligence collection and the use of spies have significant implications for modern security studies. Today, intelligence gathering remains a critical component of statecraft, and the methods used in ancient India are still relevant. Also, spies and other covert intelligence-gathering methods have become increasingly necessary, particularly in asymmetric warfare and counterterrorism. The lessons learned from the Hindu texts can help modern-day security professionals develop more effective intelligence-gathering strategies and use them more effectively.

Likewise, we have enormously benefited from the wealth of practical teachings in the Old and New Testaments. Accordingly, we can relate this learning and understanding to our modern security. The Old and New Testaments offer applicable stability, security, and territorial protection teachings that have significantly contributed to global security studies and diplomacy.

King David and Solomon's Contributions to Contemporary Security

The contributions of King David and Solomon to contemporary national and global security studies are highly significant, as their approaches to intelligence collection remain applicable in modern times. Here is how modern security studies can derive benefits from these practical examples of intelligence gathering:

1. Emphasizing Intelligence Gathering: King David and Solomon recognized the paramount importance of intelligence gathering to make well-informed decisions and safeguard their territories. In contemporary security studies, intelligence collection plays a vital role in assessing threats, identifying vulnerabilities, and formulating effective policies.
2. Understanding the Value of Intelligence Gathering: King David and Solomon comprehended that possessing timely and accurate information about potential adversaries and internal developments is crucial for making informed choices. Modern security studies can gain from this lesson by highlighting the significance of intelligence gathering in effectively evaluating threats and vulnerabilities.
3. Use of Covert Operations: Both rulers employed spies and covert operations to gather information discreetly. In modern security studies, covert intelligence operations are pivotal for monitoring adversaries and detecting potential risks.
4. Adapting to Contemporary Threats: King David and Solomon tailored their intelligence strategies to specific contexts. In contemporary security studies, adapting intelligence collection methods to address modern

threats, such as cyberattacks or terrorism, remains essential.
5. Proactive Risk Mitigation: The intelligence-driven approach of King David and Solomon empowered them to take preemptive actions to neutralize threats. In contemporary security, proactive risk mitigation through intelligence-driven policies is crucial to thwart potential attacks and safeguard national interests.
6. Protecting Borders and Territories: Their focus on safeguarding borders and territories retains contemporary relevance, as ensuring the security of national boundaries and critical assets remains a fundamental aspect of global security studies.
7. Balancing Defensive and Offensive Measures: Both rulers maintained a strategic balance between defensive and offensive measures based on insights from intelligence. In modern security studies, achieving a strategic equilibrium between defense and offense is vital for upholding stability and deterring potential aggressors.
8. Ethical Considerations in Intelligence: King David and Solomon likely considered ethical principles in their intelligence efforts. In contemporary security studies, ethical considerations within intelligence collection are imperative to maintain trust and uphold human rights.
9. Leadership and Decision-making: The effective use of intelligence by King David and Solomon showcased exceptional leadership and strategic decision-making. In modern security studies, leadership that prioritizes intelligence analysis and informed decision-making is indispensable for effective governance.

In the global fight against terrorism, contemporary security agencies utilize intelligence gathering and covert operations to uncover terrorist networks, proactively disrupt plots, and safeguard vulnerable populations. This approach draws inspiration from the proactive measures King David and Solomon employed to shield their territories from potential threats. In essence, the contributions of King David and Solomon to contemporary national and global security studies lie in their emphasis on intelligence gathering, utilization of covert operations, adaptability to modern threats, proactive risk mitigation, protection of borders and territories, balancing defense and offense, ethical considerations in intelligence, and exemplary leadership in decision-making. Drawing insights from their historical examples, modern security studies can enhance their effectiveness in safeguarding nations and communities within today's intricate and ever-evolving security landscape.

Furthermore, the Old and New Testaments stress the importance of justice, peace, and security, which are universal values that the international community has recognized. Therefore, the teachings of the Old and New Testaments on security can provide a common ground for dialogue and cooperation between different nations and cultures. Also, the texts provide practical examples of how to achieve security and stability. For example, the Old Testament's emphasis on protecting the vulnerable, including widows, orphans, and strangers, can be applied to modern-day security challenges. Similarly, the New Testament's teachings on love, forgiveness, and nonviolence can guide conflict resolution and peacebuilding.

Additionally, scholars throughout history have written extensively on security and territorial protection in the context of the Old and New Testaments. These writings have provided insights into how the teachings of the texts can be applied to contemporary security issues and can contribute to a more subtle understanding of the complex issues surrounding security and territorial protection. Finally, the Old and New Testament's teachings on security and territorial protection can contribute to diplomacy development within and between Christian and non-Christian communities. The principles of justice, peace, and security are universal values that can provide a common ground for diplomacy and cooperation.

Besides, the texts remind us that security is not an end but a means to an end. Security is essential to the flourishing of individuals and communities, allowing them to live their lives without fear and to pursue their goals and aspirations. However, security is not the ultimate goal of life; instead, it is a necessary condition for pursuing higher goals, such as justice, peace, and human flourishing. The Old Testament, for instance, underscores the importance of strategic planning and preparation, such as in the story of Joseph's interpretation of Pharaoh's dreams, which enabled the Pharaoh to prepare for the coming famine. Also, the book of Proverbs contains real-world wisdom on strategic planning, decision-making, and risk assessment, which can be applied to intelligence collection and analysis. Again, the New Testament accentuates the importance of honesty and transparency and warns against deceit and manipulation. These teachings can be applied to utilizing spies, which should be conducted with integrity and within the bounds of ethical and legal frameworks.

The Old and New Testaments' contributions to global security studies and diplomacy accentuate ethical leadership, justice, and human dignity. They remind us that security is about physical protection, promoting social and economic justice, and protecting human rights. In present-day security, we can see the relevance of these ancient texts in several ways. First, they remind us of the need to build strong, resilient communities that withstand external threats and challenges. This requires investing in social capital, building relationships of trust and cooperation among individuals and groups, and fostering a sense of shared purpose and identity. As we navigate the complex issues of modern security, we can learn from these sacred texts and inquiries to find a balance between security and liberty, ensuring that citizens can live safely and freely.

In terms of collecting intelligence and using spies, while the Old and New Testaments do not provide a specific framework for intelligence collection and the use of spies, they do contain instances and teachings that can inform our understanding of intelligence gathering in modern security contexts. For example,

King David and Solomon gathered intelligence in the Old Testament to protect their kingdom and people from external threats. He sent his spies to collect information about the enemy's plans and strengths before engaging in battle. This example illustrates the implication of collecting intelligence to identify conceivable threats and take proactive measures to deter them. It further gave them a real advantage to take preemptive measures over their adversaries.

In particular, King David utilized intelligence collection and employed spies to protect his kingdom and people from external threats. Notably, in 1 Samuel 26:4-5, it is noted that David sent spies to gather information about the Philistine army. The spies reported back to David about the location and movements of the Philistine army, which allowed him to plan his attack and defeat the enemy. David's use of spies is also mentioned in 2 Samuel 15:10, where he sends his spy to gather information about his son Absalom's rebellion. Likewise, King Solomon also utilized intelligence gathering and the use of spies for the protection of his kingdom. In 1 Kings 4:1-19, it is noted that Solomon appointed twelve officials to serve as administrators over the land. One of their duties was to gather information and intelligence for the king. These officials were responsible for gathering information about food supplies, military readiness, and potential threats to the kingdom. Solomon's use of intelligence gathering was so effective that it is said in 1 Kings 4:24 that "he had peace on all sides around him."

The contributions of King David and Solomon to modern security studies lie in their recognition of the importance of intelligence gathering and the use of spies for territorial protection. Their use of spies and intelligence collection enabled them to identify and neutralize potential threats to their kingdoms, contributing to their success as rulers. The lessons learned from King David and Solomon's use of intelligence collection and spies have meaningful implications for modern security studies. Today, intelligence gathering remains a critical component of statecraft, and the methods used by King David and Solomon are still relevant. Moreover, using spies and other covert intelligence-gathering methods has become increasingly important in modern times, particularly in the context of asymmetric warfare and counterterrorism.

In the New Testament, Jesus teaches his disciples to be "wise as serpents and innocent as doves" (Matthew 10:16), stressing the importance of strategic thinking and discernment in navigating complex situations. This teaching can be applied to intelligence gathering, where strategic thinking and discernment are necessary to gather relevant information and identify potential threats. Previous and current studies on security from a Biblical perspective have underlined the importance of ethical considerations in intelligence collection and utilizing spies, reminding us that collecting intelligence should not violate ethical principles, such as respecting human dignity and protecting innocent lives.

Furthermore, the Quran and the Prophetic tradition offer valuable stability, security, and territorial protection instructions. By carefully investigating these sources, we can understand the Islamic perspective on security and how it relates to modern-day issues. The Quran stresses the need for justice and fairness and the importance of establishing societal stability and security. It calls upon Muslims to protect their communities and work towards building a more peaceful world. Finally, it teaches that security is essential for human well-being and is one of the fundamental objectives of the Islamic system. One of the critical contributions of the Quran and Prophetic tradition is their emphasis on justice and fairness. These teachings underscore the importance of treating all individuals with respect and dignity, regardless of race, religion, or nationality. This message has meaningful implications for global security, as it promotes a world where all individuals can live in peace and security.

The Prophetic tradition, which includes the sayings and actions of the Prophet Muhammad, offers further guidance on the topic of security. For example, the Prophet Muhammad emphasized the importance of maintaining a strong defense and treating prisoners and non-combatants respectfully and kindly. Muslim scholars have also written extensively on security and territorial protection throughout history, providing insights into how Islamic teachings can be applied to contemporary security challenges. By studying these sources, we can gain a deeper understanding of the Islamic perspective on security and work towards finding solutions to the complex security challenges of our time.

The Prophetic tradition provides practical examples of how to achieve security and stability. The Prophet Muhammad, peace be upon him, established a system of governance that emphasized justice, security, and the protection of individual rights. He also taught his followers to work towards creating a just and peaceful society and to prioritize the community's welfare over individual interests. Moreover, Muslim scholars throughout history have written extensively on security and territorial protection, offering insights into how the Quran and Prophetic tradition can be applied to present-day security issues and how to balance the need for security with preserving individual rights and freedoms.

In addition, the teachings of the Quran and the Prophetic tradition offer practical guidance on achieving security and stability. The Prophetic tradition provides examples of how to establish a system of governance that prioritizes justice, security, and the protection of individual rights. These teachings can be applied to current security and diplomacy issues, providing valuable guidance for policymakers and leaders worldwide. Furthermore, Muslim scholars throughout history have written extensively on security and territorial protection, offering insights into how the Quran and the Prophetic tradition can be applied to modern issues. These contributions have helped shape modern-day discussions and practices in security studies, providing valuable guidance for policymakers and leaders worldwide.

In modern times, the issue of security has become increasingly complex, with new challenges such as terrorism and cyber threats. However, the knowledge acquired from the Quran and Prophetic tradition and past and current Quranic undertakings on security can provide meaningful guidance for policymakers, leaders, and individuals alike. Ultimately, the goal should be to create a just and peaceful society where individuals can live in security and freedom, guided by the principles of the Quran and the Prophetic tradition. One of the most significant contributions of the Quran and the Prophetic tradition to global security studies and diplomacy is their focus on justice, peace, and security. The teachings of these sources underscore the importance of creating a just and peaceful society, which is essential for the well-being of individuals and communities. The Quran also highlights the importance of trust in God as the ultimate source of security, which has imperative implications for how we approach issues related to security and diplomacy.

Islamic Contributions to Present-Day Intelligence Collection

Examples of humans (HUMINT) collecting intelligence in the Quran include Moses' mother instructing his sister to follow the whereabouts of infant Moses while he floated on a basket along the Nile River. Additionally, Hudhud, the bird (hoopoe), was used as a form of reconnaissance to spy on adversaries' territories, aiding in understanding their capabilities and vulnerabilities for combat readiness. These two captivating examples showcase the various ways intelligence collection was practiced by humans and animals.

1. **Moses' Mother Instructing His Sister (Surah Al-Qasas, 28:7-13):** Moses' mother's decision to set him adrift in a basket on the Nile River to protect him from Pharaoh's oppression highlights a strategic act of intelligence collection. Entrusting his sister to monitor the basket's journey and observe its eventual destination in Pharaoh's household allowed for critical information gathering. Her vigilance and courage led to Moses' reunion with his mother, ensuring his proper upbringing while preserving his identity and destiny as a prophet.
2. **Hudhud, the Bird, known as hoopoe (Surah An-Naml, 27:20-28):** The story of Prophet Solomon and the

bird Hudhud offers an intriguing example of intelligence collection from an animal. The Quran portrays Hudhud as a perceptive observer used to spy on the kingdom of Sheba. The bird's reconnaissance missions provided insights into the adversaries' territories, contributing valuable information for combat readiness and strategic decision-making.

The Quranic depictions of intelligence gathering from humans, birds, and other unconventional sources offer practical wisdom for contemporary security studies. These examples underscore the importance of considering diverse sources for intelligence collection, as exemplified by Moses' mother and sister, as well as the bird Hudhud. They emphasize the significance of vigilance, observation, adaptability, collaboration, and inclusivity in intelligence efforts. The following outlines how modern security studies can benefit from these practical examples of intelligence gathering:

1. **Unconventional Sources:** The Quranic examples highlight the value of exploring unconventional sources for intelligence collection. Modern security studies can enhance their practices by incorporating non-traditional means such as community engagement, open-source intelligence, and technology-driven data collection from diverse sources.
2. **Vigilance and Observation:** Moses' sister's vigilance underscores the importance of keen observation in intelligence gathering. Modern security studies emphasize training individuals to be attentive and discerning, enabling them to extract critical information from their surroundings.
3. **Inclusivity and Collaboration:** Moses' mother and sister's collaborative efforts highlight the importance of inclusivity and collaboration in intelligence collection. Modern security studies can benefit from fostering cooperation among various agencies, communities, and

stakeholders to gather comprehensive and actionable intelligence.
4. **Protection of Vulnerable Populations:** Moses' mother's actions to shield her infant from oppression emphasize the necessity of safeguarding vulnerable populations. Modern security studies can glean insights into ensuring marginalized groups' and individuals' safety and well-being.
5. **Animal Intelligence and Technology:** The Hudhud (hoopoe) narrative showcases the concept of animal intelligence applied to reconnaissance. While modern security studies may not employ birds for intelligence gathering, they can explore technological advancements like unmanned aerial vehicles (UAVs) and drones for effective reconnaissance.
6. **Strategic Decision-Making:** The use of Hudhud for reconnaissance by Prophet Solomon highlights the role of intelligence in informed decision-making. Modern security studies can recognize the value of basing strategic decisions on accurate and timely intelligence, enhancing security operations' efficacy.
7. **Ethical Considerations:** The Quranic examples underscore the ethical dimensions of intelligence collection. Modern security studies can draw from these examples to prioritize ethical principles, privacy protection, and the preservation of human rights while conducting intelligence activities.
8. **Contextual Adaptation:** The Quranic stories emphasize the need for adapting intelligence collection methods to specific contexts. Modern security studies can adopt context-specific approaches tailored to address unique challenges and threats different regions and communities face.
9. **Intelligence Integration:** Moses' mother and sister's coordination exemplifies the importance of integrating various intelligence sources. Modern security studies can explore integrating diverse data streams, including human intelligence, signals intelligence, and geospatial

information, to create a comprehensive intelligence picture.
10. **Leadership Lessons:** The Quranic narratives provide leadership lessons, highlighting the significance of wise decision-making, courage, and empathy in safeguarding communities. Modern security studies can draw inspiration from these examples to cultivate effective leadership within security and intelligence organizations.

The Quranic examples underscore the significance of intelligence gathering and its various forms, whether through human observation or the use of animals for reconnaissance. They emphasize the importance of vigilance, keen observation, and resourcefulness in gathering essential information for decision-making, protection, and preparedness. Moses' sister and the bird Hudhud serve as exemplars of intelligence collection, reminding us of the value of diligence, adaptability, and open-mindedness in seeking knowledge from diverse sources. By learning from these practical examples, security professionals can benefit from considering unconventional sources, emphasizing vigilance and observation, fostering collaboration, securing vulnerable populations, embracing technological advancements, making strategic decisions based on intelligence, adhering to ethical considerations, adapting to different contexts, integrating intelligence sources, and drawing leadership lessons.

These lessons carry historical significance and offer timeless wisdom that can enhance the effectiveness and ethicality of intelligence gathering in contemporary security environments. The Quranic narratives provide historical accounts of remarkable events and offer timeless lessons about the art of intelligence collection, strategic thinking, and utilizing all available resources to enhance the security of individuals and societies.

Regarding intelligence collection and using spies, the Quran in Surah Al-Anfal (8:60) states, "And prepare against them whatever you are able of power and of steeds of war by which you may terrify the enemy of Allah and your enemy." This verse stresses the need to be prepared, equipped, and using all available resources, including intelligence, to protect oneself against the enemy. Additionally, the Hadith of Prophet Muhammad (peace be upon him) guides the ethical and legal boundaries of intelligence gathering. The Prophet said, "Do not spy on one another, do not betray, do not be envious of one another, do not hate one another, do not desert (cut relations with) one another. O Allah's servants! Be brothers" (Sahih al-Bukhari). This Hadith accentuates the value of conducting intelligence collection ethically, accordingly, and within legal boundaries.

    The Prophet Muhammad sent a companion, Abdullah ibn Urayqit, to Mecca to gather information about the movements of the Quraish tribe, who were pursuing them. Abdullah ibn Urayqit successfully infiltrated the Quraish tribe and returned with valuable information, allowing the Prophet Muhammad and his companions to evade capture and safely reach Medina. This undercover mission was not simply an act of reconnaissance but a coup de maitre that personified the Prophet's perceptive understanding of the essence of intelligence gathering in national security.

    The mission of Abdullah ibn Urayqit to Mecca sums up a lesson that reverberates through the written account: in matters of security and survival, knowledge is power. The Prophet Muhammad's tactical leadership expanded beyond the spiritual domain to bring about the practical national security sphere. Even in peril, his brilliant move to gather intelligence indicates his masterstroke and resolute commitment to defending the emerging Muslim community. The narrative of this clandestine assignment continues to inspire the contemporary world with its far-reaching message about the essential role of intelligence in shaping the future of nations.

    In addition, the Hadith provides examples of Prophet Muhammad's use of spies for security and territorial protection. One such example is the story of Ali ibn Abi Talib, the fourth Caliph of Islam, who was sent by the Prophet Muhammad as a spy to collect information about the Banu Nadir tribe plotting against the Muslim community. Ali magnificently penetrated the tribe and returned with real-world intelligence, empowering the Muslim community and giving them the advantage to take preemptive measures to protect themselves. In an era of limited communication and quick decision-making, the Prophet Muhammad's utilization of spies underlines his creative leadership. By engaging a companion to obtain firsthand information, he exemplified the essence of strategic intelligence in shaping strategic decisions.

The contributions of Prophet Muhammad to modern security studies lie in his recognition of the importance of collecting intelligence and using spies for territorial protection. His use of spies and intelligence gathering enabled him to identify and neutralize potential threats to his community, which contributed to the success of the early Islamic state. The lessons drawn from Prophet Muhammad's use of intelligence collection and spies have significant consequences for modern security studies. Today, intelligence collection remains a critical component of statecraft, and the methods used by the Prophet Muhammad are still relevant. Moreover, spies and other covert intelligence-gathering methods have become increasingly meaningful in modern times, especially in the context of asymmetric warfare and counterterrorism.

Moreover, modern-day security professionals can benefit from these insights by developing effective intelligence collection strategies guided by ethical and legal boundaries. For example, intelligence collection in counterterrorism operations should be conducted within the legal boundaries established by international law and human rights standards. As we have seen through our examination of religious texts and ancient civilizations' perspectives on national security, the need for security and protection has been a constant throughout human history. However, the challenges we face today vastly differ from those of the past and require new approaches and strategies. While threats may have evolved, seeking security remains a fundamental concern for individuals, communities, and nations.

A new book on security studies offers a comprehensive and captivating overview of these modern security challenges, drawing on a range of perspectives and insights to provide practical guidance on navigating this complex landscape. With a focus on ethical leadership, human rights, and social justice, this book presents a compelling vision for building more just, peaceful, and secure societies. Additionally, a detailed exploration of the latest security strategies, technologies, and trends equips readers with the knowledge and tools needed to confront the most pressing security challenges of our time, including cyber threats, terrorism, and climate change.

At its core, this book emphasizes the importance of balancing security with broader ethical considerations, recognizing that security cannot come at the expense of individual freedoms, human rights, or social justice. This book contributes to security studies through its thought-provoking visions and real-world recommendations. It provides readers with a deeper understanding of our challenges and the tools we need to build a more secure, just, and peaceful world. The book also underscores the importance of recognizing the diverse and often competing interests that shape security decisions. It stresses the need for a holistic and inclusive approach to security that recognizes the interconnectedness of local, national, and global security challenges. Furthermore, this book is an essential read for anyone interested in security studies or seeking to understand better the historical and cultural factors that shape modern security practices. Its comprehensive and captivating writing style, thorough research, and insightful analysis make it a valuable contribution to the domain of national security studies.

Our examination of religious texts and ancient civilizations' perspectives on national security has highlighted enduring principles of ethical leadership, human rights, and social justice critical to building more just, peaceful, and secure societies. These principles serve as the foundation for a new book on security studies that offers a fresh perspective on the evolving security landscape. Through a comprehensive analysis of current security challenges, this book presents beneficial suggestions for applying these principles to create a safer and more prosperous future. In addition, the book offers a compelling vision for achieving security without sacrificing our fundamental values. With a focus on collaborative approaches to security, the book encourages readers to consider the interconnectedness of security challenges and the importance of building partnerships across sectors and regions. It also stresses the critical role of ethical leadership in shaping security policies and ensuring that they align with our values and aspirations as a global community.

Furthermore, studying religious texts and ancient civilizations provides valuable insights into security and territorial protection perspectives. They have significantly shaped our understanding of security and territorial protection. By investigating the correlations between sacred texts, ancient civilizations, and modern security, we can benefit from their contributions to present-day security studies. Modern states can adopt ancient civilizations' strategies and approaches to building fortifications and walls to protect their territories and learn from religious texts' emphasis on the importance of security and territorial protection to develop more effective strategies.

Hindu texts and traditions also provide numerous examples of intelligence gathering and using spies for security and territorial protection, mainly through the contributions of kings, princes, and warriors. Their use of intelligence gathering and spies allowed them to identify and neutralize potential threats to their communities and kingdoms, contributing to their success. The lessons learned from their use of intelligence collection and spies have substantial implications for modern security studies and remain relevant today. While the Old and New Testaments do not provide a specific framework for intelligence collection and the use of spies, they contain examples and teachings that can inform our understanding of intelligence gathering in modern security contexts. By learning from these teachings and incorporating ethical considerations, we can utilize intelligence gathering to identify potential threats and take proactive measures to promote global security and diplomacy.

Similarly, the Quran and Hadith offer examples of intelligence gathering and the use of spies for security and territorial protection, mainly through the contributions of Prophet Muhammad. His use of intelligence gathering and spies allowed him to identify and neutralize potential threats to his community, which contributed to the success of the early Islamic state. The insights obtained from his use of intelligence collection and spies have significant outcomes for modern security studies and remain relevant today. The teachings of the Quran and the Prophetic tradition have made significant contributions to global security studies and diplomacy and can continue to provide helpful recommendations for policymakers and leaders worldwide.

The study of security and territorial protection is undoubtedly one of the most important fields of research in modern times. Its advancements owe a great deal to the teachings of religious texts and the practices of ancient civilizations. Sacred texts like the Bible, the Quran, and Bhagavad Gita have long underlined the essence of security and protection. In addition, ancient civilizations like the Greeks and Romans developed sophisticated military tactics and fortification strategies that are still studied today. Modern security studies have made significant strides in safeguarding our communities and nations by drawing on the knowledge and wisdom of these texts and civilizations. Accordingly, the contributions of sacred texts and ancient civilizations to the study of security and territorial protection must be balanced and continue shaping how we think about and approach these critical issues.

Moreover, the wisdom gleaned from investigating ancient sacred texts can help military strategists develop pragmatic approaches to modern-day security concerns. For instance, by studying the Quran, stakeholders can better understand the social-psychological stimuli and tactics used by terrorist organizations such as Al Qaeda, ISIS, Boko Haram, etc. Comprehending their unrealistic beliefs and ideologies can help military strategists develop counterterrorism strategies that actually address the root causes of extremism. Similarly, by probing the military strategies of ancient civilizations, policymakers can better understand how to address modern-day security concerns. For illustration, studying the techniques used by ancient empires such as Rome and Persia can provide insights into maintaining a balance between military expansion and resource management, avoiding overreliance on military force, and ensuring sustainable security.

Ancient civilizations and their sacred texts have been a basis for military strategy for centuries. For instance, Sun Tzu's "The Art of War," a text written over 2,500 years ago, is still widely studied by military strategists today. The strategies and tactics in this text were appropriate in ancient warfare and still apply to modern-day military campaigns. In essence, Sun Tzu's work indicates the enduring influence of ancient civilizations and their wisdom on the evolution of military strategy. Its ongoing applicability underlines the unchanging nature of warfare's essential principles, reinforcing that history's lessons are priceless in shaping tomorrow's tactics. The text's principles of deception, intelligence gathering, and knowing one's enemy remain critical aspects of modern-day military planning.

Similarly, the ancient Indian text, "Arthashastra," contains strategic and tactical visions for policymakers and military strategists. The text provides a detailed understanding of espionage, diplomacy, and economic warfare. Examining these texts and applying their principles to modern-day security concerns can give policymakers and military strategists a fresh perspective. The text's deep emphasis on espionage highlights the ongoing implication of intelligence collection as a foundation of adequate security measures. "Arthashastra" provides a layout for convoluted information acquisition methods, underscoring the age-old truth that knowledge is power. Such doctrines remain as critical today as they were in ancient times, navigating the complexities of the current international arena.

Likewise, the text's exploration of economic warfare displays an alacritous recognition of financial strength and security interconnectedness. In an era of globalization, where economic leverage is vital in international affairs, "Arthashastra" presents a timeless lesson in harnessing economic resources as a strategic tool. The text underlines the wisdom of strategically manipulating economic resources, resonating with its applicability for current leaders managing the complex interplay of international relations and economic influence.

Substantially, sacred texts offer a plethora of information on ancient military maneuvers, intelligence gathering, and strategic planning. For example, the Hindu epic, Mahabharata, is a rich source of information on ancient Indian military tactics, including the utilization of chariots, elephants, and infantry. Similarly, the Art of War by Sun Tzu is a classic military treatise that offers wisdom into ancient Chinese warfare tactics, including deception, espionage, and unconventional maneuvers. Researching these texts provides invaluable discernment into the strategies and tactics employed by ancient civilizations that are still suitable today. Military strategists and policymakers can use this knowledge to develop more pragmatic security policies considering historical perspectives and lessons.

In closing, the information from past religious texts and ancient civilizations has helped us better understand security issues and advance our present security studies. By studying the experiences of these cultures, we have gained a priceless understanding of the need to maintain strong defensive capabilities, the dangers of overreaching and overextension, and the role of diplomacy in promoting peace and stability. As we face new security challenges in the modern world, these lessons remain as applicable and vital as ever. This contributing book on security studies is a helpful resource for anyone seeking to understand the complexities of security in the contemporary world. It provides a thoughtful and thought-provoking exploration of security issues relevant to individuals, communities, and nations worldwide.

References:

Abdullah Yusuf Ali. (2015). The Holy Qur'an: English Translation and Commentary. Amana Publications.

Brinkley, J. (2021). Israel's Security Wall. History. Retrieved from https://www.history.com/news/israels-security-wall

Frye, R. N. (1984). The History of Ancient Iran. Munich: C. H. Beck.

Gardner, H. (1978). The Kung Fu Book of Wisdom. New York: Tuttle Publishing.

Hagen, R. (2016). Ancient Egyptian fortresses and military defenses. Retrieved from https://www.ancient.eu/article/891/ancient-egyptian-fortresses-and-military-defenses/

Hanson, V. D. (2020). A wall is a country: Immigration policy in an age of walls. Basic Books.

Hornblower, S. (2014). Long Walls. In The Oxford Classical Dictionary. Oxford University Press. Retrieved from https://www.oxfordreference.com/view/10.1093/acref/9780199545568.001.0001/acref-9780199545568-e-3567

Kulke, H., & Rothermund, D. (2004). A History of India. Routledge.

Kautilya. (n.d.). Arthashastra. (R. Shamasastry, Trans.). Retrieved from http://www.sacred-texts.com/hin/kautilya/index.htm

Mahabharata. (1993). Penguin Classics.

Pandey, R. (2011). Spy and Intelligence Operations. Vij Books India Pvt Ltd.

Sahih al-Bukhari. (1997). Book of Military Expeditions. Dar-us-Salam Publications.

Sahih Muslim. (1994). Book of Government. Dar-us-Salam Publications.

Schwartz, J. (1996). The Shema: Spirituality and Law in Judaism. New York: Paulist Press.

Zhang, J. (1993). The Great Wall: China Against the World, 1000 BC-AD 2000. London: Harper Collins.

www.ingramcontent.com/pod-product-compliance
Lightning Source LLC
Chambersburg PA
CBHW061252230426
43665CB00026B/2908